The Quintinshill Conspiracy

The Quintinshill Conspiracy

The Shocking True Story Behind Britain's Worst Rail Disaster

Jack Richards and Adrian Searle

PEN & SWORD
TRANSPORT

First published in Great Britain in 2013 by
Pen & Sword Transport
an imprint of
Pen & Sword Books Ltd
47 Church Street
Barnsley
South Yorkshire
S70 2AS

ISBN 978 1 78159 099 7

Typeset in Ehrhardt by
Mac Style, Driffield, East Yorkshire
Printed and bound in the UK by CPI Group (UK) Ltd, Croydon,
CRO 4YY

Pen & Sword Books Ltd incorporates the imprints of Pen & Sword
Archaeology, Atlas, Aviation, Battleground, Discovery, Family
History, History, Maritime, Military, Naval, Politics, Railways,
Select, Social History, Transport, True Crime, and Claymore Press,
Frontline Books, Leo Cooper, Praetorian Press, Remember When,
Seaforth Publishing and Wharncliffe.

For a complete list of Pen & Sword titles please contact
PEN & SWORD BOOKS LIMITED
47 Church Street, Barnsley, South Yorkshire, S70 2AS, England
E-mail: enquiries@pen-and-sword.co.uk
Website: www.pen-and-sword.co.uk

Contents

Dedication

This work is dedicated to the memory of Jack Richards, co-author, whose sudden death in April 2013 came as the book, to which he had contributed so much, was being prepared for publication.

Driven by a deep sense of injustice at the outcome of the 1915 investigative process, Jack's tireless research into the facts underpinning the tragedy was instrumental in revealing the astonishing reality behind this complex story. He wanted the book to serve as a long–overdue, properly rounded testament for all the victims of the Quintinshill disaster, the many who lost their lives and those who were cruelly forced to accept all the blame in the service of corporate and national interests.

Hopefully, the book will serve as a fitting tribute to Jack's unstinting resolve in this regard. The final tragedy is that he did not live to see the end product of his unbounded quest for the truth.

Preface

It was the railway's *Titanic*. An accident of unparalleled proportions. When it happened in May 1915 at the remote Quintinshill signal box near Gretna on the Anglo-Scottish border it was the worst ever disaster on a British railway line. In terms of the number of people who lost their lives – well over 200 with virtually the same number injured – it remains so today.

Two crashes within minutes of each other; five trains involved – a troop train, a local passenger train, an express train from London and two freights. It led to a raging inferno fuelled by the gas used to illuminate the deathtrap-on-wheels which masqueraded as adequate transport for a battalion of Scottish soldiers en route to fight for their country in the Dardenelles but mercilessly cut down on British soil before they had sight of the sea.

This was a dreadful disaster. The victims died horribly, trapped, fatally pierced by flying splinters of wood and metal or slowly burned to death. Civilians, women and children among them, died too. Rescuers toiled valiantly and in many cases with extraordinary courage, but it was carnage.

The cause, it was said – and nothing has materially changed the view in the virtual century that has elapsed since it happened – was simple. Two young, careless, rule-breaking, signalmen – one extraordinarily forgetful – were entirely to blame. No one else. They were sent to prison for their criminal negligence. It was an open and shut case and nothing has been put forward to challenge this long-held perception. No room for doubt at all.

Until now.

Quintinshill's tragedy has never made any real sense. With its centenary on the horizon, the purpose of this book was to look behind the known facts and, with the help of previously unpublished information, to dig deep in a bid to unearth the full story – which surely was far more complex.

The digging produced some astonishing new evidence, implicating a great many more people than the signalmen who were jailed – and revealing at its core a riveting central factor which led to serious consternation in the wartime corridors of power in that crisis-torn month of May 1915.

For the sake of those who died, those who were appallingly served by the lop-sided society of post-Edwardian Britain, and for their descendants today, this is a story which really needs telling. It is time at last to reveal the full, shocking truth behind the catastrophe at Quintinshill.

Maps & Diagrams

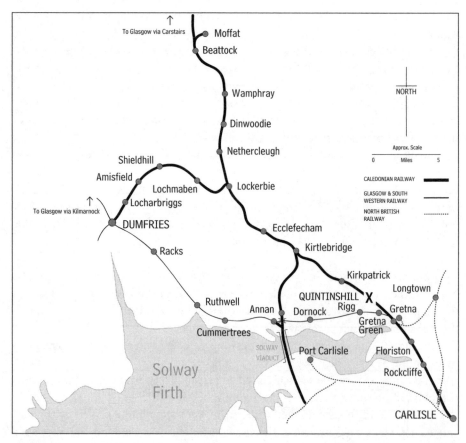

Railways in the Carlisle–Dumfries–Beattock triangle on the Anglo-Scottish border in May 1915, showing the location of Quintinshill passing loops on the Caledonian's main line north of Gretna.

Diagrammatic representation of the Quintinshill rail crash on 22 May 1915.

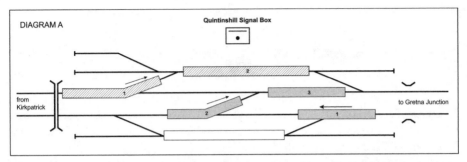

Fig A: (06.30–06.34). With the northbound freight train positioned in the down passing loop, the local train from Carlisle arrives (1) and reverses through the crossover (2) to stand on the southbound main line (3). The southbound empty coal train is directed from the up main line (1) into the adjacent loop (2).

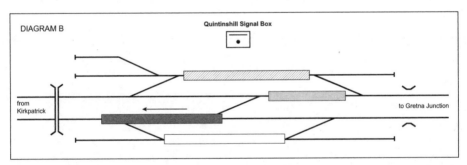

Fig B: (06.38). The northbound express for Edinburgh and Aberdeen passes safely through.

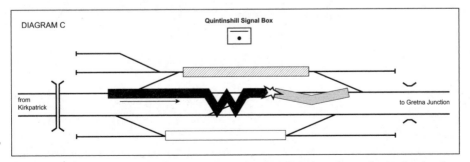

Fig C: (06.49). The southbound troop train crashes headlong into the stationary local train.

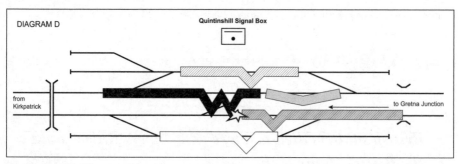

Fig D: (06.50). The northbound express for Glasgow ploughs into the wreckage which then spills onto the stationary trains in the two passing loops.

Stationery northbound freight

Northbound local

First northbound express

Empty southbound coal wagons

Southbound troop special

Second northbound express

Note: simplified representation only, not to scale.

Chapter 1

A Country in Crisis. A Disaster too Far?

*'British soldiers died last week on Aubers Ridge because
the British Army is short of shells.'*

> Sir John French, Commander-in-Chief,
> British Expeditionary Force, 14 May 1915

To understand the truth behind the worst disaster in the history of Britain's railways, to peel away the whitewash obscuring the complex realities that underpin the story of this appalling tragedy, it is essential to seek out the bigger picture. The real story of Quintinshill's tragedy is as multi-tracked as the stretch of railway line on which it occurred in May 1915.

Previous attempts to chronicle the accident at the isolated West Coast Main Line signal box have essentially been targeted at railway enthusiasts. It was, after all, a railway *cause célèbre*. But this is not merely a tragic story about trains. There is a great deal more to it than that – Quintinshill was a momentous event for Britain in a period of wartime crisis.[1]

It was all so different in August 1914 when war was declared against Germany. Large crowds on both sides of the Channel had cheered as the British Expeditionary Force set off to join its French allies to teach the upstart Kaiser Wilhelm a lesson he wouldn't forget and chase his army, which surely would be comfortably defeated, back to Berlin to lick its wounds. It would be a glamorous, fast-moving continental campaign of cavalry charges en route to certain victory – it would all be over by Christmas.

It didn't turn out like that, of course. This was destined to be a wholly different kind of war in which mechanised armies would fight themselves into a bloody stalemate. After the initial battles of 1914 both sides held an entrenched 400 mile line that stretched from the Belgian coast, through the flat lands of industrial Artois, the wide expanses of the Somme and Champagne, then into the high Vosges and all the way to the Swiss border.

Winston Churchill, appointed First Lord of the Admiralty in 1911, had enthusiastically pursued a plan for the Royal Navy to spearhead an invasion of the Gallipoli peninsula in the Ottoman Empire (modern-day Turkey). The plan was to force open the Dardenelles strait and a secure sea route to Russia, thus relieving pressure on the Czar's forces and helping to break the deadlock in the war.

Launched on 24 April 1915, the campaign quickly faltered and developed into a further deadly stalemate – regarded in retrospect as a disastrous failure – which, among other consequences, saw Churchill's removal from office. On 7 May, two weeks after the ill-fated attack on Gallipoli, the Cunard liner RMS *Lusitania*, commandeered by the Admiralty as an armed merchant cruiser, was torpedoed by a German U-boat eleven miles off the Old Head of Kinsale lighthouse on the southern Irish coast en route from New York to Liverpool. The 'Lucy' sank with the loss of 1,198 lives.

Then, on 9 May, British forces suffered unmitigated disaster, with heavy casualties and no tactical gain whatsoever, at the Battle of Aubers Ridge, south of Armentières in France. Five days later, exasperated at the lack of available ammunition, the BEF's Commander-in-Chief, Sir John French, with support from *The Times* newspaper, launched a fierce attack on the War Office.

'British soldiers died last week on Aubers Ridge because the British Army is short of shells,' he declared bitterly. Political crisis immediately ensued. Prime Minister Herbert Asquith's Liberal administration was in big trouble.

In the midst of these shattering events, on the sunlit Saturday morning of 22 May just north of Gretna on the Anglo-Scottish border, a train carrying nearly 500 Scottish territorial soldiers bound for the Gallipoli beaches via Liverpool collided head-on at high speed with a stationary local passenger train at Quintinshill on the Caledonian Railway's main line. A minute later a Glasgow-bound express from London ploughed into the wreckage.

The result was carnage. The country was appalled when news filtered through that 230 had died in terrible circumstances and another 247 had been injured, many of them seriously. It was yet another numbing event in a month of disasters. Three days later, on 25 May, the schism which had developed within Asquith's Cabinet over the 'shell crisis' in the wake of Aubers Ridge and other issues of wartime leadership forced him into unwanted coalition with the Conservative opposition. Political meltdown gripped the nation.[2]

Was Quintinshill one disaster too many for the Government? When, a week after the tragedy, disturbing evidence emerged about one of the signalmen involved – as a consequence of his arrest on a charge of culpable homicide – was a decision reached at the highest level to take all measures necessary to 'bury' the story, or at least the apparently unwelcome truth which lay behind it? Was there a conspiracy to keep it buried? Was there a rush to judgment as a result of this? Research carried out for this book points firmly to the conclusion that, in all respects, there was.

The wider issues are many and profound. Yet trains are, of course, at the heart of the story and, in setting the wider context, it would clearly be absurd to ignore the backdrop of the Edwardian railway. While the accident actually happened five years after the accession to the throne of King George V, the British railway system was very much the product of the preceding Edwardian era and, indeed, of Edwardian society as a whole.

The enormous power held and exerted by major industrial concerns was particularly evident in the railway and shipping sectors, their tentacles spreading far and wide into the political and economic fabric of the nation.

As a counterweight to this the trade union movement had gained influential power in the late nineteenth century, leading to the formation in 1910 of the Labour Party which quickly established itself as a political force.

By the close of the Edwardian era in 1910, trade unionism in the railway industry was becoming better organised. Rail workers declared a national strike over wages and conditions in 1911 at the height of what became known as 'The Great Unrest'. Two years later the National Union of Railwaymen (NUR) was formed, the result of an amalgamation of three smaller unions. The men who enjoyed the prestige of working on the locomotive footplate, the drivers and firemen, had their own, well established, union in the form of the splendidly titled Associated Society of Locomotive Engineers and Firemen – ASLEF for short – formed in 1880.

Probably no one alive today can remember what has been called the 'golden age of railways'. Express passenger trains in Edwardian Britain during the first decade of the twentieth century had reached a splendour unequalled anywhere else in the world. These were not the trains that many today would immediately link with the age of the steam railway. The modern mind more easily focuses on the gleaming trains hauled by world-famous locomotives such as *Flying Scotsman* and the streamlined record-breaker *Mallard*. Both these iconic engines were products of later eras.

Neither would a visit to one of Britain's magnificent heritage railways provide more than a glimpse of the true glory of train travel before 1914. With some notable exceptions, the locomotives and coaches that epitomised the railway traveller's experience during this long-vanished period – specifically for those using the cross-border West Coast Main Line – are represented only among the collections of the National Railway Museum in York and Glasgow's Riverbank Museum. They serve as evocative preserved fragments from a huge, proud and essential industry.

Together with trans-oceanic shipping, the mighty internal rail network functioned as the heart and arteries of Britain's mobile Edwardian age. Railways and shipping were pivotal to the early twentieth century economies of the industrialised world. Nowhere was this more true than in Britain. Without its ability to rely on these two forms of transport, both at home and abroad, the country could never have sustained its envied global empire.

Hard as it is to imagine today, just about everything – people and freight – travelling anywhere other than short distances overland went by train. It was a massive operation. In the pre-war eras of Edward VII and George V specialised railway vans and wagons were designed and provided for just about every conceivable purpose, even for touring theatre companies and circuses!

The railways continued to dominate internal transport as the major powers of Europe plunged into war on an unprecedented industrial scale in 1914. It was a war that none of the participant nations could have hoped to prosecute without the ability of their railways to supply them. Britain's extraordinarily complex rail network was absolutely vital to the war effort.

As an island nation, separated by sea and considerable landmass from the battlefields, Britain had different considerations to the other powers when it came to planning how best to use rail in wartime. On the continent railways were at the heart of battleground strategy itself. Long before the war Germany in particular had adopted a military policy utterly dependent on the quick deployment of rail-borne supply lines to battle zones.

German rail expansion, especially near the western border with France, had seen extravagant facilities provided which far exceeded peacetime levels. During a prolonged pre-war period, military considerations were paramount in the considerable development of the newly-unified nation's railways.

'As the new century dawned, Germany's military plans became more and more sophisticated, and at their core was the notion of a rapid mobilisation through the railways,' writes Christian Wolmar in his enthralling book, *Engines of War*. This comprehensive account of the role played by railways in deciding the outcome of major international conflicts reminds us that, since 1899, the use of rail as the centrepiece of German military intentions and strategy had been enshrined in what was effectively an annually revised blueprint for war. Colloquially referred to as the Schlieffen Plan, it was devised by chief-of-staff, Alfred von Schlieffen.[3]

Only by using the railways to their fullest possible extent, the plan made clear, could Germany successfully wage a war on two fronts, as it correctly anticipated having to do. The ability to supply men and materials speedily to the front line by rail would knock out the threat from France in the west in time to deal with the slower to mobilise Russians in the east.

That, at least, was the theory. It did not, of course, work out that way – 'an elaborate fantasy', says Wolmar – because of the errors of military strategy and the false political assumptions upon which the plan was based. Yet the Schlieffen Plan serves as a major reminder of the unchallenged status of rail as the period's main means of overland transport.

In Britain, too, the importance of the internal rail network in military planning was primarily its ability to get soldiers and their equipment mobilised quickly for action. However, the specific objectives were different to those of the enemy-in-waiting. The essential task for Britain's railways was to transport men, armaments and the other paraphernalia of warfare to the ports for transhipment to the continent – an operation which, up to a point at least, had been usefully rehearsed with the transfer of thousands of British troops and equipment from rail to ship through the port of Southampton during the Boer Wars at the close of the nineteenth century.

In general terms, aided as it was by the creation in 1914 of a national Railway Executive Committee to oversee wartime operation, mobilisation by rail in Britain can be said to have worked well. But the demands were intolerably heavy, both on the capacity of the track and the availability of rolling stock, a twin burden which could have been, *should* have been, but was not, alleviated by any appreciable reduction in the normal train timetable. It was thus very far from being a flawless operation.

Within a year of the war's outbreak in 1914, this dependency on the trains of myriad private companies, the need to utilise from them whatever stock happened to be lying around, sometimes with scant regard for its suitability for a specific task, would have a direct impact on the events which culminated so tragically at Quintinshill on that sunny morning in May.

However, what happened there and during the course of the disturbing events which followed the disaster cannot be properly considered on so narrow a front. There were other factors at play and to understand these it is necessary to delve more deeply into the structure and character of Britain's early twentieth century railway system – and of British society as a whole.

The trains themselves reflected the class structure. In the main there were three classes of travel: first, second and third. The treatment of third class travellers was more often than not disgraceful – uncomfortable and dirty.

The history of the conveyance of the 'lower orders' by Britain's railways is a disreputable one. More than seventy years before Quintinshill an accident on the Great Western in 1841 had resulted in the deaths of many working class passengers travelling in open trucks on a freight train – normal procedure at the time. This resulted three years later in the passing of an Act of Parliament to provide better accommodation for third class ticket holders.

The railway companies grudgingly complied with the minimum standards required by the new law. Their 'Parliamentary trains', known throughout the industry as 'Parlys', were awful and generally ran at times when only a hardy, or desperate, few would contemplate travelling. This sorry state of affairs was destined to linger long. It was still in place when W.S. Gilbert penned his famous libretto half a century later for *The Mikado*. Five of his lines neatly summarise the upper class view of these dismal trains:

The idiot who, in railway carriages,
Scribbles on window-panes,
We only suffer
To ride on a buffer
On Parliamentary trains.

It is probably unlikely that many who sing or hear those familiar lines in a modern production of the Gilbert & Sullivan classic will appreciate their true meaning. However, they would certainly have struck a chord in the Edwardian era and beyond when the 'Parly' was still the miserable lot of many a third class passenger, riding in an obsolete apology for a railway carriage which lurched along, often on just a four-wheeled frame. Those wretched third class trains were little better than mobile garden sheds![4, 5]

By comparison, the crack expresses of the day were among the best in the world, especially for the first class passenger. Painted in exotic liveries distinctively different from each other they represented the pride of their owners. Few companies exemplified this better than the Caledonian, the prestigious railway at the centre of Quintinshill's story. Referred to affectionately as the 'Caley', the company is still remembered today for its magnificent locomotives, resplendent in their glorious blue livery.[6]

Caledonian blue was a superb choice. The latest express engines of the company's *Cardean* class bore it with a particular majesty. That evocative livery colours most modern-day reflections of the Caledonian. Yet the gleaming blue of the Caley was horribly tarnished by the blackest day in British railway history and the *Cardean* class had a pivotal role in the story.

As did the conveyance of freight. It too was a factor at Quintinshill. In this Britain was far from being a world leader. Almost all the goods wagons employed by the period's railway companies were formed into loose (chain) coupled formations, sometimes of extraordinary length. Unlike passenger coaches, the only braking equipment fitted to these vehicles had to be applied manually and individually. The brake van at the rear helped to control them, but the only other method of braking while the train was in motion was that fitted in the cab of the locomotive itself.

Large numbers of these wagons were privately owned, had primitive lubrication, were often poorly maintained and were always likely to break down. They did so with monotonous regularity. Quintinshill, in common with many other locations, had special sidings in which to store defective wagons.

The 'troublesome trucks' immortalised in the pages of the *Thomas the Tank Engine* stories were not created by the fertile imagination of the books' author, the Rev Wilbert Awdry. They were real and they were, without any doubt, troublesome for far too long a period on Britain's railways!

Ponderous railway caravans, sometimes comprising more than fifty wagons crawling at little more that 15mph (at a time when passenger trains were often averaging in excess of 60mph), had to make their leisurely way across the vast Edwardian rail network, causing congestion and frequently having to be shunted into passing loops to allow passenger trains to pass them. It was not unknown for the crew of a goods train to work entire shifts just moving their troublesome trucks from one loop to another![7]

By 1915, thanks to the vast increase in rail traffic imposed by the demands of the war – up by forty per cent on the Caledonian Railway – this irksome state of affairs had become very difficult to manage. Slow-moving goods trains accounted for most of the additional movement by rail.

Despite the Boer War 'rehearsal' this was pretty much a new experience for the railways of Britain which, unlike their European counterparts, had never before been faced with the challenge of accommodating the demands of wartime on this scale. The formation of the overseeing Railway Executive was a wise move but the rail companies still retained a large measure of independence. By May 1915 vital lessons had yet to be learnt.[8]

After the war's outbreak, despite some cutbacks and an easing of train schedules, the Caledonian, in common with other companies, was fired with a 'show must go on' mentality, a determination to do whatever it could to maintain a proper passenger service. This was misplaced patriotism. In general Britain saw no reason to emulate the German model of an all-out strategic wartime railway. She had the backing of empire; she would not be humbled. Wherever possible, the express trains would run.

At all costs.

Tragically, in a quiet part of southern Scotland, the folly of such a policy on an overworked network – when combined with an unforeseen element of human frailty – would be demonstrated with awful results.

A railway can be likened to links in a chain. Its signal boxes control the chain and hold it together. But when that chain and its control systems are simultaneously stretched beyond their limits, inevitably the chain will break at the weakest link. It did so at 6.50am on Saturday, 22 May 1915.

Notes

1. The West Coast Main Line, as it is now known, comprises the major trunk route between London Euston and Glasgow Central. In 1915 it was referred to simply as the West Coast Route.
2. A total of 226 were officially listed as killed but that did not include four unidentified female victims, children possibly among them, whose bodies were found on the Anglo-Scottish express – see chapter three.
3. *Engines of War* by Christian Wolmar, published by Atlantic Books, 2012 – ISBN 10-1848871732.
4. Following investigation by the Board of Trade, Sir Robert Peel's Conservative government enacted the Railway Regulation Act 1844 which introduced the Parliamentary train to Britain. The new law compelled the provision of at least one train a day each way travelling at a speed of not less than 12mph, including stops at all stations, and of carriages protected from the weather and provided with seats; 'luxuries' for which no more than a penny a mile would be charged!
5. There was something eccentrically British about the first move away from the three-class system in 1875, the year the Midland Railway courageously – *outrageously* according to rival companies and an indignant press – reduced it to a two-class structure. Oddly, it was the intermediate second class ticket that was abolished by the Midland, leaving just first and third! The effect, however, was to improve the travelling experience for the vast bulk of the company's passengers. First and second class were merged at the lower end of the

scale, literally opening the door to first class luxury for the burgeoning middle classes, and, while third remained third, passengers enjoyed a simultaneous increase in comfort, their accommodation correspondingly upgraded. The Midland's move was a popular one but shook the railway establishment to the core. However, it would be many years before the initiative was universally matched nationwide. The three-class system remained the norm, the travelling public still rigidly segregated by status. Parliamentary trains survived on the Caledonian Railway network to become a central part of the Quintinshill tragedy in May 1915.

6. In his book, *The Trains We Loved* , C. Hamilton Ellis waxes lyrical about the trains of the Caledonian, describing them as 'the finest and most imposing aspect on any British railway in the old days. A Caledonian express with its massive blue engine and its carriages of red-brown and white was a superb sight'. (New edition published by Macmillan, London, 1971 – ISBN 10-0330027883). O. S. Nock's definitive history of the company (new edition published by Ian Allan Publishing, 1973 – ISBN 10-0711004080) incorporates a contemporary *Railway Magazine* account of the then brand-new express locomotive *Cardean* introduced in 1906 as the first in a class of just five engines. 'A handsome combination *Cardean* made,' said the magazine, 'with the seven cars of the two o'clock, all twelve-wheelers of a special design, and some of the smoothest riding stock that has ever run over West Coast metals', adding an evocative reminder of Carlisle on a typical winter's night, 'with half the city – or so it seemed – making the Citadel station the venue of its evening promenade, and *Cardean* the centre of attraction'.

7. Despite being hopelessly outdated by European and indeed global standards, the traditional British goods wagons and the Victorian methods of operating the trains they formed, stubbornly held sway well into the 1960s, a situation that helped considerably to leave railfreight an easy picking for the road haulage industry which started to flourish in the Twenties.

8. Set up in 1914, the Railway Executive Committee continued to exercise strategic control over Britain's railways until 1921, the year an Act of Parliament set in motion the grouping of the nation's many rail companies into what became known as the 'Big Four' – the London, Midland & Scottish (of which the Caledonian Railway became part), the London & North Eastern, the Great Western and the Southern. The REC was reconstituted in 1939 at the outbreak of World War Two, remaining in control until the entire network was nationalised in 1948.

Chapter 2

A Crash of Overwhelming Magnitude

'The most calamitous railway disaster in the history of Great Britain, both in overwhelming magnitude and the horror of the scenes that followed, occurred on Saturday morning on the Caledonian Railway, half-a-mile north of Gretna Junction.'

Dumfries & Galloway Standard & Advertiser, 28 May 1915

And so it remains today. A century has elapsed since the eloquently bleak summary reproduced above was consigned to print by the local newspaper in whose territory the awful drama it depicted had unfolded. Since then, despite horrific headline-grabbing – though thankfully rare – rail accidents elsewhere in these islands, no journalist in Britain has been tasked with describing a train crash of equal proportion. The truly dreadful tragedy of Saturday, 22 May 1915 half-a-mile north of Gretna in the Scottish border region has never been eclipsed.

The thought that they might soon be part of the blackest day in British railway history would not, of course, have occurred to the passengers congregating at London's Euston station late on the previous evening. They were there to join the overnight sleeping car express to Glasgow as preparations were made for its midnight departure. Hand trolleys piled with the extravagantly extensive luggage regarded as the norm by many of the train's wealthier passengers were unloaded into the accommodation provided. Food and other provisions were added for the travellers' convenience. A world war was no barrier to their comfort.

In May 1915 services on the West Coast Main Line from Euston, one of three competing routes for the highly lucrative Anglo-Scottish rail traffic, were managed jointly by two of the UK's most prestigious railway companies – the London & North Western and, assuming responsibility further north, the Caledonian.

Both companies had invested heavily in the route, providing glamorous trains that offered the last word in luxury travel for their first class passengers. The impressively appointed midnight train consisted of five sleeping cars, one brake van and seven other coaches. Each was built on modern steel underframes. At the front of the train the locomotive crew waited for the signal to clear their way into the north London suburbs on the first part of their journey.

Midnight passed and with it the prestigious train's booked departure time. Maintaining main line passenger services as close as possible to peacetime schedules may have been the aim of the companies running the trains but delays were inevitable on the overstretched rail network. It was thirty minutes into the morning of Saturday, 22 May when the elegant sleeping car express eased its way out of Euston. A half-hour's delay was annoying but nothing more. This was, after all, wartime. It was also Whitsun, and a holiday weekend was, for some at least, in prospect. The passengers settled down to sleep.

Unlike its chief rival, the East Coast route from King's Cross, the West Coast line was (and still is) a difficult route to operate. Far from being a modern railway in 1915, with complex origins dating back to the 1830s, its trains had to contend with many curves, speed restrictions and two challenging major inclines culminating in the famous summits at Shap, amid the Cumbrian mountains, and Beattock, across the Scottish border in south Lanarkshire.

As ever, the driver tried to make up the time lost to the delayed start in London. It proved impossible. After travelling virtually 300 miles through the night, the sleeper arrived at Carlisle still half-an-hour behind schedule. Here the LNWR engine and crew were released as the service was taken over by two Caledonian Railway 4-4-0 locomotives for the difficult climb ahead across the border. Both equipped with eight-wheeled tenders, engine number 140 led the assault followed by number 48, attached to the train itself – a powerful double-header.[1]

Although due to leave at 6.05, it was not until 6.37 that the night express actually pulled away from Carlisle Citadel station, heading out of England in the early morning sunlight – shortly to plunge into the dark realms of unimaginable horror.

With both this train and a preceding overnight express service for Edinburgh and Aberdeen running late, it had been decided at Carlisle to allow the first (6.17) local passenger service of the day, which would normally have followed the expresses, to go on ahead of both. This avoided seriously delaying the departure of the 'local', an important consideration because, while this was very much a local service between Carlisle and Beattock, doubling up as the morning milk train, its engine was scheduled to switch roles and adopt upgraded status at the latter station, continuing northwards at the head of a fast commuter service originating on the short branch line from Moffat up to Glasgow. The priority was to get the locomotive to Beattock on time even if it meant the local service missed its connections with the overnight expresses at Carlisle.[2]

But on 22 May 1915, as was often the case, at some stage south of Beattock the local 'Parly' train would have to be shunted out of the way to let the expresses pass.

As the overnight services from London to Scotland's great cities followed the local service on the run to the Anglo-Scottish border near Gretna, a train of vastly different character was approaching from the north. It had set out in darkness from the small station at Larbert, not far from Falkirk, to the north of and roughly midway between, Glasgow and Edinburgh in the Central Lowlands. Leaving at 3.42am, it was chiefly made up of fifteen coaches, a motley assortment of ancient (some built fifty years earlier) non-corridor vehicles – a quartet of eight-wheeled coaches, the remainder with six wheels – all of which had been borrowed from England's Great Central Railway.

In marked contrast to the stock of the sleeping car express, the underframes of these wooden-bodied coaches were built mostly of oak, a form of construction long obsolete. The train also had an assortment of six Caledonian Railway wagons and vans – including the brake van – coupled to its rear, loaded with military equipment and ammunition for the use of the passengers, soldiers of the 7th Royal Scots, en route to Liverpool and thence by ship to fight in the bloody battles history collectively recalls as the Gallipoli or Dardanelles campaign. Larbert had served as the soldiers' final training ground prior to departure. Empty, their train would have weighed 319 tons. With the weight of its armed occupants and equipment added, the tonnage must have exceeded 400.[3]

Troop trains such as this served as a fitting prelude to the horrors that awaited their cramped occupants in what would prove an ultimately doomed nine-month Allied offensive in southeastern Europe. The Liverpool-bound special train that morning, just four weeks into the Gallipoli campaign, possessed nothing of the majesty and elegance, nor anything like the comfort, of the northbound sleeper. It was at the other end of the scale entirely.

The soldiers on the train – officers and other ranks – were Territorials, part of a close-knit military unit known colloquially as the Leith Battalion in recognition of the port town serving Edinburgh from where many of them were drawn. The remainder came from neighbouring Musselburgh, just five miles away.

Not unusually for the British Army in the 1914-18 war, these friends and colleagues in civilian life – many of them linked by close family ties – were now heading as one for battle on a faraway front. Since late April the battalion, released from home defence duties in the Edinburgh district, had been assigned to the Army's 52nd Lowland Division and trained for service overseas. This elevation, according to the Royal Scots' official history, was met with rejoicing. The Scottish Territorials had craved the chance to show their mettle on the battlefield – and here it was at last. France had been the 52nd Division's intended theatre of war but when in May the 7th Royal Scots prepared at their Larbert training base for departure, it was well known among the ranks – a poorly-kept military secret – that they would be making for Liverpool. Few of the battalion harboured doubts as to where they were bound from there and that it would not be the short passage across the Channel to France.

The men had been readied for the move on Wednesday, 19 May. Their rail journey, they were told, would begin in the early hours of the following morning. But it was delayed. One of the reasons was that no carriages could be found to convey the soldiers that Thursday morning. Another was that, in marked contrast to the accommodation eventually provided on the railway, the soldiers were booked to embark at Liverpool for the Dardanelles aboard the luxury ocean liner *Aquitania*, a plan hindered when the great ship became stuck in mud on the Mersey estuary. So the departure of the Leith Battalion from Larbert had been put off for two days until the fateful Saturday morning of 22 May.

Three trains had been assembled. The 3.42 departure had led the way. It carried the battalion's A and D companies, its commanding officer and the headquarters staff. The official passenger list numbered 498 – 15 officers and 483 other ranks. They sat eight to a compartment. That, at least, was the intended norm. It is clear from some accounts, however, that the number rose to nine in some cases. Eight or nine men fully kitted-out, each with a rifle, it must have been an uncomfortable squeeze. The vans behind held most of the battalion's stores.

Scheduled to depart from Larbert two hours later, the second of the trains had been allocated to the battalion's remaining two companies, B and C, while the third, due out later in the day, was readied to convey battlefield essentials which included the 7th Royal Scots' horse-drawn transport – the animals travelling in vans with their fodder – and the battalion's field kitchens.

The 3.42's rag-tag composition reflected the enormous pressure placed on the railways of Britain to find from whatever source they could the coaches and ancillary rolling stock needed for the wartime military traffic. As noted in chapter one, while the movement of troops and their equipment around the country by rail was an obvious and entirely necessary priority, there was no properly co-ordinated strategic approach to this in Britain during the First World War. Had such a policy been in place, civilian travel could have been restricted – as happened in World War Two – with the result that newer, better and safer vehicles, far more suited to the task of coping with the military traffic, might well have been available. That they were not on the morning of 22 May 1915 would prove a catastrophic factor in the events that transpired.

Critically, virtually all of the fifteen coaches in which the soldiers travelled were illuminated by high-pressure gas stored in cylinders beneath the floors. In any mishap on a railway line, this was obviously a recipe for potential disaster. As historian John Thomas put it in his 1969 book, *Gretna: Britain's Worst Rail Disaster*, 'with the wartime shortage of stock, almost anything on wheels was acceptable'. The train allocated to the Royal Scots was clearly one not fit for purpose.[4]

If we are to believe accounts given by some of the Scottish soldiers, recorded by the press at the time and by the authors of subsequent books, the prevailing mood among the 3.42 troop train's passengers was good amid the grey light of the emerging dawn at Larbert. They were apparently in 'high spirits' as they marched to and then along the platform in full voice, singing as they made for the train's decrepit coaches to the stirring accompaniment of the pipes.

Yet as their train hurtled southwards on the early stages of its special working, timetabled to run at express train speeds guaranteed, at the very least, to give the men of the 7th Royal Scots the roughest of rides en route to the Mersey, did the mood darken? This was a train merely masquerading as an express.

This cannot be dismissed as hindsight. It was apparent whenever the train picked up speed – though this was not very often to begin with. Soldiers commented that the carriages were swaying so violently, their luggage fell from the racks and the soldiers themselves were thrown around 'with chilling prescience'. One went further. 'Surely,' he told his mates, 'there is going to be a wreck.'

Perhaps those men had recognised back at Larbert the potential threat posed by the obviously sub-standard condition of their carriages. It would probably be unwise to take the upbeat accounts of their departure at face value without question. There must surely have been serious reservations. The press were subject to strict wartime censorship which would never permit any suggestion of low morale among the armed forces. However, there are no firm alternative sources with which to challenge the published descriptions of the soldiers' early departure other than suggestions, which continue to circulate in the Scottish border region, of desertions. This is an issue better left for later analysis.

Like the northbound sleeping car express, the troop train encountered delays caused by the heavy additional demands on the network, slow-moving freight traffic in particular, as it headed southwards on the initial stage of its journey to Carstairs, where its route from Glasgow joined the line from Edinburgh for the onward journey towards the English border. It had taken a frustrating ninety-two minutes to cover the thirty-six miles from Larbert. The troop train pulled into Carstairs at 5.17 for the locomotive to take on water. By the time it left the South Lanarkshire junction station, it was running twenty-two minutes behind schedule.[5]

No doubt the driver and fireman in the cab of the Caledonian Railway engine hauling the train were relieved on reaching the lofty summit at Beattock, midway between Carstairs and Lockerbie, to find the path ahead into the border county of Dumfrieshire apparently cleared for them. There was a cautious descent of the bank, with frequent application of the brakes. It has been suggested that the driver's caution – here and very probably earlier on the journey – was prompted by his forced reliance on vacuum braking. The aged Great Central Railway vehicles his engine was hauling were not equipped for use with the more accommodating Westinghouse air brake, a system the driver was accustomed to using. Whatever the truth of this, once down the southbound gradient from the top of Beattock, the troop train quickly gathered pace. When the train passed Lockerbie, it had taken sixty-five minutes to travel the forty-eight miles from Carstairs, markedly quicker than the earlier part of the run from Larbert.[6]

The twenty-one vehicle formation may have been ramshackle but there was an altogether more impressive combination at the head of the train. The 4-4-0 express passenger locomotive, number 121, was a product of the Caledonian's St Rollox workshops in Glasgow when the company's motive power development was in the hands of John F. McIntosh between 1895 and 1914. A member of the famous *Dunalastair IV* class, it was considerably more modern than its long rake of rolling stock. At its controls was Francis Scott, who enjoyed celebrity status among the ranks of the railway's employees, having earlier been entrusted with the prestigious task of driving the trains provided for three reigning monarchs – Victoria, Edward VII and George V. A wholly different kind of fame lay ahead of Scott and his engine as they closed in on the border.[7]

Just before crossing it in the opposite direction, still ahead of the two Anglo–Scottish expresses, the local train from Carlisle had drifted into Gretna, the station on England's northern fringe separated by the border from the famously Scottish village it served. Signalman James Tinsley, who lived nearby, was late for work, his destination a signal box located a short distance down the Caledonian's main line, beyond its junction with the Glasgow & South Western's competing route northwards. An intermediate box, positioned between stations, ten miles and ten chains north of Carlisle, this was a railway outpost little known to the public at large – but that was dramatically about to change.

In the signal box to which Tinsley was headed, his colleague George Meakin, nearing the end of a tiring ten-hour night shift, had reached a decision. The express trains from London were important – the local train, very much less so. It was time for the Parly to be shunted aside, to yield to the expresses' superior status. As well as prioritising military traffic, signalmen were under strict instructions, war or no war, to give fast-moving passenger trains a considerable degree of precedence in all but the most exceptional of circumstances. They risked disciplinary action if they failed regularly to do so. There was nothing to warrant an exception on Saturday, 22 May 1915. That, at least, was the way it seemed to the men on the railway's own 'front line' that morning.

Given the pressure he was under not to delay the progress of the overnight expresses, George Meakin's decision was perfectly understandable, but it would turn out to be crucial to the shattering events that were to transpire in a very short space of time. Meakin would stop the local train outside his signal box. It would have to wait its turn in the procession northwards at this remote spot.

Quintinshill.

It was fairly routine for Meakin, nothing out of the ordinary on a busy main line. He telephoned Roger Kirkpatrick, signalman at Gretna Junction, the neighbouring box to the south, to say that he was going to halt the 6.17 from Carlisle when it arrived. Using some form of prearranged hand signal, Kirkpatrick relayed the message to James Tinsley as the latter left his home close by.

The ten-hour day shift at Quintinshill officially started at 6am. It was already well past that time, but Tinsley was not concerned about that. Thanks to a strictly *unofficial* local arrangement, he wasn't expected there until 6.30. He was, however, still short of time – too short to walk from his home to the signal box. Running might have got him to work at 6.30, but the opportunity to be taken there by train was obviously a better option. He knew from Roger Kirkpatrick's signal that the local train would be stopping at Quintinshill. Not for the first time, James Tinsley hopped aboard the engine of the 6.17 to begin his short trip from Gretna – a journey that would transport him into lasting infamy.

The fact that there were passing loops either side of the running lines at Quintinshill should have made the process of holding the local train there straightforward. But not on this occasion. Both loops had been allotted to freight trains, understandably given a low priority by Meakin as he juggled the competing demands arising from the traffic congestion on his section of the line.

Arriving at 6.14, a late-running northbound goods service had been diverted by him into the adjacent loop to clear the main line for the passenger trains behind. The prospect of the express trains – also running late – being further delayed by the plodding progress of this heavy freight train of forty-five loaded wagons, behind a moderately powered 0-6-0 locomotive, was the determining factor. Meakin calculated that the freight had insufficient time to reach Kirkpatrick, the next available passing place to the north. Thus, it had to be removed from the equation.[8, 9]

At 6.28 Meakin had been presented with a further complexity. Nearing the signal box from the north was a train of empty wagons, returning from Grangemouth on the banks of the Firth of Forth, to South Wales after delivering coal to fuel the Grand Fleet at Scapa Flow. The signalman had been told that there would be no room for the train in the Kingmoor marshalling yard at Carlisle. It would have to wait at Quintinshill, possibly for a lengthy period, until space could be allocated for it south of the border. Meakin had the southbound passing loop at his disposal. He halted the empty coal train pending the shunting manoeuvre that would allow it to proceed into the safety of the loop.

First he had to deal with the arrival, a couple of minutes later, of the local passenger train from Carlisle. With both loops now or soon to be occupied by the freights, an alternative means of shunting the 'local' away from the northbound track, thus clearing a path for the first of the late-running express trains behind it to pass, would be needed – and there was only one other option.

After it drew to a halt the train was reversed through the crossover connection from the northbound main line onto the southbound. The first express, making for Edinburgh, could now run through unhindered while the 'local' waited on the 'wrong' line, facing north on a track carrying traffic for the south. It could then be returned to its rightful line and sent on to Kirkpatrick station where a further shunt would allow it to be passed by the second express. This was Meakin's plan.[10]

Although this was something of a last resort procedure, the heavy wartime traffic demands had forced its use several times before at Quintinshill. The local train would be safe. The signalman would protect it. That was the theory.[11]

With the Parly dealt with, George Meakin cleared the signal to allow the southbound train of Welsh coal empties to run into the adjacent passing loop. James Tinsley climbed the steps of Quintinshill signal box to relieve him. This would become the most momentous shift change ever undertaken on a British railway.

It began smoothly enough when, as planned, the first of the two late-running overnight northbound expresses, the scheduled 11.45pm from Euston to Edinburgh and Aberdeen, cantered past the signal box at 6.38am. A few minutes later it ran past the Liverpool-bound troop train which was now making much better progress, clattering by the signal box at Kirkpatrick station – Quintinshill's neighbouring box to the north – at a speed the signalman there later recalled as 'very fast.' With Quintinshill's George Meakin alerted to its proximity, the troop train then made good use of the favourable gradient from Brackenhill summit.[12]

Was Francis Scott driving his hotch-potch of a train *too* fast as he raced towards Quintinshill? It has been estimated that the troop train's speed may have exceeded 70mph on the falling gradient. It was tightly scheduled and running late. No doubt frustrated by the hold-ups further north on the overtaxed railway system, Scott was trying to make up time. His engine could cope well enough but the venerable vehicles lurching along behind it were an entirely different proposition. Another man under pressure, Scott was surely taking a chance.

But the signals ahead were all cleared for him so Scott pushed on. As he approached Quintinshill, having covered the fifteen-plus miles from Lockerbie in just eighteen minutes, luck still seemed to be with him. The box's outer signal was also at 'clear'. Scott hurried on, rounding a curve which, along with the bridge beyond it carrying a road across the railway, obscured his view of the signal box until he was almost upon it. As he swung under the bridge and prepared to run past the box and its loops, his vision along the line ahead, until then masked by the curve and the presence of the goods train in the northbound loop, cleared. Francis Scott was confronted with a train driver's nightmare scenario.

Less than 200 yards in front of him, its blue paintwork gleaming in the bright morning sunshine, stood a massive locomotive. Facing his way. On the same set of rails. Was there time for it to register with driver Scott that this was an engine of the 4-6-0 *Cardean* class, pride of the Caledonian Railway? For such a locomotive to be at the head of a humble local train from Carlisle was unusual in the extreme. For it to be standing where it was, blocking his way, would have been unfathomable to Scott in the last few seconds of life left to him.

On the footplate of the local train fireman George Hutchinson was about to take a snack when he happened to glance upwards. To his horror he saw that the signal had been cleared for an approaching train from the north. The 'local' was in its way. Naturally, he alerted his driver, David Wallace. Better placed from his position to the left of the cab to see along the curve of the line, Wallace saw immediately that a train was bearing down on them at speed. It was less than a couple of hundred yards away and closing in fast. There was nothing he or

Hutchinson could do to avoid a collision. They leapt from either side of the cab and raced for cover beneath the wagons of the freight trains in the loops.

The footplate crew of the troop train had done their best to minimise the inevitable impact, reducing speed as far as was humanly possible. But, at 6.49, amid a cacophony of screaming whistles and burning brakes, their heavily-laden train hit the 120 ton locomotive head-on at an estimated speed of 40mph.

Their own engine was split from its tender, the former thrown to the right, the latter to the left. Scott and his fireman, James Hannah, both Carlisle-based railwaymen from Etterby, a mile northwest of the city, were killed instantly. Bunched together in their flimsy coaches behind the locomotive, the men of the 7th Royal Scots were left dreadfully exposed, defenceless against the resultant mayhem.

The leading vehicles catapulted over the top of the wrecked locomotive. The remainder, apart from the Caledonian vans at the rear, which remained on the rails, literally disintegrated in seconds. The Great Central coaches lay in pieces across both running lines. What had been a train more than 200 yards long was compressed into a mere 67 yards. The soldiers were jolted violently over one another, bombarded by rifles and haversacks falling from the luggage racks. Wooden splinters and flying pieces of metal ripped into their flesh, potentially as lethal as anything an enemy force could have thrown at them on the battlefield. Several of the men died this way. Many more were injured. Others were trapped.

By comparison, the local train escaped relatively lightly – though it was as complete a tragedy for two of its passengers as it was for the soldiers killed on impact. Along with its tender, locomotive number 907, which had been allocated the train – a considerable come-down from the expresses it was built to haul – as a running-in trip following overhaul, was thumped back more than forty yards. It came off the rails but remained upright. Behind it the back of the tender caved in and its coupling to the four-coach train broke, setting free the sparsely-filled vehicles, which ran back the best part of another 100 yards, safe from the catastrophic sequel that would soon emerge. But the front of the leading coach had smashed against the tender. It was here the two lives were lost.[13]

What could have happened in the signal box? The theory of signalling protection for the stationary locomotive and its local train – and for the onrushing troop train, which inexplicably had been allowed to proceed all the way to Quintinshill unchecked on the same set of rails so that a collision was unavoidable – had proved to be just that and nothing more. A theory. Not a reality.

Of course it *should* have been a reality. No properly functioning signalman presented with the sort of situation outlined to James Tinsley as he arrived for the early day shift at Quintinshill box would have failed to ensure the necessary safety precautions were in place to safeguard the trains under his control. The troop train would not have been permitted to approach the signal box until the 'local' from Carlisle had been cleared from the southbound main line. But it hadn't been. As a result, the way had been opened only for a tragedy.

By any standards this was a serious accident. Lives had been lost although we shall never know how many deaths could directly be attributed to the initial collision. Perhaps the toll of fatalities would not have been that high, relatively speaking. J.A.B. Hamilton suggested in his account that the majority of casualties might have been restricted to injury rather than outright death. It remains a moot point. What is certain is that worse, *much* worse, was soon to follow.[14]

Immediately south of Quintinshill, the London-Glasgow sleeping car service was making up for lost time on the rising gradient thanks to the combined effort of the two powerful 4-4-0 locomotives at its head, aided, as the troop train had been, by a series of clear signals. In the cabs of the engines the firemen spotted men running towards them, shouting and waving their hands in a manner which left no doubt that something was seriously amiss. Closest to the express was Douglas Graham, guard of the local train, who, shaking off the stunning effect of the collision seconds earlier, had, in his words, 'remembered that the down 6.05 express [the official departure time from Carlisle, though the sleeper was of course late] would be at hand.' Commendably, Graham had 'rushed back to the line to stop it'. But, he added, the sleeper 'was then too near'.

It was later estimated that Graham had covered 167 yards in just forty seconds. The point has been made that this was pretty good for a 46-year-old man, whether he ran over the sleepers or, more likely, alongside. It was not recorded which of the two options he had chosen. Neither would have represented an easy run. He was followed by James Benson and John Grierson, driver and fireman, respectively, of the empty coal train. Their valiant dash was equally in vain.

Driver John Cowper, in charge of the leading engine, number 140, did what he could once alerted by his fireman to the frantic signals of Graham and the men behind him. 'I immediately crossed to the left of the engine and applied the Westinghouse [air] brake with full force,' he recalled later. As number 140 shot past the exhausted Graham, Cowper looked up. 'I saw the wreckage in front of me.'

Andrew Johnstone, driving the second locomotive, number 48 (the 'train engine' in railway parlance), had slammed on his brake in unison with Cowper, but the two drivers' brave, desperate bid to avert catastrophe was never going to be enough. There was simply not enough time. Less than two minutes after the first collision, the double-headed sleeping car express ploughed into the wreckage.

Driver Cowper described the initial impact as 'not very hard.' His engine had run into the crumpled leading coaches of the troop train, strewn across the track ahead of their own locomotive. Fortunately, the collision speed was reduced by Cowper's ability to slow his train from 50mph, at the time he passed Graham, to an estimated 40mph. But, he added, there was 'a great sound of splintering wood and breaking glass, followed by a very hard blow which almost brought us to a stand'. His engine had struck a more substantial obstacle – the tender of the troop train's locomotive. It rode high into the air above a mound of twisted metal.

Cowper himself was, as he later put it, 'buried up to the neck in the left-hand corner of my engine cab by the coals from the tender, with my back to the firebox.' He revealed in the Coroner's court that, aware the closest of the wrecked coaches were burning and understandably fearful the fire might at any moment spread to his locomotive, he had 'resolved to gain my freedom by severing my imprisoned foot with a knife'. Fortunately, such drastic action was averted.

Stunned, considerably bruised 'and somewhat burnt about the neck', Cowper was helped out of the cab by his fireman, David Todbunter, and driver Johnstone. His wounds needed attention and were soon tended, along with those of many other casualties of the tragedy, in the field alongside the railway, allowing John Cowper, with remarkable selflessness, to help other injured victims. A man in his sixties, his courage has been richly and deservedly praised.

Driver Johnstone and his fireman, John Graham, cushioned to an extent by Cowper's engine in front of them, escaped almost entirely unhurt from the collision. Behind their locomotive, the modern construction of the rolling stock, markedly stronger than the coaches of the troop train, offered protection to their occupants. Most of the express train's passengers were unhurt as a result, but for seven people travelling in the train's front two coaches there was no escape. The Quintinshill death toll was mounting. Horrifically, it was soon to rise much further.

A three-train collision immediately became a five-train crash when piles of wreckage were spread violently to either side of the running lines, smashing into the freight trains which had been held in the two passing loops. Then, an already dreadful scene of desolation rapidly descended into a virtual hell on earth.

Notes

1. The designation 4-4-0 refers to the wheel arrangement of the locomotives, indicating that they were equipped with four leading wheels on two axles and four powered driving wheels, but had no trailing wheels. Similarly, a 4-6-0 locomotive, such as number 970 of the local train, would have four leading wheels, six driving wheels and, again, no trailing wheels.
2. The through train from Moffat's branch line terminus to the main line at Beattock and thence northwards to Glasgow was known as the *Tinto Express* – after the high South Lanarkshire hill of the same name.
3. The Caledonian Railway vehicles attached to the rear of the troop train included two caravan trucks, an 'open scenery' truck, two fish vans and the brake van. All except the brake were six-wheeled vehicles.
4. *Gretna: Britain's Worst Rail Disaster (1915)* by John Thomas, published by David & Charles, 1969 – ISBN 0-7153-4645-8.
5. The troop train had been halted by signals for ten minutes at Abronhill, North Lanarkshire, and was further delayed en route to Carstairs by two permanent way slacks (speed restrictions).
6. George Westinghouse pioneered the railway air brake system, activated by compressed air, in 1872. The fail-safe air brake system employed worldwide on railway networks today is based on his original design.

7. Francis Scott was a prominent figure in both professional and private life. In common with many other engine drivers of the period, he worked hard to foster non-conformist and working class movements. An elder of the Carlisle Presbyterian Church, he was actively involved in its Sunday School.

8. An 0-6-0 designation denotes a locomotive with six driving wheels on three axles but no leading or trailing wheels.

9. The northbound freight train had been timetabled to leave Carlisle at 4.50 but was delayed for a full hour.

10. It is clear that the 6.17 local train from Carlisle arrived at Quintinshill at, or just before, 6.30am. This was actually its advertised time of departure from Gretna, so it must have left the station there a few minutes early, presumably to ensure it could be put out of the way at Quintinshill in plenty of time for the northbound expresses to run past. At that time of the morning, leaving a few minutes ahead of schedule would have caused very little, if any, inconvenience to the sprinkling of passengers on the 'local.'

11. Records confirm that the process of stabling the northbound local train on the southbound running line at Quintinshill to allow faster trains to pass had been adopted four times since the previous January.

12. J.A.B. Hamilton (see below) suggests that it wasn't until the troop train came down the incline from Brackenhill summit that driver Scott was able to make any significant headway in his bid to recover lost time.

13. Number 907, the most prized of the locomotives involved in the two collisions, was later able to travel by rail to the Caledonian's St Rollox works in Glasgow. There was great reluctance on the company's part to write off such a valuable asset, especially as number 907 had only just received a general overhaul. However, the damage caused was found to be too serious to warrant repair. The engine was scrapped and not replaced. Also written off was number 121, of the troop train, but in this case a replacement engine *was* built by the company – identical to its predecessor in both design and number.

14. *Britain's Greatest Rail Disaster: The Quintinshill Blaze of 1915* by John Thomas, published by Allen & Unwin, 1969 – ISBN 10-0046250034.

Chapter 3

Fire and Rescue

'They looked more like the remnants of a corps that had just emerged from a deadly battle than the survivors of an accident occurring within a few hours' distance of their home.'

Dumfries & Galloway Standard & Advertiser, 28 May 1915

The real horror of Quintinshill lay not in the fact of the first collision, nor indeed in the second. Both were, of course, serious – bad enough on their own. But it was what happened immediately after the second collision that produced the ultimate catastrophe and accounted substantially for the huge loss of life which ever since has set aside the events of 22 May 1915 as a railway disaster without precedent, or matching sequel, in Britain. It was a massive contributor. Yet it can be encapsulated in a single word. One solitary, devastating element:

Fire

The antiquated troop train was a tinderbox on wheels. That it was ever permitted to transport soldiers – or anyone else for that matter – at express train speeds was a disgrace which cannot be excused by the exigencies of wartime. The soldiers and others who died at Quintinshill were led to their doom by a lack of foresight and compassion arguably as shameful as that exhibited by the military strategists who sacrificed thousands of young lives in battle for the sake of a few feet of contested land.

Of course the disaster was not solely the fault of the planners who condemned the 7th Royal Scots to ride in a mobile death trap – as this book will reveal, there were many other failings by many other people, few of which have ever been noted – but the condition of the early morning troop train from Larbert was nevertheless a fundamental factor.

In the immediate wake of the multiple crash that factor was all too horribly exposed.

'The scenes which followed beggar description,' reported the *Dumfries & Galloway Standard* in its remarkably detailed, evocative eyewitness account.

'After the dreadful crash had shattered the restful quiet of the surroundings and had proclaimed its message of destruction there was a sudden hush as if Nature herself stood aghast at the hideous spectacle. Then it was all chaos and confusion.'

A series of explosions blasted out an ominous response to the five-train collision. The gas cylinders beneath the fragmented floors of the troop train's splintered coaches had blown. Burning coals from one or more of the ruptured fireboxes of the wrecked locomotives – most probably from the troop train's engine – quickly ignited the escaping gas. In seconds, the twisted debris was engulfed in a massive firestorm. In the scattered homes nearby some local people wondered if the German forces of Kaiser Wilhelm had launched an invasion.

There was also a belief, though it was soon dispelled, that the explosions had been caused by ammunition stored on the troop train. It was fortunate indeed that the vans loaded with large amounts of military projectiles had been coupled to the rear of the train. If these vans had instead been marshalled at the front, it does not seem too fanciful a suggestion that the entire neighbourhood might have gone up in smoke – including the signal box and, with it, any hope of determining key causes of the disaster. In fact, the ammunition was quickly eliminated from becoming a major exacerbating factor in an already appalling drama.

As the *Dumfries & Galloway Standard* reported, 'immediately after the collision a number of the men of the ammunition section ran to the wagons in their stockinged feet and, wearing only their shirts and trousers, for they had been sleeping with most of their clothes off, they uncoupled the wagons and pushed them back, and then took the ammunition to a bank some distance away, out of harm's reach.'

The extent of further death and destruction averted by this courageous act of quick thinking on the part of the soldiers can only be imagined.

It is clear from the evidence and undisputed that while the exploding gas cylinders greatly intensified the blaze, the conflagration was first ignited by 'live' coals from the locomotive of the troop train and then, separately, by those spilling out from the express train's leading engine.

The *Standard's* report continued: 'There was a medley of horrible sounds that the worst delirium could not equal. In the midst of the wreckage were four great engines broken and twisted as if by some giant hand. From one of them, propelled by some unseen force, came huge pieces of metal which were sent high into the air and fell to earth with great violence, rendering rescue work in the vicinity impossible.'

It would appear from this that the Dumfries paper's reporter, or someone he spoke with on arrival at the crash site, may have witnessed the explosion of a locomotive's boiler, or possibly one of its cylinders, the means by which stored steam power is converted into motion. If so, it is an intriguing aspect of the Quintinshill disaster that no other chronicler of the events has since referred to.

The report provided a graphic depiction of the human tragedy: 'Arms and legs protruded from the debris; cries for help, and in some cases even for death, were heard on all hands [sic], but many of these had to go unheeded because of the raging flames. What the ultimate fate of some of the imprisoned sufferers was can only be imagined, but a considerable number of them must have been burnt alive.'

Such accounts – and many others, equally graphic – were seriously at odds with remarks made later in the report of Lieutenant Colonel Edward Druitt, of the Railway Inspectorate, the officer quickly appointed by the Board of Trade to conduct the official inquiry into the accident. 'The wreckage of the troop train was so excessive,' he wrote, 'that probably all those not rescued before the fire reached the coaches in which they lay were dead, or at any rate insensible, so it may be confidently hoped that few, if any, were conscious when the fire reached them.'

Druitt added that he had been told by more than one person that 'they were struck by the absence of cries for help from the wrecked coaches of the troop train and by the great fortitude of the injured.'

While the reference to the wounded men's courage is beyond dispute, the point has been made by other writers that either Colonel Druitt was trying to soften the awful realities of the crash for the sake of the victims' families or he had been grossly misinformed. Whichever of the two applied, this official assessment was about as wide of the mark as is possible to imagine. The human suffering at Quintinshill was dreadful. Fire was at its heart.

'Flames which looked scarlet in the sunlight,' bringing 'death and destruction in an inconceivably short space of time' and 'ghastly white smoke.' Reporters vied for the most descriptive accounts of the desolate scene. One was struck by the 'strangely incongruous mingling of human cries of anguish with the sweet trill of the mavis [thrush] and the blackbird as they poured forth their morning song from the neighbouring trees.'

While fatalities among its own passengers had, mercifully, been restricted, the impact of the northbound sleeping car express train's collision had clearly had a profound effect on the soldiers' chances of surviving the shattering demise of their troop train. The *Dumfries & Galloway Standard added*: 'The express had in its impetuous rush torn up carriages of the troop train and would seem to have cut off and destroyed many soldiers who were making their escape, as their remains were found huddled in groups along the side of some of the carriages.'

Survivors would later tell incredible stories of how they escaped the wreckage of their train. 'I had only just lain back to go to sleep when, all of a sudden, the carriage seemed to crumple up like a melodeon,' recalled Piper Thomas Clachers in a gripping account. 'Fire shot up before my face. It must have been gas; it was such a sudden big flame. I went down amongst a lot of woodwork. My foot was jammed and the door was locked. Then we got a second bump and another carriage came on top of us, and there was fire all around. Then something broke and there was a hole above. An Irish fellow shoved a drummer boy up through it. There was an engine – I think it was the engine of the local train – just against us, with the driver on it. He got hold of my hand and pulled me up, and another too. My hands and face were badly burned but I did not know it then and started to help others. It was an awful sight right enough.'

Peter Cumming, at 15 the youngest member of the 7th Royal Scots involved, was sound asleep when the troop train ran into the stationary 'local' at Quintinshill. Years later he recalled being woken up by the 'terrific crash and the stuff falling all about.' Located in a coach half way down the train, he was unhurt but the vehicle was wrecked. He scrambled out by climbing through a pile of debris. 'On the left side of me was a truck laden with coal [from the freight train held in the loop]. I was putting out my hand to grab it when another crash came and there we were among the wreckage again.'

For a second time the young soldier found himself clambering up the debris of his carriage compartment, 'through a little sort of tunnel affair,' but he quickly realised that his left foot was caught. 'I gave it a tremendous drag and freed it. I put my hand on the coal truck again when a bloke behind me yelled, "give me a hand, give me a hand." I reached out my hand and gave him a tremendous tug and he came free as well. I scrambled over the truck and dropped onto the track.'

Peter Cumming escaped with scratches and bruises and in later life would pursue a successful career as a policeman. Not so fortunate was his brother, John, two years his senior. Grievously hurt, he died later of his injuries in hospital at Carlisle. Their father, a long-serving 49-year-old sergeant, although part of the battalion heading for Gallipoli, was not on the stricken train.

A trio of NCOs – a sergeant, an armourer staff sergeant and a corporal – had been fortunate in the allocation of accommodation. They had travelled first class, just the three of them in a compartment midway down the train. Making the most of the space, they had been sleeping in relative comfort. The first crash had smashed the windows, leaving them dazed but otherwise unhurt. It hadn't seemed too serious a situation; they could quite easily have got out safely. 'Then the express came upon us,' the corporal told the press later in hospital.

'What happened I cannot exactly say, but I was violently thrown and the next moment I found myself among a mass of wreckage with the staff sergeant over me. My head was down and my feet were pointing upwards. We were imprisoned among the debris and there seemed no way out, so the sergeant suggested that we should keep still until help arrived. Very soon we became conscious of a smell of burning which came from underneath the wreckage and this at once stirred us into action. The staff sergeant, one of whose legs was broken, began to clear a way through the entangled mass, which in a short time burst into flames. It was with great difficulty that we succeeded in getting clear. My right leg was firmly held and, although it was already very painful, I had just to wrench it away. In doing that I made the injury worse, but it was only by doing it that I was able to effect my escape. At last we got out of the wrecked carriage...'

The escape route led them directly onto the top of their train's locomotive! They crawled over it – 'although how it came to be in that particular place I don't know,' added the corporal – and were confronted with a scene of appalling devastation. 'When we looked around an awful scene met our eyes. Mixed up with the wreckage we could see bundles of bodies. Many others were fearfully mutilated and from underneath the pile came the moans and the cries of the victims. It was such a terrible sight that I fainted twice before I was removed.'

Some soldiers had jumped from the troop train, without serious injury, onto the 'four foot way' (the space between the tracks) following the initial collision. For a short while those men were safe, survivors alongside the mound of debris. But they were also stranded, vulnerable, and given no time to avoid becoming victims as the express from London ripped into the wreckage and took their lives. Quintinshill was the cruelest of tragedies. Men escaped, their lives apparently saved – and then, within seconds, without mercy, they were cut down.

However, for one soldier at least the impact of the express on the initial crash was a blessing. In preparing his account in the 1960s J.A.B. Hamilton was able to speak with several surviving eyewitnesses. Among them was Peter Skea, a private with the Royal Scots who had travelled in the leading coach of the troop train. 'We went right over the top of the locomotive,' he said, recalling the initial collision. 'Its funnel was no more than two feet away and flames were already belching out. I couldn't move. Then the express came and cleared everything out of the way. I scrambled out and dropped ten feet, then I climbed up onto the tender of one of the express train's engines. My right leg was broken in two places and both arms were burned right up to the armpits. My face too – burned skin was hanging like grapes from my chin. But I felt no pain, either then or later.'

For some of the Royal Scots the fact that there had been a double collision was lost amid the confusion. 'It seemed as if we toppled over and were falling down the embankment with the wreckage on top of us,' recalled James McCullough, a member of the battalion's pipe band, seated in the third coach. 'I don't know whether this was due to the first or the second collision; in fact, I didn't know there had been two collisions until later in the day when they told us in hospital.'

Knocked unconscious, McCullough came to lying on the embankment. 'I had been pitched through a window and a piece of skull had been cut out by the glass.' Speaking to Hamilton half a century later, he added: 'I remember being carried into the field where we had to wait a long time before the rescue people came.'

Other survivors were completely oblivious to what had happened. Corporal Thomas Gleave, for example, woke up in hospital ten days after the disaster after losing consciousness in one or other of the collisions. He had no idea where he was. Neither had he any recollection of having been in an accident. He can perhaps be counted as one of the more fortunate victims. Those who did remember the crash were destined to carry the mental as well as the physical scars for a very long time.

Prior to the arrival of any medical professionals, there had been an immediate local response to the plight of the crash victims. The *Dumfries & Galloway*

Standard interviewed several of the rural community who had rushed to the crash scene. Among them was Andrew Sword who lived half a mile from the signal box. He was working in a field belonging to farmer Hugh Mackie, his employer, when his attention was seized dramatically by the thunderous impact of the initial collision on the nearby railway line. He described being 'paralysed' as, looking up, he witnessed the northbound express plunge into the mire.

'Like a flash it was into the other two,' he said, 'dug into the middle of them, and raised a hill of wreckage. The flames spurted out of the wreckage higher and higher. There were bursts as if something was exploding. Bits of debris were hurled high into the air. Little tongues of flames, like bursting rockets, shot up.'

This was no fanciful, exaggerated account. Many others on the scene, then and later, provided dramatic corroborative evidence of the sheer volume of burning wreckage. One, a doctor from Carlisle, recalled 'iron girders heaped and twisted in fantastic shapes, and wreckage perhaps forty feet in the air, all burning.'

Andrew Sword managed to steel himself. 'With a great effort I moved and ran across the fields to the wreck. I found speed as I moved and raced across the fields like mad. But not as fast as a young fellow who reached the scene first.' The identity of the 'young fellow' was not disclosed by the *Standard*, nor by the Carlisle-based *Cumberland News*, which also carried extensive coverage of the disaster, or the other newspapers – local and national – which devoted many column inches to the story. What, if anything, he was able to do remains a mystery.

There were, however, plenty of others able to add their own 'take' on the tragedy. Early arrivals also included John and Andrew Mackie, the farm owner's sons. The brothers' testimony painted a graphic picture of human despair.

'As I approached the flaming wreck I saw people running out from the London train,' Andrew Mackie told the reporter from the *Standard*. 'Looking closer, I saw that they were soldiers,' he recounted. Maybe the Royal Scots had gone to the aid of the passengers on the express or had found an escape route via its carriages. More probably, Mackie had seen some of the off-duty Army personnel, home on leave, among the express train's own passengers who, having escaped injury on the sleeper, were helping immediately with the rescue. From the accounts of eyewitnesses, the fact that the bid to save lives was so quickly mounted after the second collision owed a great deal to the presence of these soldiers.

Aided by tools – notably axes, crowbars and saws – from the nearby farms, the ad-hoc rescue mission concentrated on the remains of the troop train. Soldiers and civilians joined forces as its carriages, or what remained of them, were ferociously smashed to smithereens to free those trapped inside. 'I heard voices,' added Mackie. 'Someone shouted, "help me out of here." I rushed up and, seeing a piece of wood on the way, smashed the window… another man came up and we pulled the man and two others out.' It was just the start.

'The next man I rescued had his back and both his legs broken,' Mackie recalled in his moving account of the drama. 'He cried out in agony when I only touched him. We got him out in spite of his cries as the flames were coming up.'

The *Dumfries & Galloway Standard* stressed that railwaymen on the spot and the local people who rushed to help did the best they could in the most trying of circumstances. It was an uphill task. 'Attempts were made to douse the flames using water from the tenders of the locomotives, but such attempts were almost futile.'

Professional medical assistance was not long in arriving. Among the first on the scene was local GP, Dr P.M. Carlyle – destined to play a major role in the disaster's aftermath – accompanied by his wife. 'Other local doctors and nurses joined him,' added the *Standard's* report of this huge local news story. But it was the lack of fire-fighting expertise and equipment that would prove so costly.

Arriving at the crash site on his motorcycle, Andrew Mackie's brother, John, immediately turned tail on seeing the flames, returning home to fetch a fire extinguisher. Sadly, it was found to be of little use so Mackie went home a second time, accompanied by two soldiers, and returned with a small hand pump.

'We poured water on the flames, but some of the injured shouted for us to stop because we were drowning them.' The deadly hazards were accumulating at Quintinshill. Splintering wood, fire, water and then suffocation caused by the smoke billowing out from the burning horsehair cushions in carriage compartments which had quickly been reduced to virtually escape-proof prison cells.

The well-rehearsed, co-ordinated responses to large-scale emergencies that exist today were not available to the victims of Quintinshill. Indeed, the absence at the crash scene until well after the event of emergency service aid was another factor behind the appalling death toll. The fact that the signal box stood in a remote location with poor road access was an obstacle to the prompt arrival of ambulance and fire crews. But other determining factors were at play.

It was not until 8.10 that a Caledonian Railway emergency train arrived from Carlisle. Sending this vital help by rail on a, by now, cleared main line made sense, and the railway company deserves commendation for organising it in a relatively short space of time. Relatively, but not actually. Assembling and equipping an emergency train with ambulance staff, essential medical supplies and several more doctors could not be done at the flick of a finger.

Later, the number of doctors was swelled by the arrival of several from further afield, including Glasgow and Edinburgh, some of whom made the journey – the best part of one hundred miles in some cases – by road. How they managed to get there, given the inadequacies of road access, without the roadside petrol or servicing that exists today, was little short of a miracle. However, judging by contemporary press reports, in some cases at least travelling by road was the more reliable of options.

The first rescue train may have been relatively well organised but, as the *Dumfries & Galloway Standard* told its readers, subsequent attempts to bring in emergency medical resources by rail were beset by all manner of problems. The newspaper reported how four Dumfries doctors, responding to an appeal by the Caledonian company, left the town's station on a special train at 10.10 to render assistance. It turned out to be what the *Standard* called 'a most excruciating experience.' Routed along the Caledonian's (now closed) branch line via Lochmaben, the train reached the main line without incident, ready to head southwards, but it was then held at Ecclefechan station for nearly an hour.

'This, it transpired, was because a directors' train from Glasgow had dropped the back spring of the engine and the line was closed until it had been sought for and recovered,' recorded the *Standard,* adding: 'The obstacle being removed, the [Dumfries doctors'] train proceeded to Kirkpatrick station, still three miles away from the scene of the disaster.'

Things were about to get frustratingly worse. The reason this time was down to human, rather than mechanical, failing. It was a pity those Caledonian directors who had set out from Glasgow to see for themselves the extent of the disaster and whose own train had inadvertently stalled the doctors' progress, were not around to sort it out.

The doctors' train had pulled into Kirkpatrick at 11.45. There it stayed. 'On inquiring the cause of this delay,' said the *Standard*, 'the medical gentlemen were informed by a none too courteous official that all the injured had been removed and their services were therefore not required. The official stated that he had been instructed not to allow any train to proceed along the line. Neither was any facility offered for their return to Dumfries. It was only after some trouble and a threat to commandeer the train, as one of the doctors was required for military duty in the afternoon, that arrangements were made to send it back.'

But two of the doctors, having got that far, were not going to be put off by officialdom. According to the press report, Doctors Hunter and Donnan, along with two ambulance workers, took to the tracks – walking along the three-mile stretch of railway to reach Quintinshill about 3pm. There, the *Standard's* readers were told, 'in spite of the discouragement they had received,' the doctors 'rendered most valuable assistance during the afternoon in rescuing bodies from the wreckage.' It is arguable whether or not the pair might have been able to rescue lives rather than dead bodies had they been able to arrive earlier.[1]

The reasons behind the failure to get firemen to the scene at the time they were most needed were more complex. Although news of the disaster was received in Carlisle within minutes via the railway's communications network it has been said that no one thought to tell the city's fire brigade! Consequently the firemen did not begin fighting the blaze until 10am, by which time it was beyond their control, spewing out massive flames, roaring like a furnace, burning virtually without smoke. No doubt this was every bit as frustrating and heartbreaking for the fire brigade as it was for the anguished comrades of the trapped men and the first band of rescuers who had longed for their arrival. Once there, the Carlisle firemen worked valiantly in the continuing rescue operation.[2]

There are conflicting accounts as to who eventually alerted the brigade and, in so doing, brought them, albeit belatedly, to the fearsome Quintinshill blaze.

J.A.B. Hamilton suggested in his book that a sailor, a passenger on the express from London, hitched a lift by road to Carlisle and informed the police there that a fire was raging at the collision site. On checking with the city's railway authorities at Citadel station, the Chief Constable, Colonel Eric de Schmid, who also served as chief fire officer, was told that they believed the fire was now out. It took the arrival in Carlisle of a second caller to challenge that response. The wreck was still ablaze. At 8.55, in some haste and woefully late, the fire brigade was dispatched on the awkward ten-mile journey to the signal box.

Elements of this version of events are challenged by the *Dumfries & Galloway Standard* which reported that it was John Mackie, rather than the unnamed sailor, who first brought news of the fire to Carlisle. According to the newspaper he travelled there by motorbike. The fire brigade, he said, were unwilling to come out at first because they were waiting for an official call-out from the railway company. His powers of persuasion, aided no doubt by a graphic depiction of the true situation, did the trick and they were mobilised. There may be truth in both stories. Mackie may well have been the second caller.

It hardly matters. The pertinent point here is that, had communications within the city been better and had the information circulated been more reliable so that the Carlisle firemen were sent to Quintinshill earlier that morning, the dreadful fate of some of those burnt to death in the inferno might have been averted. But it is impossible to say this with any certainty. The fire engulfed the wreckage so quickly that even the speediest of brigade responses might still have proved too late for many of the victims. It remains, however, a disturbing aspect. Yet this was another issue Colonel Druitt did not see fit to highlight in the report of his Board of Trade inquiry into the disaster with an appropriate recommendation as to future railway company procedure in the event of an emergency.

That it was a further hour and more following dispatch from Carlisle before the brigade was able to put its fire-fighting skills to work at Quintinshill was not the fault of the firemen. On arrival at the scene it was soon realised that a hose would need to be run back half a mile to the River Sark in order to 'tap' the water needed to tackle a blaze of this size. So the fire had raged for more than three hours before the water of the Sark was trained upon it. Three jets were used by the brigade – by then, too little, too late.[3]

On the field alongside the railway – the makeshift reception area for the dead and wounded alike – the demands on the expanding team of rescuers had been relentless. 'By motor cars and special trains, doctors, Red Cross men and nurses had been brought to the scene,' the *Dumfries & Galloway Standard* reported. 'The area in the vicinity of the wreckage was indeed like a battlefield. From the edge of the blazing pile stretcher bearers, working at top speed, brought those rescued from the flames. On the bright green of a field to the west of the line the dead were laid up in rows, while all energies were diverted to the saving of the living.' It was an increasingly desperate struggle against time.

While he waited in the field for help to arrive, wounded soldier James McCullough spotted a lone woman – a farmer's wife he thought, looking back on the event half a century later – running along the embankment. 'She was in hysterics and kept throwing her apron over her face to hide the things she could see.'

And little wonder. 'Lying nearby,' the former soldier recalled in his vivid account of that never to be forgotten morning, 'was a man called Hoskins, who had been in my compartment, with his head through part of the wire fence. His leg was broken and the wire had caught between the bone of the leg and the flesh. John Gale, a sergeant-cook, came and tried to pull him clear. I remember shouting, "for God's sake, leave him alone". His screams were terrible. Another Scot – Merriman his name was – lay nearby beside the wire fence. He was not dead but terribly hurt and shouting and screaming too. At last they got him out over the fence and laid him in the field and a nurse came along with a doctor. The doctor knelt down beside Merriman and told the nurse, "you'd better look after this other fellow", and called for two men to cart [Merriman] away. He was dead.'

Quintinshill reverberated with the utter despair of men at the extremity of human suffering. Take, for example, the chilling account of an eyewitness who, reported the *Dumfries & Galloway Standard*, recalled 'one imprisoned soldier who shouted through an aperture – "for heaven's sake, shoot me, Jock". Some say that an officer complied with his agonised request... but corroboration is lacking.'

In fact, there *was* further evidence. It came in part from a local farmer who spoke movingly and graphically of 'the terrible cases... of men who had been scorched by the flames and were suffering agonies that we could not alleviate, for nobody could get near them and, even if they could have done so, rescue would have been impossible owing to the wreckage beneath which they were buried.' The farmer added with an understandable shudder: 'These men were in the death throes and so terrible was the agony they were undergoing that they were praying for their would-be rescuers to shoot them and thus end their misery.'

More telling was the eyewitness account of Piper Clachers: 'I saw a private lying under an engine tender with just his feet and part of his legs sticking out. He asked to be shot, as he could not recover... an officer shot him with a revolver.'

It is, even today, a sensitive issue. There is no absolute proof in official records that any 'mercy killings' of this nature were actually carried out. Yet the stories persist and the precise recollections of reliable eyewitnesses such as Piper Clachers suggest at the very least the probability that several of the trapped Royal Scots were in this way spared the appalling agony of being burnt to death thanks to officers who used their pistols to bring a swift end to the soldiers' suffering. There is now an acceptance among the custodians of regimental records that it did happen. If so, unpalatable though it may seem, history surely should now record it as a perfectly justifiable act of compassion on the officers' part.

For at least one of the hopelessly trapped Royal Scots, the 'mercy' of a quick release from indescribable pain was self-inflicted. Stressing that, but for the rapid spread of the fire, 'a large number of lives would have been saved, ' Sapper George Robertson told how 'a man, as the flames reached him, cut his throat to escape death by fire. His arms were free but his legs were fixed by the wreckage.'

Piper Clachers may have witnessed the same tragic event – or another very much the same. 'A private was caught between buffers and jammed,' he recalled. 'There was fire all around him. I saw him cut his throat with his jack knife.'

Desperate situations call for the most desperate of remedies – and this was possibly never more true than at Quintinshill that morning.

Michael Moscroft, a young railway porter at Gretna, saw such a remedy at first hand. On a day's leave, he had hurdled a hedge and torn across fields to reach the crash scene as soon as it was obvious that something disastrous had taken place. The second local railwayman to arrive at Quintinshill – the first was a lengthman – it is said that he remained there, without rest or food, for the next twenty-four hours. His graphic recall of that time was reproduced in J.A.B. Hamilton's book:

'I held one poor fellow while Roger Kirkpatrick, the local joiner, amputated his leg with an ordinary saw. An officer held his shoulders while I steadied the leg.' The backdrop was just as ghastly. 'By this time practically the whole train was engulfed in the fire and one could hear the moans of the injured and the dying.'

The rescue operation was laced throughout with improvisation. This was a scene worlds apart from the well-appointed hospital wards in which many of the doctors were usually employed. At Quintinshill those engaged on providing medical aid had to make do with whatever resources were to hand. The joiner's saws used to amputate a man's leg was not the only example of this, as an account from the *Dumfries & Galloway Standard* made clear.

The paper quoted Private W. Reed, a Canadian soldier serving in the UK with the Montreal Field Ambulance who, having survived the second crash, used his skills to help the rescue bid. The harrowing scenes following the collision were 'too horrible to describe,' but he managed to recall 'men pinned down in the wreckage in such a way that the only means of saving them was by amputation of their limbs… one poor soldier had been caught by both hands in smashed woodwork of a carriage. The flames were approaching him rapidly and he was squirming under the intense heat. It was impossible to extricate him and his arms had to be amputated just above the wrists. A razor was used in the operation.'

These may have been the first of the many amputations of limbs that were deemed necessary as a last resort in order to free the trapped victims. Fortunately, most were carried out in a more professional manner by the team of doctors following their arrival from towns and cities to the north and south. They brought with them surgical tools and, just as importantly, supplies of morphine.

They also brought a determination to do everything that was humanly possible to save lives. Of necessity in many cases this involved a degree of extraordinary improvisation. Telling the story of how their city's doctors had responded to the emergency, the *Carlisle Journal* reported that 'in their work at the scene of the disaster, and in various hospitals, the doctors rendered a service that cannot be overrated. Only now is it possible to realise what they have accomplished.' As soon as news of the disaster reached Carlisle the city's doctors were notified, joining the first emergency train dispatched to the crash site.

The *Journal* quoted from an interview carried out with one of Carlisle's medics – a Dr Edwards – by a reporter from *The Scotsman*, the widely-read Edinburgh-based daily: 'When I reached the scene of the disaster all was confusion. The smash had occurred an hour before [sic] and the injured men who had been rescued from the debris were lying in the fields either side of the line.'

Added the *Journal's* second-hand account: 'The first [thing] the doctors did was to go round these men and attend them. They had been roughly dressed by their comrades who had used the emergency bandages they carry in the lining of their coats. Considering the circumstances, the railway organisation [the train and its contents] was wonderful. We had a splendid supply of lint and antiseptics. There were three surgeons on the ground – Dr Lediard, Dr Paul and Dr Edwards – and their services were immediately required. I saw Dr Paul amputate one leg of a soldier who was lying in the field where I was working and I believe he had to amputate another…'

But what the journalist called 'the most dramatic piece of work' was one in which Dr Edwards took the centre stage.

The newspaper story described how one of the doctors patrolling the scene, a Dr Sheenan, had proved invaluable in finding men still lying under the debris. 'On this occasion he crawled underneath a wagon of the goods train and discovered that, on the other side, imprisoned amid great piles of wreckage which the fire was steadily approaching on three sides, there were still living men.' The report added grimly: 'The living and the dead were in a confused heap.'

Dr Shoeman immediately summoned assistance. The dramatic report added: 'It was obvious that an operation would have to be performed if one man was to be got out. He lay underneath two dead men and one living man, and these first had to be removed before he could be got out. One of his legs was hopelessly pinned in the wreckage and the fire was at that moment burning the lower part of both his legs. He was a brave fellow. He never murmured. "Just lie still for a minute or two and we will have you out all right," the doctors told him, and his reply was quite calm: "Well, try not to be long about it. I am getting pretty fed up."'

If the man's life was to be saved the imprisoned leg would have to come off. A surgeon was called for. Dr Edwards happened to be the only one available. 'He collected his knives, but was compelled to borrow an ordinary carpenter's saw for the operation,' the report continued. 'Dr Matthews, another Carlisle doctor, accompanied Dr Edwards to apply the chloroform. Both had to crawl beneath the goods truck in order to get to the 'four foot way' where the poor man lay. Railwaymen armed with levers and crowbars followed to assist them in the operation.'

Somehow they managed to remove the imprisoned leg. The reporter who recounted this story was moved to comment that 'surely never was such an operation carried out under such terrible circumstances. I am not exaggerating when I say that the doctors worked in momentary danger of their lives. Very close to them the fire was raging. While they worked, the flames were beginning to lick the outside of two gas cylinders two yards away. The railwaymen levered the wreckage as much as they could to allow the doctors to perform their work.' Sadly, this superhuman collective attempt to preserve life was all in vain. Although released, the unfortunate soldier died shortly afterwards. But there was no time to dwell on that. There was unfinished business.

Taking up the story, the *Dumfries & Galloway Standard* told how Dr Edwards returned to release the other trapped man, 'but in this case both legs had to be amputated and it was scarcely hoped from the first that the man, who had been pinned beneath a gas cylinder, would survive. The operation was performed amid the scorching heat of the flames and the only protection the doctor had was the water from the fireman's hose which was kept playing around him until the ordeal was over. Dr Matthews shared the danger by creeping beneath the wreckage to administer chloroform, and so intense was the heat that the chloroform mask caught fire.' It appears that, in this case, the soldier's life was saved.[4]

Incidents such as these illustrate perfectly how extraordinary heroism – both on the part of the victims and those who battled so valiantly to save their lives – pierced the pervading gloom of this dreadful tragedy with the shining light of humanity at its very finest. It is imposible to overstate. The *Dumfries & Galloway Standard* chose as good an adjective as any to describe the work of the rescuers – noble. It was inarguably that above all else.

Added the *Standard*: 'Many risked life and limb to save others, but there were instances where certain death would have resulted from any attempt to extricate the injured from the debris, which in places reached a height of twenty feet. No battlefield could have surpassed the scenes of carnage and destruction.' It was a sentiment echoed by many others. Was Quintinshill really *worse* than the trenches?

One man with first-hand experience of both certainly thought so. A member of the Army Service Corps home on leave from France, who survived the second crash, told the Dumfries newspaper that the scene he had witnessed that morning had been 'worse than anything he had seen in the trenches. People were lying about injured in the most terrible manner and blood was to be seen everywhere.' The point can be argued, of course, but Quintinshill was at least a parallel.

Human destruction can take many forms. It was hardly surprising that some victims of the disaster, while escaping serious physical injury, were mentally broken by it. A soldier helping with the rescue operation described one such incident some ninety minutes into the fire when it was believed that no one left among the wreckage had survived. 'When I was working near to the wrecked engines,' he said, 'a man appeared. He had freed himself before his escape was observed. He stood dazed-like, then tried to walk... but we saw a queer look on his face and then he began to run about wildly. We guessed he had lost his reason. One of our number caught hold of him and, having calmed him, led him away.'

Another soldier? Or a passenger on the express? It was not revealed. Whatever his identity he is unlikely to have been the only survivor affected in this way. Quintinshill was a potentially mind-numbing experience for all who witnessed its horrors. Those soldiers who escaped without the sort of injuries that would otherwise have prevented them needed immense courage and discipline in order to help with the rescue operation. Time and again these vital battlefield qualities were in evidence as the Royal Scots worked tirelessly to help their stricken comrades. The general impression given was that the soldiers, following the inspirational leadership of their commanding officer, Lieutenant Colonel William Carmichael Peebles, did not just pull their weight but performed heroically, displaying a level of gallantry that would have marked them out for distinction in battle.

That Colonel Peebles was able to inspire his men to such heroic effect was down not only to his leadership qualities but also to the fact that, as befitted his status, he had not been forced to travel in a crowded compartment but in one which afforded him the luxury of being able to lie at full stretch on the seat. On the initial impact the seat was pushed hard against the one opposite as the troop train's carriages telescoped violently . It has been suggested that, had the CO been forced to adopt a sitting position, his legs would probably have been broken, or severed, between the seats.

But the dark forces governing the tragedy of that bright spring morning were no respecters of rank. The disaster counted officers as well as their men among its calamitous military toll and there was little chance of escaping injury, or worse, in the troop train's leading coach, irrespective of status. Thomas Clark, a second lieutenant sharing a compartment in that first coach with four other officers, spoke years later of being 'deluged with water' from the tender of number 121, the train's locomotive, its side torn open by the initial impact. Much worse was to follow. 'The second train [the express from London] smashed into our carriage and I passed out. The next thing I remember was lying in the field with a broken pelvis and a dislocated hip joint,' he recalled.[5]

All five officers in that compartment were injured but, relatively speaking, they were fortunate. The three officers in the next compartment to Clark's were all killed. Major James Hamilton, commanding A Company, Captain John Mitchell, his second-in-command, and Lieutenant Christian Salvesen were the only Royal Scots officers to lose their lives in the disaster. It seemed a sad commentary on the scale of the double collision and more particularly the fire which followed, to read in several accounts of the disaster that no trace of any of these three officers was found. Sadder still, perhaps, was the emergence of evidence, now preserved at the Royal Scots Regimental Museum, to disprove this widely held assertion – in the case of Lieutenant Salvesen at least.

The vivid recollections of Lieutenant (later Captain) George Haws, a Quintinshill survivor, were recorded in a detailed typescript by his father and now form part of the museum's archive. 'George picked up the arm and shoulder of one officer and looked at it,' records the document. 'He knew the tunic [i.e. the identity of its wearer – Salvesen] and told me that his brother was lying out on the field waiting for him to come… George said that he had not the heart to go and tell the brother, who was wounded, that his relative was ground to pieces under the wreckage.' It remains today a matter for grim conjecture how many others were similarly spared ghastly details of a relative's death.[6, 7]

By mid-morning, all hope of freeing survivors from the burning debris was abandoned. 'I wrought amongst the wreckage until about 10.30 when it was said that all the living had been recovered,' recalled Andrew Mackie. 'For the rest of the forenoon we did nothing but recover bodies. The soldiers were brave chaps. Many of them, injured themselves, were trying to help their comrades and the sailors, too, worked desperately hard to rescue as many as they could.' The sailors were from the London train. Mackie added that, in common with many of their fellow passengers on the express, hardly any of them had been injured.'

That these men from the Royal Navy performed so admirably was no surprise, but it was perhaps a touch ironic. Naval parties travelling to the far north by rail from London were effectively segregated at the time from other passengers, and especially from Army personnel, apparently because of complaints about their significant presence (and possibly their exuberant behaviour) on the West Coast route. This would eventually be redressed when the railway authorities allocated the Navy its own trains for the journey up to Scotland, but in May 1915, so far as naval and other passengers were concerned, it was very much a case of 'never the twain shall meet!' Thus the sailors travelled at the rear of the trains – and this was clearly the safest place to have been for those heading north towards Quintinshill on the midnight express.

An enduring story recalls how one sailor, ignoring the convention, took up a seat in the front carriage of the express. He was promptly given his marching orders by the other passengers and told to join his mates at the back. He did so. At Quintinshill that front coach was smashed to pieces in the second collision. At the train's rear, the sailor survived unhurt to help with the rescue – a lucky man.

The sailors and the majority of their fellow express train passengers were also fortunate in that the all-metal underframes of their train's carriages endowed it with a degree of crash-worthiness almost totally absent in the troop train. Only the front three coaches were derailed. The fourth, a sleeping car, while remaining on the rails, was destroyed by fire – its attendant, Samuel Dyer, was among the eight occupants of the express officially acknowledged to have lost their lives – but the rest of the train, sufficiently robust to withstand the impact, was propelled clear.

As a result the number of deaths on the express was mercifully restricted. But there were narrow escapes and it was not just on the troop train that many owed their survival to the gallantry of fellow travellers. Escape was not easy from the second sleeping car. Commandeering a large axe, a group of passengers who had avoided injury smashed through the carriage roof – and were confronted immediately with a problem. In order to free those among the trapped occupants – men and women – who could not otherwise be reached, they needed ropes to haul them up and to pull wreckage away from several who were pinned to the floor. None were available. In desperation wire was cut from the line-side fencing and used instead. It is unclear how many passengers were saved in this way and spared the agonies of being burnt to death. For others in the front of the express nothing could be done.

Apart from Dyer, the seven other identified passengers who died were mostly serving officers of the armed forces back in the UK on leave. Three – Captain Robert Findlay and Lieutenants James Bonnar and John Jackson – were from the 9th Argyll & Sutherland Highlanders, a Territorial battalion of the Scottish regiment. Lieutenant Commander Charles Head was a Royal Navy officer serving with the torpedo boat HMS *Vesuvius* while Assistant Paymaster William Paton was attached to the Royal Naval Division, men who fought as an infantry unit in Kitchener's New Army. It has been recorded that Paton was on his way home to Scotland on compassionate leave to console his mother on the death of another son in the Dardenelles. He was pulled alive from the wreckage but died on his way to hospital.

The two remaining express train passengers known to have died were both civilians – 43-year-old civil engineer Herbert Ford, who worked as a crane department manager at Arrol's works in Glasgow, and James McDonald, aged 48, a Glasgow-born London jeweller, travelling in the first class sleeping section with his wife, en route to Glasgow to bury his father when disaster struck.[8]

'Both were thrown on the floor when the collision occurred and afterwards the roof fell in upon them, but at the same time the floor of the carriage collapsed,' wrote local historian Gordon Routledge in his 2002 book, *The Sorrows of Quintinshill*. 'Almost providentially as far as they were concerned,' he added. 'Both of them were able to crawl out onto the railway in their nightclothes. One of Mr McDonald's arms was very much lacerated and he was bruised about the face and body. Mrs McDonald was injured about her hands and legs...' The couple had lost everything they had with them and, while they survived the collision to become the only civilians – among the many soldiers – taken to Carlisle's Cumberland Infirmary, Mr McDonald died there later of his multiple injuries.

This, at least, was the official toll of victims from the express. But this is an aspect of the tragedy that has always needed further examination. Others were killed. The *Dumfries & Galloway Standard* reported that 'some of the bodies recovered, even in the earliest stages, were scorched beyond recognition [but] there is little doubt that women, too, perished among the express's passengers and this is borne out by the fact that a lady's hand, with a bangle still decorating the wrist, was seen hanging from an aperture in one of the ruined coaches. A lady's shoe was also observed in a bundle of articles pulled from the wreckage.'

Who was she? No name was ever given, but the most widely held view suggested the tragic possibility that the mystery female may have been one of four members of a single family who perished in the crash. Worse, it seemed likely that they might all have been children or young adults. This disturbing story is examined in a later chapter.

That Quintinshill claimed the life of at least one woman is beyond doubt. And, tragically, she died with the only acknowledged child victim of the disaster. Rachel Nimmo (28) and her son, Dickson, not yet two years old, were the only fatalities among the handful of passengers on the local train. Together with her husband, also named Dickson, and the couple's two older daughters, the young mother had travelled overnight from Newcastle, where they lived, changing trains at Carlisle for the journey across the border on the early morning local service.

A poignant passage in the *Dumfries & Galloway Standard's* report quoted eyewitness Mrs Sword (presumably the wife or mother of Andrew) who was among the first local residents to offer help at the scene of the accident: 'When I reached the railway there were a number of injured soldiers lying in the field. I carried water to them, giving them drinks and washing their wounds. There was a man, a draper from Newcastle, beside the soldiers. He was staring at the [local] train and I went up to him. He said to me, "my wife and child were along with me in the train, but she left me to go to another carriage to put the bairn to sleep. Then there was a collision and both of them are dead". My heart bled for the poor man as he had seen the burnt bodies of his wife and bairn taken out of the wreck.'

Leaving the remainder of the family behind well down the train, Rachel Nimmo had taken her son to a compartment close to the front – too close, as it turned out, to escape the fatal consequences of the troop train running into the 'local' at Quintinshill signal box. The bodies of mother and child were taken later that day to Gretna, where their three stricken relatives were also accommodated overnight, and were eventually returned to Newcastle for burial.

Other women passengers on the express suffered at Quintinshill. The *Dumfries & Galloway Standard* reported that 'two ladies belonging to Glasgow were released by the exertions from a band of soldiers and civilians after having been pinned down under the wreckage of the Euston express for twenty minutes'.

But it cannot be stressed enough how comparatively safe were the majority of the express train's passengers compared with the men of the 7th Royal Scots in their decrepit troop train. It was a distinction that dominates any present-day analysis of the Quintinshill death toll; a discrimination that sits astride the terrible events of that May morning like a prejudiced judge in a court of law.

Oddly, the vital difference in construction between the three passenger trains involved at Quintinshill was apparently not seen as a major factor by Colonel Druitt at the Board of Trade inquiry. He failed to refer to it. The *Railway Gazette* saw things differently. In September 1915 the influential rail industry journal, in its eleventh year of publication, declared 'the contrast in the behaviour of the rolling stock [to be] an object lesson [Druitt had] failed to bring out'.

The *Gazette* compared the respective weights of the three trains involved, noting that the troop train weighed, empty, almost 434 tons while the stationary local train's empty weight was nearly 219 tons and the express, 608 tons. 'The first collision was sufficiently severe to drive the local train engine for 42yds, and in the second collision the express pushed the tender of the troop train and all the debris surrounding it ahead for 30yds,' the journal reflected in its detailed analysis of the Quintinshill disaster. Yet, added the *Gazette*, while the fifteen troop train vehicles had collapsed from a length, including the engine, of 213yds to one of about 67yds, the rear nine of the express train's coaches 'were but little hurt by the collision; only the first three were seriously damaged.' The explanation was simple. 'The express's vehicles were all, but one, built with underframes composed entirely of steel, whilst only four of the fifteen on the troop train were so built,' the remainder having only steel sole-plates.[9]

The antiquity of the vast majority of the troop train's rolling stock and the fact that most of its vehicles had only six wheels, a further obstacle to rigidity, was also noted by the *Railway Gazette*. Did nobody in officialdom ever seriously consider the possibility of a crash? The answer to that must be, no they didn't – and it was the troop train's unworthiness for travel, let alone a crash, which contributed so prominently to Quintinshill's sorrow.

It was a sorrow all too evident in the hastily improvised mortuaries at the farm buildings closest to the scene of the tragedy and at Stormont Hall in the nearby village of Gretna Green which offered the most convenient accommodation for the bodies of those who had lost their lives. Laid out side-by-side, Quintinshill's dead, the majority of whom had awaited their troop train's departure just a few hours earlier with exuberant resolve, now awaited, silent, broken and motionless, the arrival of special trains from Carlisle and Glasgow. Those trains, which must surely rank among the most sombre ever to be dispatched on a British railway line, eventually brought their coffins. The rows of unmarked black boxes lay empty for a while as a large team of undertakers organised the transfer of the victims' remains. It was a harrowing task even for men so well-versed in their professional calling.

There were so many bodies that the largest makeshift mortuary, a large barn, could not hold all those who were carried in procession to it. So, of necessity, men were laid, shrouded, behind the building until they could be moved – the grim overspill of the grimmest of disasters. But it was not a question of finding a coffin for every victim. Some were filled with the remains of up to three victims, their bodies reduced to little more than ashes.

The dead could not tell of their suffering and the living had little appetite for doing so. Certainly not the soldiers. Overlooked on the railway embankment by the breakdown gangs who had arrived with the mechanical means to clear the mountain of charred debris – and by a large crowd of sightseers, having to be held behind boundary fences – roll calls were taken on the blood-drenched meadow of the remaining troops of the 7th Royal Scots. The poignancy was captured by the considerable journalistic skills of the reporter from the *Dumfries & Galloway Standard*.

'During the forenoon the survivors of the troop train were mustered on two occasions and those who witnessed the second roll call will not easily forget the awful tragedy of the spectacle,' he wrote. 'As smartly as it was possible in the circumstances the men came up from all quarters. A sergeant, wearing a civilian cap in place of the glengarry [Scottish regimental cap] he had lost, marshalled them into line. In front stood a group of officers, not more than half-a-dozen. The one who had sounded the whistle was a young man, tall and strong, his clean-cut face smeared with dirt and smoke. He had no jacket and was bare-headed. With his shirt sleeves rolled up, and his puttees [cloth lower leg coverings] disordered in such a way that the calf of one leg was exposed, he gazed around in a half-dazed fashion, evidently overcome by the fatigue caused by the broken sleep and ceaseless labours. He was looking around to see if any stragglers were still about. Doubtless he hoped and prayed for a large muster…'

If so, this was a forlorn hope. All the troops who were left had responded to his call.

'The sergeant, with accustomed military precision, shouted his orders,' added the report. 'The men formed up in double file. In the two lines were only a small number of men out of the 450 or 500 who had set out on the journey. No more pathetic picture could be imagined. It only required the hand of a painter to immortalise it as one of the historic incidents in the military annals of the nation.'

There was no painter on Quintinshill's field, but photographs were taken. The roll-call of the battalion's survivors *has* been immortalised. Historic. Heroic. Pathetic.

'Not a single man, from private to officer, presented a spruce appearance,' the *Standard's* report continued, 'but the soldierly bearing was there, despite the stained and tattered tunics. Some of them were bootless, some had no cap, many bore bruises on their faces and all of them were palpably worn out. As one viewed the spectacle one almost doubted its awful reality. They looked more like the remnants of a corps that had just emerged from a deadly battle than the survivors of an accident occurring within a few hours' distance of their home.'

It is hard to imagine what thoughts were running through the minds of those men. Possibly they were too dazed, too exhausted, to think of anything at all. The

Standard provides the best analysis: 'While the roll was being called four other privates arrived and fell into line. The list having been completed, the young officer ordered the men to stand easy. Then, with a kind consideration for their physical condition, he informed them that they might sit and rest. All availed themselves of the opportunity and the officers, one by one, followed suit.

'Even though freed from the regulations of the parade, the men hardly exchanged a word. They lay prone on their backs or rested on their elbows, watching the melancholy procession of stretcher bearers carrying the dead. By this time seventy bodies had been recovered and still there were more to follow.'

A great many more.

Notes

1. There was an element of confusion in the *Standard's* otherwise magnificent reportage as to the identities of the two Dumfries doctors who walked along the track to Quintinshill. While the paper initially identified them as Doctors Hunter and Donnan, its report subsequently referred to 'Mr Nabb and Mr Laurie... rendering most valuable assistance at the disaster scene'.

2. Carlisle was not formally granted city status until 1974 but has been colloquially, and widely, known as the Border City for much longer and is thus referred to as a city throughout the book.

3. Also known as Sark Water, the River Sark forms part of the western border between Scotland and England although most of its short length lies entirely within Scotland. The Scottish bard Robert Burns immortalised the river in his poem, *Such a Parcel of Rogues in a Nation*.

4. The extraordinary contribution to the rescue operation by the large team of doctors who went to Quintinshill is worthy of fuller recognition. In his 2002 book, *The Sorrows of Quintinshill*, local historian Gordon Routledge recorded many of their names. They included Mr Balfour-Paul and Drs Airken, Beard, Bird, Edwards, Lediard, McDonald, Morrison, Murphy and Sheehan (from Carlisle); Drs Denny, Marwick and Taylor (Longtown); Dr Symingtom (Brampton); and Dr Anderson (Canobie). As the *Dumfries & Galloway Standard* made clear, others attended from the Scottish side of the border – see footnote one, above. Routledge also recorded the on-site attendance of a Nurse Stephens from Carlisle and members of the city's Men's Voluntary Aid Detachment and described how a local confectioner, Mr G. Wheatley, 'allowed his car to be used as a base for the supply of bandages etc'.

5. Second Lieutenant Clark spent three weeks in the Cumberland Infirmary at Carlisle recovering from his injuries before returning by train to Edinburgh. Within a short space of time he had joined his battalion comrades in Gallipoli and remained on active service with the Royal Scots for the rest of the war – a true survivor. On the 70th anniversary of the disaster in 1985, approaching his 90th birthday, he was believed to have been the only Quintinshill survivor still alive (but see chapter 15).

6. The Salvesen brothers were members of one of Edinburgh's greatest commercial dynasties. The family-run Christian Salvesen company based at Leith was founded in 1872 and became a major European player in the twin fields of transport and logistics before its

multi-million pound takeover by the France-based Norbert Dentressangle organisation in 2007.

7. The remaining nine of the battalion's seventeen officers all escaped injury principally because they had been allocated seats in the less vulnerable middle section of the troop train.

8. To an extent the eight men on the London express who lost their lives are the forgotten victims of Quintinshill. The names of the five who were serving military officers do not feature on the memorial at the mass grave in Edinburgh's Rosebank Cemetery. They were buried at various locations elsewhere. The graves of the three officers of the 9th Argyll & Sutherland Highlanders are all in Dumbartonshire – Captain Findlay's in the private cemetery at Boturich Castle, Lieutenant Bonnar's in Helensburgh Cemetery and Lieutenant Jackson's in Dumbarton Cemetery. Of the Navy victims, Lieutenant Commander Head was buried at the Western Necropolis near Glasgow and Assistant Paymaster Paton, at the city's Cathcart Cemetery.

9. A sole-plate, or solebar, is a beam fixed to the sides of a railway vehicle onto which the bodywork is mounted. This apart, most of the troop train's vehicle underframes were made of wood.

Chapter 4

The Days after Disaster

*'The heap of ruins on the line were still afire, and the
smoke, which spread itself like a pall over the scene,
smelt of more than smouldering wreckage. It was
tainted with the odour of burning flesh and bones,
sickening, nauseating, One felt that it could only last a
little longer then the nightmare would pass.'*

Dumfries and Galloway Standard & Advertiser, 28 May 1915

On Quintinshill's field of despair the wounded awaited transportation to hospital. Doctors, perspiring under the unforgiving sun, sleeves rolled up, worked without ceasing to prepare them. As soon as a man was dealt with and considered ready for moving he was dispatched. The undamaged rear coaches of the express train were utilised as a rail-borne ambulance for an initial journey behind a summoned locomotive to Carlisle.

Fifty-two of the most seriously injured were taken from the blood-drenched grass on this train, arriving in the city at 10.42. Two more trains were sent from Carlisle to collect further victims during the course of the morning. On returning to Carlisle, two of these trains were reversed and propelled a short distance along the tracks of the North British Railway (the start of the Waverley route to Edinburgh) to a siding, recently constructed at a canal-side location, providing easy access to the nearby Cumberland Infirmary. That, at least, was a blessing.[1, 2]

Privately-owned road vehicles, some of which, laden with stretchers, had been utilised for the unenviable task of removing bodies to the side of the railway line and to the makeshift mortuary, also helped with the hospital transfer. The local press were moved to commend 'the readiness in which men brought out their motor cars and placed them at the service of those in charge'. One man, it was noted, had driven his car between Carlisle and a point close to the site of the disaster throughout the day 'and had had nothing to eat'.[3]

Nothing stood still for long at Quintinshill in the aftermath of the crash. There was continual movement of people, trains, cars and lorries as the bid to rush the wounded to hospital continued without pause. Time and again the vital part played by the local community – and by many from Carlisle and towns in the vicinity – featured in the mass of press coverage. It was given unstintingly by people who could not fail to be moved by the plight of so many casualties. An estimated 300 injured victims could at least rely on what the press called 'the unsparing efforts of all,' but for some it was no more than a final comfort. Mortally wounded, beyond further help, they died on their way to Carlisle.

Some succumbed on the first ambulance train which arrived in Carlisle at 10.12am and drew into the canal siding some fifty minutes later. It was met there by a team of nurses, railway officials and many other volunteers. Everything possible was done to move them from the train to the nearby infirmary. When stretchers ran short at the siding, wheelbarrows were hurriedly pressed into service as improvised conveyances for the less seriously hurt. There were, it seems, plenty of volunteer barrow-pushers among the local people who had gathered to help. When the barrows ran short, ladders and planks were used. Others were carried in a coal wagon converted into an ambulance. The arrival of the fire brigade from Carr's Biscuit Factory was a godsend. The *Carlisle Journal* reported how they 'threw themselves wholeheartedly' into the task of assisting the injured on the final stage of their journey. But the death toll rose still further before some could reach the hospital.[4]

In some cases motorised forms of conveyance were found for the transfer from siding to hospital. Recalling more than half a century later how, as a seriously hurt stretcher case, he was among the initial fifty-two soldiers taken to the canal-side in the undamaged coaches of the express train, Private Peter Skea remembered that 'buses came to take us to the Cumberland Infirmary. While we were waiting [to be boarded], a nurse came along and was about to step over me. I didn't like the idea of her stepping over my burned face so I got up to let her pass. She played up all sorts – stretcher cases are not supposed to be able to stand up!' But he added: 'We made it up later in the infirmary!'

By noon all three ambulance trains despatched in the morning had reached Carlisle. The *Carlisle Journal* recorded the arrival in the city of the one train that was not routed to the canal siding, terminating instead at Citadel station shortly after 11am with a large number of casualties, mostly soldiers. Many, according to the *Journal's* story, had 'blackened faces… some were placed on railway barrows and were taken to the entrance of the station, where motor cars and vans were waiting, in which they were removed to the various local hospitals.'

Inevitably this sudden influx of casualties, many of them badly injured, imposed a severe strain on the resources of the Cumberland Infirmary. The hospital was accustomed to accommodating injured military personnel but had only a short time before admitted a large number of wounded soldiers returned to the UK from the front line in France. On 22 May the building became so congested that the superficially injured from Quintinshill were treated outside at the side of the road. By noon the hospital had dealt with 180 cases.

While the infirmary continued to serve as the main reception point for the wounded, other local hospitals – and a variety of alternative establishments – were also asked to find bed space for some of the less seriously injured. In fact they were given no choice; their accommodation was commandeered by the military authorities, working from an emergency headquarters at the County Hotel, who deployed doctors, many brought in from a considerable distance, and Red Cross workers as staff.

It was a logistical challenge. Twenty of the injured went to the city's Chadwick Hospital where the usual patient provision was exceeded by no fewer than seventeen! To make room there for the injured soldiers, some of the hospital's patients, wounded in France, were taken into private homes, including the local vicarage. Within a few hours the Central and Viaduct hotels were effectively functioning as hospitals, along with Carlisle Castle, Chadwick School and Fusehill Workhouse – and, when *their* space was exhausted, other smaller buildings were utilised.[5]

Back at the Cumberland Infirmary space was at a premium as the hospital authorities struggled to cope with the huge number of casualties brought to its doors, via rail or road. To make room for them, existing patients who could be moved were sent elsewhere while others were put two to a bed. Beds were also made up on the floors and rooms were converted into overspill wards.

'Carlisle was like a front line city as Red Cross wagons rumbled through the streets with loads of bandaged, blood-stained soldiers,' wrote author John Thomas evocatively. 'By the afternoon its capacity was exhausted, and injured men fit to travel were sent on to Glasgow and to hospitals in Penrith, Lancaster and Preston.'

According to the *Carlisle Journal*, the transfer of patients to Penrith took place on the Tuesday evening, twenty-four hours after the hospital authorities in the Cumbrian market town had been asked by their Carlisle counterparts to make arrangements to receive several wounded men temporarily accommodated in the city's hotels.

'The townspeople of Penrith assembled in large numbers at various points to watch the arrival of the men, who were conveyed in three motor ambulances, the journey occupying two hours,' the *Journal* reported, adding that the ambulances were met on the Carlisle road by a local doctor who organised the onward distribution of the men among 'three auxiliary hospitals.' It appears that these were set up in two of Penrith's public halls – the Wordsworth and St Andrew's – and at Skiddaw Grove in Keswick, seventeen miles west of Penrith. Most of the men treated at these locations were burns cases though some were suffering from crush injuries. Illustrating further the wide range of involvement in the medical emergency, members of the Voluntary Aid Detachment (VAD) field nursing service helped out at all three makeshift hospitals.[6]

The extent of the demands placed on the Cumberland Infirmary was well illustrated in a report made soon after the Quintinshill disaster by the hospital's house surgeon, Dr W.A. Anderson, in which he described being alerted in a telephone message from the Caledonian Railway at 7.45am to 'a serious accident near Gretna.' Unsurprisingly, the company's immediate request was for doctors, stretchers and dressings to be sent to the crash site. According to the *Carlisle Journal,* Dr Anderson 'conceived that it was not his duty to leave the infirmary, but he at once despatched the head porter with dressings and all the spare stretchers, and having obtained the matron's permission, a sister and one nurse. In the meantime, the matron set about preparing every available bed.'

The surgeon's report revealed that the injured began arriving at the infirmary, by car, shortly after nine – but, as with the confusion which stalled the fire brigade's response, a breakdown in communication had occurred. The hospital had been officially notified that only thirty beds would be required. Some victims with comparatively slight injuries were admitted at first, but these were subsequently transferred to other institutions leaving the requested thirty beds free.

'The injured arrived in quite unexpected numbers,' reported the *Carlisle Journal* in its summary of the house surgeon's report. 'Seventy-two were hurriedly examined and admitted to the wards or temporary accommodation in the nursing home; forty-three were treated in the casualty department, and about sixty-five, suffering from trivial injuries, were interrogated or examined at the roadside. So that, in all, about 180 injured were dealt with by the hospital staff before midday.'

Dr Anderson provided details on those patients whose removal from the infirmary was deemed essential in order to cope with the unexpected influx from Quintinshill. It seems they too were soldiers, among the twenty-four admitted the previous weekend from France. As officer-in-charge, Anderson had been ordered to forward as many of these men as possible to the general hospital in the Liverpool suburb of Fazakerley in order to relieve the congestion in Carlisle. Eleven were transferred on 24 May, leaving thirteen as in-patients at the infirmary.

This extraordinary movement of hospital patients was not one-way traffic. Dr Anderson noted that, in return for transferring some of the less seriously hurt Quintinshill victims to accommodation elsewhere in Carlisle, the infirmary had 'received cases requiring immediate operation' from those establishments. The logistical challenge imposed that weekend on the city's medical authorities was immense. Fortunately it was matched by the supreme collective response of doctors, nurses and ancillary staff. 'The work performed by the whole of the nursing staff has been beyond all praise,' the *Carlisle Journal* was proud to remark.[7]

By the morning of Tuesday, 25 May, the Cumberland Infirmary was still treating sixty-six victims of the disaster – three officers, sixty-one non-commissioned officers and privates, and the McDonalds, the only two civilians admitted to their care. The number had been reduced not only by the various transfers elsewhere but also by the loss of ten more soldiers – eleven if another who died on the way in is counted – whose injuries were so terrible they could not be saved.

Carlisle's coordination of the sudden influx of the disaster's victims extended to the military depot at the city's medieval castle. 'Unostentatious but extremely valuable,' was how the *Carlisle Journal* summed up the work of the depot upon whose officials and clerical staff 'a great deal of strain was placed... inured as they have been to congestion of work during the great rushes of recruiting.' They had, said the *Journal,* 'worked with a will far into the night.'

The depot had served as the initial point of report for the injured soldiers brought to Carlisle by car. 'Although accommodation might have been found there for most of the injured, the medical staff to cope with such an emergency was wanting,' added the report. So most of the wounded had been sent elsewhere although the depot did manage to find accommodation for ten men in its own hospital – a number quickly reduced to nine when one critically injured soldier died on being removed from the car which had brought him to the castle.

The task of helping officers of the 7th Royal Scots compile an initial list of soldiers involved in the disaster – uninjured, injured and dead – fell to the staff in the depot's orderly room. They had 170 names on the roll by nightfall but it is unlikely the list was entirely accurate. At one stage only eighty-three dead men had been identified. Almost as many bodies had been recovered but were unrecognisable. Fifty officers and men were listed as missing.

These stark particulars were forwarded to Major General Sir John Spencer Ewart, head of the British Army's Scottish Command, the War Office and the headquarters of the Royal Scots. With the list far from complete and constantly changing, throughout the next day depot staff were besieged with inquiries from anxious relatives. Eventually, the compilation of names and the answering of external queries was taken over by members of Carlisle Citizens' League using information from railway officials and the heads of the various hospitals.

The Citizens' League volunteers were themselves at the heart of Carlisle's 'front line' that weekend. A key task for them was to provide much needed comfort for the injured prior to the arrival in Carlisle of the men's relatives from Scotland. On the Saturday practically the entire membership of the League was helping in the removal of the injured to hospital. They also provided – and in some cases served – the extra food required at several of the places to which the wounded were taken, helping too with the onward distribution to other accommodation of some of the men discharged from the infirmary after treatment.

At 4.30pm on Saturday the remnants of the battalion involved in the disaster finally left Quintinshill for Carlisle, their arrival eagerly anticipated in the packed city streets by local people determined to give the soldiers the warmest of sympathetic receptions. The approaches to Citadel station were lined by the crowds as word spread at 5pm that the train had arrived. Probably those Carlisle citizens were surprised when the soldiers emerged from the station. They could not fail to have been impressed. The Royal Scots were not being transported in any form of conveyance. They were not struggling along on foot. They were marching, proudly, defiantly. The cheers rang out in Carlisle.

The men were allowed to wash, eat a meal and have a medical examination while in the city and were then ordered to rest. But not for the night. At 2am on Sunday they were paraded outside Carlisle Castle. The story is told that they were passed by the lieutenant general commanding Scotland as he left the castle by car. The Royal Scots dutifully saluted. The officer stopped his car, got out and returned the salute. The soldiers then marched to Citadel station to board a train made up entirely of first class coaches, each compartment occupied by just two passengers. There weren't many of these exhausted soldiers on their exclusive train as it travelled through the night – seven officers and fifty-seven other ranks. Liverpool was still their immediate destination; Gallipoli remained their destiny. More than 200 of their comrades were now believed dead. Around the same number lay wounded in hospital across 200 miles of northern Britain.[8]

For some of the Leith battalion Carlisle was but a few fleeting glimpses. The other half-battalion – B and C companies – had reached Liverpool on the second troop train to embark on their sea voyage aboard the ocean liner *Empress of India*, which had been substituted for the *Aquitania*. Barred from the Caledonian main line by the earlier tragedy at Quintinshill, the train had been re-routed around the area of the disaster via the Lockerbie-Dumfries branch line before running into Carlisle and then out again en route for the Mersey. News would have filtered through to the soldiers – although not the full extent, it seems – of their comrades' tragic fate. It must have been a sombre journey.

But not, of course, as mentally draining as that which later carried the remnant of A and D companies towards the waiting ocean liner. 'It was a nightmare trip,' recalled one soldier. 'Our nerves were shattered and every time the train slowed or took a corner we gasped and braced ourselves for the worst.' Finally, at 2.45am on Sunday, this torturous ordeal was over for the beleaguered troops as the special pulled into Liverpool's Edge Hill station, as far as its silent occupants would be taken by rail.

The top brass were there in force to meet them – Brigadier William Scott Moncrieff, commanding the 156th Infantry Brigade of which the 7th Royal Scots formed part, and the brigade staff, together with the battalion's second-in-command, Major A.W. Sanderson, and other officers who had reached Liverpool with the men of B and C companies on the diverted earlier train. It has been recorded that the men were met too by the regimental sergeant major, who had also travelled on the second train from Larbert, thus avoiding the tragedy. When he saw the pitiful remnant arrive he broke down in tears.

What happened next to the men who had endured the horrors of Quintinshill is difficult to understand. It seems from at least one eyewitness account that carriages were available at Edge Hill as sleeping accommodation for the battalion. Other men slept on the platform, rolled up in their blankets. Neither facility appears to have been extended to the Quintinshill survivors. Instead, they were put to work sorting equipment salvaged from the disaster which they had brought with them. 'I am quite sure there was flesh stuck to some of it,' recalled one of the group, Alexander Thompson, many years later, testimony recounted by J.A.B. Hamilton. Later still, wrote Hamilton, the shattered soldiers were ordered to carry equipment aboard the ship. Why the apparent lack of consideration for men who manifestly deserved it in abundance?

Hamilton suggests, and he is probably right, that it can only be explained by a lack of appreciation on the part of those in authority of just how severe the tragedy had been. On board the *Empress of India* the men were allocated to their mess decks. They retired at last, to rest. 'Only then,' added Hamilton, 'did the message arrive to say that, except for the seven officers, none of the men were to sail.' The instruction had come from the War Office. Someone had deemed the presence of the officers to be essential in Gallipoli. This was hard on them – very hard – but at least mercy had finally been extended to their men.

'The effect of the shock was so overwhelming that, when the survivors arrived in Liverpool, all the NCOs and men were sent home,' records the Royal Scots' regimental history. The men's release, it appears, was at the instigation of their CO, Colonel Peebles. It is hard not to conclude that they should never have been sent on to Liverpool in the first place, let alone put to work when they got there.

Not that release from the sea voyage marked the end of their misery. Once again, surely feeling utterly wretched, they were marched through the streets of Liverpool on the Sunday morning to Lime Street station, their sorry state only too apparent. 'Whilst marching back,' remembered one of the survivors in an interview with the *Edinburgh Evening News* forty years later, 'we were stoned by street urchins who, because of our ragged condition, no doubt mistook us for German prisoners.'

From Lime Street they travelled, eventually, back to Scotland, reaching Edinburgh Waverley station at 10pm. There to witness their arrival, the *Evening News* was moved to comment the next day that, when the men were lined up on the platform, 'it was evident from their appearance that they had had experiences of a nerve-shattering character... and the state of their uniforms bore testimony to the work they had undertaken after the smash. They were not permitted to converse with the few persons who were on the platform when they arrived.'

Instead, the men were quickly transferred to a fleet of waiting cars which took them to the capital city's Craigleith Hospital for a night's rest and observation. Relief at last.

Back at Quintinshill the wreckage had smouldered on into the morning of Sunday, 23 May. The saddest of sights, but for many an irresistible spectacle. The news had spread – and so, too, had the crowd of fascinated onlookers, gawpers, drawn to this out-of-the-way railway outpost like pins to the most powerful of magnets. It was impossible to tell how many had gathered there. 'Thousands of people,' reported the *Cumberland News*, adding that 'the final removal of the wreckage was watched with keen interest.'

Carlisle's firefighters continued the process of damping down the debris until they had been doing so for a full twenty-four hours. Large gangs of men worked to clear the blackened, battered carriages. Locomotives and tenders were piled unceremoniously at one side of the track, clear of the down (northbound) line where they would remain for two more days. By 7pm on Sunday evening crane operators from Carlisle and Motherwell working, respectively, at the south and north ends of the still blocked (southbound) line, had cleared this too.

With damaged track relaid, the railway was declared fit for re-opening. An hour or so later the first train to run past Quintinshill since the multiple collision – the up Limited Mail from Glasgow due in Carlisle at 8.14pm – proclaimed the line's return to normality in what, by any standards, was a remarkably short period of time. The diversionary routes – the Glasgow traffic had used the Glasgow & South Western route as far as Dumfries and thence the branch to the main line at Lockerbie during the blockage while the Edinburgh trains followed the North British line via Hawick – had been needed for less than two days.

Throughout the weekend the spectators were enthralled. They were also a major problem. 'From near and far people travelled on Sunday to Gretna,' reported the *Carlisle Journal*, while the *Cumberland News* described the scene on the ten miles of highway between Carlisle and Gretna as 'remarkable... the roads were black with cyclists and motor cars most of the day. Many trudged on foot in the broiling hot sun'. The level crossing over the railway at Longtown, just short of the border, seriously hindered the sightseers' progress, the *Carlisle Journal* likening the endless procession through that small town to 'the breaking up of a Derby Day crowd'.

Major congestion, especially on the restricted approaches to the crash site, was inevitable. Orchestrated by their chief constable, Dumfrieshire's police sought to identify those with a legitimate right to be there and to keep those without any at a reasonable distance. Chaos threatened as they struggled to maintain the protective cordon thrown around the site. The lanes and hedgerows in the immediate vicinity were lined with people.

While the press coverage, local and national, in the wake of the disaster covered just about every conceivable detail, there was one notable exception, something that would certainly have jarred with the 'heroism among the horror' tone of the overall reportage.

In terms of the unstinting, selfless work and devotion to duty carried out by so many at the scene of the disaster and then at Carlisle and elsewhere in the immediate aftermath, Quintinshill undoubtedly brought out the very best in human nature. Sadly, it also produced an element of the very worst. The police had moved quickly to control the crowds of onlookers at the site and prevent them from encroaching on the rescue operation, but photographs taken at the time show clearly that many people trespassed onto the field used as the reception area for the victims and, worse, there are anecdotal reports of looting which appear to be well-founded.

Harry Frost, a Carlisle man, recalled as an 80-year-old on the fiftieth anniversary of the disaster in 1965 how he arrived at the site on the Saturday. 'It

was a terrible affair,' he said in an interview. 'When I got there in the afternoon…
there were billy cans, bayonets and all sorts of things strewn about the fields.
People were picking up souvenirs but I didn't touch anything. When I got back
home my wife asked me what I had bought back and I said, "I have seen enough
without bringing anything back to remind me." I shall never forget it. I saw a
fellow picking up 2/- (two shilling) pieces… they were all welded together.'

Who were the looters? That they were not local people is strongly suggested
in the recollections of survivor, Lieutenant George Haws, recorded by his father
(see chapter three): 'More than once [George] expressed his gratitude for the way
the residents of Gretna acted in alleviating the suffering of the injured – so very
different to the middle class who came out from Carlisle and other places out
of curiosity and souvenir hunting.' They came, according to the Haws memoir.
'sweeping down on the place, and were nothing but a lot of thieves and pilferers'.

Some said the looting continued on the Sunday. Whether this was true or
not, the contemporary press accounts reveal the presence of a potential hoard of
rich pickings for those tempted to return home with a memento of what, it was
already abundantly clear, had been a truly momentous event.

'Pathetic souvenirs lay all around,' the *Carlisle Journal* informed its readers.
'A large box of chocolate bearing the name of a Princes Street [Edinburgh] firm
was found. It had not been broken open but lay in a melting state. Novels and
periodicals were found here and there amongst the wreckage, one paper bearing
signs that it had been held in a desperate clutch, so it lay in its crushed state, just
as a man would hold it. It bore the name of W. Ballie.' It seems highly improbable
that Private William Ballie, as he read his paper on the troop train, would have
considered the possibility that he was about to become part of a story that would
dominate the pages of many periodicals to come. Quintinshill claimed his life and
that of his brother, Andrew, a fellow private.

The *Carlisle Journal's* list of Quintinshill's 'souvenirs' also included a bundle
of regimental papers, with a tag bearing the inscription, 'for use on board ship.'
The remains of rifles, charred until only the lock and barrel remained, dotted the
site along with bayonets and the remnants of glengarries, greatcoats and tunics.

Amid it all the bodies of still more victims were pulled from the debris. Mainly
soldiers, of course, but also the remains of the troop train's driver and fireman,
Francis Scott and James Hannah. The last body of them all was found around
noon. But this was not the final retrieval of human remains. Early on Sunday
afternoon men working with the breakdown gang made a gruesome discovery: a
man's foot. To whom had it belonged? No one knew. There was no way of telling
in May 1915. This pitiful remnant of human life, a final token of carnage, was
buried alongside the railway track close to where it had been found.

When the press in Edinburgh and Glasgow carried the story of the disaster –
in less detail than the newspapers of the border region, perhaps, but sufficient to
convey the extent of the tragedy – the Scottish nation was stunned. And in Leith,
the home of the 7th Royal Scots, it was a hammer-blow without precedent.

John Thomas wrote eloquently in his 1969 book on the crash of the shock waves which descended on the port town: 'If the Quintinshill affair was the greatest catastrophe in British railway history, it was also the bitterest blow ever suffered by Leith as a community. Relatives of the soldiers congregated at the drill hall in Dalmeny Street seeking news; at length a list of the dead arrived and, before being posted outside the hall, it was read out loud from a window to the relatives assembled in the street. It was followed soon by a longer list. On Sunday morning the ministers of Leith and Musselburgh gave the names of the known casualties from their pulpits: dead, injured and missing.'

The term 'missing' was extraordinarily hard to accept in the context of an accident on Scottish soil. In France it would have been easier – to a degree – to accept. In the Dardenelles it would have been more understandable, but in *Scotland?*

The gloom in Leith was all pervasive. At one stage 2,000 local people had gathered outside the battalion's headquarters in the desperate wait for news. On the Sunday afternoon the military authorities arranged for a special train to run from Edinburgh to Carlisle for the benefit of relatives anxious to visit the injured. The *Carlisle Journal* told how a considerable number assembled at Edinburgh Waverley station, 'where Major Smith, of the 7th Royal Scots, intimated that the train, which would leave at 4.30, was primarily for those who had received messages saying that their relatives were injured. He strongly advised those who had not received word to stay at home. He also stated that bodies were being bought to the city that night. This information induced a goodly proportion of the relatives to abandon their contemplated journey to Carlisle.'

When the train pulled out of Waverley, however, around 160 relatives had been provided with tickets for the journey. With them went the Reverend William Swan of South Leith Parish Church who also served as a chaplain with the 7th Royal Scots. The ties between the battalion and the local community were many and close, and now more than ever, those ties were interwoven as one as Leith struggled to come to terms with the tragedy tearing at its heart.[9]

That some who had heard nothing of the fate of a husband, son or brother chose to ignore the major's advice to stay behind is beyond doubt. Those people travelled south in hope; perhaps there *would* be news when the train arrived at Carlisle. Others, with news of a loved one's injury, travelled without guarantee that their condition had not worsened, removing him from the names of the wounded to that of the dead. Uncertainty and anxiety accompanied them all across the border – and arrival in Carlisle at first served only to increase the tension.

The relatives from Leith were assembled on the platform at Citadel station to hear an officer of the 7th battalion read out an updated list of all the dead and injured, together with details of the various locations at which the latter were being treated. As a man's name was called, his relative – more than one in some cases – stepped forward. For several, relatives of soldiers taken to the military hospital in Preston, this meant a further journey, again specially arranged, was in prospect. On the spot, the *Carlisle Journal* later reported that 'it was a nerve-trying experience for many as the names were being read…' And for some of the women it was too much. 'They gave way under the strain,' added the *Journal*. For those who had to endure listening to the lengthy list without hearing the name of a loved one, the Carlisle newspaper chose a simple term: 'pitiable'.

Their menfolk were still missing. Was this worse or marginally better than for those whose hopes of comforting an injured relative were dashed by the news that, as so many had feared when they set out, the soldier in question was now dead? In some cases, there was not even the body of a loved one, confirmed as a fatality, to visit. Arrangements had been made for the running of another special train, this time heading north to Edinburgh and Leith, returning many of the slain. Tragically, it had left Carlisle by the time the grief-stricken relatives arrived.

Scenes described by the *Edinburgh Evening News* as being 'of the saddest description' gripped Leith when news spread on the Sunday evening of the impending arrival of that first trainload of Quintinshill's victims. 'The news was responsible for the gathering of large crowds in the neighbourhood of the Central station,' reported the *Evening News*. 'None were admitted to the station except those who had authority from the military headquarters. Between eight and nine o'clock soldiers lined each side of the street, and shortly before half past nine the ordinary traffic was suspended and there was a procession of funeral vans, motor ambulances and motor cars, which passed up the carriage way to the station, where the train containing the dead was at this time waiting.'

Underlining once again how hard it was at that stage to identify, or even quantify with any accuracy, the dead, the train arriving at Leith Central contained 106 coffins, but in only fifty-three cases could the men they carried be positively named. Some of the coffins contained the remains of more than one man. 'As the first van of the sad procession left the station the soldiers reversed arms, and as the procession turned into Leith Walk heads were uncovered and the most complete silence prevailed,' the *Evening News* told its readers.[10]

With the coffins carried in a number of slow-moving Red Cross vehicles, that sombre procession, suggested the *Carlisle Journal* which had followed the story north, 'might have been the setting for the homecoming of victors, but for the unwonted silence of the onlookers, which conveyed the sorrowful significance of the occasion. There was the murmur of voices, but none of the animation of military displays, and the only harmonious note was provided by the noisy laughter of young children, thoughtless of the sad circumstances.'

And so the men of the 7th Royal Scots were brought for the last time to their familiar drill hall, their coffins lining its walls overnight awaiting the final salute.

With so many of the bodies reduced to badly charred remains, the decision had been taken to allow relatives to view only the outside of the coffins. 'On the coffins of those who had not been identified it was touching to see flowers placed by the relatives of those whose sons have not been heard of since the disaster.

It was somebody's boy that was inside the black shell if it was not their own,' reported *The Weekly Scotsman*. Partial access to the coffins was probably for the best but the tears of grieving loved ones could not be similarly restricted.

The next morning saw most of the surviving remnant of the battalion's A and D companies discharged from their overnight stay in Edinburgh's Craigleith Hospital and allowed to return home to Leith and Musselburgh on fourteen days' leave – but not before undergoing what must surely have been another painfully sad ordeal in the afternoon. They assembled to pay their respects to the first of their comrades who had died in, or soon after, the rail disaster – the number widely reported in the press was 102 – to be given a funeral service followed by burial on a corner site at Rosebank Cemetery, close to the border between Edinburgh and Leith. It took three hours for this mile-long funeral procession from the battalion's Dalmeny Street headquarters to pass the silent crowds behind massed troops lining streets which, incongruously, were in festive dress for Queen Mary's birthday on 26 May.

A sad oversight indeed. A reader of *The Scotsman* no doubt voiced the opinion of a great many in Scotland's capital when he wrote that, 'when every heart in the city was aching, and many were breaking, Edinburgh was bright with flags fluttering gaily top-mast high'. No one had thought to lower the flags to half-mast.

Two batteries of field artillery transported the soldiers' coffins draped with the Union Jack. Representatives of each of the regiments stationed in the area walked with them. At Rosebank, with what *The Weekly Scotsman* called 'imposing military pageant,' the 100-plus victims of what the press had decided should henceforth be known as 'the Gretna Railway Disaster' were laid to rest in the presence of huge crowds. 'In death they were not divided. They were buried in a common grave, dug by soldiers' hands as though they had fallen on the field of battle,' reported the weekly paper, before making one of the first calls for a permanent memorial.

'No funeral like this has been seen in Edinburgh or Leith within living memory, either as regards the number carried to the tomb at one time or the amount of national and local sympathy the event has evoked,' added *The Weekly Scotsman*. 'The authorities paid to the deceased citizen soldiers the highest military honours it was in their power to show.' There were several thousand troops on parade for the occasion. Indeed, the northern military presence could not have been any higher in rank, extending right up to Major General Sir John Spencer Ewart, head of the British Army's Scottish Command, and his staff. Other dignitaries included several officials of Leith, magistrates and council among them, the Lord Provost of Edinburgh, the Moderators of the Church of Scotland and the United Free Church Assembly of Scotland and the Bishop of the Episcopal Church. A pipe and drum band played what the press described as 'impressive dirge-like strains' while relatives of the dead, many of these weeping women, had summoned up the courage to follow their men to the grave. This was a local community truly united in grief.

The trench dug for the communal grave into which the coffins, still covered by the national flag, were lowered was more than twenty yards long. The Royal Scots' regimental chaplains led the committal prayers before a large military firing party broke the silence with a resounding gun salute and the trumpets sounded *The Last Post*. 'The funeral of these brave men, many of whom faced a worse death than on the battlefield, was in all respects deeply affecting and will remain indelibly engraved on the memory of all those who witnessed it,' *The Weekly Scotsman* reflected.

It was, of course, only the first, albeit by far the largest, of a series of funerals held for the victims of Quintinshill. On the Tuesday the remains of three more soldiers were interred, privately, in Edinburgh's Eastern Cemetery, Easter Road. On the Wednesday another nineteen coffins were borne, with military honours, from the battalion HQ at Leith to Rosebank. Once again large crowds turned out to witness it. At that stage no further deaths among the Royal Scots had been reported, with the hospitalised patients said to be progressing favourably. But it was impossible then, and it is impossible now, to state with absolute certainty how many of the 7th battalion were actually represented among the remains interred at Rosebank. The precise fate of many will never be known.

South of the border, Carlisle was also in funereal mood. Thousands of people had lined the route from the city's Etterby township to the nearby Stanwix Cemetery to witness the funeral procession organised for local railwaymen Francis Scott and James Hannah, driver and fireman of the troop train. At its head walked 100 of the men's Caledonian Railway colleagues from Carlisle's Kingmoor locomotive depot, followed by a large number of children from Etterby Mission Sunday School of which driver Scott had been superintendent. In place of the Union Jacks which adorned the Royal Scots' coffins in Leith, those containing the two railwaymen were covered in what the newspapers reporting the event called 'beautiful floral tributes'.

The considerable number of people who processed behind relatives and friends spoke of the heavy sense of shock felt in Carlisle at the loss of two highly-regarded citizens, each of them carried to their grave by a quartet of their colleagues – drivers in the case of Scott and firemen for Hannah. From the upper echelon of the Caledonian's hierarchy, the railway company's representation at the funeral, among other key officials, was notable thanks to the particularly high-profile presence of William Pickersgill, its Locomotive, Carriage and Wagon Superintendent since 1914.[11]

The funerals of those fatally injured in the express and local trains (see chapter three) claimed the headlines elsewhere but attention switched back to Leith with the arrival on Saturday, 29 May of sixty-eight survivors who had spent the week since the disaster recovering from their injuries in hospitals at Carlisle, Longtown and Penrith. They had left Carlisle by hospital train that morning. When it pulled into Edinburgh Waverley, its arrival time a matter of public knowledge in Leith, it was met by a large gathering of the men's relatives and friends – rather too large, it seems. The *Cumberland News* reported that they had to be 'barricaded out of the platform in order that the Red Cross men might carry out their work unhampered. There were twenty-six stretcher cases, but even the worst of them faced the matter bravely and acknowledged the passing greetings of their friends.' Most were able to walk unaided to the waiting transport laid on, mainly by the Red Cross. Their injuries, noted the press, were 'mostly in the head and hand.' The returning Royal Scots were then taken to Craigleith Hospital to rest.

Meanwhile, in Glasgow, the destination for a small number of the disaster's victims, two coffins sent by train from Edinburgh had attracted particular attention from the press at the city's Central station on the night of Monday, 24 May. The *Dumfries & Galloway Standard* reported that both contained the remains of children. One bore a label, identifying the single body inside as that of an 'unrecognisable' female child. The other, just as pathetically, was labelled, 'three trunks, probably children.' Thus was born the enduring mystery of Quintinshill's lost children, one that has never been conclusively solved.

In his book, John Thomas suggests that the two coffins had initially been taken to the Royal Scots' drill hall in Leith along with those of the battalion's dead. He adds that no children had been reported missing and the remains were sent to Glasgow in the hope that somebody would claim them. But nobody did – and nobody ever has done. The Caledonian Railway interred them with moving ceremony in Glasgow's Western Necropolis the following Wednesday. And there the mystery has lain.

As noted in chapter three, the evidence suggested that the four children – if children they were – had travelled on the express from London. Were they in the sleeping car that was destroyed by fire? And why did their tragic demise apparently fail to provoke a flicker of interest from family or friends? Theories have been put forward based mostly on nonsensical logic and fanciful conjecture. But has the truth finally emerged? There seems a good chance that it might have. In chapter fifteen the most compelling explanation so far is examined.[12]

The body of the only identified child victim of the disaster, Dickson Nimmo, had been taken from the site in a wagon, along with that of his mother, Rachel, to the church at Gretna before being returned home to Newcastle on 26 May.

If the terrible events of Saturday, 22 May 1915 touched the hearts of the local communities in Leith, Carlisle and elsewhere, they also reverberated around the British nation. Messages of sympathy flooded in from all quarters. On the 25th the press reported a message from the reigning monarch, George V, on behalf of the Royal Family. 'Please express to the Royal Scots the heartfelt sympathy of the King and Queen, with all ranks, in the loss of gallant comrades through this terrible railway accident, and assure the bereaved families how much their Majesties feel for them in their overwhelming sorrow.' It would not be the last statement from the office of the sovereign on the Quintinshill disaster as a web of events gathered pace in its wake.

Something rather more tangible than sympathetic words was thought in royal circles to be more appropriate for the injury victims. Queen Mary asked the Caledonian Railway what they thought might be suitable gifts. It is unclear why the Queen's approach should have been made to the railway company rather than to the Royal Scots or the hospital authorities. The Caledonian management took the sensible course of referring the royal query to the hospital administrators who advised that cigarettes, chocolate and fruit would be most acceptable. On the Wednesday after the disaster the gifts arrived in Carlisle and were distributed among the various hospitals accommodating the injured.

But the gift most coveted by the men's relatives, by the bereaved families and by the people of Leith in general was a permanent memorial to Quintinshill's fallen. A year later in May 1916, after the considerable sum of £4,000 had been raised through public subscription, their wish was granted. Nearly 2,000 congregated by the communal grave at Rosebank to witness the dedication by Lord Rosebery, honorary colonel of the 7th Royal Scots, of a magnificent Celtic cross memorial made from Peterhead granite. Several firms in Leith closed that afternoon as a mark of respect and to allow employees to attend the service. In front of them stood local dignitaries and armed forces representatives. To ensure they had first claim on the available graveside space relatives and friends of the fallen were issued with admission tickets.[13]

But just about every element of public life in Leith's tight-knit community – from the special constabulary to the boys' brigade and boy scouts – was represented. Appropriately, the guard of honour was provided by men of the 7th battalion. Poignantly, many of those who had survived the horror of the disaster, several since discharged from the army and still carrying their injuries, walking with the aid of sticks and crutches, were present for the three o'clock dedication.

No doubt the pipes of the King's Own Scottish Borderers, later joined by a combined choir of more than 100 voices from different churches in Leith, added further to the poignancy of the occasion, as would the words of the town's provost, Malcolm Smith. 'Leith,' he said, 'will never forget the tragic fate which befell her battalion on its way to fight for king and country in the greatest war in human history.' The memorial had been erected 'in order that those who come after us, as also those who live today, may see and realise something of the feeling of admiration entertained towards those who are ready to endure hardness as good soldiers and to lay down their lives for their country in a great cause'

The public generosity which had provided the monument to the 7th Royal Scots had also funded provision, in that pre-NHS era, of a hospital bed in Leith and the setting up of a fund to help those in financial need as a result of the accident.

A lot had happened in the year since the disaster. Blame had been apportioned (as the following chapters of this book will detail). Lord Rosebery therefore felt justified in his own address to refer to the 'criminal blunder' which had precipitated the tragedy, causing three trains to crash and, in an instant, leaving 'that gallant fellowship' of Royal Scots 'crushed, dying and dead.' And so the memorial was unveiled, buglers sounded their call, the 7th battalion's guard of honour presented arms, prayers were said, *The Dead March* was played and the large gathering sang the national anthem before Roseberry walked solemnly to the foot of the cross to lay a commemorative wreath and bring the ceremony to a close.

There are other memorials elsewhere to the victims of Quintinshill, but it is to the granite cross at Rosebank, with the names of the men of the 7th Royal Scots who died inscribed on ten bronze panels set into the adjacent cemetery wall, that the people of Leith have returned to remember their battalion's fallen at the subsequent memorial services held annually since the memorial's dedication. Those panels list the names of 214 victims – the combined total of confirmed, identifiable fatalities and the many others, their remains never found, who were classed as missing, presumed dead.

To this number must be added the eight people who lost their lives on the express, the footplate duo on the troop train and Rachel Nimmo who died with her baby on the local train. This brings the overall total of fatalities to 226. It is a disputed figure. The final tally should almost certainly be 230 if the 'lost children' are included. The official number of injured victims was put at 246. In truth, there were a great many others – relatives, friends and whole communities – who suffered as a result of this, the worst-ever rail disaster in Britain.[14, 15]

On the day the memorial to the 7th Royal Scots was dedicated at Rosebank Cemetery in 1916 there was no sign of the bright sunshine that a year earlier had cast a mocking illumination on the ghastly scenes unfolding at Quintinshill. Instead, on a grey afternoon, the drizzle wept for the Leith Battalion and those who had been cut down with them. Where did the blame lie?

Notes

1. The canal-side siding had been built for the specific purpose of transferring to the Cumberland Infirmary wounded servicemen returned to the UK from the continental war front. The siding had been laid along the route of a former canal which had closed in 1853.
2. The Cumberland Infirmary had opened in 1841 and was extended in 1870. In 2000, extensively rebuilt as Carlisle's principal hospital, it became the first in the country constructed under a Private Finance Initiative (PFI) when it was opened by Prime Minister Tony Blair.
3. The gallant transporter of so many of the wounded from Quintinshill to Carlisle was named in the local press as a Mr Johnston, of Messrs Little and Johnston, a local firm based in the city,
4. The first dead body removed from the ambulance train at Carlisle Citadel was that of express train casualty, Assistant Paymaster William Paton (Royal Naval Division) – see also chapter three.

5. Originally constructed as a school, Chadwick became a military auxiliary hospital during World War One – as did the hospital at Carlisle Castle (which served as regimental depot of the Border Regiment until 1959). Fusehill had opened as a workhouse in 1864, later becoming a hospital. It was re-branded a general hospital in 1946 and was closed in 2000 on the completion of the new Cumberland Infirmary. Its site is now occupied by St Martin's College.

6. The subsequent death of Lance Corporal Robert Scott Dawson at Penrith triggered a separate coroner's inquest there on 15 July. It was attended not only by officials of the Caledonian Railway but also by George Meakin and James Tinsley, the signalmen at Quintinshill. See chapter twelve.

7. It was reported that Dr Anderson's retired predecessor, Dr Bennet Clark, on hearing of the accident, immediately set out from Edinburgh to help with the emergency, arriving in Carlisle the same afternoon. His contribution in the treatment and care of the injured, was said to be 'invaluable.'

8. The reference to fifty-seven other ranks among the remnant of A and D companies was recorded by Colonel Peebles. Other sources have suggested a higher figure – up to eighty-eight – but this seems unlikely.

9. Provost Malcolm Smith, the ceremonial head of the then independent (from Edinburgh) Leith community was among those who watched the relatives' train depart from Waverley for Carlisle.

10. Leith Central was the four-platform terminus of a short branch line from Edinburgh Waverley opened by the North British Railway in 1903. It was closed to all traffic in April 1952.

11. As Scott's home was in Etterby Road and Hannah's in Scaurbank Road their corteges linked up in Etterby Street and wound their way in long procession to the cemetery for the service.

12. Sir Charles Bine Renshaw, chairman of the Caledonian Railway, and Sir Thomas Dunlop, Lord Provost of Glasgow, were among those attending the burial of the unknown victims.

13. The choice of Peterhead granite for the memorial carried an irony which was almost certainly lost on those who attended its dedication. The granite might conceivably have been quarried by James Tinsley during the term of imprisonment he served for his part in the disaster!

14. Other memorials exist on the railway bridge adjacent to the crash site and in Gretna Green.

15. See chapter fifteen for memorial inscription and appendix one for a full list of those who died in the disaster.

Chapter 5

The Signalman who Forgot

'I forgot about it after I jumped off the engine and it never entered my mind again until after the accident had happened.'

Signalman James Tinsley at the
Board of Trade public inquiry, 25 May 1915

A one-sentence admission simple and straightforward. Reproduced above, it has stood for nearly a century synonymous with Quintinshill as the truthful, reliable explanation for the disaster. Signalman James Tinsley somehow had wiped from his memory the train in which, only minutes before, he had travelled to work and which had then stood helpless outside his signal box as he invited the Royal Scots' troop train to run headlong into it, triggering the catastrophe of 22 May 1915. 'I forgot about it.' It has never made sense.

How could this possibly have happened? Why has it been so universally embraced as the cause of the disaster? Tinsley's admission lies on the surface, exposed for all to see. To reach the root causes of Quintinshill's tragedy there is a need to dig some way beneath. The roots take us in several directions, the first back to the construction in 1903 of the isolated signal box, essentially to relieve congestion on the increasingly busy Caledonian Railway section of the West Coast route between England and Scotland. The box was responsible for a section of line between Gretna Junction and Kirkpatrick and controlled passing loops either side of the double track, allowing slow-moving freight and local passenger services to be safely stored out of the way while faster trains ran through without hindrance, a practice which is still followed today on every main line railway.

During the six months which preceded the disaster war demands had seen a substantial increase of traffic on the national rail network. On the West Coast route through Quintinshill it had risen by as much as forty per cent. Naturally this had imposed extra demands and consequent strain on those tasked with coping with the additional wartime traffic while simultaneously maintaining peacetime passenger train schedules.

George Meakin (31), who regularly worked the box with James Tinsley, was an experienced hand who had been on the Caledonian payroll for seventeen years. On Friday, 21 May 1915 he had arrived at 8pm to work the ten-hour night shift. In peacetime this would have been a fairly routine duty with little traffic to deal with in the small hours. But the war had intervened and Meakin's job had significantly changed. He now faced something of an uphill struggle to keep things moving. In his strategic position he had to make quick on-the-spot decisions.

Meakin's modern-day counterparts benefit from the assistance of traffic controllers who are able to assess the overall traffic situation across a wide area and advise signal boxes accordingly. Meakin had no such support. In common with all other signalmen of the period, he had to cope as best he could by relying on a system of bell codes, telegraphs and a telephone link with neighbouring signal boxes. There is considerable evidence to suggest that, had a train control system been available to him, the accident might never have happened.[1]

At 6am, towards the end of his long shift, George Meakin had a complex traffic management situation on his hands. Too many trains in all the wrong places. It was not affected by the passing of a train of empty coal wagons from the north at 6.04, but the complications quickly set in. Close behind was another lumbering train of empty wagons heading for Carlisle – and hot on its heels, travelling at speed, was the 7th Royal Scots' late-running troop train. Meakin had been told that there would be no room at Carlisle's Kingmoor freight yard for the empty trucks approaching his box. There was no point sending the train south and it was about to block the progress of the troop special. So Meakin would need to direct it into the adjacent up (southbound) passing loop, freeing the line for the Royal Scots' Liverpool-bound train to pass through.

The down (northbound) line was also very busy that morning. As described in chapter two, the two Anglo-Scottish expresses to Edinburgh and Glasgow were running late. To keep the line clear for these prestige services Meakin had diverted another slow-moving freight, heading north, into the adjacent passing loop at 6.14. So far, so good. It was company policy not to hamper unnecessarily the progress of expresses and troop trains. The freights could wait.

Meakin probably cursed – with good reason – when alerted that a decision had been taken at Carlisle to send the 6.17 local train, stopping at all stations to Beattock, ahead of the two northbound expresses in order to ensure its locomotive's ability to haul the important commuter service off the Moffatt branch line from its main line junction at Beattock to Glasgow. Getting the engine to Beattock on time was the limit of Carlisle's concern. The fact that at some point just across the border it would have to relinquish right of way to the expresses was not their responsibility. Instead, it would fall entirely on the shoulders of George Meakin at Quintinshill – and he had virtually run out of space.

Told that the first express had left Carlisle at 6.27 and aware that it would rapidly catch up with the local train, Meakin's options were severely limited. Delaying an express train was not among them and neither was hindering the progress of a troop special. But his passing loops were allocated and making its ponderous way between these two priority trains was the local service from Carlisle. He had to get it out of the way. So, as described in chapter two, Meakin had decided to stop the 'local' at his signal box and facilitate its shunt through the cross-over points to the up (southbound) line. It could be held there, temporarily on the wrong side of the track, to allow the first express to pass through.

To avoid delaying the southbound troop train, the local service could then be returned to its rightful down line and sent on to the next signal box at Kirkpatrick station where the shunt could be repeated to permit the second express to run past – unorthodox but not unheard of in this period of intensive traffic management. Of the twenty-one previous occasions it had been necessary to shunt the 'local' at Quintinshill, four had involved a move onto the southbound line. Irksome it might have been, but it would not unduly have fazed a signalman with the experience of George Meakin. And, in principle, it would not expose any of the trains involved to danger so long as the signalling safeguards were in use. Given the circumstances, Meakin's solution made sense.

But it was complicated by the fact that before it could be fully implemented – with the train protection safeguards in place – Meakin, ending his overnight shift, would be handing over responsibility for the operation of the signal box to James Tinsley. Not that he would have had any qualms about doing that – Tinsley (32) was a reliable, capable signalman himself – but within minutes this entirely manageable situation would descend into an abyss of unimaginable chaos.

That shift change should have occurred at 6am but for some time, as noted in chapter two, Meakin and Tinsley had been operating an unofficial change-over system which allowed the man coming on shift in the morning to arrive up to half-an-hour late. 'We expected each other between six and six-thirty,' Tinsley would later admit in a written statement. It would appear, however, that the arrangement was rather more one-sided than Tinsley suggested. Meakin, who lived close to the signal box in the Soringfield area of Gretna, said that Tinsley 'would sleep in a little; he was in the habit of coming in late'. Whatever the precise nature of the arrangement, it was clearly in breach of company regulations.

In order to conceal it, the two men had concocted a cover-up which was both simple and effective. Whichever of the two was on the night shift would jot down on a sheet of paper all train movements from 6am onwards. When the other man arrived, late, to take over the signal box, it was a simple process for him to copy the details recorded on the paper into the box's official train register, thus giving the impression that he had clocked on for his morning shift at the correct time. This was a deceit which is impossible to defend.[2]

Certainly, it did nothing but harm the interests of both signalmen when it came to apportioning blame for the disaster – during the judicial process itself in 1915 and ever since in the eyes of those who have chronicled the events for public consumption. Yet, in common with so many aspects of the Quintinshill tragedy, this is something that has always lacked the thoroughness of 'forensic' examination in order to determine how much of a factor it actually was.

An arrangement often portrayed as a secret known only to the two men involved was actually nothing of the sort. Evidence would emerge to show that it was apparently well known to Tinsley's next-door neighbour, fellow signalman Robert Kirkpatrick, in the station cottages at Gretna where Kirkpatrick manned the junction signal box, Quintinshill's adjacent box to the south. Occasionally, when Meakin decided to stop the local train at Quintinshill, as he did on that fateful Saturday in May 1915, he would tip Kirkpatrick off so Tinsley could hitch a ride on it at Gretna, saving himself a walk of around two miles.

Therefore, when Meakin rang Robert Kirkpatrick that morning to let him know he would be stopping the 6.17 local train from Carlisle at Quintinshill, the second part of his message was well rehearsed: 'The boy will get a ride this morning.' Kirkpatrick would certainly have been aware that Tinsley was due on shift at 6am and, having overslept, was clearly not going to make it to Quintinshill on time. He had seen him hurrying from his nearby cottage towards the station at Gretna where the local train was waiting at the platform. To Tinsley's evident relief, Kirkpatrick had opened a window of his signal box and, acting on Meakin's message, had directed the out-of-breath signalman onto it.

There is more than a hint of routine about this. Indeed, in a statement he made later, Kirkpatrick would admit that he had assisted in getting a late-running Tinsley to work in this manner on 'four or five' previous occasions.

Did this knowledge of Tinsley's late starts extend higher up the chain of command? It seems likely. On the early shift that morning was his manager, Alexander Thorburn, stationmaster at Gretna and another close neighbour of the Tinsley family. Thorburn would later deny knowing anything about the late shift change arrangement, but he was definitely on the station platform that morning to see the local train leave so it is highly likely that he would also have seen Tinsley.

As described earlier, Tinsley did not travel the short distance to Quintinshill in a carriage. He climbed into the cab of the locomotive, technically another breach of company regulations; it would appear that quite a few of the Caledonian's procedures were being given somewhat scant regard that morning. Maybe the cab ride was just too tempting to resist as Tinsley was welcomed aboard by driver David Wallace and his fireman, George Hutchinson. Experienced Carlisle men, they had been detailed a dream of a locomotive in 4-6-0 *Cardean* class number 907. To a Caledonian railwayman the five *Cardeans* in the company's fleet were the 'cream of the crop' and 907 was in immaculate condition, returning to service on this humble running-in turn after a general overhaul intended to restore it for 'top link' express train duty.

James Tinsley could not fail to have been impressed as, no doubt, the footplate crew showed off their mighty charge, resplendent in its magnificent Caledonian blue livery, revealed to its best effect against the backdrop of that sunny May morning, the shimmering jewel in the Caley's locomotive crown. It should have been an unforgettable experience for him to ride in the cab of such a prestigious engine as number 907. Yet that stylish ride to work and the locomotive on which he rode – indeed the entire train – seems instantly to have slipped his memory.[3]

There would be reminders aplenty of the local train while it was halted at Quintinshill, as if he needed them, and despite his statement – 'I forgot all about it after I jumped off the engine and it never entered my mind again until after the accident had happened' – he clearly *did* remember the train's presence from time to time. But it was only fleeting, never constant, and not at the *crucial* time. The key truth behind the Quintinshill disaster lies within this infamous statement but, as this book will show, it is not the truth it appears to be.[4]

Meanwhile in the signal box, Meakin's ability to implement fully the safeguards to protect the stationary local train were restricted not only by a failure to conform with safety regulations that would damn him in the eyes of those who sought justice and explanation, but also by the volume of traffic on the line to the north. Usually, when the need arose to shunt the 6.17 local service in the manner adopted that Saturday morning, he would have relied on a newly-introduced signalling provision known as 'blocking back' designed to protect a train standing on the main line. He would have contacted the signal box to the rear – Kirkpatrick, two miles to the north – and sought the go-ahead to block the section of line between the two boxes. If this was agreed, both signalmen would have recorded this in their train registers and no other train would have been permitted to enter the section until Quintinshill withdrew the blocking back. Not on this occasion.[5]

Meakin never sent the blocking back signal to Thomas Sawyers in the Kirkpatrick box. According to the rule book, this would have to have been done *before* the local train was shunted, not afterwards. He couldn't have blocked back anyway, he would later explain, because the section of track from Kirkpatrick was still occupied by the train of empty wagons heading back ultimately to the South Wales coalfields but initially to the passing loop Meakin had allocated for it at Quintinshill. Blocking back was impossible to implement while a train was in section. It would have to wait until the coal empties were safely installed in the loop. Meakin, due off shift, would need to explain the situation to James Tinsley.

Blocking back was not the only potential weapon in Meakin's train protection armoury. He could have – and company regulations stipulated that he should have – used a signal lever collar, a simple device slipped over the handle of a lever locking it out of use. Had he done so it would have prevented use of the signal clearing the line from the north so that nothing could proceed to Quintinshill.

Evidence would later emerge that lever collars were rarely used in this signal box nor, it would appear, at other cabins elsewhere in the southern district of the Caledonian's network. Signalmen were mostly content to rely on their experience and familiarity with the section of line under their control when it came to operating their signals. Meakin clearly thought the device unnecessary to automatically protect a train which Tinsley, when he relieved him, would surely be bound to safeguard – having only minutes before hopped off its engine.[6]

George Meakin's undoubted failure, through circumstance and arguably understandable rule infringement, to apply either the blocking back procedure or the lever collar were not in themselves fatal errors. He had no reason to suppose the stationary local service and the trains speeding towards Quintinshill from north and south would not be safe in the hands of his signalling colleague once the traffic situation was explained to him. The troop train, although approaching on the same track as the local train, was still far enough away for Tinsley to keep it from running through until the 'local' had left the scene. The expresses would be provided with a clear run past the signal box. Meakin would not for a second have doubted Tinsley's ability to see to this. Tragically it was this that would turn out to be the fatal miscalculation on his part.

The local train from Carlisle was halted at Quintinshill by George Meakin at 6.30. James Tinsley dropped down from its locomotive as it was negotiating the crossover. It would have taken him a matter of seconds to arrive at the signal box and it is generally accepted that he was in the box by 6.32. Apart from Meakin, he was met there by Thomas Ingram, brakesman of the northbound goods train stored in the down passing loop. Ingram had been there for about fifteen minutes, ostensibly waiting to find out how long his train would have to wait. In all probability, with little else to do, he was passing the time of day with Meakin. His presence is key to establishing what happened next.

By common consent Tinsley went straight from the door to the signal box's level frame. Taking off his jacket, he placed his packed lunch on a nearby shelf – something he would later recall in remarkable detail despite forgetting so much else – and went over to Meakin's side. Just as he should have done, Meakin carefully explained to Tinsley the traffic situation. He went into great detail according to the later testimony of brakesman Ingram who was standing close by. Meakin detailed the position of all trains in the vicinity of the box. We can be confident that Tinsley would have been told of the plan to dispatch the local train northwards between the two expresses. We can be equally sure that it went out of Tinsley's head almost immediately. Indeed, he would make no mention whatsoever of the entire conversation with Meakin when later questioned.

With everything explained, at 6.33 Meakin was offered the first Anglo-Scottish express from the signal box at Gretna Junction. Accepting its approach, he immediately offered it forward to Kirkpatrick and when Kirkpatrick had accepted it, cleared his signals for its approach. His final act on duty was to see the train of Welsh coal empties into the southbound passing loop as planned. This was completed around 6.34. Meakin replaced the signal permitting access to the loop and closed the points behind the train. Then someone in Quintinshill box sent a 'train out of section' signal to Thomas Sawyers at Kirkpatrick to let him know the train of empty wagons was clear of the main line.[7]

Who sent the message has exercised the minds of countless people ever since. Tinsley recorded in the train register the fact that it had been sent but would later say that it was not he who had actually sent it. If, despite this denial, he *had* done so, it would imply that he had assumed control of the box from Meakin around the time the empty wagons were being secured in the loop. The fact that Tinsley recorded the bell signal in the book tells us nothing – the train register that morning would be full of entries made in Tinsley's own hand but copied from Meakin's original notes as part of the men's late shift change cover-up.

'Tinsley stated that he entered the "train out of section" for the Welsh empty wagon train from memory,' the Caledonian Railway's Assistant Superintendent, Robert Killin, would later comment. 'The question is – how far does his memory take him? Memory of what? Who, according to his recollection, gave the signal? It seems probable that, if he is speaking truthfully, he heard Meakin give it and he wrote it down in the book.' Killin then made the obvious point about the signal box's register. 'This train register book, having been manipulated... it is impossible to tell from it who gave this signal.'

This is undoubtedly true. The identity of the sender is unprovable. Questioned later, George Meakin was equally adamant that it wasn't him, though he seemed to trip himself up at one stage by suggesting that Tinsley did not take over the box until 6.36, two minutes *after* the signal was relayed to Kirkpatrick, and claimed he had not heard it being sent by anyone else – i.e. Tinsley. These less than convincing responses have led many people to conclude that Meakin must have been the sender. 'I think there can be no doubt whatever that it was Meakin who sent the signal,' wrote J.A.B. Hamilton in his widely-read account of the accident. 'Tinsley would certainly have remembered taking over in the middle of a sequence of operations... [Meakin] had not heard Tinsley give the signal, yet it had been given. This was as good as an admission by Meakin that he gave it.'

This argument is flawed. To suggest that a signalman capable that morning of forgetting the presence a few yards away of the very train he had just arrived in 'would certainly remember' anything at all is, at the very least, a questionable assertion.

It would have been routine for the signalman at Quintinshill, after directing a train into a loop, to send the 'train out of section' message to Kirkpatrick, the signal box in the rear, and then cancel the 'train on line' indication on the block instrument in his own signal box. On that morning of course the southbound line was not obstacle-free. It was still impeded by the presence of the 6.17 local train from Carlisle.

James Tinsley would firmly state that 'someone' had restored the block instrument to normal. A fatal error unless it had been followed immediately by blocking back. A signalman relying on the indications on the block instrument would assume the main line from the north was clear for the approach of another train. Especially a signalman who had forgotten about a stationary train blocking the way.

So who changed the indicator? For Meakin to have done so would imply that he, too, had forgotten the local train's presence. That is surely stretching the realms of credibility well beyond the limit. Unsurprisingly, he would later deny any suggestion that he had done it. Yet Tinsley, although insisting that it *had* been changed, would also repeatedly deny changing the instrument himself. In theory brakesman Ingram, the third man in the signal box at that time, could have done it – it would of course have been a highly irregular act on his part – but nobody has ever seriously put this forward as a possibility.

At 6.35, with Meakin now off duty, relaxing in the south corner of the signal box, scanning the pages of the newspaper Tinsley had brought with him to work, the pair were joined in the box by another visitor, the local train's fireman, George Hutchinson. He arrived just as Tinsley was about to start copying into the train register the detailed timings jotted down for him by Meakin. Hutchinson had climbed the steps to the box to carry out rule 55 – an official reminder to Tinsley that his train was standing on the main line. It is clear that he thought this a mere formality as Tinsley, just a few minutes earlier, had been riding with him in the cab of the locomotive. Tinsley handed Hutchinson the pen and showed him where to sign his name in the train register.[8]

This was the correct procedure. However, it seems Tinsley was already in a muddle with the train book. He failed to ensure that Hutchinson signed on the page recording the movement of trains on the down (northbound) line or to leave an empty space above for him (Tinsley) to copy details from Meakin's piece of paper. This gave the impression that Hutchinson had arrived in the box half-an-hour earlier than he actually had. Clearly these were the actions of a man in a state of confusion. But then Tinsley seemed to recover his composure to some extent, explaining to Hutchinson that he would keep the 'local' where it was for a few minutes before sending it northwards to allow the two night expresses from London to pass.

Clear proof, despite his later evidence that he hadn't given the local train a second thought after he stepped off it, that he had suddenly remembered the 6.17 was on the main line – even if he had apparently forgotten Meakin's instruction to let it go *between* the expresses. What on earth was going on in his head?

Tinsley then started to copy Meakin's notes into the register. But at 6.36 the box to the south, Gretna Junction, signalled him that the first northbound express from London was approaching. Correctly, he acknowledged this, and at 6.38 the train for Edinburgh passed safely.

At this juncture, Meakin, fireman Hutchinson and brakesman Ingram were all still in the signal box with Tinsley. There is little doubt that they were talking together. However, all would later deny that Tinsley was distracted by the discussion, though Meakin would note that his fellow signalman 'joined slightly' in it. Despite this, the suggestion that Tinsley's erratic behaviour that morning was partly due to his being engrossed in animated chatter quickly gained a wide currency that has endured ever since. Tinsley was not noted as much of a conversationalist and all the evidence suggests he took little part in the talk.

With the first express dealt with, Tinsley, no doubt prompted by the presence in the box of Hutchinson, had again remembered he had the local train blocking the southbound line. Hutchinson recalled later in a statement what happened next: 'After the 5.50 [the booked departure time from Carlisle of the late-running Edinburgh express] had passed, Tinsley had a conversation on the telephone with someone at another signal box. He then informed me that he would have to keep us for the 6.05 ex-Carlisle [the advertised departure time for the Glasgow service] to pass. I asked him if it had left and he said, "yes, passed number three signal box at Carlisle at 6.40." I went back and informed driver Wallace.'

In his statement Tinsley gave a rather briefer account: 'I said to my mate, "there will be another express to come" and he said, "yes". That was after the first one passed. I rang number three cabin [at Carlisle] and asked the boy where the second express was. He said it passed him at 6.40.' No reference there to him informing Hutchinson of the situation. Presumably he'd forgotten that, too, when he made his statement. As for his comment to Meakin, was this merely a casual observation or was it a question from a man unsure of a situation that had only just been outlined to him – a further indication of the muddle he was in?

What seems certain, judging by what he told Hutchinson, is that Tinsley had disregarded Meakin's plan to release the local train in advance of the second express, It is, however, impossible to say whether this was down to forgetfulness on his part or whether he had decided to change the plan and keep the 'local' where it was until both of the Anglo-Scottish trains had passed the box. As with so many things in this story, no one ever thought to question him on this.

Hutchinson and Ingram left the signal box together around 6.40. On the way out they passed William Young, brakesman from the train of empty coal wagons held in the southbound passing loop. Young had come up to the box to ask Tinsley how long he was going to be kept there. He also wanted the Quintinshill signalman to telephone Carlisle with a request for a relief man. 'My day's hours were just about up,' he would later tell the Board of Trade inquiry.

On entering the box, Young saw Tinsley sitting at the desk writing up the train register. 'I spoke to Tinsley and asked him how long I was going to be kept. He did not answer,' added Young at the inquiry. Why didn't Tinsley reply? He was certainly well within earshot. The only conclusion, judged on his general behaviour that morning, is that James Tinsley was absorbed in a world of his own.

Getting no response whatsoever from Tinsley, William Young went to the back of the box to look at pictures mounted on the wall. The subject matter was poultry. 'They interested me because I used to be in the poultry line,' he would recall, adding that at that time Meakin was still reading the newspaper. 'I did not ask about any wars.' This was not the random quote it appears at first glance to be. It was a response to a specific line of questioning. Hutchinson, it was suggested – and still is in some quarters – was party to the conversation in the box which had now assumed lively proportions between no less than five people – Tinsley, Meakin, Young, Ingram and Hutchinson. The topic was the latest war news in the press. Since this was supposed to have taken place just a few minutes before the accident, great importance was, and is, attached to it, the argument being that it must have further distracted Tinsley, his mind already on the task of covering up his late start, from his signalling duties.

The theory about the noisy five-way discussion on the war is arrant nonsense. As noted there were only three railwaymen in the box, Ingram and Hutchinson having both returned to their trains. As this book will demonstrate there is now plenty of evidence to support this. At no stage were there five men in the signal box at the same time. Of the trio who were left, Meakin was quietly reading the paper, Young was looking at the poultry pictures and Tinsley was working at the desk.

If Tinsley wasn't distracted by animated chatter in the critical nine minutes leading up the initial crash, was his absorption in copying Meakin's notes into the register the reason he forgot about the local train's presence, as many would have it? Not according to Tinsley, of course, with his insistence that the 'local' had been erased from his memory the moment he had stepped off it, although, as noted earlier, there is very little doubt that the stationary train flashed in and out of his memory throughout the period he had control of the box prior to the crash.

In the context of trying to establish the effect on subsequent events of Tinsley's note copying, a close examination of the process involved – closer than was carried out at the time – reveals some interesting results. There were about fifteen sets of figures to enter into the train register. This would have taken him about three minutes at the most, a statistic easily verifiable by repeating the process today. It seems safe to assume that he was keen to get this done as quickly as possible and he insisted in his statement that he'd finished before the crash.

But had he?

A later study of the train register revealed that copying in the notes was still proving a struggle for Tinsley, as apparently was everything else. The book was not fully written up and – if he was attempting to make a good forgery – he was failing badly. If this effort had been typical of the standard of forgery used by Tinsley during the years the practice of covering up the late shift change had been in being, it is hard not to conclude that it would have been uncovered long before.

This could not have been typical. On the morning of 22 May 1915 it was different. Signalman Tinsley was adrift in his own private chaos. And in a matter of moments this would manifest itself for all to see amid destruction and death.

As he laboured at the register bells rang in the signal box at 6.42, an alert from Kirkpatrick's Thomas Sawyers offering Tinsley the 7th Royal Scots' troop train – in other words, checking if the section of line to Quintinshill was clear for it to run through. It wasn't, of course. Standing outside Tinsley's signal box, just thirty yards away from him, the local train was still blocking the main line to the south. Had he turned round and glanced out of the window overlooking the track he would have seen it there. He didn't. But this was not in itself the careless blunder it seems and was made out to be in the aftermath of the disaster.

All signalmen who worked at Quintinshill did so with their backs to the railway line – this was how the box and its lever frame were designed – and used the two side (north and south) windows, rather than the one in the front with its panoramic view above the track, to check signals and the movement of passing trains. Tinsley would certainly have noticed the stationary local train had he looked out of the south window but he had no other reason to do so. He needed only to glance out of the north window to see the first express pass through and to check his signals in advance of the troop train's approach. That would have been the operational norm. No need to use the south window at all. Thus he missed another opportunity for being reminded that the troop train's progress should have been halted because of the presence of the 6.17 from Carlisle.

Thomas Sawyers knew nothing of the blockage ahead. Neither did Francis Scott and James Hannah on the footplate of the troop train. And James Tinsley had once more forgotten all about it. Acknowledging the bell code alert from Kirkpatrick, he indicated that the line was clear for the troop special. Having done so, Tinsley went back to the desk to record in the train register the signal he just given for the troop train. In front of him (because it had been written on the wrong page) was the signature of George Hutchinson, the local train's fireman, just two lines above. Yet another reminder – how could he possibly miss it? Surely, this would have reminded him?

It didn't. At 6.46 Tinsley was offered the second northbound express – the Glasgow sleeper – from Gretna Junction. He sent his colleague at Gretna a signal accepting its onward progress. Seconds later Kirkpatrick box alerted him that the troop train from the north was entering the section under his control. He immediately offered it forward to Gretna. The signalman there accepted it and Tinsley cleared his signals for it. The troop train cantered forward. Returning to the train register, he recorded the signals he had just sent. Again, Hutchinson's signature just above was there to remind him of the local train's blocking presence. Again, fatally, Tinsley missed it.

So how did he explain this extraordinary lapse when questioned later on his performance? He didn't. Again, nobody bothered, or thought, to ask him about it.

Collision was now inevitable. At 6.49, unhindered by the signals which should have prevented it, the Royal Scots' troop special ran headlong with deadly force into the local train – the train that Tinsley forgot – just outside the signal box at Quintinshill. What had been an out of the way border outpost on the railway network had begun its terrible slide into the unwanted realms of disaster and infamy.

For any signalman functioning normally there was but a single response to a situation such as this – throw every signal immediately to danger. It should have been an automatic reflex just as a motorist would slam on the brakes in the event of a collision on the road. James Tinsley was not functioning properly. Far from it. Instead, he ran directly to the front window of the signal box.

It was left to George Meakin, on the point of leaving the box, to react. Rushing to the lever frame, he screamed at Tinsley, 'Good God Jamie, what have you done?'

Tinsley was flummoxed. 'Oh God, George, what is wrong? The levers are right and the signals are all right,' he yelled, a response that betrayed his abject inner turmoil.

According to later testimony, Meakin, understandably shaken to the core, screamed back at him, 'Man, you've got the Parly [the local train] standing there!'

Tinsley's response to that was truly pathetic. 'Good Lord, whatever shall we do?'

There was, of course, something he could – and certainly should – have done if he had been in his right mind. James Tinsley could have stopped the second crash. The second of the northbound expresses was travelling at 60mph towards Quintinshill but it was still fifty-three seconds away from reaching the signal box.

The distant signal, with its early warning function, was 1,029 yards to the south; the home signal guarding the immediate approach, 207 yards away. Had the distant signal been immediately pulled to danger at the moment of impact it is likely, despite the express train's close proximity to it, that somebody in the cab of one or other of its two locomotives would have seen this in time for the brakes to be applied. Even if they missed the distant signal's warning, on such a clear morning the home signal at danger would have been visible some way off and would have given the footplate crews at least a chance of reducing speed considerably and possibly pulling up altogether. But it required the most immediate of responses from the signal box to make any of this a possibility.[9]

James Tinsley was incapable of such a response. George Meakin wasn't. He tried desperately to save the situation. Pushing Tinsley aside, he threw the distant signal to danger and – as far as can be deduced from later testimony – every other signal controlled by the box on both of the main line approaches to it.

But it was too late: Meakin rushed down the signal box stairs and saw that his frantic endeavours had not been enough. He watched, horror-struck, as the London-Glasgow sleeping car express smashed, just over a minute after the initial collision, into the wreckage. As the shocking devastation began to envelope the freight trains stored in the passing loops, George Meakin – unlike James Tinsley, still in a daze and continuing to do absolutely nothing – kept his head.

It was essential to warn other signal boxes and inform the Caledonian's higher operating authorities of the disaster. Meakin ordered Tinsley to alert the boxes while he sat down to write and send as quickly as he could emergency telegraph messages. But relying on his colleague to do anything correctly at this point was asking a lot. Tinsley failed to send the correct 'obstruction danger' signal to either of the neighbouring signal boxes.

Later, Roger Kirkpatrick, signalman at Gretna Junction, the box to the south, would tell the Board of Trade's public inquiry that he had been offered the troop train at 6.47 and, when it failed to appear, he had asked Quintinshill (Tinsley) where it was. Tinsley told him to put his signal to danger. Kirkpatrick did so immediately. Naturally, he then asked Tinsley what was wrong. The response was a long time coming.

For two to three minutes he was kept waiting for information before learning from Quintinshill that 'there's been a smash up here.' A little later Tinsley asked him to 'send for the station master; send for the platelayers – send for everyone.' From this, it would appear that still Tinsley had failed to send Gretna Junction the 'obstruction danger' signal – Roger Kirkpatrick had, in effect, to ask for it. Confusion held Tinsley in a vice-like grip and it was getting tighter, although it would appear from the train registers that he did finally send 'obstruction danger' to both adjacent boxes at 6.53.

Inexplicably his next act was to send a routine signal to the box north, Kirkpatrick, as if nothing untoward had happened, *after* he had sent the danger signal. 'I received the 'obstruction danger' signal at 6.53. I got this signal before I got the 'train entering section' signal' for the 6.05 [from Carlisle – the Glasgow sleeper] – I am certain of that,' Kirkpatrick's Thomas Sawyers was later quoted as saying in the Board of Trade's inquiry report. If any further proof was needed of James Tinsley's highly disturbed mental state, this was surely it.

Without doubt, something clearly was desperately wrong with signalman Tinsley.

In his 1969 account of the Quintinshill tragedy, J.A.B. Hamilton commented: 'What would a psychologist make of such a mental blackout? We can only speculate.' That speculation has continued ever since, unanswered, an enduring puzzle.

But there was an answer and it was known at the time – and then buried, expunged from the official historical record along with so much else about this shocking disaster and its causes. On Friday 28 May, less than a week after the accident, a sequence of disturbing events, until now a closely guarded secret, began to unfold – and with this the key to why the usually capable James Tinsley floundered so woefully in his familiar signal box on that tragic day in 1915.

It has taken a century to get to the truth of this. It was never supposed to emerge. But finally it is time to make sense of something that has never made sense before.

Notes

1. In all signal boxes of that period (and still in a few today) routine messages relating to the movement of trains were sent from one box to another by a series of codes tapped out and relayed by bells.
2. The train register book was used by signalmen to record manually the details of all train movements and related signals controlled by the signal box – see appendix two.

3. Introduced in 1906, the five Caledonian Railway 903 (*Cardean*) class 4-6-0 express passenger engines were designed by John F. McIntosh and built at the company's St Rollox works in Glasgow. At the time of their construction these were the most powerful locomotives in Britain.

4. James Tinsley made this extraordinary statement at the Board of Trade inquiry in Carlisle on 25 May 1915.

5. The 'blocking back' signal had only recently been adopted. See later chapters for a full explanation of why George Meakin considered it impossible to employ this signalling safeguard on the morning of the disaster.

6. Signal collars were metal discs, coloured red, that could be fitted over a lever controlling a signal, locking it out of use when that signal was set at 'danger.' It was impossible to pull the lever to clear the signal while the collar was in place, thereby physically preventing its use at the wrong time. Signal collars, which had to be applied manually, are still used today in some circumstances – see picture.

7. A 'train out of section' signal was sent as confirmation that a train was clear of the section of line controlled by a signal box. Trains had to be kept at a safe distance from each other. To facilitate this railway lines were divided into sections which normally could be occupied only by one train at a time. These sections were controlled by an individual signal box. When a train left his section the signalman would inform the box in the rear by means of a bell coded signal.

8. If a train was stopped on the main line by a signal the driver of that train, after a short period of waiting, was required to send his fireman to the signal box to remind the signalman that the train was there and to ascertain the cause of the delay. This was known as rule 55. Some aspects of the rule are still used today on the rail network. If a train is held at a signal for some time the driver will contact the signalman – usually by radio – for an explanation.

9. The distant signal was the first signal a train driver saw on the approach to a signal box. If the signal was pulled off, indicating the line was clear, the driver could expect the home (or stop) signals ahead would also be off. If the signal was left in the 'on' (danger) position, he would expect to be stopped at the first home signal. This required a distant signal to be positioned a full braking distance from the home, taking into account gradients and speed limits.

Chapter 6

The Arrest of James Tinsley

'Two police officers were sent to arrest Tinsley on Friday, but they were met by a medical certificate... stating that the man was unable to be removed, or could only be removed in an ambulance wagon.'

Annandale Observer 31 May 1915

Unsurprisingly, there was utter disbelief in Britain that an accident on such a horrendous scale could have occurred on the nation's railway network, widely regarded – with some justification – as the finest in the world.

Although subject to censorship to guard against sinking public morale, coverage in the press was keeping the civilian population up-to-date with the war's progress – and when the enemy was seen to commit a particularly shocking atrocity the front pages of the popular press would ensure the nation knew all about it. Thus it was with the sinking of the RMS *Lusitania* by a marauding German U-boat eleven miles off the Old Head of Kinsale, Ireland, on 7 May 1915, just two weeks before the Quintinshill disaster, killing 1,198 of the 1,959 people on board. Patriotism was stirred by the press coverage, the *Daily Mirror*, for example, filling virtually its entire cover with a picture of the great ocean liner beneath the chilling heading, 'The Huns carry out their threat to murder'.

This, of course, was an out-and-out act of war, the result of direct enemy action. It was appalling, outrageous – particularly as so many of the casualties were non-combatant civilians – yet it was possible, just about, to appreciate that in the context of a world war such events were possible.[1]

It was different with the disaster at Quintinshill signal box. This appeared to the nation to have been a 'home-made' tragedy, entirely out of keeping with the recurring combatant horrors of twentieth century global warfare. Where was the enemy in this? As author John Thomas put it in his 1969 book on the tragedy: 'That anything as frightful as Quintinshill could happen on a British main line railway produced a profound sense of shock.'

It took a little longer to sink in than it would in today's multi-media world of twenty-four hour news coverage – and as it did in December 1988 when 243 passengers and sixteen crew lost their lives in the bombing of Pan Am flight 103 above Lockerbie. Just seventeen miles from Quintinshill this handed Dumfries and Galloway the rare distinction of having two of Britain's worst twentieth century disasters happen on its 'doorstep'.

The coverage of major news in 1915 was solely in the hands of the printed press, slower to spread the word than its media rivals today but nonetheless thorough. Although considerably restrained when compared with modern standards, speculation in the press after Quintinshill was rife. Probably fostered by general disbelief that such a disaster in wartime could have been an accident at all, suggestions of sabotage by enemy agents were being propounded in print and even considered as a possibility by British security authorities. However, the focus was primarily on the apparent failings in the signal box – and particularly on James Tinsley.[2]

Unwisely he had consented in the immediate aftermath of the accident to an interview with the local press. There were no direct quotes from him in the *Carlisle Journal's* report, headlined 'A signalman interviewed,' and the newspaper's Dumfries correspondent's report was not overly convincing as a first hand account. While it correctly described Tinsley as a Yorkshireman who had 'been five years at the Quintinshill cabin.' it wrongly gave his age as 35, three years older than he actually was.

The *Journal's* report from Dumfries went some way to feeding the public appetite for details with their first crumbs of insight into the operation of the signal box at the heart of the story. The journalist described the track layout and the situation that, according to the unnamed correspondent, had confronted Tinsley on 22 May when 'both loop lines were filled by goods trains and he had no alternative but to place the Carlisle local train on the up line to allow the Euston expresses to go past…Tinsley stated that this was done regularly.' It was, of course, George Meakin, not Tinsley, who had shunted the 6.07 from Carlisle through the Quintinshill crossover.

Details of how the 'local' had stood on the southbound line until it was hit by the troop train, and how 'the Euston express, drawn by two powerful locomotives, dashed into the wreckage,' were correctly outlined for the *Journal's* readers, who were then told that Tinsley was 'obviously deeply concerned about the awful nature of the accident and said the worst of it was the terrible loss of life.' Whether these were James Tinsley's actual words – if they were, why didn't the *Journal* directly quote him rather than resort to reported speech? – will forever remain a mystery.

But the Carlisle newspaper did correctly dispel one rumour, denying a report that Tinsley had been arrested in connection with the tragedy almost as soon as it had happened. Anecdotal evidence, however, does suggest that both he and Meakin were escorted from the scene by police.[3]

What is certain and well documented – although it has never before been made public – is that James Kissock, Dumfrieshire's Depute (deputy) Procurator Fiscal, immediately opened investigations in preparation for a fatal accident inquiry, a form of inquest, as prescribed by Scottish law. A recently discovered archived statement from Charles Morrison, a police inspector based in the town of Annan, not far from the scene of the disaster, confirms that Kissock wasted no time. The statement was made in precognition, the practice used in Scotland for taking a witness statement in advance of a trial which cannot be offered as evidence but provides an advocate with pre-knowledge of what is likely to be said in court.[4, 5]

In his statement, preserved in the National Archives of Scotland, Morrison said, 'During the evening of 22 May and continuous dates I assisted the Procurator Fiscal Depute, James Kissock, and in concert with other officers made inquiry as to who was the cause of this collision and the loss of life.'

Kissock moved rapidly to establish cause and responsibility. In a letter dated 24 May to the Crown Agent in Edinburgh, and now filed at the Scottish archives, he wrote, 'Referring to my communication with Mr Smart [an officer in the Crown Office] this forenoon, I now enclose a number of precognition [statements] by railway servants, showing the circumstances of the accident. Although these are yet incomplete they show that the accident was caused by the failure of memory on the part of James Tinsley, the signalman on duty at the signal cabin at Quintinshill.' Thus Tinsley had been formally identified for the first time as the sole culprit.

Kissock added in his letter, 'He has not yet been arrested. It is considered improbable that he will abscond. I understand that the books kept in the signal cabin will show the times of the various signals etc. on the morning of the accident. These books are required for the private inquiry by the Caledonian Railway today and the Board of Trade inquiry tomorrow. I shall be glad to have any instructions or advice on the matter.'

For Kissock to have arrived at this unreserved conclusion it seems clear that Tinsley had been interviewed at a very early stage as part of the legal process. Frustratingly, *his* precognition statement does not survive in the archive.

Was Kissock being pushed by public opinion to rush his investigation and achieve a result? Disbelief was turning to anger as news spread around the country of the extreme nature of the disaster at Quintinshill. Vengeance was in the air. It was somebody's fault – and somebody had to pay.

In truth, the causes of railway accidents can seldom be explained easily. It is hardly ever as simple as that. Railways are complex, highly specialised transport systems. Many factors and many people are involved. But, on the face of it, James Tinsley's inarguably lamentable performance in the signal box probably did appear to present an open and shut case. However, while Kissock was well within his rights under Scottish law to investigate, to come up with such a simple explanation and almost immediately act on it seems overly premature – a knee-jerk reaction.

It would surely have been more circumspect for him to have waited for the outcome of the Board of Trade's public inquiry, due to open south of the border in Carlisle the following day – Tuesday, 25 May – before determining so conclusively that he had the right man solely 'in the frame'.

With the Board of Trade inquiry duly opened and the accident's key events and apparent causes aired in public (see following chapters), Kissock evidently received a response to his letter from the Crown Agent, returning the precognition statements. That reply is now lost to the record, but the Scottish archives do contain Kissock's letter of acknowledgment, dated 28 May, in which he notes an instruction from the government office in Edinburgh to obtain and execute a warrant 'for the apprehension of Tinsley, the signalman, on a charge of culpable homicide'.

Kissock wrote that 'a warrant has accordingly been obtained today, and Tinsley will probably be brought before the sheriff [in Dumfries] tomorrow forenoon, at eleven o'clock'. The deputy fiscal added, 'In view of a probable application for bail by the accused, I shall be glad if Crown Counsel will indicate whether this application should be opposed, and if not, what minimum amount of bail should be accepted. If you could give me instructions by wire or telephone tomorrow morning, I should be obliged.'

A rail disaster was wholly new territory for the forces of law in Dumfries and Galloway. James Kissock concluded by making clear that he was writing on the suggestion of the Dumfries sheriff, 'who also considers it desirable to have an indication of Crown Counsel's opinion on the matter of bail'.

This sent the Crown Office staff in Edinburgh scurrying off to find some sort of precedent elsewhere in Scotland. On 29 May Kissock received his reply by wire: 'The only suggestion that Crown Counsel can make with regard to bail is that the precedent of the Gourlay case (Elliot Junction Disaster) be followed. In that case the bail was fixed at £300 and was found.'

In December 1906 a two-train collision at snow-bound Elliot Junction, on the North British Railway main line in Forfarshire, had resulted in the deaths of twenty-two people and injuries to several others. George Gourlay, driver of one of the trains involved, was sent for trial at the High Court in Edinburgh to answer charges that he had driven his express train in a reckless and culpable manner. Not an exact parallel with Quintinshill but similar in that both led to allegations of primary fault on the part of the railwaymen principally concerned – a satisfactory precedent for setting bail.[6]

Armed with the approval of Crown Counsel, Kissock made his move on Friday, 28 May. Accompanied by a police colleague, Inspector Morrison travelled from Annan to arrest James Tinsley at his home in the station cottages at Gretna Junction. It did not go according to plan. Morrison was soon contacting his superiors with news of an unexpected twist, a situation relayed the next day to the Procurator Fiscal's office in Dumfries.

Tinsley had not been arrested. In a later precognition statement, Morrison recalled what had happened: 'At 7pm on Friday, 28 May 1915 I arrived at Gretna, having got instructions to assist in apprehending the accused James Tinsley on a charge of culpable homicide, but I found him apparently unwell and his relatives informed me that Dr Carlyle of Kirkpatrick [the same doctor who had helped with the rescue work at the crash site] had been attending him and left instructions that Tinsley was not to be interviewed or spoken to by anyone. They told me that the doctor had mentioned that, if care was not taken, his brain might be affected.'

The message passed on to James Kissock's Dumfries office by the police was, in one major respect, rather more specific. Scribbled down at the time and preserved undisturbed ever since, it was hugely significant in the overall context of the Quintinshill story, but – along with most of the details relating to Tinsley's arrest – it has never before featured in its telling.

'When the constables went to apprehend Tinsley yesterday they found him unwell, apparently. His own medical attendant said that he had had epileptic fits since [the] collision – that these might develop into acute mania and [he] could only be removed in an ambulance. He has been left under supervision since by the police, and it is now proposed to send an independent medical man and a motor ambulance from Dumfries to have him conveyed to Dumfries if he is fit to be removed,' explained the police.

The message concluded by raising the possibility that Tinsley might *not* be declared fit and asking if the Procurator Fiscal's office had any objections to the course proposed or any suggestions from Crown Counsel.

That specific reference to epileptic fits was, or should have been, a crucial piece of evidence. Yet the possibility of epilepsy as an explanation for Tinsley's erratic behaviour in the signal box would feature only obliquely in the subsequent judicial process – and not at all in any of the published accounts of the disaster. Was it the key missing piece of the Quintinshill puzzle?

On receipt of this surprising and, no doubt, unwelcome development, it would appear that there was a flurry of messages – telegrams and telephone calls – between Crown Counsel and Kissock's office. The outcome was recorded in a handwritten memo which survives in the same file of documents at the Scottish archives. Sent from Dumfries and dated 28/29 May, it outlined for the police the Crown's decision on how to proceed:

'Crown Counsel wishes him [Tinsley] to be examined at once by an independent medical practitioner, but [the police] will await his report before having him removed to Dumfries. He will only be removed if the report justifies it; in the meantime the police will keep him under surveillance.'

The precognition statement given later by Inspector Morrison details how this now delicate situation was handled: 'I was instructed to keep him under supervision and did so with other officers until 1.45pm on the Saturday, 29 May. Chief Constable Gordon then arrived with Dr James Maxwell Ross, the County Medical Officer, and Dr John Ritchie, his assistant. After an examination by these doctors, Tinsley was taken into custody.'

Following the story every step of the way, the *Dumfries & Galloway Standard* reported the arrest, and what happened after it, to its astonished readers. Calling it 'a sensational sequel' to the disaster, it outlined the background to the arrest and the unexpected intervention by Dr Carlyle before describing in detail how the arrest was finally secured by the police:

'The two officers were left to keep Tinsley under supervision and, acting on the instructions of the Crown Counsel, Mr Gordon, the Chief Constable, proceeded to Gretna on Saturday afternoon with a motor ambulance. He was accompanied by Dr Maxwell Ross, Chief Medical Officer for the county, and Dr Ritchie, his assistant and a specialist in tuberculosis.

'Having examined Tinsley, they expressed the opinion that he was quite fit to undertake the journey and he was then told to get up and dress himself. In a few minutes he was put into the ambulance and conveyed to Dumfries.'

The *Standard's* report – shared with the *Annandale Observer* – continued with an evocative account of events at the other end of Tinsley's ambulance ride to Dumfries: 'The wagon arrived at the Sheriff Court-House in Buccleuch Street shortly before three o'clock in the afternoon. There were few people in the street at the time and Tinsley was scarcely noticed during his transfer from the wagon to the building, although several passers-by seemed to recognise him. His appearance, pathetic in the extreme, was such as to inspire the utmost sympathy. His face was pale and wan, and he appeared to be on the verge of collapse. He had to be assisted into the building by the Chief Constable and Dr Maxwell Ross.'

More detailed coverage of the court appearance and its outcome appeared in the *Cumberland News:* 'He was brought before Sheriff Campion and went afterwards to Dumfries prison pending further inquiry. During his appearance before the sheriff, Tinsley completely broke down and was in tears. The charge… was one of culpable homicide and it was understood that there were five names [of victims] mentioned in the charge, those of the driver and fireman of the troop train and three military officers who were killed instantaneously in the collision. Tinsley, we understand, did not make any statement, Mr James Kissock, [depute] procurator fiscal, appeared for the Crown and Mr J.M. Haining appeared in Tinsley's interest.'

The report elaborated on Tinsley's apparent condition throughout the short formal proceedings, which lasted only a few minutes. 'Tinsley suffered from complete nervous breakdown; he sobbed fitfully and his body shivered convulsively,' the *Cumberland News* told its readers, adding that, having arrived at the prison, Tinsley was admitted to its hospital.

On Monday, 31 May, James Kissock filed a report of the arrest to the Crown Agent confirming that Tinsley had been 'committed for further examination,'

Kissock reported that the accused railwayman had been released on bail amounting, as Crown Counsel had advised earlier, to £300.

Tinsley's medical condition at the time of arrest was unsurprisingly a key feature of Kissock's letter. According to the deputy fiscal, Dr James Maxwell Ross, acting in his capacity as surgeon to Dumfries County Police, 'certified that Tinsley was suffering from nervous collapse but not to such an extent as to make him unfit to be removed to Dumfries.' That Tinsley, given his dreadful predicament, had broken down in this way would have come as no surprise. There was no hint here from Kissock of any specific underlying health issue despite the fact that his office had been alerted over the weekend to the signalman's post-collision epileptic fits.

It seems pertinent to ask – how thorough was Maxwell Ross's examination of Tinsley at Gretna and why was there no apparent reference in his assessment to the epilepsy mentioned by Tinsley's own doctor? Was there, in fact, a deliberate attempt by someone to conceal this?

If this were true, the attempted cover up was certainly not helped by a report in *The Scotsman*, the influential Edinburgh-based daily newspaper, on 31 May. In its coverage of Tinsley's arrest, the paper told how 'the Dumfrieshire Police on Saturday arrested James Tinsley… in connection with the disaster on the Caledonian Railway near Gretna… where a troop train was wrecked. Tinsley was the signalman on duty when the accident happened. He was arrested at his home and, as the man is subject to fits, he was conveyed to the police headquarters [at Dumfries] in a motor ambulance.'

Epilepsy may not have been specifically mentioned by *The Scotsman* but the reference to fits would have been close enough to cause something approaching panic in the mind of anyone anxious to keep any hint of Tinsley suffering from the condition away from the eyes of the public. We can only wonder at the source of this apparent leak to the national Scottish press.

The records show that the ambulance arrived at Tinsley's Gretna Junction home at 1.45pm. Just over one hour later it was drawing up at Sheriff Court House in Dumfries. Research into ambulances of the period suggests a probable average speed of 25mph might have been possible during the journey of fractionally under twenty-five miles, bearing in mind that the roads from Gretna Junction were little more than dirt tracks in 1915 before the main road was reached. This would have left little time for a proper medical examination and it seems reasonable to assume that it was not carried out at Tinsley's home at all. Maybe it took place at the police headquarters, if *The Scotsman's* reference to the ambulance calling there first was correct. More probably, it was conducted later in the prison hospital.

Newspaper reports suggest that Tinsley had to be carried into the ambulance such was his pitiful state. If this was so, he surely was in no fit state to be taken to court. Frustratingly, it is impossible to check any of this with the contemporary medical records from the prison hospital. All those for that period have been lost. We are left to speculate on an arrest that, on the face of it, seems rushed and utterly heartless. Possibly this harsh treatment of James Tinsley was linked to the emotions of the arresting officers who, just a week before, had witnessed at first hand the appalling nature of the disaster at Quintinshill. It would certainly have been fresh in their minds when they were sent to Gretna to pick up the man who, it was now well known in the locality, had been breaking rules – his late shift change arrangement with Meakin – and was widely thought to have caused the carnage.

The successful application for bail by Tinsley's solicitor did not procure his release from prison until the Monday afternoon, two days after the court hearing. It took that long to guarantee the £300 fixed by the sheriff, a huge sum for the period. The National Union of Railwaymen stepped in to act as guarantors. According to James Kissock's report, Tinsley 'left Dumfries with the 3.15 train to Lockerbie, in company with his wife and a friend, and subsequently arrived at his home in Caledonian Cottages, Gretna.'

But was this true? Did Tinsley really go home? His address at Gretna Junction was Station (not Caledonian) Cottages. It could, of course, be merely an optional name for the Caledonian-owned cottages, but there is a twist. Records show that, not long after the accident, the Tinsley family had been moved by the Caledonian company to 4 Caledonian Buildings in Carlisle, a property owned and managed by the company for their employees. Could it be that it was to this address rather than his home at Gretna that Tinsley was headed after his release from prison in Dumfries? More importantly, why did the Caledonian Railway re-house Tinsley in Carlisle?

The fact that the company had by then suspended him from duty but kept him on the payroll was one thing – the action that might have been expected from a responsible employer – but moving Tinsley away from the remoteness of Gretna into the comparative urban glare of Carlisle suggests something else. Was the Caledonian Railway anxious to keep a close watch on Tinsley? Was 4 Caledonian Buildings something of a 'safe house'?

There seems little doubt that *someone* was looking after Tinsley in the weeks that followed his initial court appearance. Whatever the precise nature of his medical condition at the time of his arrest, James Tinsley was a sick man. Photographs taken of him in the immediate post-disaster period present the figure of a man in very poor health, thin and drawn, looking much older than his 32 years. Yet, just one month later, when he was next photographed, his appearance had changed out of all recognition! He looked younger, healthier and markedly more at ease – a remarkable transformation from the earlier image.

It would seem from this that the Caledonian had gone to great lengths to improve his health, appearance and demeanour. Why would they do this? Tinsley was charged with causing by far the worst event in the company's history. Why extend to him such apparent hospitality? The simple answer is that it was very much in the company's interests, and those of senior staff considerably higher up the chain of command than James Tinsley, to do so.

There is good reason to suspect that Tinsley had epileptic fits after the 22 May collision. The long-hidden evidence from his doctor, while second-hand in its recording, seems unequivocal. This prompts the obvious question – did he suffer from epilepsy *prior* to the disaster? And if that were the case the Caledonian Railway would have faced enormous and, on the face of it, entirely justified public criticism and probable formal censure for employing a man with epilepsy in a signal box on one of Britain's busiest and strategically important main lines.

It does not seem fanciful to suggest that the Caledonian would have been made aware of Tinsley's reported epileptic fits in the wake of the tragedy. The article in *The Scotsman* alone would have alerted them to the possibility and they would not have wanted this to become common knowledge. The potential for corporate embarrassment, and worse, was huge – this was the biggest disaster in the history of Britain's railways. If the hypothesis is developed – and with good reason it will be in the following chapters of this book – it was clearly the case that, in order to look after its interests, the Caledonian Railway had first to look after James Tinsley and present him to the world as an otherwise healthy young signalman who had somehow 'lost his head'.

Advice from a leading professional in the field of epilepsy suggests that if Tinsley *was* suffering from epileptic fits after the disaster, the probability is that he had a pre-existing epileptic condition. This opens the door to the next logical line of enquiry – did epilepsy contribute to the accident? When considered in the light of Tinsley's otherwise inexplicable mental blackout in the signal box, this seems a plausible explanation for what happened on that fateful day.

Quite apart from the certainty of Caledonian corporate embarrassment, a revelation such as this, had it leaked out, carried the potential for damaging public morale at this crucial period of the war. What would have been the reaction if it were shown that the regulatory standards on one of the nation's key transport arteries were so lax as to allow a man with a serious medical condition of this nature to work in a strategically vital role? It would not have looked good. Sending men from Britain to risk their lives for their country amid the uncertainties of war was one thing. Not being able to guarantee their safety before they left was quite another.

If, as we firmly believe, James Tinsley was suffering from epilepsy at the time of the crash, there are other questions to ask. How did he cope with his condition prior to the accident in what had become a very demanding job? And, if the Caledonian Railway knew nothing about his epilepsy before the disaster, how did Tinsley manage to conceal it from them and to what extent – if any – were the company's signalmen medically examined?

An analysis of the story's development during the summer months of 1915, the subject of the following chapters, makes two things abundantly clear. A medical condition of some sort had played a fundamental role in the unfolding of this shocking tragedy, but the responsibility for the Quintinshill disaster was not solely down to the signalmen – George Meakin as well as James Tinsley – who would eventually be punished for it.

Notes

1. Arguments over the legitimacy of the *Lusitania's* sinking raged between the two sides in the conflict throughout the war years and the liner's fate remains a controversial topic to this day. Germany stressed that the ship was carrying rifle ammunition and other materials essential to the British war economy on its eastbound transatlantic crossing, and was therefore a legitimate military target. The heavy loss of civilian life – men, women and children – was naturally the focus for the then neutral USA, many of whose citizens were among the victims, and Britain, where public opinion quickly united in condemnation of the enemy.

2. Among the sabotage theories was a story that German agents had interfered with the signals. The police investigated a telegram that suggested the accident had been planned – see chapter fifteen.

3. The anecdotal evidence from local sources suggested that Tinsley and Meakin were escorted from the signal box for their own safety after a Royal Scots officer had entered the box and attempted to shoot them. There is, however, no formal evidence to substantiate the claim.

4. In Scotland a Procurator Fiscal still acts as the public prosecutor. Dumfries and Galloway is one of the eleven areas of the country over which a Procurator Fiscal exercises jurisdiction today.

5. Born at Lochruthon, Dumfrieshire in 1869, James Kissock attended Edinburgh University in preparation for his career as a solicitor which would eventually see him appointed Depute Procurator Fiscal for Dumfries. When, having transferred to Banff, Aberdeenshire, as Procurator Fiscal in 1917, he retired in 1945, he was described as 'a scrupulously fair prosecutor,' regarded as honourable and clearly well liked. Away from his legal duties, he was a former member of Dumfries & Galloway Students' Society and served for a period as sessions clerk at St Mary's Church, Dumfries. He was 46 at the time of the Quintinshill disaster.

6. The Board of Trade inquiry into the accident at Elliot Junction – located between Arbroath and Carnoustie on the Dundee-Aberdeen main line – identified primary cause of the crash as the failure of driver Gourlay to heed instructions to drive with caution in the December blizzard.

Chapter 7

Colonel Druitt's Incomplete Inquiry

'It has been suggested that, if you had been all right, you would have put your signals to danger at once, for what it was worth. You don't know you did that?'

'I cannot state that. I only know they were put to danger afterwards.'

James Tinsley's exchange with G.A. Lightfoot,
his solicitor, at Board of Trade inquiry, 25 May 1915

Outside the country's rail fraternity, professional and enthusiast, the highly specialised work of HM Railway Inspectorate in Britain is relatively little known.

Its origins date back to 1840 when, under the provisions of the Railway Regulation Act, the Board of Trade began appointing inspecting officers to oversee safety on Britain's rapidly expanding rail network. Recruited exclusively from the railway operations division of the Royal Engineers, they were all commissioned army officers with considerable experience. Their key tasks were to inspect new railways to ensure their worthiness for the envisaged traffic and to investigate rail accidents reported to the Board of Trade.

Over a period lasting nearly 170 years – until its responsibilities were taken over in 2009 by the new Rail Safety Directorate – the Inspectorate distinguished itself both in the eyes of the public and, eventually, the railway operators. From the start it was normally the Inspectorate's practice to hold its investigations in public on behalf of the Board of Trade. Its reports were likewise published and so became available to anyone who wished to read them.[1,2]

At the head of the Inspectorate was a chief inspecting officer. Some of the more notable holders of the post – particularly Captain Sir Henry Tyler (1870-1877) and his successor, the legendary Colonel William Yolland (1877–85) – campaigned vigorously during their respective tenures of office for improvements in railway safety, sometimes in the face of hostility from railway companies whose expansionist policies not infrequently were pursued ahead of concerns for passenger safety and the avoidance of accidents.[3, 4]

Seemingly unimpeachable while it was in operation, and certainly highly respected in retrospect, the Railway Inspectorate occupies hallowed ground in the annals of Britain's railways. For the most part, this legacy is well deserved. But its documented involvement – and that of the Board of Trade generally – with Quintinshill, although it has never been questioned before, casts a murky shadow over the whole business of rail accident investigation in the early twentieth century.

That the Inspectorate would have a key role to play in the aftermath of the disaster was obvious. As early as 24 May, just two days after the accident, the press were reporting an immediate start to the inquiry process – and naming the officer granted the distinction of weighing-up the evidence at this historic hearing in Carlisle. On reflection, his appointment comes as something of a surprise.

'The inquiry, I was officially informed,' wrote a *Glasgow Herald* journalist, 'will be opened tomorrow. Lieutenant-Colonel Druitt RE; Inspecting Officer of Railways, who will conduct the proceedings, arrived [in Carlisle] from London this afternoon, and arrangements have already been made for his visit of inspection.'

For an inquiry into an accident in which more people had lost their lives than in any preceding British railway disaster, the Chief Inspecting Officer – the grandly named Lieutenant Colonel Pelham George von Donop – would, in retrospect, seem the obvious candidate to investigate the causes. Admittedly, he was approaching the end of his career, but this was surely a matter that merited the attention of the Railway Inspectorate's top man. The choice of 56-year-old Edward Druitt to hear the inquiry in Von Donop's stead can therefore, at least on the face of it, be regarded as puzzling.[5]

Eschewing any speculation on such matters, the contemporary press stuck to the facts. The *Glasgow Herald's* reporter added: 'The inquiry will begin at eleven o'clock, and two hours earlier Colonel Druitt will be conveyed by special train to the scene of the accident, ten miles to the north of the city [Carlisle]. Plans of the railway will be furnished to him and he will be fully conversant with the locus [location] of the disaster before the proceedings are entered upon. The inquiry, as expected, will be open and I am informed that it is likely to last more than one day. A large number of witnesses will be examined. Most of the officials engaged in the inquiry arrived at nine o'clock this evening.'

Opening an inquiry so soon after the crash smacks of indecent haste, but this was the usual practice for a major railway accident in 1915. The investigative hearings would be convened at the earliest possible date following the event – and then adjourned to allow further evidence to be taken before proceedings were resumed and the investigation continued in possession of all the relevant facts.

This, no doubt, would have been the general perception of how the process would evolve when, at 11am on Tuesday, 25 May, Colonel Druitt, who had visited the scene of the disaster the previous day, opened his inquiry at Carlisle's impressive County Hotel, just outside the city's historic Citadel station. The large assembly included representatives of the Caledonian Railway and their West Coast partners, the London & North Western Railway. Also present were legal teams for the railwaymen involved with the disaster and the employers, and a large contingent from the national and local press which had already devoted many column inches to the story – the *Carlisle Journal*, the *Cumberland News* and the *Dumfries & Galloway Standard*.[6]

The scrupulous and incisive reporting of the local newspapers – particularly the Cumberland and Dumfries titles – would much later prove pivotal to unravelling a startling truth behind the inquiry process, effectively hidden for a century.

All eyes among those on the press benches, and among the packed gathering in the hotel's function rooms generally, were on the two Quintinshill signalmen, George Meakin and, in particular, James Tinsley who, it was now known, had been interviewed by the police on the day of the accident.

Proceedings began with a statement from the Caledonian's General Manager, Donald Matteson, on behalf of the company's chairman and directors, expressing their 'great regret' about the accident and 'deep sympathy' for the relatives and friends of the many casualties – killed or injured – and for the injured themselves. 'The company,' added Matteson, 'especially deplores the deaths of and injuries to those gallant soldiers who were travelling to the south in the service of their king and country.'

Rightly, there was an expression of the company's gratitude from Matteson for 'all those who acted so valiantly in the rescue,' but the opening statement was rounded off by the Caledonian manager reiterating how deeply his employers deplored what had happened, 'and the painfully distressing results.'

The company's formal expression of remorse was suitably matched by G.A. Lightfoot, the solicitor appointed by the National Union of Railwaymen to represent the interests of its members. 'Of all classes of men at the present time,' said Lightfoot, 'perhaps railwaymen would be most moved by this terrible occurrence, associated as they have been during the last ten months so much and so directly with the movement of troops on the various railway systems.'

The solicitor's engagement had been personally handled by Jimmy Thomas MP, the NUR's wily chief activist, a man destined to play a key role in subsequent events. Thomas had visited the crash site on the Sunday and, aware the apparent circumstances of the disaster posed a potential threat to the union members at its heart, he had acted quickly to safeguard their interests. 'Under the circumstances I recognised the necessity of engaging the best Carlisle solicitors I could,' Thomas reported to senior NUR colleagues. He had chosen the city's Saul & Lightfoot legal practice, of which G.A. (known as Lionel) Lightfoot was a partner. Thomas was at the inquiry to witness his man in action.

Once Colonel Druitt had added his own words of sympathy on behalf of the Board of Trade, the inquiry began in earnest. Altogether, nineteen witnesses were called. All but one – Lieutenant Colonel J.C. Bell, a Royal Scots officer – were railway professionals. Surprisingly perhaps, no one from the fire brigade or the police was called. Neither was any evidence sought during the course of the day from the many doctors present at the scene or the civilian rescuers. Any of these people could have added pertinent information as to how many of the victims had died. Perhaps Druitt considered the sort of input they could bring to the inquiry was beyond the realms of determining the causes of the disaster – yet many of the railway witnesses who were called *did* provide details not only of the crash itself but also their personal involvement in the rescue.

A more likely explanation for this apparent imbalance in the taking of evidence from witnesses is that the Carlisle hearing was intended to serve only as the preliminary to a full-scale inquiry, following the established Board of Trade practice, with Druitt's objective restricted to establishing just the main facts.

Much of the evidence given has been used as a basis for the reconstruction of events in Quintinshill signal box detailed in chapter five. The inquiry heard from Roger Kirkpatrick, signalman at Gretna Junction, how George Meakin had alerted him that the late-for-work James Tinsley would be needing a lift up to Quintinshill in the 6.07 local train from Carlisle on 22 May, and how, later that morning, having been offered by Tinsley the troop train from Larbert at 6.47, he had after six minutes queried its whereabouts when it failed to appear. The inquiry's first slice of drama followed when Kirkpatrick recounted Tinsley's response – to put the signals to danger – and explained how he had then waited for up to three minutes for an explanation from Tinsley before the Quintinshill man finally revealed that there had been a smash… 'send for everyone'.[7]

From Kirkpatrick the signalman the inquiry spotlight then fell on Kirkpatrick the signal box as Thomas Sawyers, the man operating the cabin to the north of Quintinshill on 22 May, as he had done for the past three years, gave his short statement. Sawyers (35) recounted the critical train movements and related signalling communications. Apart from confirming that the troop train had run 'very fast' by his box on its doomed lunge towards Quintinshill, the most telling revelation from Sawyers was that it had taken Tinsley a full three minutes to send him the 'obstruction danger' signal following the initial collision.

Thus the inquiry's opening phase had already succeeded in painting the bleakest of scenarios for James Tinsley when Colonel Druitt called a short temporary halt to the proceedings so that he could attend the opening of the Carlisle Coroner's inquest – one of two that would be held on the English side of the border – at the city's police office. When he returned to resume the inquiry it was time for Tinsley's colleague George Meakin to take centre stage.

The press noted that the 31-year-old signalman appeared 'worn and anguished' as he began by outlining his seventeen year career with the Caledonian, culminating in his permanent posting three to four years ago to Quintinshill, a signal box in which he had previously worked for two years in a relief capacity. It was therefore a box – and a stretch of railway – he knew very well.

The shift system operated at the box was quickly the focus of attention. Meakin confirmed that he had started work at 8pm the previous evening and was due to finish his night shift at 6am before handing over to Tinsley to work the day shift until 4pm when a relief signalman would take control until 9pm. Those were the official times but Meakin was immediately put on the spot when the inspector asked him what time he had *actually* ended his shift on 22 May.

'My mate relieved me at about 6.33am.'

'How is it he was late?' asked Druitt.

'I cannot exactly say,' replied George Meakin. 'He would sleep in a little. We made it our duty to change between six and half past six. He was in the habit of coming in late. On Saturday morning he came on the engine of the 6.10 local train.'[8]

Meakin had no option other than to admit that the late shift change arrangement with Tinsley was entirely unauthorised – one they had agreed between themselves – before the questioning turned to the critical events in the signal box.

Reading from Quintinshill's train register book, Meakin recounted the position of all the trains involved, explaining that when the local service arrived at the box, the empty coal train preceding the troop train southwards, and needing to be shunted aside because there was no room for it at Carlisle's Kingmoor marshalling yard, had not yet entered the passing loop and was waiting at the home signal. By 6.34, he told the inspector, he had it safely in the loop. The signal and points controlling the loop were then replaced for the adjacent main line.

Druitt's next questions were key. The coal empties had been put out of the way but the southbound main line was still blocked by the local train. 'Did you tell him [Tinsley] about the local train being put through the crossover road to the up road?'

'Yes.'

'When did you hand over the working of the cabin to Tinsley?' asked the inspector.

'At 6.35 or 6.36,' replied Meakin. 'At that time there was a train on each of the two loops. I gave up duty at 6.36.' Stabling the train of coal empties had been his final act on shift. Now the questioning turned to the vital period that followed:

Druitt: 'What did you do then?'

Meakin: *'I sat down and read the newspaper.'*

'Did you talk to Tinsley?'

'There were a few remarks passed, sir.'

'Did you read the newspaper to him?'

'No I didn't, but I passed one or two remarks.'

'Was there anyone else in the cabin at that time?'

Yes, brakesman Young of the Welsh empty train. He stayed in the cabin until the collision occurred. He came into the cabin as soon as his train was in the loop.'

'What did he come into the cabin to do?'
'He did not say.'
'Is it the usual thing for men to come into the cabin?'
'Yes.'
'And stay there all the time?'
''Well, some stay for a short time and some don't.''
'Was there anybody else in the cabin?'
'Yes, the fireman of the 6.10. He came and signed the book and stayed for about four or five minutes. The brakesman did not sign his name in the book. The other brakesman was in the box and stayed for about ten or eleven minutes.'

This somewhat convoluted response has apparently confused other commentators on the Quintinshill tragedy – among them authors John Thomas and James Hamilton – into believing that there were four people in the signal box at the same time distracting Tinsley. In fact a close study of all the known facts shows that there were never more than three at one time as detailed in chapter five. Thomas Ingram, brakesman of the goods train held in the northbound loop, was there when Meakin handed over to Tinsley, soon joined by George Hutchinson, the local train's fireman. But both left the box around 6.40, just as William Young, brakesman of the empty train of coal wagons in the other (southbound) loop, arrived. How many at the inquiry appreciated this is a matter for conjecture. George Meakin's response was hardly an aid to clarity. Colonel Druitt allowed it to pass into enduring confusion as he asked Meakin:

'Did you pay any attention to what your mate was doing?'
'No sir, not after I left off work. The first warning of anything came when the troop train was running past the box.'
'What was the last bell signal you took on the block instrument before you gave over the work to your mate?'
'I accepted the 5.50 from Carlisle [the London to Edinburgh train, which passed Quintinshill safely at 6.38]. *I gave "train out of section" for the local train.'*
'After you had put the empty coal train into the loop did you give "train out of section" for it?'
'No Sir.'
'Although you replaced the points?'
'Yes'
'Why did you not complete the movement?'
'My mate was working at the block instrument then.'
'On the block instrument there is an indicator lock. Did you do anything to it?'
'No, I did not release it.'
'That lock must be released deliberately?'
'Yes sir, I did not give the blocking back signal for the local train because the empty Welsh train was not going out of section then. It had started to come into the loop.'
'Why did you not complete the work before handing over?'
'Because my mate had started to work at the block, sir.'

'Yes, but you ought to have completed the operation.'

'Yes, but he had started working with the block, sir.'

'Yes, but you ought to have seen what he was about. Why is it you did not see that he sent the blocking signal?'

'I understood that he would do that himself.'

Was this a fair line of questioning on the inspector's part? Meakin's shift was finished and his mate had taken over the box. It was not his duty to oversee him. Colonel Druitt was on safer ground when he raised the issue of the signal collar:

'You passed the slow train to the up line. Did you make use of the signal collar?'

'No sir.'

'Why not?'

'It is seldom we make use of them.'

'And what are they given you for?'

'We thought the blocking back signal would do.'

'But you never gave the blocking back signal.'

'No, not on this occasion.'

Meakin was planting himself in a tight corner with this set of answers; he needed help. Realising his predicament, his solicitor, Lightfoot, came to his rescue. 'Witness had had an exceptionally busy night,' the lawyer told the inspector. 'He moved the slow [local] train onto the up line because he had already got the up and down loop lines full. His mate got off the engine of that train before it arrived on the up line. His mate knew it was going onto the up line. He would pass it coming back again through the road [facilitate its later shunt].'

Lightfoot added: 'The lever collar was there to ensure the safety of the train, to indicate its presence on that particular line and to protect it. Witness did not use the collar,' A statement of fact – and, on the face of it, not at all helpful to Meakin's cause. But then, having set out the 'case' against his client on this specific point, Lightfoot immediately set up the most obvious line of mitigation by asking Meakin directly, 'Had you every reason to believe that Tinsley himself, having got off the engine of that train, knew perfectly well where it was?'

'Yes,' replied Meakin. 'The fireman from the 6.10 local on the up line was in the box.'

Lightfoot was also able to help Meakin add substance to his weak earlier response ('he did not say') as to why empty coal train brakesman William Young was in the box. Young, said Meakin this time, had gone there to check how long he and his train might be detained. As for any suggestion that animated discussion, or anything of the sort, might have taken James Tinsley's mind off his duties once he had assumed operational control – a theory that has in much more recent times acquired a large degree of support – Meakin was adamant that this was not the case. 'There was no nonsense going on in the box.'

That assertion by Meakin was to a large extent supported by William Young's own evidence. He confirmed there were never more than four men in the signal box at one time. The 26-year-old goods brakesman was unequivocal. As he was going into the box, he met fireman Hutchinson and brakesman Ingram just as they were leaving. Entering the cabin, he told the inquiry, he saw Meakin reading a newspaper while James Tinsley was 'busy with his book and the phone'. Thereafter, Young contributed little else of real substance to the inquiry.

Druitt: 'Was he doing that all the time?'

Young: '*I cannot say exactly.*'

'What was Tinsley doing in regard to working the instruments?'

'*I don't know.*'

There was little of note either from Thomas Ingram, apart from confirming his presence in the box – as in Young's case, to check how long his train might be delayed – when Tinsley arrived to take over from Meakin. Brakesman Ingram would be more forthcoming, and rather more helpful to Meakin, at the subsequent inquest, but, if his contribution to the inquiry lacked drama, the next witness, the man everyone present wanted to hear, more than made up for that.

When James Tinsley was called, he got as far as confirming his age as 32 and the fact that he had been a signalman for more than eight years, the last five of which had been spent at Quintinshill. At this juncture Lightfoot, clearly aware that criminal proceedings were being prepared against his client, advised him that he did not need to give his evidence in public and warned him appropriately on several other points. Tinsley, for reasons known only to himself, chose to ignore the advice. He would give his evidence in full public hearing.

Clearly a man in considerable distress as he provided his account of the events which culminated in the disaster, Tinsley nevertheless appeared to be holding nothing back, responding to Colonel Druitt's questioning in an apparently frank manner.

He began by admitting candidly that it was his usual practice to travel to work on the local train from Carlisle if he had received word from the signalman at Gretna Junction – as he had on 22 May – that the train was going to be stopped and shunted aside at Quintinshill. He made no secret of the fact that this was bound to delay his arrival for duty in the signal box beyond the scheduled start time.

It was as if this palpably frail young railwayman was anxious to get the whole appalling episode off his chest and bring what was clearly an ordeal for him to a swift close as he responded to the inspector's grilling. But Tinsley's next two replies to Druitt were as confusing as, apparently, they were open and frank:

Druitt: 'In order to help you not giving yourself away, you entered in the train book that you had come on at 6am?'

Tinsley: '*Yes, between six and half past, six. I used to make a note of the time of the train on a piece of paper – a telegraph form.*'

'And what did you do?'

'*I used to copy them into the book.*'

Possibly this was the result of journalistic misinterpretation, but Tinsley's statements in this passage of his evidence clearly referred to the usual practice in the signal box rather than to the specific events on the morning of 22 May. Under the unofficial arrangement he had struck with Meakin there would have been no need for Tinsley to note the time of his train's arrival on a piece of paper. It was the role of whoever was ending the night shift in the box – whether this was Meakin or Tinsley – to cover for his incoming mate's late arrival by jotting down all train movements for later copying into the train register.

Whether Tinsley's response was correctly reported by the press is now a matter for conjecture. Whatever he said, Colonel Druitt seems not to have challenged him on it, though unsurprisingly he did seek more detail on the late shift change, and his next questions secured responses which were specific in content:

Druitt: 'Was it generally about half past six when you came on duty?'

Tinsley: *'Nearly always about that time. On this particular morning I came on board the local passenger train from Gretna. The Gretna signalman gave me a signal and I understood the train was going to be shunted. On arrival at Quintinshill I got off the engine as it was proceeding through the road* [the crossover connection] *from the down line to the up line, so I knew the train was being crossed on to the up main line. The train was standing on the up main line when I got into the box.'*

'When you got to the box what did your mate tell you?'

'He said there was a train signalled on the down line, the 5.50 [Edinburgh] *express from Carlisle.'*

'Did he tell you anything about the running of the troop train?'

'Yes sir, he told me it passed Lockerbie at 6.32.'

'And about the empty wagon train?'

'He told me Kingmoor [marshalling yard at Carlisle] *was blocked out, and it* [the empty wagon train] *was coming into the up loop. The first signal I got on either block was at 6.38 for the 5.50 express from Carlisle. I accepted it on the down line, entered it as passing Quintinshill at 6.38 and gave the 'train entering section' signal to Kirkpatrick* [box] *at 6.38. On the up road the first signal I gave was for the special troop train. I had nothing to do with the coal train.'*

There is more than one problem with Tinsley's evidence here. The late-running Edinburgh express which should have left Carlisle at 5.50 could not have been offered to him (from Gretna, the box to the south) at 6.38 if, as he said, it passed Quintinshill at that time; it would have to have been earlier. A study of the relevant page from the train register book records its actual acceptance at 6.33, when it was immediately offered forward to Kirkpatrick box. The express is shown as entering the section under Quintinshill's control at 6.36 before passing the box there two minutes later and was out of section at 6.42. Once again, the apparent discrepancy could have been an error in the press reporting – 6.38 instead of 6.33 – or, if it was reported correctly, James Tinsley, hardly in the best frame of mind for accurate recall, may simply have become confused.

George Meakin would later say that it was he who accepted the express from the south at 6.33 and offered it onwards as Tinsley had only just arrived for work. On the balance of probability, it seems likely that Meakin, despite saying that he made no further entries on the sheet of paper after 6.30, included the Edinburgh-bound express train's acceptance in his notes for Tinsley to copy into the book. The handwriting used for the relevant register entry was clearly that of Tinsley.

The significance of all this, of course, was to establish precisely at what time the operation of the signal box was handed over from Meakin to Tinsley and who was doing what during the changeover period. Thus Colonel Druitt persisted with questions aimed at clarifying the situation: He was anxious to determine which of the two signalmen completed the process of transferring the train of coal empties from the main line, out of section, into the up passing loop.

Druitt: 'You are quite sure you did not give the "train out of section" for it?'

Tinsley: *'I am quite sure, sir.'*

'And if your mate says he did not?'

'Well I did not, sir. The first I sent was [for] *the troop train offered at 6.42 and I accepted it. I offered it to Gretna at 6.46 and received the "line clear" signal at that time. I pulled all the signals for it.'*

Tinsley's recall of events was, utterly haphazard. Irrespective of who sent the 'train out of section' for the empty coal train, there is no doubt that he had done so for the first of the two northbound expresses, alerting Kirkpatrick box at 6.38. While this was indicative of Tinsley's performance under examination – as erratic at the inquiry as it had been in the signal box a few days earlier – it stands as little more than detail when compared with the substance of the next segment of Colonel Druitt's examination of the hapless signalman's evidential account:

Druitt: 'Did you forget about the local train?'

Tinsley: *'Yes sir.'*

'When you went to the block instrument on the up line, how was the indicator when you first touched it?'

'The block was in its normal position.'

'It was not showing red?'

'No sir.'

'Someone must have put it back?'

'Yes, but I am quite sure I did not put it back.'

Tinsley's apparent argument that, because the indicator in the signal box was not set to 'train on line', he had no reminder of the local train obstructing the southbound main line, was deservedly accorded little credibility by the inspector. Whether or not George Meakin should have applied the blocking back procedure, and whatever the indicator was set to, the obvious fact remained: James Tinsley had only just got off the train in question. Why would he need reminding that it was there? Thus the scene was set for the exchange now enshrined in the realms of folklore.

Druitt: 'The fact of the slow train being on the up line did not enter your mind at all after you took control of the box?'

Tinsley: *'I forgot about it after I jumped off the engine and it never entered my mind again until after the accident happened.'*

Quite probably the most extraordinary statement ever made to explain a major disaster of any nature, Tinsley's now infamous words flew in the face of the facts. Colonel Druitt did not have the benefit of all the evidence that would emerge via the later judicial process, neither was he privy to the ream of witness statements that would be given in precognition as a precursor to criminal proceedings. Together, this would paint a startling picture of a man in a muddle whose awareness of what was going on around him – and especially that of the local train's close proximity – was fleeting intermittently in and out of his mind.

But Edward Druitt had heard testimony at his inquiry that Tinsley had been handed several reminders of the stationary train's presence. If, somehow, he had *still* forgotten all about it at the crucial time, then something must have been seriously amiss with him. He could not have been functioning properly. James Tinsley must surely have been unwell. But the inspector either missed the underlying implication of what Tinsley had told him or he chose not to pursue it. Instead, apparently in the belief that his witness was mentally stable but extraordinarily slapdash in his behaviour, Druitt tried, with unspoken incredulity, a new line of questioning seemingly aimed at hammering home the point.

Druitt: 'The engine of the slow train was not thirty yards away from you. If you had looked out of your [front] window you could not have helped seeing it.

Tinsley: *'If I had happened to look out of the window it might have called my attention to it.'*

'It is not your custom to look out of the window?'

'We can see all our signals before we pull them off.'

'Did you not look along the line before you pulled your signals off? Something might have got on the line. Is it not your custom to look along the line at all?'

'We would not have time to run to the window every time a train came. We can see our signals from where we pull them, and the line too.'

Here Druitt was displaying an apparent lack of knowledge about the methods used by Caledonian signalmen in boxes of this design. As noted in chapter five, it was the practice to rely on the box's side (end) window – at Quintinshill and elsewhere on the network. Tinsley's evidence on this point was perfectly correct. An independent railway expert would have supported this. None was called. Neither did the Caledonian Railway, well aware of the practice, come to Tinsley's aid. At the inquiry and during the subsequent legal process the company made no attempt to intervene on this key issue. Tinsley was 'hung out to dry' by his employers – and Colonel Druitt sought no clarification on the matter.

Druitt: 'What time were you offered the second express?'

Tinsley: *'At 6.45* [it was actually 6.46]. *I accepted it at the same time and offered it to Kirkpatrick* [box], *where it was accepted. I got the "entering section" for it at 6.48.'*

'When the collision between the troop train and the other [local] train occurred did you realise that the express was just approaching?'

'I knew the express would be at the back of it, after it [the collision] *happened.'*

'Did you put your down signals to danger at once?'

'They were put to danger as soon as the accident happened. I cannot remember now who did it. I cannot remember whether I put them to danger myself or not.'

Again Tinsley's struggle to recall anything clearly was obvious, or at least it seems that way today. Possibly his inability to remember whether it was he or Meakin who had put the signals to danger following the initial collision – later evidence would show that it was the latter; Tinsley simply froze, unable to do anything – was put down at the inquiry to understandable shock in the wake of the disaster. Certainly, Druitt missed another opportunity to delve more closely into the reasons for the signalman's memory lapses as he returned to the theme of who else was in the signal box and the effect their presence may have had:

Druitt: 'Your mate was still in the box when the collision occurred?'

Tinsley: *'Yes sir.'*

'Was anybody else in the box when you arrived at it?'

'The brakesman [Ingram] *from the 4.50 was there and the fireman of the local passenger train* [Hutchinson] *followed me up shortly after. I gave him the pen to sign the book.'*

'That ought to have reminded you of the local train.'

'Yes it ought.'

'Did the brakesman of the empty wagon train [Young] come in while you were there?'

'Yes sir.'

'What were you doing between the time of your arrival at the box and the accident?'

'I said to my mate, "there will be another express to come" and he said, "yes". That was after the first one passed. I rang number three cabin [at Carlisle] *and asked the boy where the second express was. He said it passed him at 6.40.'*

That Tinsley chose to confine his answer so narrowly is baffling or perhaps a further indication of his patchy recall. It is worth noting that this brief verbal exchange with Meakin is the only recorded conversation between the two prior to the initial crash, adding no weight at all to the case, still argued today, that Tinsley was distracted from his duties by chatter in the signal box. He had, however, missed the chance to further discredit the argument by failing to point out that brakesman Young did not enter the box until Ingram and Hutchinson had left.

Druitt: 'When did you enter the times of the trains which had passed between six and half past six and which you had not dealt with?'

Tinsley: *'I went to the desk where the book was after taking off my coat and putting my piece* [lunch] *down, and looked on the telegraph form to see what trains were marked down. Then the fireman* [Hutchinson] *came up.'*

'Are you accustomed to make use of the lever collar when there is a train standing – to protect it?'

'Just in case of a train being put off to the loop.'

'When a train like this is crossed from one line to another, do you use the collar then to block the signals?'

'*No.*'

'Why not? Why don't you carry out your instructions?'

Tinsley had no answer to this. He could have argued that it was Meakin who should have applied the collar but, aware that the collar, despite company regulations, was very seldom used at Quintinshill, he said nothing.

Druitt: 'Do you make use of the blocking back signal?'

Tinsley: '*Yes sir.*'

'You did not use the blocking back signal when you arrived in the box because you had forgotten about the local train?'

'*After the train was put through I thought the blocking back signal was being done.*'

Despite his travails in examination, Tinsley on this occasion had given a perfectly fair response, one which showed that he understood the blocking back regulations while Colonel Druitt did not. As noted in chapter five, under the rules blocking back had to be applied *before* the train it would be safeguarding on the main line could be moved into place. Meakin had been unable to implement the process because the relevant section of line was still occupied by the empty coal train, but Tinsley may have assumed that Meakin *had* blocked back and could not justifiably be accused of not doing so himself once the shunting manoeuvre involving the local train had been completed – the rules forbade this.

Having slipped up for a second time on a technical issue, Druitt returned to old ground as once more he asked Tinsley if he was sure he had not given the 'out of section' signal for the empty coal train. Again, Tinsley was 'quite sure' he hadn't. Druitt then enquired of the signalman what time he had taken absolute control of the box – he had given his first signal at 6.38, Tinsley replied – and whether it was Meakin who had sent the 'out of section' signal for the local train.

Tinsley responded to this with an unequivocal 'yes sir' although the signal almost certainly would have been sent by Meakin before Tinsley arrived in the box and the latter could not, therefore, have known this for a fact. He was on equally shaky footing when, once again, he told the inspector he had accepted the first northbound express from Gretna and had immediately given the 'train entering section' signal to Thomas Sawyer in the box to the north at Kirkpatrick.

Tinsley's responses to Colonel Druitt ended with his telling the inspector he didn't suppose there would have been a minute between the two collisions. Then the signalman's examination took on a wholly new slant when, finally, it touched on his mental state at the time of the accident thanks to the intervention of G.A. Lightfoot, the solicitor representing the interests of Tinsley and his fellow NUR members. It is an arguable point but, from the way Lightfoot framed his questions, he may have suspected an underlying health problem – although on 25 May the spectre of epilepsy had yet to rise above the parapet.

Lightfoot: 'When you recognised what had happened after the first collision was there anything you could have done effectively so as to prevent the second collision?'

Tinsley: '*There was not time, sir.*'

'But, as a matter of fact, supposing there had been anything you could have done, were you in a condition to do it?'

'Yes sir, if there had been time I would have done it.'

'Were you yourself or were you in a state of collapse?'

'No sir, I was all right at the time.'

'It has been suggested that, if you had been all right, you would have put your signals to danger at once, for what it was worth. You don't know you did that?'

'I cannot state that. I only know they were put to danger afterwards.'

'May Meakin have put them to danger?'

'I don't know.'

Tinsley may have insisted that he had been 'all right,' but Lightfoot had planted the possibility of some sort of medical malfunction affecting Tinsley in the signal box. He took it no further. If he and whoever had suggested it to him – a perplexed railway professional perhaps – did suspect a pre-existing illness of which Tinsley's employers were unaware, it was a potential minefield for a nervous witness under examination for his role in a dreadful tragedy. We are left to conjecture as to why Lightfoot mentioned it at all, however obliquely, unless he was referring merely to the possibility of his client being in a state of shock.

It is hard to gauge the truth about this, but two things are very clear. Colonel Druitt did not see fit to pursue at his inquiry the possibility of Tinsley's being unwell – for whatever reason – at the time of the accident and no trace of Lightfoot's questioning of him on the matter was published in the final Board of Trade inquiry report. Indeed, it is only thanks to the diligent press reporting of the Carlisle hearing that we are able to reproduce this fascinating exchange now.

The solicitor now did his best to provide Tinsley with at least a degree of mitigation by suggesting the congested track layout at Quintinshill might have hindered visibility.

Lightfoot: 'Would the fact that the empty train on the loop line standing immediately in front [of the signal box] not rather prevent you from seeing the up line?'

Tinsley: *'A wee bit.'*

'You could have seen the up if you had looked for it, but the presence of the empty train might have prevented you seeing the passenger [troop] train?'

'A wee bit.'

Having achieved relatively little from that set of questions, Lightfoot changed tack. He now sought confirmation from Tinsley that the signalman had produced the train register book for local train fireman George Hutchinson to sign as required under the company's rules. Tinsley said he had indeed done so. The fact that he had handed Hutchinson the wrong page of the register – for up line movements rather than the correct down line page – was not raised at the inquiry. It was only later, when the case against Tinsley gathered pace, that it became an issue.

Lightfoot, with the awkward task of having to juggle the interests of more than one client, asked Tinsley to clarify whether or not he had been the responsible signalman at that time. 'I had not begun to mark up the book then. I marked up my book and then I signed on,' Tinsley answered. It was an ambiguous response. While he may not formally have signed on for duty the very fact that it was Tinsley who handed the register book to Hutchinson for signing was a pretty strong indicator, among others, that he was by then effectively running the signal box

If this appeared to help George Meakin, the next intervention at the inquiry did nothing of the sort. It came from Thomas Pettigrew, the Caledonian Railway's Superintendent of the Line, apparently in the form of a prepared company statement. Tinsley, said Pettigrew, 'did not interfere with the Welsh empty [train] at all, or the indicator lock. It was standing 'off' [indicating a clear line] when he got the troop train belled to him, and he accepted it.' In other words, according to the company, there was little doubt that Meakin had set, or left, the indicator at 'clear,' thus allowing the troop train – in theory, at least – to proceed into calamity.

Pettigrew's motive for taking this line can only be conjecture but it appears that the Caledonian company may have had Meakin rather more than Tinsley in their target sights when it came to apportioning blame for the accident. If, by now, they too suspected an illness affecting Tinsley – and again it can only be conjecture – then gunning for Meakin would perhaps have made sound commercial sense. It would certainly not have been in the company's interests to see an employee working in a busy main line signal box with an apparently destabilising medical condition exposed as the chief culprit. Either the blame could be deflected chiefly against Meakin or, if Tinsley's guilt was so overpoweringly obvious, any health issues would need to be kept hidden so that the Caledonian Railway could escape censure for taking him on to the payroll.

It remains a hypothesis – but within a matter of days the railway company would be faced with the reality of confronting a situation precisely along those lines.

The line superintendent had one more contribution to make to the inquiry. He repeated a question already put to Tinsley – had he put the signals to danger after the first collision. 'I may have put the up line signals to danger but I am not sure about the down line signals,' replied Tinsley. Another vague, unhelpful response. Later evidence would show clearly that, in a totally flummoxed state, he had done neither.

Tinsley's ordeal was over, at least for the moment. The press reported nothing further from him. The remainder of Druitt's public examination of the facts that day saw the recall to the witness stand of George Meakin for further clarification as to who had done what in the signal box. There was no doubt in Meakin's mind that it was not he who had given the 'out of section' signal for the empty coal train once it had been positioned in the loop – just as Tinsley was arriving to relieve him. Meakin was adamant that his final act on duty was to replace the points controlling the loop to their normal position, restoring right of way to the main line.

Tinsley, he said, was at that time standing at the block instrument at the other end of the signal box – he had gone to it as soon as he arrived. There was a hint of inconsistency here for Meakin had apparently forgotten that, before anything else occurred at changeover, he had briefed Tinsley on the current local traffic situation.

Either this was not spotted by Druitt or Pettigrew – who seems to have taken on the mantle of representing the Caledonian company's interest despite the presence at the inquiry of their corporate lawyers – or they both ignored it as Meakin's re-examination continued. What remained of this didn't take things very much further. Meakin remembered only his mate looking at the block instrument; he did not recall seeing him manipulate it – releasing the lock to clear the line from the north.

Pettigrew: 'You did not hear the "train out of section" signal at 6.34?'

Meakin: *'I did not hear the signal.'*

'Your attention would surely be drawn to that as a signalman?'

'I never heard it.'

'Did you release the lock?'

'I never touched the lock.'

'You never interfered with it?'

'No.'

'Someone must have done it. It was at 6.34 that the "train out of section" was given. That must have been given by the other signalman. The other signalman says he did not take charge of the box until 6.36.'

'He was standing at the block when I put the points back. He was in the box at about 6.32.'

This was getting the inquiry nowhere. It would have been better served had Pettigrew seen fit to educate Colonel Druitt of the normal operating procedures in Quintinshill signal box and others like it on the Caledonian system – the fact that signalmen, working with their backs to railway, did not rush to the front window every time a train went past, relied on their block instruments and tended to use only the side windows to check signals and train movement. That would have been useful – for Lightfoot, too, who seemed similarly unaware of these matters – as would the fact that the railway company's supervisors were very well aware of this.

Meakin's re-examination did provide him with the chance to say what he had been able to do, while Tinsley floundered, in the period immediately following the initial collision. He said he could 'well remember' putting the down (northbound) distant signal to danger before the second crash occurred in his desperate bid to warn the approaching Glasgow express, but was unsure whether he had done the same with the home signal in the short time at his disposal.

George Hutchinson, the local train's 30-year-old fireman, faced something of a predicament when he was called to give evidence. Confirming his presence in the signal box prior to the accident, aware that his northbound train was standing on the southbound line, he accepted that it had been his duty to see that the protective signal collar was on the relevant lever before he left the box. He could do little else but admit that he had not done so. Solicitor Lightfoot came to his aid with a line of questioning that strongly suggested that, while Hutchinson was technically in breach of company regulations, there had seemed very little need for him personally to ensure that the collar was in place.

Lightfoot: 'You knew that James Tinsley had come off your train and you depended on him for seeing that the collar was put on the lever?'

Hutchinson: *'Yes and that helped me forget.'*

'Knowing that he had just come off your train, you were not worrying about it?'

'No sir.'

That hardly let Hutchinson off the hook, but it was a fair point to make on his behalf – though it helped neither Meakin, who should have secured the collar in the first place, nor Tinsley, who Hutchinson might reasonably have expected to have checked it was in place. This passage in the proceedings underlines just how tricky a task Lightfoot had been handed in representing the interests of all three of the railwaymen who faced the most awkward of the questions at the inquiry.

One witness faced no awkward questioning at all – though he certainly should have done. Robert Killin, Assistant Superintendent of the Line with direct jurisdiction over the Caledonian route through Quintinshill, was a man destined to take a key role in the protracted aftermath of the disaster. This was his first involvement. On the face of it, what he told the inquiry must have seemed to the uninitiated a concise and authoritative summary on behalf of the railway company of the failings which had culminated in the tragedy. In truth, it was an extraordinarily shabby piece of manipulative and highly selective analysis which aimed – successfully – to absolve the company from any share of the blame.

Relying on an apparently prepared statement, his appraisal singled out the inarguable breaking of company regulations by Meakin, Tinsley and Hutchinson and played heavily on what he clearly regarded as incompetence on the part of the two signalmen. In so doing Killin studiously avoided any hint of irregularities or poor practice of any sort by the Caledonian itself, particularly with regard to failings in the company's own inspection regime. The evidence which is now available, and which this work will later expand upon, shows clearly that this was a cover-up, the first stage in ensuring that the full weight of responsibility and censure would fall on three – later reduced to two – employees.

In what would become a feature of his contribution to subsequent hearings, Killin quoted from company rules in a highly creative manner, incorporating bits which supported what had undoubtedly become 'his case' while selectively excluding those which detracted from it and implied any corporate fault. He did it very well. He was never challenged. Never shaken. Never found out. Two examples from his evidence to the Carlisle inquiry serve to illustrate this.

Killin told Colonel Druitt that 'the signalman who signalled the Welsh empty coal train should have given the "train out of section" for that train when he had the train safe inside the loop and he had reversed the points to the up main line.' This was incorrect, misleading and unfair to Meakin. Killin would later be forced to concede – at the subsequent inquest – that Meakin was in fact under no obligation to see any operation through once his shift was over. It was the responsibility of Tinsley to send the signal once Meakin had reversed the points.

Also desperately unfair on Meakin was Killin's statement with regard to the blocking back procedure. 'The indicator lock on the block instrument should not have been released,' said Killin correctly, 'but immediately the "train out of section" signal was acknowledged he should have given the blocking back signal to Kirkpatrick [box] and the indicator lock should have been kept on all the time. He should have given this signal personally or, if his mate was taking part in the work, he should have seen that these signals were given by his mate.'

Once again, Killin would later – but not at the inquiry – be forced to agree that Meakin was not required to oversee his mate's work once his own shift had ended. More seriously, Killin had based his remarks on a redacted summary of the Caledonian's blocking back rule, ignoring the part which made clear the procedure had to be carried out before the local train from Carlisle had been shunted onto the opposite line. It could not be done afterwards. Apart from this shockingly misleading statement, Killin, unsurprisingly, offered no support for or appreciation of Meakin's explanation for not being able to block back in the first place – because the empty coal train was still moving on the section to be blocked.

Was avoiding a widening of the blame the main objective for the Quintinshill signalmen's immediate boss, Alexander Thorburn, Gretna's 42-year-old stationmaster, when his turn came to give evidence? It certainly seems that way. Whatever went wrong in the signal box it was unlikely to have been the result of equipment failure, or any supervisory shortcoming on his part, he attested.

Druitt: 'Do you visit the signal boxes sometimes?'

Thorburn: *'Yes sir, as often as circumstances permit.'*

'How often; once a week?'

'It just depends on how much work I have to do. I have two stations to look after as well as Quintinshill and that takes up a great amount of my time.'

'You have always found things worked properly at Quintinshill?'

'That is so.'

'When were you last there?'

'I don't know the date, but it was not a week ago.'

Such a vague answer should certainly have been challenged. If Thorburn had inspected the signal box only days earlier, he would surely have remembered when, especially in the light of such dramatic subsequent developments. Yet he was apparently questioned no further on this and, while his weak response was reported in the press at the time, when the official Board of Trade inquiry report was published in September, it had been replaced by something altogether different, a much sharper version of events suggesting a markedly higher degree of professionalism on the part of the Gretna stationmaster and his superiors.

This would have the effect of safeguarding corporate interests which undoubtedly had been threatened at Carlisle where Thorburn had either ignored, misread or forgotten the Caledonian's script in his pathetic response to Colonel Druitt.

It would seem reasonable to speculate that the railway company's senior management must surely have been appalled by Thorburn's muffed lines. He couldn't have received a better prompt when, minutes earlier, Robert Killin had given his own evidence. 'The stationmaster was required to visit the signal box as often as his duties permitted, and records of his visitations were entered in the train register book', Killin was reported in the press coverage as telling the inquiry.

'This book showed that the stationmaster visited the signal box on Tuesday, 18 May at 1pm, four days before the accident happened, and an inspector for the southern district visited the signal box at irregular times without notice. A record of *his* visits showed that on these occasions there were no irregularities of any kind. In this way the box was visited on 19 May twice, at 3.12 in the morning and at 9.20, and the train register books showed that, within one month prior to that time, three visits were paid at various hours on different days.'

Killin added that, in addition to the visits made on the district inspector's behalf – visits that, in retrospect, can certainly be regarded as extremely unusual – the inspector had in January personally carried out a spot check at the cabin.

All very precise – yet perplexing at the same time. Again, it begs the question, why couldn't Thorburn remember precisely the date of his last inspection visit to Quintinshill? Killin was clear enough about it. This should certainly have raised eyebrows at the inquiry. But then so too should the majority of what Robert Killin outlined to Colonel Druitt in Carlisle. His use of the phrase 'on these occasions' at least hinted at the possibility that those words were very carefully chosen – had irregularities been apparemt on *other* visits to the signal box?

Some may dismiss this as conjecture with very little foundation but, when considered in conjuction with the substance of Killin's remaining evidence, the suggestion that the Caledonian Railway may have harboured concerns about the operation of Quintinshill signal box prior to 22 May 1915 does not seem too fanciful a proposition. Why else would the company carry out no less than three inspections at the box just days before the accident – one by stationmaster Thorburn and two by the district inspector's man – within a period of less than twenty-four hours? Robert Killin had made clear that this was very far from the norm.

Had Thorburn detected something on the 18th which led to the district officer's double inspection the following day at times when he could see both signalmen in turn? If the company *did* have concerns – about James Tinsley's health and performance, perhaps – clearly they had done nothing about this before disaster struck. Not the sort of thing they would have wanted aired in public.

And it never was. The evidence on signal box inspections would conveniently be standardised so that the Caledonian's officers were eventually saying the same thing and, while this would still beg clarification as to why so many inspections were made, no questions would ever be asked and no answers given.

Thus the day-long hearing drew to a close. It had exposed rule-breaking by Meakin, Tinsley and Hutchinson and implied a degree of incompetence on their part but had conspicuously failed to consider as potential contributors to the disaster the wider issue of corporate failure despite evidence which at least hinted at the possibility. Neither during the course of the day had Edward Druitt touched upon matters related to railway operating policy during wartime, such as the stubborn insistence on maintaining express passenger schedules and, equally importantly, the use of antiquated coaching stock for high-speed troop transport.

Thanks to G.A. Lighfoot the possibility of James Tinsley's being unwell at the crucial time had been introduced into the equation – but then brushed to one side.

But Druitt, at least to an extent, can be excused for the narrow confines of his inquiry. The conclusion must be that he regarded the Carlisle hearing as an initial step only. He had taken preliminary evidence pending a more comprehensive examination at a later date. He was entitled to do so under the inquiry system of the day. It was the norm for public inquiries into major rail accidents. Certainly the press reporters came away from Carlisle under no illusion that the process was complete. The *Dumfries & Galloway Standard* reported that the inquiry was not closed but had merely been adjourned.

This fact has never before been acknowledged by Quintinshill's historians. That is no surprise. There is no mention of an adjournment in the official Board of Trade inquiry report. But then, neither is any reference made in the report to a good deal of what was reported to have been said at the Carlisle hearing. There is no doubt the inquiry *was* re-opened but whether Edward Druitt played any part in it is a moot point. The report compiled after its conclusion is preserved in the archives as the official record. It was put together by – and is filed away today on his company's headed paper – by Thomas Pettigrew, line superintendent of the Caledonian Railway. There is not a hint of company failure or shortcoming of any sort in any of its pages. No corporate blame is attached.

And nowhere is there any reference at all to James Tinsley suffering from epilepsy, or any other pre-existing medical condition, at the time of the accident, even though by the time the report was finalised and published this was a distinct probability known to the forces of law – and to the Caledonian Railway.

Notes

1. HM Railway Inspectors was eventually absorbed into the Department of Transport before, in 1990, being transferred to the Health & Safety Executive (HSE), assuming new powers which saw it monitor the health and safety at work of railway staff. High Court judges now presided over its accident inquiries, with a greater accent on determining responsibility and guilt. The Inspectorate was transferred again in 2006 when it was merged with the Office of Rail Regulation, finally losing its long-held legal identity when its functions were taken over by the new Rail Safety Directorate in 2009. Its inspectors continue to be known as HM Railway Inspectors.

2. If criminal proceedings were being considered the Board of Trade would usually conduct its investigation in private so as not to prejudice any legal outcome. When Colonel Druitt opened his inquiry James Tinsley had been interviewed by the police but had not yet been arrested or charged. Interestingly, in the case of the inquiry into the 1913 Ais Gill disaster on the Settle & Carlisle Railway, when legal proceedings were in prospect, the initial session was held in private but the inspecting officer, Colonel Sir John Pringle, bowing to the intense public interest, broke with convention and held the subsequent two sessions of his inquiry in public.

3. The last man with a Royal Engineers background to hold the position of Chief Inspecting Officer was Major C.F. Rose, who retired in 1988 shortly before the Inspectorate's transfer to HSE.

4. During his term of office, Colonel Yolland led the inquiry into the infamous Tay Bridge railway disaster of December 1879 when the centre section of the bridge collapsed in a storm as an express train was crossing, killing everyone aboard, an estimated 75 people. The bridge was condemned by Yolland and board of inquiry colleagues as badly designed, built and maintained.

5. Edward Druitt, who enjoyed a prominent career with the Royal Engineers, received a public school education at Cheltenham College,. However, despite his privileged background, his life was not without trouble and tragedy. Both his mother and grandmother suffered from mental illness which confined them to asylums where both women ended their lives. Druitt's brother Montague, a lawyer and well-known cricketer, had similar health issues and in 1888 his drowned body was found in the Thames. Montague's death at the age of 31, treated as a suicide, gave rise to suggestions that he had committed the murders attributed to Jack the Ripper.

6. The County Hotel alongside Carlisle Citadel station has since been renamed the Hallmark Hotel. The former name is now used by another of the city's hotels which is located in the Botchergate district.

7. An experienced hand, Roger Kirkpatrick had been in the Caledonian's employ for thirteen years, the last of which he had spent in the signal box at Gretna Junction, close to the station cottages where he lived as James Tinsley's next door neighbour.

8. Meakin's apparently confusing reference to the 6.17 local train actually leaving Carlisle at 6.10 was correct. It was the normal practice when, as happened on 22 May, one or more of the two overnight expresses from London was running more than fifteen minutes late. The 'local' could then make some progress before being shunted aside to allow the late-running fast train to pass.

Chapter 8

Doubts and Determination in Dumfries

'An honest man is the noblest work of God.'

Alexander Pope (1688-1744)

The name of James Tinsley will understandably forever be synonymous with the Quintinshill disaster, but relatively little has been written of Tinsley the man. Yet the background, character and condition of the 32-year-old signalman are crucial to a proper understanding of the extraordinary tragedy on 22 May 1915.

Contemporary press coverage provided tantalising glimpses. These have subsequently not received from historians the attention and scrutiny they merited. Chroniclers of Quintinshill's tragedy ignore the newspapers at their peril.

It is a near certainty that the circumstances of Tinsley's arrest on 29 May would have given considerable cause for concern in the neighbourhood of his railwayman's home at Gretna. This slight man, who was clearly seriously unwell, had been dragged from his home in a pitiful condition and literally carried into the courtroom at Dumfries. shivering convulsively, unable to speak or possibly even to understand the gravity of the situation confronting him.

Tinsley's obvious distress and ill health had not spared him from the wrath of Scottish law enforcers apparently intent on immediate retribution for the huge loss of life. His arrest was both crude and cruel.

Yet Tinsley was a family man with a wife and three young children, a man with no previous criminal record, someone who was later described by the arresting police officer, Inspector Charles Morrison, as 'honest, steady and industrious'. This description is about as far removed as possible from the deceitful, unreliable, slapdash image of him conjured up during the investigative process.[1]

Tinsley was born in 1883 at the north Yorkshire market town and cathedral city of Ripon, one of the thirteen children of a hard working and respected local family. He grew up in the town but found employment initially in Leeds, nearly fifty miles to the south, where he obtained work as a footman at Lyddon Hall which survives today as halls of residence for students at the city's university.[2]

Tinsley was destined for better things. He married Hannah Moore at Knaresborough in 1903. The couple lived for a short while at nearby Harrogate before James joined the staff of the Caledonian Railway as a pointsman, the precursor to his eventual career as a signalman. On appointment he was posted to Lockerbriggs across the Scottish border in Dumfrieshire. By 1910 he had graduated as a fully qualified signalman and had started work in Quintinshill's main line signal box. The 1911 census found him living in Station Cottages at Gretna with Hannah and their three children, all boys. It seems clear that Tinsley was an able man with an aptitude for the job and a natural desire to do his best for his young family, to whom, by all accounts, he was devoted.[3]

Nothing appears to have survived with regard to Tinsley's health prior to the May 1915 disaster. Indeed, so far as formal documentation is concerned, there is a disturbing absence of any meaningful reference to his medical condition – even in those places where that sort of information would normally be expected. The authorities who dealt with the various strands of investigation in 1915, and their consequences, seem collectively to have brushed this to one side.

With the exceptions of his solicitor's queries at Colonel Druitt's inquiry hearing in Carlisle regarding Tinsley's health, a famously oblique comment on epilepsy by his advocate at the High Court trial (see chapter eleven) and the specific reference to epileptic fits in the scribbled note from the county's police to Dumfrieshire's Depute Procurator Fiscal's office – a document only recently discovered and never used as evidence in 1915 – the only clues to the illness, or to anything which might account for Tinsley's 'forgetfulness' in the signal box on the morning of the tragedy, are excluded from the Quintinshill archive.

However, as we have shown, there is no doubt that the press covering the story at the time were aware, to varying degrees, that Tinsley was suffering from a serious medical condition in the days and weeks following the accident beyond that of the severe shock to be expected as realisation of the scale of what had happened sank in.

And, if something aside from shock was ailing him in the aftermath of 22 May, it would have been reasonable for the press to assume that, whatever this was, it had afflicted Tinsley prior to the accident and might have been a contributory cause. Suggesting outright before the investigative process had reached any conclusions that a pre-existing medical problem had been a causal factor would have carried too high a risk for the newspapers. It was enough to note, as *The Scotsman* had done – a point immediately picked up by Edinburgh's evening press – that Tinsley was 'subject to fits' at the time of his extraordinary arrest.

Surprisingly perhaps, given the extent of their coverage of the disaster generally, and Tinsley's arrest specifically, the local newspapers in Dumfries and Carlisle did not venture into comment or speculation about his health issues. So from where did the Edinburgh-based papers get the crucial 'fits' angle?

The most plausible explanation is that the information was leaked to the city's newspapers by someone in the Lord Advocate's Edinburgh office. That James Kissock, Dumfries' Depute Procurator Fiscal, telephoned the Lord Advocate, Scotland's Crown Counsel, about Tinsley's fits as soon as he learnt of this after the aborted arrest attempt on Friday, 28 May is an established fact (see chapter six).

It would not have been surprising, given the very high profile of the case, if this startling news had spread quickly around the office before someone there, either out of perceived duty or possibly pecuniary interest, but surely not inadvertently, tipped off *The Scotsman* and the city's evening papers. This might explain why the remainder of the British press carried only the official story that Tinsley had been arrested but made no reference to his propensity to fits. The scoop, it seems, was exclusively restricted to journalists in the Scottish capital, who ran it on Monday, 31 May, two days after the arrest had taken place.

Thus the newspaper on Quintinshill's 'doorstep,' the *Dumfries & Galloway Standard*, missed out, a bitter pill to swallow for a journal that had so diligently reported every move in the story up until then. We can surmise that there would have been both anger and frustration in the paper's Dumfries editorial office. And there would surely also have been an attempt on the bi-weekly *Standard's* part to run the 'fits' angle in its next available issue the following Wednesday, 2 June.

If so, the attempt failed. Had the authorities put the dampers on the apparent leak, indeed on the whole Quintinshill story itself? This can only be conjecture but one thing is certain – it was the *Dumfries & Galloway Standard* alone which kept the story in the news when, following the revelations in the Edinburgh papers, all press reporting of the disaster abruptly ceased until the Carlisle coroner's inquest, adjourned after a brief opening, began in earnest on 23 June. The otherwise total abandonment of the story suggests the Dumfries paper was probably defying a high-level ban on reporting the morale-sapping tragedy's aftermath, an arguably understandable piece of wartime censorship by the Government, but the *Standard's* editor seems to have been a man on a mission.

He may have lost out on one major aspect of the drama, but it is thanks to the outstanding journalism of his remarkable local publication – which survives today – that we are able nearly a century later to peek beneath the story's surface into other aspects of the tragedy which were hidden at the time. If there was an official ban on continuing news reports (though it has to be said that no documentary proof survives to confirm this) the *Standard* technically observed this – by allowing comment instead in the form of readers' letters.

Established in 1843 to 'advocate and defend the principles of the Free Church of Scotland,' the *Standard* was Liberal in its politics. Its editor in 1915 was William Dickie (42), a local man from the town of Annan, fifteen miles from Dumfries. Joining the paper as an apprentice compositor (typesetter) he had switched to journalism and progressed through the ranks to assume the editor's role in 1914. Deeply religious, Dickie was a prominent figure in the Scottish Presbyterian movement – specifically the United Free Church – whose professional instincts as a newspaperman were evidently influenced by his faith. When, aged just 46, he died in August 1919, his obituary in the *Standard* would note that he had lived his life according to the poet Alexander Pope's eighteenth-century observation that 'an honest man is the noblest work of God.'[4]

If William Dickie was following his guiding principles in May 1915, and it seems highly probable that he was, it would have required considerable courage. Fortunately for him, when it came to understanding the complexities of railway matters, the *Standard's* editor had something – or rather, someone – else to guide him. His brother was employed in a senior role as a traffic inspector by the Caledonian Railway's bitter rival, the Glasgow & South Western.

Formed from an amalgamation of smaller companies in 1850, the G&SWR served a triangular area of southwestern Scotland, operating to Glasgow and Stranraer via Dumfries from its southern boundary at Carlisle. In 1876 the company grew in importance as a result of an alliance with the Midland Railway following the start of passenger services further south on the new Settle-Carlisle line. This partnership saw the introduction of Anglo-Scottish services over the G&SWR route in direct competition with the Caledonian.[5]

Having a senior railwayman as a close relative, a man who would certainly have owed no allegiance to the predominant Caledonian company, would have given William Dickie vital insight. Of course his brother might have welcomed the opportunity to kick the Caledonian rival while it was down, but his knowledge and perspective would certainly have widened the key areas of debate.

There was disquiet among many railwaymen from an early stage at the way events were unfolding in the post-crash period. The day-long Board of Trade inquiry hearing in Carlisle on 25 May, and the bleak prospects it heralded for Quintinshill's two signalmen, had been well reported in the press. Four days later, James Tinsley's arrest had seemed premature, possibly unjust, to many in the rail industry. It had aroused sympathy for Tinsley's plight among his peers and – if we go by the first in a series of readers' letters on the tragedy published by the *Standard* – from at least some of the industry's management figures.

Exactly one week after the tragedy, on Saturday, 29 May, William Dickie devoted several column inches to a letter from an anonymous correspondent in Dumfries who signed off simply as 'Railwayman' but gave every impression that he held a supervisory post with whichever company it was who employed him. The heading – 'Wholesale and Flagrant Neglect of Rules' – suggested the content would be rather more than a narrow condemnation of James Tinsley.

'Sir, I hope you will be good enough to allow me space in your paper to call attention to several points which emerged in the course of the Board of Trade inquiry on Tuesday into the Gretna disaster, as reported in your issue on Wednesday.

'My object... is to show that the lamentable accident of Saturday last was not due to the failure of only one man to do his duty, but to the wholesale non-compliance with the railway company's rules and regulations. It will appear rather disquieting to the ordinary traveller when some of the most flagrant breaches of the rules are set down; and it is exasperating to think that if any one of the men had performed their clear duty in one small particular the terrible holocaust would not have taken place. The errors may be briefly described as follows…'

Unfortunately, what did follow from the anonymous correspondent got off to a shaky start when he suggested that the 'section clear' signal had not been sent by Quintinshill back to the Kirkpatrick box after the train of empty Welsh coal wagons had been shunted into the southbound loop and, because of this, signalman Sawyers at Kirkpatrick should not have cleared the main line for the approaching troop train. As noted in previous chapters, the signal *had* been given at Quintinshill though it was never clarified whether this was done by Meakin or Tinsley. The next point made by 'Railwayman' was rather more valid:

'Before the 6.10am local passenger train was allowed through the crossover Meakin should have sent the 'blocking back' signal to Kirkpatrick and the signalman there would have known to have stopped the troop train at Kirkpatrick.'

The key word here is 'before.' This was the point that had been missed at Colonel Druitt's hearing, and would continue to be ignored in all strands of the investigative process – that, according to the Caledonian's rule book, Meakin could only have blocked back to Kirkpatrick before the local train was shunted onto the southbound main line. What the *Standard's* correspondent failed to mention was that Meakin was in an impossible position. He had to get the 'local' out of the way to free up the northbound track for the two expresses from London. It had to be done quickly but blocking the line southwards from Kirkpatrick was not possible because the empty coal train was still on that stretch of line. Once he had moved the local train the rules forbade blocking back.

So Meakin had broken the rules to avoid hindering the progress of the expresses – and it was the Caledonian's policy to give those trains absolute priority.

It was an imperfect point from 'Railwayman' but at least it made clear, for anyone motivated to read between the lines at least, that Meakin was caught between the proverbial rock and hard place. Failure to block back was not his fault.

The point was made inadvertently, of course. While not seeking to exonerate James Tinsley – he had, after all, broken rules – the letter writer was determined to demonstrate that others, Meakin among them, had been at fault apart from the signalman who clearly had been targeted by the Scottish legal authorities. And, ran his argument, when it came to the rule-breaking failure to use the signal collar, a good many others were caught up in the loop. His letter added:

'As soon as the passenger train had come through the crossover, the collar ought to have been placed on the lever, which would have effectively locked the signals and rendered impossible the pulling of the signals for the troop train.'

This, as noted earlier, had been Meakin's responsibility, but 'Railwayman' then widened the net:

'The fireman of the 6.10 local passenger train [George Hutchinson] went to the signal box for the specific purpose of seeing that his train was protected and he signed the book provided to show two things – (1) that the signalman had performed his duty in placing the collar on the lever; and (2) that the act was performed. Neither of these things was done.'

The correspondent then directed his evident ire and incredulity back to James Tinsley:

'[He] travels by the passenger train, leaves it standing facing the cabin not thirty yards away in clear daylight and yet he pulls the signals for the troop train to come on. "Most extraordinary" some people will say; but no doubt due to the fact that he had arrived half an hour late and had from forty to fifty entries to make in his book [the train register] from the telegraph form on which his mate had taken a note of the workings of the trains during the half-hour.'

This was gross exaggeration, hard to understand from an obviously experienced railwayman who must surely have been aware that the number of train movements Tinsley needed to copy from Meakin's notes would have been far fewer. The correspondent was similarly off-beam with his next statement – that there were 'four railwayman in the box in addition to Tinsley.' As we have shown they were never all in the cabin at the same time. This quartet of men, he added:

'…understand the whole system of signalling while the troop train is being belled, while Tinsley is pulling his own signals, and yet not one of these practical men – two of them held up because of this very troop train, and all aware that there is only one road, and that for the London express – raises a question as to the sounding of bells and the drawing of levers. This is surely inexplicable; and the point was not cleared up [at Druitt's inquiry opening] on Tuesday.'

Indeed, it hadn't. This suggested the writer had been at the Carlisle hearing and was illustrative of how shallow and incomplete Druitt's inquiry proceedings on 25 May had been. Warming to his theme, the *Standard's* correspondent then stoked up his fire and, with a series of incisive comments, proceeded to fan the flames:

'There are people who call for the arrest and punishment of the persons responsible for the accident; but it may be difficult to lay hold of all who are really responsible…It is well known that many of the rules laid down by railway companies are honoured in the breach rather than the observance.

'Take, for example, the rule which requires signalmen to place a collar on the lever when there is a train standing on the main line. I have been on the railway for over forty years and, while everyone knows the rule, has seen the collar provided, and admits to the effectiveness of it, I have never once seen it used; and I venture to suggest that many railwaymen would have the same story to tell.

'As a matter of fact, some of the rules and regulations in special circulars and in the working timetables [governing all traffic on the line, as opposed to the public timetable] alike are consistently ignored. But they have their use. If they are broken and nothing happens the company is conveniently and consistently blind. And then, in the case of an accident, the company turns round and says, 'our regulations are there and we did not know they were not being carried out."

'No doubt the high officials of the Caledonian company never dreamed of the extent of the laxity that has prevailed and there is little doubt that, as a rule, the safeguards are not violated in the flagrant way that they were on this occasion. Indeed, if it were otherwise, accidents would be more numerous.

'It is to be hoped that this terrible accident will be productive of good – that the travelling will be made safer than it is today. One way in which it could be accomplished would be for the railway companies only to have rules that they intended to be carried out and to see that they are rigidly enforced.'

'Railwayman' dated his letter 28 May, the day before it was published and thus one day before James Tinsley's arrest. Was there collusion between the writer and the editor? It is doubtful whether anyone in the employ of the Caledonian would have risked writing it. Far more likely is that the writer worked for the G&SWR. Might it have been instigated – or possibly written – by Dickie's brother?

Whatever its origins, this was powerful stuff. It stands to this day as one of the very few examples of public condemnation of what, in modern parlance, would be called a systems failure on the Caledonian Railway – indeed, on the railway industry as a whole, the sort of deep-rooted breakdown which underpins many industrial mishaps. Such failures usually come to the fore during official causal investigation. The *Standard's* correspondent, it seems, was drawing attention to the disturbing fact that this appeared unlikely to happen in the rush to judgment following the Quintinshill tragedy. He was right.[6]

The provocative letter was certain to attract comment – and William Dickie was not afraid to allow the space in his newspaper to publicise this. In the next issue of the *Standard*, on the following Wednesday, 2 June, the Dumfries paper carried a second reflective letter on the disaster, signed just as vaguely as the first, by a correspondent calling himself 'Electrical Operator.' He opened his robust response by suggesting that 'Railwayman' 'appears to be too self-assertive, and comes to conclusions for which he has no authority. Besides, is he justified in remarking on a case which is *sub judice*?'

Tinsley's arrest on a charge of culpable homicide had been made public by the time this letter was written, or at least published, but 'Railwayman' would not have been aware of it when his own letter was penned for the 29 May issue, so the suggestion of *sub judice* was incorrect although the editor saw no necessity to point this out. That aside, the crux of the letter was soon apparent as it continued:

'As a railwayman he ought to have a fellow feeling and try his level best to ward off the keen edge of public antipathy to the poor signalman or signalmen involved. How does he know that all the four men, including Tinsley, who were in the signal box were well acquainted with the belling and block working? I do not think so.

'Although he hits the railway companies, and rightly so, about rules and regulations being made to suit the companies and not the servants, he seems to hold a brief for the companies.

'He omits to add – and he ought to know, seeing he has forty years' experience – how signalmen are harassed about detentions [delays], some of even a single minute, to trains, and how they are harassed with circulars and supplementary applications of rules and instructions. A signalman's work is no bed of roses and those whose work does not require responsibility on anything like the footing of a signalman, should pause before casting a stone at their fellow workers.'

Once again the wider responsibility for the disaster had been raised, this time in a direct reference to the insistence of the Caledonian – although it was not alone – in maintaining as closely as possible the peacetime schedules of its principal trains and, as with George Meakin on 22 May 1915, the problems this inevitably caused for harassed signalmen trying to juggle this ridiculous corporate priority with the vast amount of additional wartime traffic on their tracks, a root cause of the tragedy that never formed part of the investigative process.

The *Standard*'s two correspondents were arguing from somewhat different perspectives but the cumulative effect of what they had written added up to one thing – public embarrassment for the Caledonian Railway. Some sort of corporate response was by now probably inevitable. It came on Saturday, 6 June.

The final letter in this series of correspondence was published in the weekend issue of the Dumfries paper. It came from Thomas Sawyers, the duty signalman on 22 May at Kirkpatrick, the box immediately north of Quintinshill. Sawyers took issue with the point made by 'Railwayman' a week earlier that, having received no 'section clear' signal from Quintinshill, he should not have invited the troop train on. This, he wrote, amounted to 'an unwarrantable insinuation' against him and, burning with indignation, he set about putting the record straight:

'Two inquiries have been held, namely the railway company's and the Board of Trade's [see following chapter for clarification] and I have given evidence at both these investigations. The Board of Trade inspector will shortly issue his official report and the public will then have the opportunity to judge as to the person or persons responsible. Perhaps 'Railwayman' could have been better employed than making an erroneous remark until the completion of the official inquiry.'

Sawyers was fully justified in making this defence; it was not his fault that the southbound main line was blocked, nor was he aware of it when he signalled the doomed troop special onto the section of track north of Quintinshill. But the language used in this letter hints at some level of corporate involvement in its construction and it is probably not stretching the imagination too far to suggest that this was part of the Caledonian Railway's developing strategy – and of those in higher authority – to avoid a widening of the investigative scope beyond the events inside Quintinshill signal box on that fateful Saturday morning.

As noted, nothing more on the tragedy appeared in the *Standard* – nor in any other journal – until widespread coverage of the story recommenced later in June at the time of the Carlisle coroner's inquest re-opening, but, aside from covering the key official processes, the Dumfries newspaper did carry one curious tailpiece on 7 July which once again hinted at a lack of official openness.

Dramatically headlined 'Gretna Disaster –'Facts Confidential and Secret.' It related to a legal hearing well outside the paper's circulation area, a civil action brought in the name of Private Michael Gaffney of the 7th Royal Scots for damages from the Caledonian company. It was held before Andrew Anderson – a noted Scottish judge with the judicial title of Lord Anderson – at the Court of Session.

The damages sought by representatives of the soldier, from Albert Street, Edinburgh, were for the injuries he had received at Quintinshill, injuries from which he had subsequently died. There were, of course, countless civil claims against the railway company by, or on behalf of, disaster victims. The accident had happened on the Caledonian system and, whatever the contributory causes and who was specifically responsible for them, the company was bound to be the target for those seeking a degree of financial recompense. This particular case was intriguing because of what had been said on the company's behalf in court.

Its legal representative, reported the *Standard*, 'said that the main defence was that the railway company had been taken over by the Government [in the guise of the Railway Executive Committee]. The company desired not to lodge defences until they had submitted them to the Government, because the defences would disclose a number of matters regarded as confidential and secret.' He sought, and was granted, a fourteen-day extension period for lodging a defence. What those secret and confidential matters were is now a matter for conjecture. The claim, along with many others, was eventually settled but the *Dumfries & Galloway Standard* published nothing further on the matter.

We can never be sure how much William Dickie knew of the reasons behind the Quintinshill disaster. His early death removed any hope of finding this out in the years that followed. Dickie's integrity, both as a man and as an editor, had inspired him to widen the debate on the tragedy in a bid to get to the truth, but his decision to run the story on the civil action – as far as he could – seems to have been his last throw. He had got as close as anyone, then and since, to uncovering the web of complicity that before the year was out would leave the hapless James Tinsley and George Meakin wriggling in its trap as others went free.

Was Dickie himself part of a counter web of doubters concerned that the rush to judgment was stampeding everything in its path that threatened to upset the convenience of an easy, narrow targeting of rule-breaking signalmen? In Dumfries, as tight-knit a community then as it remains today, the tragedy at Quintinshill would have dominated discussion. It is probably fair to assume that rumour and suspicion – perhaps even knowledge – of wider responsibility would have informed much of the talk. In this context the local newspaper's editor would have been a key figure, an outlet for expressions of communal concern.

Awareness of James Tinsley's apparent illness would certainly have aroused feelings of unease in the district. It is highly unlikely to have remained within the confines of Depute Procurator Fiscal James Kissock's office even before the Edinburgh press got hold of the story. The circumstances of Tinsley's dramatically controversial arrest would surely have spread around Dumfrieshire like wildfire.

Should a man with a medical condition such as his be facing trial for the deaths of Quintinshill's victims? Given the nature of his reported illness and the probable effect it had on him at the time, could his evidence be relied upon if, as happened, others in the signal box were also targeted by the Scottish legal process?

That there were doubters seems clear. In Dumfries and in Edinburgh too where someone had almost certainly leaked to the press the confirmation of Tinsley's fits.

Yet the endeavours of William Dickie and those others who doubted for more than one reason that justice was truly being served could not hold back the onrushing juggernaut of official blame and divert it from its narrow, chosen path.

Notes

1. Inspector Morrison made his remarks on a requested referee inquiry form, further noting that Tinsley was 'a respectable, working man. He has no criminal propensities to my knowledge.' But the police officer added that Tinsley's temperament was 'nervous and excitable.'

2. Built as a fine private house in 1892 when James Tinsley was nine, Lyddon Hall would still have been a relatively new building when he took up initial employment there as a footman.

3. Tinsley's affection and concern for his wife and young children is evident from the two letters he wrote to Hannah which survive in his prison file at the National Archives of Scotland.

4. The *Dumfries & Galloway Standard* was founded by George Henderson of Nunholm, Dumfries, and twenty-seven other shareholders. It was owned in 1915 by Thomas Hunter (1839-1919), who had started work in his teens as an apprentice printer to Henderson and was eventually appointed company manager before assuming ownership. He was later succeeded as owner by his son.

5. Apart from their competing routes to Glasgow, the Caledonian and G&SW rail companies were also bitter rivals on the River Clyde, vying for trade in the lucrative operation of ferry services.

6. Systems failures are often the direct result of corporate shortcomings. They demonstrate the failure of management to ensure that safety systems are robust, operate properly and are both efficiently maintained and effectively enforced. Notable examples in recent times include the sinking of the cross-channel ferry *The Herald of Free Enterprise* in March 1987 and the Piper Alfa oil rig disaster fire in the North Sea in July 1988. Both were key factors in the legislation which prompted the Corporate Manslaughter and Corporate Homicide Act of 2007.

Chapter 9

Whitewash: The Secret Inquiry

*'Is it worthwhile spending money on these inquiries? Is
any purpose served thereby that would not be served by
allowing the railway company itself to hold the inquiry
and publish its own report at its own expense?'*

New Statesman, 29 November 1913 –
a comment on the Ais Gill disaster inquiry

Filed at The National Archives in Kew is a report that purports to represent
the findings of the Board of Trade's inquiry into the Quintinshill disaster.
For those researchers who have not delved into the contemporary press
coverage – and it would appear that very few, if any, have done so – it has stood for
nearly a century as the only source of apparently factual evidence from Colonel
Druitt's investigation at Carlisle on behalf of the BoT. The fact that it differs,
in some places significantly, from what the newspapers reported in May 1915
suggests a degree, to put it mildly, of manipulation. If so, by whom?[1]

The answer to that appears obvious. As noted in chapter seven, the substance
of the archived report is filed on the Caledonian Railway's prominently headed
notepaper. On the face of it this seems disturbingly sinister. Was the railway
company, rather than the Board of Trade, responsible for the report's content?
Dig a little deeper and the suspicion is reinforced. Unlike the press accounts of
Druitt's hearing in May 1915, which at least had raised the possibility of James
Tinsley's being unwell in Quintinshill signal box immediately prior to the accident
and suggested that the company's inspection regime and line management might
have left a lot to be desired, the official report hints at neither.

This absence in the document of crucial evidence from Druitt's 25 May
Carlisle hearing, apparently dismissed and expunged, is exacerbated by the fact
that much of what does remain from those proceedings has been summarised in
narrative form with very little direct witness quotation under examination. In
this way the report puts the cause of Britain's worst ever rail crash down to the
negligent and slapdash behaviour of front line railway servants who, despite their
experience and fitness for the work, had between them made catastrophic errors

in the signal box. Nobody else was to blame. There was no other explanation. It was as simple as that. If this archived report was an act of subterfuge on behalf of the Caledonian company, it was very successfully carried out. Nobody until now has seriously challenged this official version of events.

But if, as it appears on first reading, the document at Kew represents the conclusions of a private inquiry by the railway company, it would have to have been adopted by the Board of Trade as the 'real thing' and filed as such.

Documentation exists to show that the proceedings which culminated in the archived report began on Monday, 24 May, only two days after the accident and one day *before* Druitt began taking evidence in Carlisle. No records appear to have survived to document specific investigative events on that day but, in the evening, Caledonian officials travelled down to Carlisle for Druitt's hearing the next day and probably stayed overnight, as he did, in the County Hotel.

Thus these apparently separate strands of inquiry converged. The single outcome was the document now in the archives at Kew. It shows that the completed report, signed by Colonel Druitt, was forwarded by him on 17 June to the assistant secretary of the Board of Trade's Railway Department in London. Confusingly, while Druitt appears to be writing from the department's own Whitehall offices, its address on the report's typescript appears near the top of the clearly-headed Caledonian Railway paper. Druitt's opening paragraph notes that the report has been produced in compliance with a Board of Trade order issued on 22 May, the day of the accident. It is evident from a footnote appended to the report that copies were not distributed to the company until 17 September, exactly a week before the trial of the men held responsible for the accident.

There is no other inquiry report into the disaster in The National Archives nor, it would seem, anywhere else. So far as the custodians of the British nation's records are concerned, this *is* the real thing. So what are we to make of the report? The word 'conspiracy' shrieks out from its pages. There is very good reason to reach such a conclusion. But it's not quite as black and white as that. Detailed analysis would suggest a more complex picture.

In order to sharpen the image it is necessary to examine more closely three fundamental factors – first, the whole system of Board of Trade inquiries into major railway accidents as it applied in 1915; second, the dire predicament confronting the Caledonian company hierarchy in the immediate aftermath of the accident, its motive for deceit, if deceit there was; and third, the knock-on overall effect of the accident on the British nation and the governance of the country at a time of heightened wartime tension.

Although, as outlined in chapter seven, railway inspecting officers with the right to investigate accidents had been appointed by the Board of Trade since 1840, it wasn't until the passing of the Railways Act of 1871 that the board's accident inquiries were legalised by Parliament. Railway companies were required to comply with the statutory powers granted to the Board of Trade's railway inspectorate under the terms of the Act. They were obliged to provide the inspectorate with official returns of all accidents on their networks – immediately in the case of the more serious type of incident. The inspectors were given the power to summon railway company officers and staff as witnesses and to require them to produce all forms of documentation deemed relevant to establishing an accident's cause.

Accident returns from the period are now preserved among the archives at the National Railway Museum in York. It is clear from these that the Board of Trade did not investigate every accident brought to its attention by the rail companies. In many cases it simply published the results of the companies' own investigations into the causes. This procedure even extended to some accidents in which railway employees had been killed. A coroner's inquest, or its Scottish equivalent, a fatal accident inquiry – there were examples of both after the Quintinshill disaster on the Anglo-Scottish border – might conduct wider investigation, but in several cases the evidence and conclusions published by the railway company concerned was considered sufficient for the purposes of the inquiry. In other words, a railway company was effectively able to examine itself!

However, in the event of a major accident, usually involving multiple fatalities, it was normal for the railway inspectorate to conduct an independent inquiry, and when this happened it was usually held in public.

Crucial to understanding the inquiry system is an appreciation that inspectors appointed to oversee an examination into the causes of an accident were allowed a long leash. Though the ultimate say remained with the Board of Trade, and was used on several occasions to override their conclusions or recommendations, individual inspectors had the power to run their inquiries more or less in the manner they considered best served their purposes.

It was they who decided whether or not the investigation by the railway company concerned was sufficient and, if not, whether an independent inquiry should be held in public. If separate legal proceedings were in progress, or in prospect, the inspectors were within their rights to hold the inquiry in private, without the presence of the press or public, and were able to delay publication of their report and its conclusions in order to avoid prejudicing any legal outcome.

This right to privacy was not always adopted. The precedent had been ignored in 1913 when Major John Pringle was appointed by the Board of Trade to hear an inquiry into another high-profile rail crash – at Ais Gill on the Settle-Carlisle route of the Midland Railway. After opening his examination on the railway at Kirkby Stephen station in private, and despite the possibility of legal action being taken against the driver of one of the two trains involved in the crash – in which sixteen people died and another thirty-eight were injured – Major Pringle, bowing to intense public interest, had conducted the subsequent two sittings of his inquiry in open session.[2]

We are left to speculate as to why Druitt did not adopt the same strategy with his adjourned inquiry, especially as, in this case, the opening session had *not* been held in private. The immediate targeting of James Tinsley by the Scottish legal authorities, quickly followed by his extraordinary arrest on 29 May and appearance in court on a charge of culpable homicide, would clearly have been a factor, but was pressure from a higher authority exerted on Druitt? Continuing to air the background to this most tragic of railway accidents in public, risking further revelations of malpractice on a vital transport artery in the midst of a world war, carried the potential for undermining public confidence not only in a major railway company but in the nation's rail system as a whole.

Soldiers had died in large numbers on British soil. Was the nation's rail infrastructure up to the task of underpinning the war effort? Public morale was at stake. As noted in chapter one, this was certainly not going to help the governance of a country in a state of turmoil following the schism in Asquith's Liberal government and formation on 25 May of the unwanted coalition which replaced it. The more or less simultaneous Quintinshill tragedy truly had come at the worst possible time for the beleaguered premier's struggle for political survival.[3]

It is worth reiterating that the railway network was largely under the co-ordinating control of the Railway Executive Committee, set up by Parliament in 1914. Organising the movement of troops was a key part of its responsibility. Therefore the Government could not simply pass the buck for a major disaster on the railway network to the private company on whose tracks it had occurred. It had a degree of 'ownership' itself and with it a responsibility to ensure reliable and safe operation. Quintinshill posed as much of a threat to public trust in Asquith's cobbled together coalition as it did to confidence in the Caledonian Railway. And for one prominent politician this was especially awkward.

Thomas McKinnon Wood (60) had served as Liberal MP for Glasgow St Rollox since 1906. His constituency, in the city's northeast, included the Caledonian's foremost locomotive workshops and its adjacent carriage and wagon works, making the railway company easily the most important industrial concern and employer in the area. McKinnon Wood was also a very prominent member of Asquith's government, both before and after the 1915 crisis, having been appointed Scottish Secretary in February 1912.

McKinnon Wood would later play a significant role in the Quintinshill story. It is probable his involvement began at an early stage. Indeed, it is hard to see how he wouldn't have become almost immediately involved given his twin Parliamentary roles. Was he behind a deliberate move from the top to shut down the story, halting intrusive questioning and comment which threatened seriously to embarrass – at the very least – the interests of those he represented at both constituency and national level?[4]

If so, it worked. With a notable exception, newspaper coverage of the dramatic accident abruptly ceased. Even allowing for legal considerations such as the law on *sub judice* following Tinsley's arrest, the almost total sudden disappearance of reportage suggests some sort of government edict. Neither did the press and the public in general get a sniff of a continuing inquiry process – whether this was effectively part two of Colonel Druitt's examination or a private separate inquiry carried out by the Caledonian and then filed as the official Board of Trade report.

It is impossible now to state with any certainty which of the two it was. What can be said with absolute certainty is that the document preserved at The National Archives reflects evidence taken at a later date, subsequent to the Carlisle hearing, evidence that was clearly heard in secret.

On the face of it the published report suggests a wider scope of investigation – it included evidence from twenty-six witnesses, five more than were heard in Carlisle. Evidence taken from expert railway witnesses was there in abundance, though each of those specialists was in the employ of the Caledonian company. Typically for Board of Trade inquiries of the period, at which the inspector himself was regarded as the sole independent expert, railway expertise from sources outside the Caledonian sphere of influence is conspicuous by its absence.

Given the fact that the archived report is documented on Caledonian Railway notepaper, the likelihood is that the proceedings upon which it is based were held on company premises, most probably the Central Hotel in Glasgow, which formed – and still forms today – the imposing station frontage of the Caledonian's Glasgow Central main line terminus. Edward Druitt may well have been present to hear the evidence presented but, if he was, it is hard not to conclude that his hands were tied by higher authority.

Again, it all smacks of a conspiracy to conceal the full facts and serve the interests of just about everybody concerned – the Government, the Caledonian and its managers, the British railway system as a whole and the public. Everybody, that is, except the railwaymen at the heart of the story.

The inquiry process was under fire at the time. It was a far from perfect procedure and the cracks were apparent before the outbreak of war. Holding sessions in private was not without its perils. It had certainly backfired at Major Pringle's Ais Gill inquiry when those barred from the initial private hearing at Kirkby Stephen – at the behest of the Midland Railway – included the National Union of Railwaymen's leader, Jimmy Thomas MP, adding considerable fuel to a long-running dispute about the refusal of railway companies on whose tracks an accident had occurred to permit union representatives at inquiries. Thomas was not a man to be brushed aside lightly. Turned away from the hearing, he responded by giving an impromptu press conference on the station platform to the intense embarrassment of both the Midland company and the Board of Trade.[5]

No barrier was imposed to prevent Thomas attending the opening of Colonel Druitt's Quintinshill inquiry in Carlisle, though it seems doubtful that he was involved at all in the proceedings held subsequently in private.

The Ais Gill examination represents something of a watershed in terms of public confidence – or the growing lack of it – in the inquiry process. Some of the reaction to its deliberations and findings were scathing in the extreme.

In his fascinating book, *Respectable Radicals*, Professor David Howell records how 'even such a respectable and cautious Labour figure as Arthur Henderson was moved to criticism.' Noting that the inquiry had been 'little more than a farce... the outcome was inequitable', Professor Howell quotes from a report in a December 1913 edition of the *Derby Daily Telegraph* which set out the dismissive comments of the man who would soon become Labour's first-ever Cabinet member in Asquith's wartime coalition: 'The company is saved from serious criticism while the servants are seriously indicted.' The report was 'worthless' except for its demonstration of 'an obsolete system.' It highlighted 'beyond contest the predominating influence of the railway companies. They are all powerful before the supine and inept administration of the Board of Trade.'

Commenting on this in his book, David Howell adds: 'For Henderson this was a robust reaction. In part it perhaps reflected the place occupied by railway companies, not just in Labour but also in Liberal demonology. They were seen as powerful and often autocratic corporations which were unenlightened on labour questions and ready to place shareholders' interests above everything else. Within the House of Commons the 'railway interest' was dominated by reactionary Tories.' Thus we have the political context which is essential to understanding the varying industrial perspectives surrounding the mighty British railway industry of the period.

There seems little doubt that the interests of its shareholders were uppermost in the minds of the Caledonian's directors in the wake of the Quintinshill disaster. The company went out of its way to eliminate any suspicion of systemic corporate failure. From this surely inarguable truth it is not too mighty a leap to the conclusion that the crisis-ridden wartime British Government was complicit in the conclusions which masquerade as an impartial Board of Trade inquiry report at The National Archives in Kew.

Colonel Druitt was little more than a nominal supervisory presence once the inquiry process acquired secret status and the Caledonian Railway was granted an apparent free hand to dominate proceedings, manipulate the evidence and reach a set of conclusions that in no way suggested fault in its managerial and ultimate corporate structure and systems. The company absolved itself from blame, unhindered by any damaging press intrusion while in the process of putting together its inquiry report for Board of Trade adoption. The newspapers, probably by decree, dropped the story until the Carlisle coroner's inquest, the larger of the two held in northern England, which began in earnest on 23 June, a week after the Caledonian had forwarded the report to the Board.

It seems inconceivable that any of this could have happened without the compliance of Asquith's troubled government. It might, and certainly should, have been a different story in peacetime – even an obsolete inquiry system would have been hard-pressed to save the Caledonian entirely from censure – but this was wartime and there were overriding considerations for the Government. Conveniently, ready-made scapegoats, men seen as of little if any consequence in the grand scheme of things, were there for the taking. They had undoubtedly broken company regulations and were easy to nail as the architects of disaster once their employers were themselves freed from the need to play by the rules.

Initially the Caledonian acted in a manner that would be expected of any major railway concern in the event of a disastrous accident on its premier main line. Senior management and directors needed to see for themselves the extent of the carnage at Quintinshill, hence the private train which carried them to the remote signal box on the day of the tragedy. But they were, not unexpectedly, beaten to it by the company's senior man in the area, Gretna stationmaster Alexander Thorburn. Advised at 6.55am by the station's signalman that there had been a crash, it seems he had run to Quintinshill, arriving there at 7.15. No doubt shocked by the appalling devastation, he nonetheless wasted no time in going straight to the signal box.

With the benefit of the evidence that would later emerge of James Tinsley's erratic behaviour and apparent confusion, it is easy to speculate that Thorburn was very probably deeply disturbed by what he discovered in the box. It is therefore hard to accept that his version of events, given in a sworn witness statement, is an accurate account of what actually happened.

'I… saw James Tinsley, the signalman. He was perfectly sober and in his usual good health,' Thorburn would state. The signalman, according to Thorburn, told him, with extraordinary understatement, that 'this is a serious business' but the stationmaster then added that 'I didn't speak to him.'

This extract from Thorburn's precognition statement for the High Court has an air of unreality about it. Especially hard to believe is that Tinsley would not have been asked by his immediate boss how such a dreadful event had occurred. Thorburn must surely have spoken to him. Given what would soon be known of Tinsley's true state of health, it is not difficult to construct the hypothesis that Alexander Thorburn's evidence was an attempt to hide the truth and spare him and the company the embarrassment, and consequent censure, of employing a man with a pre-existing medical condition that, had it been known, would have prevented his recruitment. The fact that Tinsley had evidently not told his employers about it would not have offered much in the way of comfort for the company.

They should have ensured his health was up to the demands that would be placed on him as a matter of routine in any of their signal boxes, let alone one controlling a section of one of the nation's most important routes.

Thorburn had apparently not been questioned on this post-crash episode in the signal box when Colonel Druitt opened his inquiry in Carlisle. Either that or he *was* questioned and the press covering the hearing all chose to ignore it, which seems highly unlikely. The visit to the box was recorded, however, in the document now archived as the Board of Trade's official inquiry report. Yet in the evidence from Thorburn which forms part of the preserved record the stationmaster did not refer to Tinsley's state of health, whether good or bad, at the time he (Thorburn) arrived in the cabin. Indeed, he made no specific mention of talking to Tinsley at all.

'I went to the signal box to ascertain [he does not say from whom] what had been done in the way of getting assistance, and found that most of the stationmasters near at hand had been advised to send assistance – doctors, ambulance men and materials…' reads Thorburn's recorded evidence.

The lack of any reference to Tinsley's sobriety, his 'usual good health,' which Thorburn was anxious to mention in precognition, is, on the face of it, baffling. But if we follow the hypothesis that the Caledonian Railway was intent on giving the impression Tinsley was functioning normally at the time of the accident, perhaps the prevailing corporate view was that it was probably better, safer, not to mention his health and mental stability at all.

To be fair to Thorburn, he does deserve some credit, according to the recorded evidence, for helping to co-ordinate the Caledonian's rescue operation. 'I took the [undamaged] engine of the 4.50am goods train and went to Kirkpatrick to open single line working up to the point of obstruction in order to be in a position to bring the trains with assistance from that end [the north] as soon as they arrived,' he said, adding that he then returned to Kirkpatrick with all the wagons of both the goods train and the empty coal train that it was possible to remove from the crash site.

While there is no justifiable reason for questioning the accuracy of Thorburn's account of his involvement in the rescue, a cynical viewpoint would be that the inquiry report was motivated by a desire to stress the 'plus factors' for the Caledonian and bury any hint of corporate failure. The impression from the report is that, after a very shaky start in Carlisle, the stationmaster had managed to get his act together. In contrast to his unconvincing response to Druitt about his last inspection visit to Quintinshill prior to the accident – 'I don't know the date, but it was not a week ago' – the official inquiry report eliminated any suggestion of doubtful recall.

'I made a point of visiting Quintinshill signal box in turn with the other signal boxes as frequently as my duties would permit, sometimes twice per week but not less than once per week, and have always found things in very good order. I have also visited the signal cabin occasionally at night, the last time about 10pm about two months ago. I last visited [the] signal box on 18 May, four days prior to the date of the accident…' read Thorburn's now very precisely recalled account.

The stationmaster's apparent leap during the inquiry process from vagueness to absolute clarity on the inspections issue was replicated in statements he made for the Carlisle coroner's inquest in June and the High Court trial in Edinburgh, which followed in September. In the former he recalled, imprecisely, visiting Quintinshill box 'three or four times a month' during the previous eighteen months.

The stationmaster added: 'I have never visited at six o'clock in the morning. It never occurred to me to go when the signalmen were changing [shift]. I have gone there at ten at night. I was not aware that the signalmen were not keeping to the appointed hours. When they sign their names in the [train register] book they put the hour at which they sign opposite and I check these from time to time.'

In his precognition statement for the High Court Thorburn adopted a far more professional, and very much more detailed, approach in outlining his inspection regime, now recalling – as happened with the second of his contrasting Board of Trade inquiry accounts – the crucial point that he had last inspected the signal box prior to the crash on 18 May and even providing the time of his visit that day – 1pm.

Once more this raises the recurring questions about Thorburn's testimony. Why hadn't he remembered the 18 May inspection when preparing his deposition for the coroner or when giving evidence before Colonel Druitt in Carlisle? Was he simply being more thorough in his later statements? Had his memory been jogged?

Or had Thorburn been directed by somebody higher up the Caledonian Railway's line of command to 'firm up' his wobbly earlier evidence and steer the company away from potential meltdown onto safer ground? The more his statements on this and other key issues are studied and compared, the more likely this appears to be. Judging by the Board of Trade report it appears he had finally learnt his lines. His statement on the inspection regime was now more or less in accord with that of assistant superintendent of the line, Robert Killin – though Thorburn still made no reference to the two visits undertaken to Quintinshill box on behalf of the railway's district inspector the day after his own inspection check. Those visits had been 'flagged up' by Killin at the inquiry's opening in Carlisle.

Why did Thorburn not mention them? It can, of course, only be conjecture but if, having discovered something of serious concern about the operation of Quintinshill box, it was Thorburn who called in the district officer, his apparent reluctance to refer to this later in evidence might not be so difficult to understand. It would have avoided potentially awkward questioning as to what precisely he had discovered, why it had not come to his attention before and why nothing had apparently been done about it in time to avert the tragedy of 22 May.

Maybe Thorburn had been alerted to a problem with James Tinsley when he inspected the box on 18 May. Or had he earlier detected, or been told of, a development in his near neighbour's health which threatened his ability to work properly? Had this prompted Thorburn to visit the box on the 18th and subsequently call for an inspection visit at district level? Considering that his station house at Gretna was literally across the road from Tinsley's home at the heart of the small railway community, this seems highly likely. The community lived cheek by jowl. Keeping secrets from the neighbours was unlikely.

What Thorburn may have known or belatedly discovered about Tinsley's illness is impossible to say, though it seems inconceivable that he could have known nothing about it. The only certainty here is that he was never asked, so far as the record tells us, about any of this in examination or invited to explain why there had been so many visits to the signal box in the week preceding the disaster.

Had he been properly questioned about this, stationmaster Thorburn might have been exposed not only as an inept manager but also as a liar – or at the very least, a man very economical with the truth – and a breaker of company rules himself. In breach of regulations, he had failed to keep records of his signal box inspections. It appears that he was relying on his memory alone – and deleting from it any of the bits that might have got him into trouble. No wonder his bosses, or somebody representing their interests, had apparently stepped in to erase from the record the feeble words of a man whose signal box inspection regime was in danger of being revealed as an unmitigated failure.

As noted, apart from being the Quintinshill signalmen's immediate superior, Thorburn was a near neighbour of James Tinsley's at Gretna's station cottages. Yet in his evidence preserved in the published Board of Trade report he claimed not to have been aware of the Quintinshill pair's unofficial late shift change arrangement. His ignorance of the illicit practice, he explained, was due to the fact that Gretna's station porter, rather than he personally 'usually passes [clears for departure] the 6.17am local train from Carlisle unless… I have cash to send to Lockerbie Bank by it – and I had not much opportunity of finding this out' – a statement that surely indicates inept management or plain deceit.

Thorburn was not in a position to observe George Meakin's early morning routine as Meakin did not live in the same neighbourhood, but he must surely have been aware of Tinsley's given that the latter lived so close to his own home. 'I understand he took care to keep out of my way when he was late in coming out,' said the stationmaster in his recorded inquiry evidence. While Colonel Druitt would eventually reveal his own incredulity about this barely, if at all, believable statement, Alexander Thorburn seems not to have been openly challenged on it throughout the Board of Trade's inquiry process – but then, neither was he apparently challenged when, in June, he provided an embellished account of the same story in the statements he made for use at the Carlisle inquest.

In these he insisted that he had never seen Tinsley going for the early morning local train when late for work – nor had he ever seen the signalman get on the train. At the inquest itself he claimed that Tinsley, on his furtive route to the station, would 'go behind the railway and I would have no chance of seeing him if he got on the engine of the slow passenger train.' Asked to expand on this feeble remark, he said Tinsley would 'go by the road to get on the engine, and at the station the water tank would prevent me from seeing [him] on the engine.'

It all seems highly implausible if not downright ridiculous. If Thorburn had known of Tinsley's supposedly devious route to the station, then he must have been aware of the signalman's motive. Indeed, if he knew of Tinsley's route, then presumably he saw him take it. Tinsley might have been temporarily obscured from view by the water tank but if he had stayed behind it he would never have got on the train! He did, of course, several times, and the truth is that Thorburn, or any member of the station staff assisting in clearing the train for departure, would have to have had a clear view of the locomotive and anyone climbing aboard from wherever they stood on the platform. Perhaps Thorburn could have elaborated further and explained these apparent anomalies – though it's difficult to see how – but he was never asked to.

With Thorburn denying he had ever witnessed Tinsley take the early morning local train to work, it should have followed that he would specifically have denied seeing the signalman entering the cab of the magnificent Cardean class locomotive when it paused with the local service on the morning of 22 May. However, the surviving evidence from him on this point, while vague and contradictory, does not constitute such a denial. It strongly suggests the opposite.

Was Thorburn on the Gretna platform that morning? Did he see the local train leave? As far as can be gleaned from the press reports, he was not asked to confirm or deny this by Colonel Druitt or anyone else when the inquiry was opened at Carlisle, and the official Board of Trade report makes no mention of it one way or the other, but the stationmaster's statements for the coroner are more revealing.

'On that particular week I was on duty every morning. I saw the 6.29 [the local train's departure time from Gretna] go out,' said Thorburn in what appears to be clear-cut confirmation that he saw the ill-fated local service depart on the 22nd.

It comes as no surprise that when it was Thorburn's turn to give evidence at the Carlisle inquest he back-tracked to a significant extent, now claiming that he was 'only on the platform twice that week' to see the slow passenger train leave the station at 6.29. Not only did this apparently contradict his earlier written statement for the coroner but also, astonishingly, it appears that nobody at the inquest thought to ask him whether those two days had included the morning of the 22nd.

In that later statement Thorburn had stopped short of lying to the coroner about his presence on the platform that Saturday. If he was there, and he surely was, he could hardly have denied it outright – that would clearly have risked contradiction by others, notably Gretna signalman Roger Kirkpatrick, who, fully aware of the late shift change arrangement, had signalled Tinsley onto the train and would have been aware of the stationmaster's proximity. In fact Kirkpatrick's own statement for the Carlisle coroner provides the strongest indication that Thorburn *was* present when the local train pulled out of Gretna station:

'Witness could not see the platform of the station very well from his cabin so he could not say whether the stationmaster was aware that Tinsley got on the engine.'

Roger Kirkpatrick's evidence might not have proved that Thornburn witnessed Tinsley's departure on the 22nd but it most certainly countered any suggestion that the stationmaster was anywhere other than on the station platform at 6.29 that morning . He was there for one purpose – to see the local train out of the station. Thorburn's woolly evidence at the Coroner's Court – neither saying he was or wasn't on the platform that Saturday – appears to have been designed to cloud the whole issue. Clarity, within touching distance had the right questions been asked at the inquest, was neither achieved nor sought. Yet another travesty.

If the Caledonian was, as we believe, trying to cover its tracks and stay free of censure, Thorburn was a huge liability, a man whose statements were seriously tainted by contradiction and vagueness – a man who had clearly failed as a manager.

And if the Caledonian – with the support of higher authority – was seeking to avoid embarrassment, Thorburn would surely have been seen as the weak link in its chain of corporate defence. The company could not afford the focus of failure to move away from the men at the foot of its hierarchical pile, those directly under Thorburn's control. If that focus *had* shifted, just how high might it have gone?

Was Thorburn's own manager, District Traffic Inspector William McAlpine, at fault for allowing, or maybe not recognising, such apparently slack supervision? Interestingly, the recorded inquiry testimony of both Meakin and Tinsley includes an insistence from both signalmen that their rule-breaking shift change arrangement was done without the knowledge of either McAlpine or his superior, District Superintendent W.H. Blackstock. It is hard not to believe that the specific references to these officers was part of a Caledonian Railway attempt to distance the company's senior management from any blame.

How fallible was the Caledonian company's supervisory structure overall? The provocative reader's letter published anonymously on 29 May in the *Dumfries & Galloway Standard* had suggested 'wholesale' non-compliance with the railway company's rules and regulations across the Caledonian system. The company's defensive strategy was consistent – cut off the chain at its lowest link.

Thus, so far as the inquiry was concerned, the mealy-mouthed Alexander Thorburn was effectively rescued from himself. The archived report goes as far as it can to present him as an efficient manager, a man with his finger on the pulse of his supervisory function who, despite his best efforts, was deceived behind his back by men willing to go to any lengths to disguise their shoddy working practices. He had fulfilled his role, had done nothing wrong. According to the report he was just another innocent victim of Britain's worst rail crash.

There is nothing in the Board of Trade's report which suggests Thorburn's fragility in the defensive chain. It would be tested further in other strands of the 1915 investigative process and, when the dust had settled, the Caledonian would punish him for it – but in terms of the disaster itself he would never be brought publicly to book nor have to answer for any contributory ineptitude on his part. This stands as one of the most shameful scandals of the Quintinshill tragedy.

Further up the chain of command, the corporate defence was handled with greater aplomb. Middle management – people like District Traffic Inspector McAlpine, for example – were bypassed and do not feature in the official inquiry record. Instead, senior management figures were relied upon to provide a far more sure-footed, more consistent, approach in the presentation of evidence than Thorburn had been with his. They did not disappoint, but that did not mean they were any fairer on their company's servants in the signal box.

From the inquiry report it seems that District Traffic Superintendent Blackstock took over corporate control of the emergency situation from Thorburn on his arrival at Quintinshill from Carlisle at 8.10am. Naturally he used the signal box as his 'command post' and his detailed description of the dramatic rescue operation is included in the report. His account suggests that he was fully occupied in his co-ordinating role throughout the whole period he was there. If, despite this, he did find time to speak with the signalmen, and surely he would have done at some stage, what they said to him forms no part of his recorded evidence. Blackstock was no bit player in the story, however. Many years later he would posthumously add a revealing and, for the Caledonian, damning, insight.

According to the archived report the company's assistant superintendent of the line, Robert Killin, backed Thorburn's professed ignorance of the rule-breaking shift change. 'The stationmaster at Gretna... was not aware of the practice,' he asserted almost as soon as he began giving evidence, quickly adding that 'the higher officials were necessarily ignorant of it.' Those officials included himself of course. If Thorburn really hadn't known of the arrangement, his superiors almost certainly would not have been aware of it either – though they should have kept closer watch on him – but was there any real need for Killin to mention this? It is yet another example of the company's managers going out of their way to distance the Caledonian from any of the blame.

Killin was as anxious to stress the failings of the signalmen as he was to distance senior management from any responsibility. 'The position, therefore, was that the men had no authority to depart from the specific instructions of the company as to change of shift,' his inquiry testimony reads. That Tinsley and Meakin had broken the rules was inarguable – and Killin's overriding objective seems to have been to hammer home their unquestionable guilt on this matter. Determined as he undoubtedly was to deflect any desire on the part of investigative bodies to look further up the corporate structure for the contributory causes of the disaster, the shift change irregularity was a gift for him.

And the Caledonian Railway was in serious need of acts of unintentional benevolence such as this in the wake of the tragedy. When the special train summoned by the company from Glasgow arrived at Quintinshill around 10am on the morning of the accident it must have been immediately apparent to Robert Killin and the other senior managers who had travelled with him that the Caledonian had on its hands an accident of unprecedented severity. Before long it would surely have dawned on him that the scale of the crash was matched by the enormity of the predicament confronting the corporate interests of his employers. This was a situation which required very careful handling if the railway company was not to become deeply embroiled in the fall-out.

According to Killin's precognition statement and later evidence to the High Court, his first task was to interview the signalmen. Under oath he said that he found both men, though clearly upset, 'in an ordinary state of health.' As with Alexander Thorburn's account of his discussion in the signal box with Tinsley and Meakin, the document filed as the official Board of Trade report makes no mention of this. Again, the question of Tinsley's health and mental state is expunged. It reads as if Killin had had no direct contact with either man on the day of the accident, Yet, according to Killin's witness statement for the High Court, he asked Tinsley while in the signal box to explain the cause of the crash.

The reply would certainly have given Killin cause for concern over the signalman's fitness for work that morning: 'I forgot about the local passenger train on the up line and I brought on the troop train.' Killin was possibly the first to hear of Tinsley's extraordinary memory lapse. Obviously puzzled, he pressed Tinsley on the point. 'He knew it [the local train] was there but it escaped his memory entirely,' was Killin's statement for the Scottish judiciary records.

It must have been obvious to him that Tinsley could not have been functioning properly. Something was wrong with him. Though it was certainly not without precedent, experienced signalmen did not usually forget they had a train standing on a main line, especially one right outside the box, while another was bearing down on it. Yet Killin's statement for the court was virtually comment-free. He raised no possibility of any underlying cause for Tinsley's memory lapse.

And according to the Board of Trade inquiry report, it was not even a matter worthy of mention.

Robert Killin's only aside on Tinsley's forgetfulness (noted in chapter five) related to the disputed question of which of the signalmen had sent the 'train out of section' signal for the Welsh coal empties to the box to the north, Kirkpatrick, once that train had been stabled in Quintinshill's southbound loop. Tinsley, it will be recalled, claimed that he had recorded the signal in the box's train register but said it was Meakin who had actually sent it. It was this remark that had prompted Killin's comment, 'The question is, how far does his memory take him?'

A fair point, but not one apparently deemed worthy by Killin, or possibly his superiors, for inclusion in his evidence to the resumed – if that's what it was – inquiry, now preserved at Kew. Again, it appears only in his statement for the court.

In that statement Killin added that, having spoken to Tinsley in the signal box with George Meakin standing close enough to hear clearly the conversation, he then called the latter over for questioning. Meakin's immediate response was to say that 'Jamie forgot all about the local train being on the up line and brought on the troop train' – more or less an exact repeat of Tinsley's own astonishing admission. What Robert Killin made of this is not recorded – anywhere – and therefore does not feature at all among the evidence in the Board of Trade's inquiry report.

The fact that Tinsley most certainly *had* forgotten all about the local train could not be avoided – it would consistently remain his simple, albeit extraordinary, explanation for the accident – but the impression given by the Board of Trade's official account is that his Caledonian Railway superiors had decided to leave him to tell the world all about that without in any way elaborating on it themselves and inviting awkward questions about what might have lain behind it. He forgot about the local train. End of story.

According to the inquiry record, Killin's evidence was all about rules, regulations and procedures – how these were impeccably maintained by senior management and shamefacedly broken by the men in the signal box. Thus, he backed stationmaster Thorburn not only on the shift change irregularity but also on his signal box inspection regime while repeating his condemnation, made initially to Druitt in Carlisle, of disregard in the box for crucial safety issues such as the rules governing lever collars and blocking back. Killin over-egged and sliced up the evidence on both counts.

With regard to the signal box inspection regime, his detailed outline of supervisory visits made to Quintinshill cabin, provided for Colonel Druitt's open session and now belatedly corroborated up to a point by Alexander Thorburn, was enshrined in the Board of Trade's report. Thus the bit that Thorburn left out, where Killin noted the two visits made on 19 May by the district inspector's assistant – 'the object of these… being to see that the company's regulations are obeyed and that there are no irregularities of any kind' – forms part of the unquestioning published record.

Was this meant to convey the impression of a supervisory system taken very seriously by the Caledonian Railway and diligently carried out? Probably it was, but if slapdash operation of Quintinshill signal box and blatant disregard for company regulations on the part of the signalmen was held to be the single cause of the accident, why had this not been picked up on one of the many inspection visits which the company maintained had revealed nothing to concern them? The probability remains that something disturbing *had* come to light, hence the two district level inspections on the 19th, but nothing was done.

The failure by George Meakin to use the signal collar to protect the local passenger train was an undeniable breach of regulations. Another gift for those concerned with holding him and Tinsley entirely responsible for the disaster. 'When the… train was being shunted through the road [crossover] the signalman who authorised that movement should have placed a lever collar on the lever of the up main line home signal and this collar should not have been removed until the local passenger train had been cleared off the main line,' reads Robert Killin's evidence in the report. Signalling staff, he adds correctly, had been advised in April 1912 of the need for signal collars in a company circular.[6]

This, at least, was consistent, a point made repeatedly by the Caledonian throughout the investigative and judicial process in 1915. Technically, they were right to do so. Morally, the company was surely at fault for ignoring the fact that Meakin hardly needed a signal collar to remind him – and Tinsley – they had a train standing just a few feet away right outside the signal box on the southbound main line, the very train in which Tinsley had just travelled to work.

Consistent too was Killin's evidence, recorded in the Board of Trade's report, on Meakin's failure to use the blocking back procedure – it was as unfair to the signalman as Killin's statement on the same issue had been when Colonel Druitt opened his inquiry in Carlisle. In fact, it was word for word the same. Evidently this was one issue where it was felt expedient to reproduce faithfully in the published document the evidence given at Carlisle. The reasoning behind this would appear to be simple – no amount of manipulative amendment to the evidence could have made matters significantly worse for Meakin on this point. Once again his failure to block back was presented without the mitigation it deserved.

Thus a crucial part of the evidence in the inquiry report is Killin's insistence that Meakin, having secured the empty coal train in the southbound loop, should immediately have given the blocking back signal – or made sure Tinsley did so when the latter relieved him – to keep the up line back to Kirkpatrick clear of traffic and the stationary local train safe at Quintinshill on the same track.

Conveniently, Meakin's case that company rules neither made it his duty to complete the task once his shift ended or supervise its completion by his mate was ignored by the Assistant Line Superintendent. As was Meakin's perfectly legitimate point that he couldn't have blocked back because he had already moved the local train to make way for the Edinburgh express behind it and Caledonian rules forbade blocking back once that manoeuvre had taken place. Neither could he have blocked back earlier as the train of empty coal wagons was still making its way to the passing loop along the section of track concerned and the required permission from Kirkpatrick box had not been given.

If Killin's selective quotation of his company's blocking back rule had been shockingly misleading when he made it in Carlisle, to find it enshrined in the official report is little short of criminal. Its stark message that George Meakin had, to a large extent, invited the initial collision because he had not blocked back has remained unchallenged until now as a key cause of the Quintinshill tragedy.

But it's worse than that. It appears that the Caledonian went to even greater lengths to hoodwink Druitt, the Board of Trade and anybody reading its report about the blocking back rule. Shamefully, it was disingenuous in the extreme.

In the report's preamble Druitt quoted from two sections of the relevant company rule, To add further substance to this, he attached the exact wording of these extracts, sections (a) and (c), cut and pasted from the rule book. It is clear from surviving documentation that this was all he was shown by the railway company. Taken on their own, sections (a) and (c) did imply that one or other of the Quintinshill signalmen should have followed the rule and blocked back to Kirkpatrick, just as Killin had asserted. There was nothing in those two sections which implied otherwise. However, had the crucial missing section (d) been forwarded to Druitt by the Caledonian, this would have shown that the rule could not have been enforced for precisely the reasons explained by George Meakin.

Robert Killin was not the only senior Caledonian manager to visit Quintinshill signal box on the day of the accident. Also there was the man with the ultimate responsibility for signal box supervision, the company's Chief Inspector, Andrew Binnie. He would surely have been deeply concerned about the implications of what he was told on arrival. If we accept the Caledonian's version of events, all reports from Binnie's inspection team prior to the crash had indicated that the cabin was being run efficiently by its regular signalmen with the high degree of professionalism he, and the company, would have expected from its experienced operatives. Yet now Binnie was confronted by a raft of apparent lapses and suggestions of bad practice.

What would that have said about the inspection regime in the southern district of the Caledonian system? From Andrew Binnie's point of view, the potential for embarrassment – for his department in general and for him personally – would have been immense.

If, on the other hand, the inspections carried out in the box a few days previously had revealed matters of serious concern to his southern district officers which had not been acted upon – whether Binnie was aware of this or not – his mood would almost certainly have been even darker. Either way, and it remains a matter for conjecture, this was a desperately serious state of affairs.

We get an idea of how Binnie sought to deal with this by studying his precognition statement for the High Court. In this he substantially backed Robert Killin's assessment – but Binnie went much further in condemning George Meakin. He declared that Meakin didn't completely finish his shift in the cabin until 6.38, five minutes later than the signalman claimed Tinsley had formally relieved him and at least two minutes before, according to Meakin, Tinsley actually took over the box's operation. No real corroborating evidence was ever produced in support of this apart from a suggestion that Meakin may have helped his mate at 6.38 by taking a telephone call. Binnie, however, was apparently intent on putting Meakin firmly in the frame for affecting crucial decisions taken after his professed time for handing over full operation of the cabin.

In his statement for the court Binnie said that he had 'pressed Meakin a bit harder than witness Killin did as to who performed the movements between 6.25 and 6.38. His admissions made it quite clear to my mind that he was the person who had done so and that Tinsley was speaking truthfully when he stated that 6.38am was the time of his first signalling movement. Meakin's one desire appeared to be to get out of responsibility for having performed any signalling movements after Tinsley entered the box at 6.33.'

This suggests that Binnie's aim was to draw Meakin more deeply into the mire while sidelining Tinsley as far as possible from the major blame – a policy which might be expected from a nervous witness afraid that exposing Tinsley as the main culprit could lead to difficult questions about his mental instability and thus invite cross-examination as to the Caledonian company's ignorance of it.

Maybe it was considered too risky a strategy when the case came to court in September. Binnie's statement, which conflicted with eye-witness accounts confirming an earlier hand-over of control by Meakin, was not used directly in evidence at the High Court. And there is not a single word of evidence from Andrew Binnie among the pages of the Board of Trade's archived inquiry report.

It is worth reiterating why the Caledonian might have harboured a desire to shift the emphasis of blame away from James Tinsley, at least to the point where he and Meakin could be shown to be equally culpable. During the course of the inquiry procedure events had conspired to seriously threaten the company's corporate interests. It had become clear something was wrong with Tinsley on the morning of the disaster. His solicitor had hinted, albeit obliquely, at this with his words to the signalman before Druitt in Carlisle – 'it has been suggested that, if you had been all right, you would have put your signals to danger at once' – and Tinsley's subsequent arrest in an ambulance had considerably fanned the flames of corporate unease. When the Scottish press covering the arrest talked of him being 'subject to fits' the alarm bells would certainly have been ringing loudly in the boardroom of the Caledonian Railway.

A signalman prone to fits, presumably suffering from the effects of a medical condition of which his employers, although they should have done, had no prior knowledge, was being named as the prime culprit behind this dreadful accident. If Tinsley was to 'carry the can,' it would almost certainly follow that he would drag down the company with him. This would have become even more obvious when the Caledonian, having carried out a reconstruction of the accident, confirmed, no doubt to its horror, that the second collision could probably have been prevented had Tinsley done as he should have done and put all his signals to danger as soon as the Royal Scots' troop special had collided with the stationary local train. The situation would have deteriorated further if it were shown that Tinsley's immediate superior, Alexander Thorburn, *had* been aware of his illness.

For a railway company intent on staying clear of any corporate blame, it would clearly have made sense to attempt a muddying of the investigative waters by bringing George Meakin more into the frame and easing the pressure on Tinsley, especially when other aspects of examination – notably the woeful performance as a witness by stationmaster Thorburn – were threatening to heap further layers of corporate discomfiture on the mighty Caledonian Railway empire.

Central to the Caledonian's defence was keeping Tinsley's health issues out of the equation altogether. According to the official inquiry report, the only witness to comment on the subject of the signalman's well-being was James Tinsley himself, insisting that he was 'in a fit condition to do anything I could have done and I was all right at the time.' As his solicitor had inferred in Carlisle – though it was erased entirely from the report – he clearly had been nothing of the sort, which raises the question, was Tinsley himself part of a conspiracy to conceal the truth about his illness and the effect this had on his performance in the signal box on 22 May?

The clear message from the report is the explanation that has endured ever since – that Tinsley was in perfect health. He had simply forgotten the local train. Nothing in his inquiry testimony, nor in the evidence given by other witnesses, suggests otherwise. After hopping off the train on arrival at Quintinshill, 'all recollection of [it] escaped my memory' is enshrined in the report as his unchallenged explanation. How did he account for this extraordinary memory lapse? According to the report, he didn't.

Tinsley would suggest only one reason for his infamous lapse: 'The only thing that I can account for my forgetting the "local"... was my mind being occupied by entering the times of the trains.' He offered this concession in a statement, not made public until after the High Court trial in September. The inquiry report does not refer specifically to this statement, despite its providing an alternative explanation in Tinsley's own words, supporting the suggestions of negligence, to a pre-existing medical condition affecting his judgment in the cabin.

Colonel Druitt had no need of such an admission – he had reached the same conclusion without it in a three-part condemnation of Tinsley and Meakin among his conclusions to the inquiry report. 'This disastrous collision was... due to want of discipline on the part of the signalmen, first by changing duty at an unauthorised hour, which caused Tinsley to be occupied in writing up the train register book, and so diverted his attention from his proper work; secondly, by Meakin handing over the duty in a very lax manner; and, thirdly, by both signalmen neglecting to carry out various rules specially formed for preventing accidents due to forgetfulness on the part of signalmen," he noted.

So here it is in a nutshell – the causes of the Quintinshill disaster officially explained. Historians have relied on those three key inquiry conclusions ever since. Certain things were done by the signalmen which should not have been done. Other things which should have been done by them were not. This is undeniably true but there is no proof that any of the rule infringements direcly contributed to the tragedy. Nonetheless, these were the factors which combined to condemn the men concerned as the culprits of disaster.

And no one else.

Colonel Druitt did give short shrift in his conclusions to Alexander Thorburn's surely ridiculous claim that he knew nothing of the illicit late shift arrangement. 'I find it hard to understand how it had not come to the knowledge of the stationmaster at Gretna during the fifteen months he had been stationed there, as Tinsley lived in the station cottages,' Druitt noted.

But this was as near as he got to criticising the Caledonian's supervisory structure or any of its officers above the level of the men manning the signal box. There was no comment on the suspect inspection regime and failure to record supervisory visits, nor did Druitt question why company rules governing safety precautions – the use of signal collars, for example – had not been enforced. He had in addition failed to check the rules on blocking back, accepting, it seems, what the railway company had told him.

Astonishingly for an inquiry into an accident of this magnitude, Druitt made no new recommendations in order to avoid similar incidents in the future. 'The circumstances attending this disastrous collision, as far as the troop train is concerned, were altogether exceptional,' he noted, 'so, with regard to suggestions for preventing the terrible results from arising from fire breaking out in wreckage after a bad collision, I need only refer to the recommendations already made in previous accident reports, the most important of these for coaching stock on main lines and for express trains etc.'

Stock should be constructed of steel, 'as far as possible, with shock-absorbing buffers,' he wrote, adding that any timber or other combustible material used should be rendered non-inflammable while special attention should be paid to the construction of the doorways, 'so that the doors shall not jam when a collision occurs. Bars across windows should be easily removable, and windows [should] be capable of being opened to their fullest extent.' Druitt noted that some railway companies were already taking steps to comply with the recommendation for non-inflammable timber. He seemed content with this, urgency conspicuously absent.

It was lacking, too, from another of the recommendations forwarded from previous reports – that electric lighting should be provided in all new stock while gas lighting in existing coaches was abolished and replaced by electricity at the earliest opportunity. But, added Druitt, while this was now underway, it 'must necessarily be a slow process spread over many years.'

A third key recommendation was that tools and apparatus for extinguishing fires should in future be provided in all brake vans, sleeping saloons and other special use vehicles. This was a practice, he noted, already being introduced in expresses. He did not mention troop trains.

These recommendations clearly made sense but none were innovative. Especially noticeable by their absence were any specific suggestions to avoid the use of poor quality rolling stock for transporting military personnel and for preventing troop trains from being operated at speeds for which their age and condition rendered them entirely unsuitable and unsafe.

Nor did Druitt see fit to comment on the policy pursued, as far as possible, by railway companies of maintaining as a priority peacetime express train schedules – another contributory cause of the Quintinshill tragedy.

Most conspicuous of all, of course, was the absence of any reference by Druitt to James Tinsley's state of health at the time of the accident. By the time the inquiry report was forwarded by him – or was it the Caledonian Railway? – Tinsley's propensity to fits had been publicised in the press. It was surely a matter, above all others, deserving of investigation and comment. It received neither. The overriding cause of the disaster was ignored.

It is possible to appreciate why secrecy was adopted after the inquiry's opening – though the fact that the ultimate findings and conclusions were seemingly those of the Caledonian Railway remains difficult to grasp – but if ever a railway mishap merited unhindered public scrutiny from start to finish in order to establish the full facts and culpability, it was Quintinshill, the most serious rail accident of them all. There is no record of any public proceedings beyond the Carlisle opening. From that point onwards establishing the truth – the whole truth – behind this calamitous event was sacrificed in the interests of preserving what, in a lop-sided society caught up in the whirlwind of war, was regarded as the greater good.

Even allowing for the possibility that Edward Druitt was simply exercising his right to 'go private' with a continuation of his inquiry, one conclusion can firmly be drawn about the Board of Trade's report. A single word suffices.

Whitewash.

Notes

1. The inquiry report is preserved at The National Archives with the reference number MT6/2423.
2. John Wallace Pringle (1863-1938) had reached the rank of major with the Royal Engineers when, in 1900, he was appointed to the Board of Trade's railway inspectorate. At the onset of war in 1914 he became a deputy director of railway transport with the temporary rank of colonel. The rank was confirmed in 1916 when he returned to the inspectorate as chief inspecting officer, a post he held until, four years after receiving a knighthood, he retired in 1929.
3. Prompted into being in 1915 by the Shell Crisis, sometimes dubbed the 'Great Shell Shortage', and disastrous naval defeat at the start of the Dardenelles campaign, and plagued throughout by widespread criticism of his weak, vacillating leadership, Asquith's shaky coalition government survived until December 1916 when David Lloyd George succeeded him.
4. Thomas McKinnon Wood (1855-1927) had previously served for a short period under Asquith as Financial Secretary to the Treasury before taking over as Scottish Secretary in February 1912. He was transferred back to his former post at the Treasury in July 1916, remaining in post while simultaneously serving as Chancellor of the Duchy of Lancaster until the fall of Asquith's coalition in December 1916. Two years later, he lost his parliamentary seat.
5. Although Thomas was barred from the secret hearing, his legal appointee, G. A. Lightfoot, did attend.
6. The Caledonian's most recent guidance on blocking back and the use of signal collars were contained in a document relating to block telegraph regulations which had been circulated to signalling staff in April 1912 by the company's General Superintendent, T.W. Pettigrew.

Chapter 10

The Coroner's Triple Indictment

*'What you must ask each other is this: could there be
any greater negligence on the part of railwaymen than
to disobey explicit rules which are a vital part of... a
system which any ordinary man must know is framed
to protect your fellow subjects from a death such as
presented to your minds in this disaster.'*

*Thomas Slack Strong, Coroner, to the
Carlisle inquest jury, 24 June 1915*

When the offices of Carlisle legal practice Bright, Brown & Strong closed
in 1999 a search of the basement below revealed a large collection
of documents, some with obvious historical interest. Saved from
destruction, the papers were placed in the care of Cumbria County Council's
archives service.

Surfacing, literally, among them was a previously hidden and entirely unique
perspective on the Quintinshill rail disaster in the form of the depositions
prepared for the June 1915 inquest before the Carlisle coroner, Thomas Slack
Strong, a former senior partner in the law firm. Those statements have shed
important new light on many aspects of the tragedy, especially the events in the
signal box on 22 May, and have been used – for the first time in this context – in
the preparation of this book. They include the only surviving witness statement
given by James Tinsley.

History thus owes Strong's former legal practice an enormous debt of gratitude
for safeguarding this invaluable archive of evidence. It seems probable that their
preservation was ordered by Strong himself. He was by all accounts proud of the
way he ran the inquest and, when he died at the age of 81, his obituary in the
Cumberland News made particular reference to this role as a career highlight for a
man the newspaper described as 'one of the outstanding personalities of the district
for many years.' Historians, Quintinshill author John Thomas for one, have been
equally fulsome in their praise of Strong's part in the investigative process.[1]

But, while we may make full and good use of those revealing unearthed documents today, Coroner Strong seems not to have done the same in 1915.

Indeed, in most respects his inquest turns out to be just as incomplete as the Board of Trade inquiry. Why, for example, did the lamentable failure of the fire brigade to respond quickly, something which drew serious criticism at the time either side of the border, not feature in his examination? The underlying cause of the inferno, primitive gas-lit coaches, wasn't examined either. It was highlighted in the press coverage, the *Carlisle Journal* using its leading article on 25 May to draw attention to it. Strong made only brief reference to it – and then only to urge the jury to leave such matters as the future use of gas on trains to the Board of Trade.

These were surely highly relevant to any investigation into the deaths of the twenty-seven Quintinshill victims the Carlisle inquest was concerned with – those who had died within the city's boundaries from their horrific injuries, so many of which, directly or indirectly, were the result of the fire.

It seems extraordinary that Coroner Strong did not take any of this into account, but he was, of course, far from being the only public official who failed to do so. To find an explanation for these apparently inexplicable omissions there is a need to consider once more the broader context of wartime Britain in the trouble-torn year of 1915, a time when individuals, especially those of the working class, were expected to pull their weight in the national interest – and to carry the full burden of responsibility for tragic failure irrespective of shortcomings at corporate level.

The rise of trades unionism, the voice and influence it gave to the working man, outraged and frightened the elevated social classes. Industries essential to the war effort were not immune to disputes with the workforce. In the eyes of many this amounted to blackmail and in some cases was even regarded as treachery. Coroner Strong probably saw it that way.

A man with colourful personality and steely determination, he no doubt was genuinely trying to get to the truth behind Quintinshill's disaster. But the coroner was a man of his time and his investigative perspective was narrow.

Prior to Quintinshill he had officiated at a September 1913 inquest into the deaths of victims of the disaster at Ais Gill, high in the Yorkshire Dales on the Settle-Carlisle route, in which two trains, heading south from Carlisle in the early hours of 2 September on the first stage of their respective journeys to London, straggled up the formidable gradient towards Ais Gill summit behind locomotives with barely sufficient power for the task. The first train stalled on the climb, seriously delaying its progress; the second ploughed into it from behind, with catastrophic results.

Rules had been broken. The main cause was generally regarded as being the failure of the second train's driver to proceed with caution, having failed to observe several signals which should have kept him at a safe distance from the train in front. The crew of the leading train were also at fault, for failing adequately to protect its rear with prescribed safety methods.

These were undeniable errors but, as with the troop train at Quintinshill, wooden-bodied, gas-lit coaching stock was a key factor in the crash and in the subsequent fire which led to sixteen fatalities and thirty-eight injuries, a higher toll than would otherwise have been expected. The Midland Railway's policy of relying on small locomotives and the use of poor quality coal were among other corporate issues brought into question, both at a separate inquest in Leeds – where some of the victims had died – held the day before the Carlisle hearing, and at the Board of Trade inquiry.

While the Leeds inquest determined that Samuel Caudle, driver of the second train, was chiefly responsible, the jury noted that 'we do not consider in the circumstances that it amounts to culpable negligence.' In line with the Board of Trade, they felt the negligence and contributory causes to have been a lot more widespread than the failings of just one man. Rejecting the coroner's view that Caudle should be indicted on a manslaughter charge, the jury returned a verdict of death by misadventure – despite being asked three times by the coroner to retire and reconsider this![2]

In Carlisle the next day Coroner Strong tried his utmost to succeed where his counterpart at Leeds had failed. His conclusions were based entirely on the rule book. Company rules had been flouted. That was enough. The individual railwaymen who had broken the rules, Caudle in particular, were to blame – full stop. Mitigating circumstances and contributory corporate failings formed no part of Strong's summing-up to the inquest jury. Caudle was duly indicted on a charge of manslaughter by the court.

In the event, while a trial at the Cumberland Assizes upheld the charge, a plea for leniency was accepted by the judge, due in no small part to the circumstances and contributory factors identified by the other investigations – not least the corporate failings on the part of the Midland Railway.

Now, in 1915, Strong was considering the far more devastating consequences of another railway disaster with rule-breaking servants of a railway company at its heart. Were Tinsley, Meakin and fireman Hutchinson, the three men who undeniably had flouted Caledonian regulations, already guilty in Strong's eyes before his inquest got down to business on 23 June following its brief opening and adjournment on 25 May? Does this explain why his investigation was so narrow and why crucial aspects of the disaster, such as the failings of the signal box inspection regime, were ignored by him? He had his ready-made culprits. Working class men who had let down their superiors, passengers and the nation.

Why look further?

Coroner's courts are no strangers to railway and other industrial accidents, but their scope and methodology has changed significantly since 1915. At that time a coroner's jury retained the power to commit someone for trial, a right seldom exercised after the mid-1930s and formally withdrawn by the Criminal Law Act 1977. Coroners' juries, once universally used, are rarely called upon today in England.[3]

However, in today's litigious environment the evidence taken at inquests can often be the precursor to claims made against those found to have been corporately responsible, partly or wholly, in an individual's death. This would have seemed strange to early twentieth century Britain. Rarely, if ever, did a company face charges as a result of an accident resulting in the death of an employee. A verdict of misadventure would have been the norm.

Neither did fatal accidents involving employees on the railways necessarily require a Board of Trade inquiry. It was left to the railway company itself to investigate the cause and merely present its findings to the coroner. Strong would have been used to such procedures and, as there was no notion of corporate liability, he would have been inclined to accept those findings as presented. It is therefore no real surprise that at his Quintinshill inquest he clearly took the Caledonian word without demur.

In considering the context of Coroner Strong's inquiry it is important to note – a factor not fully appreciated by writers on the disaster – that the public had been presented with a narrow understanding of the likely causes.

The Board of Trade's public inquiry in Carlisle had revealed 'astonishing facts,' to quote the newspaper headlines, about James Tinsley's failure to remember the presence of the local train outside his signal box. It was well known that there had been a series of irregularities on the part of both signalmen and that Tinsley had subsequently been arrested.

The fact that he had been taken to court at Dumfries in an ambulance was also public knowledge but the virtual blackout on press coverage since then had prevented anything other than speculation as to the reason for this. Suggestions of corporate failure had been mooted in the local press but that was as far as it went. For the most part, public incredulity and outrage had the one narrow focus – negligence in Quintinshill's signal box.

The citizens of Carlisle had seen the appalling results of the tragedy at first hand. It is not hard to imagine their desire for explanation and a thirst for justice to avenge the fate of the victims. An inquest provided the route for this – but did the city, or anywhere else in England, have the jurisdiction to hold such an inquiry, with the power to indict the perceived perpetrators for criminal trial? The accident, after all, had happened across the border in Scotland. Most of the victims had died there.

North of the border, where James Tinsley had already been charged with culpable homicide by James Kissock, the Depute Procurator Fiscal in Dumfries, the law was different. Under the Scottish process the arrest and charge had preceded the country's inquest equivalent, a fatal accident inquiry.

It is clear from correspondence classified for a century in 1916 as secret but released by The National Archives in 2012 following a Freedom of Information Act application by the authors, that neither Kissock nor Scotland's chief prosecutor, Lord Advocate Robert Munro, wanted a separate inquest in England with the power to indict. They argued for the right to pursue criminal proceedings under their own legal system without the complication of a simultaneous process south of the border. Referred to the Home Office, their case was overruled. The Carlisle inquest would be allowed to proceed without restriction following the usual English process.[4]

If Coroner Strong felt he had all the credentials and the necessary background information to crack this one, if the truth he sought was, in his mind at least, pre-destined – that the disaster was solely the result of flagrant rule-breaking on the part of working class railwaymen in the signal box – he was helped by what seems to have been an extraordinary intervention by the Caledonian Railway. If his mind was open to persuasive argument and he was willing to consider all possibilities in his quest for the truth, then that very same act was lying in wait to thwart him.

As described in chapter six, the evidence of that intervention came, literally, in the form of James Tinsley – his dramatic metamorphosis from the pathetically haggard figure shivering convulsively at the Sheriff's Court at Dumfries a month earlier, into the smartly dressed young man who appeared to be the picture of health as he arrived at Carlisle coroner's court on 23 June. Tinsley looked so different that some recent commentators on the tragedy, having studied photographs of him at both hearings, have assumed that the images cannot possibly be of the same man and that the picture taken at the inquest is actually of his mate, Meakin!

Far from appearing crushed by the terrible burden of responsibility – the only man at that stage charged in connection with the slaughter at Quintinshill – Tinsley looked relaxed, almost carefree. Any risk of another courtroom collapse had been eliminated. There would be no risk of his later being declared unfit to stand trial, thus opening the door to press speculation, censor or no censor, and potential corporate embarrassment. No hint was evident of the extreme stress he would still have been expected to display just a month after the disaster – stress that would certainly not have helped an underlying medical condition such as epilepsy.

Along with the British nation as a whole, Coroner Strong was being deliberately deceived. James Tinsley would face the processes of the judiciary as an apparently fit and healthy, if criminally forgetful, young man.

As we have argued, he must surely have been complicit in this subterfuge. In exchange for being the Caledonian Railway's first (though not the last) sacrificial lamb, submitting to whatever penalty lay in wait, he and the family to which he was devoted would be protected by the company so that the otherwise very real prospect of long-term unemployment as a man believed to be suffering from epilepsy, family destitution and possibly even the dreaded workhouse, would be banished. This is the only plausible explanation. It was a mutual understanding, a pact on which, as events transpired, both sides would ultimately deliver. It can be said with conviction that the Caledonian had done a very good job on him.[5,6]

That Tinsley's health was an issue in the weeks preceding the Carlisle inquest is undeniable. Surviving documents include one which refers to the fact that access to him was at that time restricted because of concerns for his condition. A letter from the Caledonian Railway in response to an inquiry on 17 June from Coroner Strong reflected the company's view that 'it would be as well that you should arrange with Mr Lightfoot [Tinsley's solicitor] for the attendance of Tinsley at the inquest as he is presently under suspension from his duties owing to the state of his health.'

While this does not in itself necessarily suggest anything other than understandable shock, it is interesting to note that the coroner had been informed of Tinsley's health problems before the inquest yet, in line with everyone else who attended the hearing, made no reference to it in the court.

Another document surviving from the pre-inquest period is a letter, or part of it, sent apparently – although the remnant which survives does not make this clear – from the railway company's solicitor, D.L. Forgan, to a colleague in his Glasgow office. Oddly, it was clearly sent from Coroner Strong's office in Carlisle. Forgan it seems had travelled south to prepare for the inquest but it is impossible to say why he was writing from the coroner's premises; it might just have been a matter of convenience.

The letter provides evidence that the target, in the eyes of the company, was widening beyond James Tinsley to include both his fellow signalman, George Meakin and George Hutchinson, the local train's driver.

'I have seen the various witnesses today,' wrote Forgan, 'and I have also had a talk with Mr Lightfoot with the view of ascertaining whether Tinsley, Meakin and Hutchinson will give evidence unreservedly as they did at the Board of Trade inquiry. He told me his idea was that they should not do so but [instead should] decline to answer any incriminating questions, though he was to reconsider this.

'That being so, it seems to me it will be necessary to bring all the witnesses who were at the Board of Trade inquiry, and which were included in my list to you, with the exception of Guard Leggat [the troop train's brakesman] who gives no material information. We may be able to dispense with some of them as the inquest proceeds but I don't think it would be safe for them to be absent as my information goes at present. I should be glad therefore if you will arrange for the attendance of them all except Leggat.'[7]

The solicitor's second request in his letter was more problematical: 'Some of the jury may ask for the production of the Gretna stationmaster's periodical reports showing his inspection of the signal boxes, and it would be well to have them at the inquiry in case they are asked for.'

Unhappily for the Caledonian, stationmaster Thorburn hadn't kept any records, despite this being a requirement laid down in company regulations. Rule 96, covering the supervision of signalmen, was clear enough:

'The stationmasters will be held responsible for seeing that the signalmen perform their duty in a proper manner, by night as well as day; and in order to maintain a proper supervision over the men in this respect, it will be necessary for the stationmasters to visit the signal boxes, by night as well as day, reporting to the district superintendent, in writing, at the end of each month, that they have done so, giving dates and particulars.'

As noted in chapter nine, Thorburn had relied solely on his – distinctly unreliable – memory at the Board of Trade inquiry. There would be no inspection records to produce at the inquest, nor later in the year when the judicial process reached the High Court in Edinburgh. No doubt with this point in mind, five days after the inquest the Caledonian's superintendent of the line, Thomas Pettigrew, was confirming the lack of records from Thorburn and seeking crumbs of comfort in a letter to Forgan:

'The stationmaster does not appear to have made special reports of his inspections of the signal boxes under his supervision, but he signed the signalman's train register book at each signal box on the occasion of his visits.'

Broken rules were covering the Caledonian Railway like a shower of confetti. The result was a mess. Thorburn's inspection failings, typical of his lax supervisory regime, along with the lies and half-truths exposed by his examination at the Board of Trade inquiry, were little short of spectacular. The rules also required him to ensure that signalmen within his jurisdiction were performing their duties in a proper manner and to report any infringement. Alexander Thorburn, of course, had done neither .

The company's district superintendent, W.H. Blackstock, had also fallen down on his responsibilities by his failure to see Thorburn's reports were sent.

It is obvious today that things were very slack on the Caledonian system at Gretna and at district level in Carlisle. It is equally obvious that such a bad state of affairs would prove extremely embarrassing for the company if Coroner Strong chose to dig deeper at his inquest than Colonel Druitt (or whoever was pulling his strings) had done at the Board of Trade inquiry.

Sadly, it is just as plain today that, even if the Carlisle coroner did choose to probe beneath the surface, the Caledonian Railway was determined to deny him, as far as it possibly could, the opportunity to dig out anything other than the conclusion the company itself – and higher authority – was seeking. Its officers had done their own bit of investigating. Their target was widening but it was not going to extend beyond Quintinshill signal box.

A sign of how things were going to pan out at the inquest had come at its formal opening on 25 May when, according to the press coverage, the jury foreman, Fred Telford, spoke emotively 'on behalf of the jurymen and himself

– and he might say they were representing the city of Carlisle,' rightly praising the citizens for their collective response to the tragedy and the courage of the wounded survivors. Feelings were running high.

When Coroner Strong resumed his Carlisle inquest in a packed town hall the press were there in force; the photographs of Meakin and the transformed Tinsley were taken. It had all the makings of a momentous event.

Before any evidence was heard, Strong and the jury had been taken by special train to the crash site where the track layout and the workings of the signal box were explained to them by Assistant Superintendent of the Line, Robert Killin. No doubt he explained the blocking back rule. We can only speculate as to how much of its complexities he strategically omitted.

A separate stark reminder for Strong and the jury of the disaster's continuing tragic outcome had followed when they were taken to the Cumberland Infirmary for the formal identification of Private Michael Gaffney who had died of his injuries during the preceding night. Finally, the party was returned to the town hall for the resumption of business at 11.15.

What followed over the next two days shed little new light on the accident and its causes. In essence it was a re-run of the Board of Trade's public inquiry just a month earlier. The focus was narrow, falling mainly on the evidence of Tinsley, Meakin and, to a far greater extent than at Druitt's inquiry, on fireman Hutchinson. Wider issues were again ignored.

But it is worth the telling as an illustration of how a powerful railway company enjoying widespread respect and admiration among the upper reaches of British society was able to draw on that high regard as a willing ally in order to manipulate so thoroughly the whole investigative process.

Once more the suspicion is reinforced that the Caledonian Railway was now desperate to drag George Meakin as deeply into the mire as it possibly could as part of a strategy to deflect the glare of attention, and its worryingly serious implications for the company, away from Tinsley. The twin spectres of the blocking back and signal collar rules hovered menacingly above Meakin as the knife was sunk firmly and repeatedly into him by the tone of the evidence and the interventions of Coroner Strong, who it seems safe to assume had been misled by Killin at the site visit.

He had the company's rules in front of him – those bits the Caledonian had seen fit to provide him with – and made a point of reading out the relevant sections to the court whenever signalling procedure was mentioned, but it is doubtful in the extreme whether his or the jury's understanding of the complexities was sufficient to properly grasp their meaning.

Things were awkward for Meakin from the start. The evidence of Roger Kirkpatrick, signalman at Gretna, reminded the court that troop trains had precedence over all other traffic, failing to add that, nonetheless, the Caledonian was still striving to maintain its express passenger services at peacetime levels – the crux of Meakin's problem on 22 May. When Kirkpatrick then referred to blocking back, from which his own signal box was exempt, the coroner halted his evidence to read out an extract of the rule to the jury. However, just as Colonel Druitt had been led to do in the preamble to his inquiry report, Strong quoted only from the rule's section (a), leaving out the sections that backed up the action taken by Meakin.[8]

Kirkpatrick was asked by the coroner if he used lever collars. 'Yes,' came the reply. It would be unfair to imply that the witness was lying here but this was precisely the response the Caledonian would have wanted their man to give. Rightly or wrongly, it made George Meakin, who hadn't used the collar on 22 May, appear decidedly second-rate, a point quickly hammered home by Strong when he read out the relevant rule in its entirety.

Before he had uttered a word, Meakin was clearly in need of help. Solicitor Lionel Lightfoot, representing his interests as well as those of Tinsley and Hutchinson, came to his aid by seeking from Kirkpatrick his own interpretation of the blocking back rule. 'Before they caused any obstruction either inside or outside the home signal they must get permission from the box to the rear,' the Gretna signalman told the lawyer.

Lightfoot then asked a specific question about the rule. In part, the exchange that followed underlined the crucial point about when blocking back was possible, but for the most part it can only have confused the court.

Lightfoot: 'Supposing you were the signalman in charge of a box and concerned in moving a train from one main line to another, do you give the blocking back signal before you place the obstruction on the line or afterwards?'

Kirkpatrick: *'Before'*

'Do you say it is the duty of the signalman who moves the train from one line to the other before the movement is commenced?'

'It depends on the circumstances.'

'Suppose there is one train standing at the home signal, you must give it [the blocking back signal] before you commence the movement of the train?'

'Yes – it might be different if there was another train standing at the home signal. I could not give that signal before I commenced the movement. I would give it after I had cleared the other line. It would be necessary to put the indicator on in that case. In the ordinary case I would give the blocking back signal before I commenced to put the obstruction on the line, but in the case where I have a train standing at the home signal in my rear, I do not give that blocking back signal in fact until that train in the home signal is clear. In any event I would not alter the indicator lock.'

It is not hard to imagine the expressions of utter bewilderment in Carlisle Town Hall after that. The coroner, his jury, the lawyers and all but the signalmen in the courtroom surely could not have understood a word of it! Whether they picked up on the two most salient points of the whole exchange – the need to block back *before* obstructing the line and to seek permission first from the signal box to the rear, along with the reasons Meakin was unable to do either – is hard to tell. The likelihood is they didn't.

Robert Killin's probably selective interpretation of the rule when he addressed coroner and jury at the crash scene would not have made those key points clear and they were then lost without trace amid the mass of evidence. Which begs the question: why didn't Lightfoot challenge Killin on the rule at Quintinshill and query everyone else who later similarly misquoted it? We should probably not be too hard on the solicitor for his weak defence on this point and, indeed, on others too. As at the earlier inquiry hearing, he had been handed the invidious task of representing more than one client and clearly had to be careful when coming to the defence of one man that he didn't then shift the emphasis of blame onto another.

The jury would have had far less difficulty understanding Roger Kirkpatrick's next response, this time to Coroner Strong. It was short and succinct – and it twisted the knife still further into the hapless George Meakin: 'The man who put the obstruction on the line must put the collar on. That was the proper thing to do,' he told the coroner. Whether intentional or not – and the suspicion is that the evidence had been rehearsed at the company's behest – Kirkpatrick was sticking to the Caledonian's script. This also looks to have been the case with the next witness, Thomas Sawyers, signalman at Kirkpatrick, the box to the rear (north).

Sawyers reiterated much of what Roger Kirkpatrick had told the court, including the rule on signal collars, but pushed Meakin into an even tighter spot by saying that, when a change of duty was taking place, it was the job of the man who had orchestrated the movement of a train, as Meakin had done with the local service, to give the necessary [blocking back] signal and affix the collar to the signal lever. In other words, there was no doubt about it – Meakin was at fault for failing to follow train safety procedure. Yet again his understandable reasons for not having done so were not defended or even raised by Sawyers or indeed by Lightfoot.

When, following non-contentious evidence from other witnesses, Meakin finally rose to give evidence – having been told by the coroner that he need not provide answers that might incriminate him – he inevitably found himself under considerable pressure from Coroner Strong. It was an awkward inquisition on the rule-breaking irregularities, real or perceived, relating to his shift change arrangement with Tinsley and his failure to block back or use the signal collar, in essence the same questions he had faced at the Board of Trade's inquiry. His responses were similarly in line with what he had told Colonel Druitt a month earlier.

There were exceptions. Prompted by Thomas Sawyers' evidence, the coroner pushed home the point that Meakin should have completed the operations in hand before handing over responsibility for the box to Tinsley. 'Well, I would never be done if I kept on,' he replied honestly and with absolute justification – he was not required to do this under the rules. Sadly for Meakin his words probably did not impress the coroner or jury.

It was much the same with the next set of questions fired at him by Strong, this time on the vexed issue of the supposedly off-putting chatter in Quintinshill signal box with various train crew about the latest war news immediately after James Tinsley had arrived in the box to begin his shift.

Strong: 'Was there any discussion with these brakesmen as to the war?'

Meakin: *'Yes, we were all talking together.'*

'Is it the practice for brakesman and others to come into the box for news?'

'No, not war news – they come to see how long they are going to be shunted for.'

Like many others since, including authors such as John Thomas, who have used it to base their case for blaming Meakin and Tinsley entirely for the disaster, the coroner seems not to have appreciated that there was never more than one of the two brakesman in the box at the same time. Thomas Ingram left as William Young arrived and, while fireman George Hutchinson was there with Ingram – something else Strong seems not to have taken on board – he too was departing the signal box when Young entered. There was no challenge from Lightfoot. There has been none since.

Harassed by the coroner, let down by his solicitor, Meakin was soon subjected to questioning from a new interrogator. It helped neither him nor the court. Jury foreman Fred Telford was the source, revealing that he had little understanding of the situation with which the nineteen-man jury were confronted.

Telford: 'Which was the most important train that morning?'

Meakin: *'The troop train is supposed to be the most important.'*

'It is run like a royal train?'

'Yes.'

'Knowing that, why did you cross the local train over? Why didn't you hold up the express?'

'Because I expected the local train would follow the 5.50 express.'

This, of course, had been Meakin's intention – to hold the local train on the up (southbound) line while the first, Edinburgh-bound, express passed through on the down line and then release the local service in front of the Glasgow express to avoid delaying the troop train as it headed south. Telford, clearly struggling to work all this out in his mind, tried to clarify things:

Telford: 'But the local train was in.'

Meakin: *'Yes, it had been shunted.'*

'Why did you put an obstruction on the line when a royal train was coming?'

'Well, we're supposed not to delay these expresses in the morning.'

'Have you received any instructions to that effect?'

'We have had word, we are supposed to keep a clear road for them.'

This otherwise ridiculous exchange should at least have served some purpose. Firstly, by underlining the predicament facing Meakin in trying to satisfy the competing, often unworkable, demands from his masters to give both troop trains and expresses precedence over all other traffic; and secondly, by making it clear that his planned solution would not have delayed the southbound troop train at all. Both points were in need of clarification. That should have been down to Lightfoot. He uttered not a word.

Without that clarification this passage of evidence was misleading, As John Thomas put it in his book: the jury foreman 'was somewhat unfair to Meakin. In war as in peace the signalmen had been impressed with the importance of keeping the expresses on time. Nor were troop trains ever officially described as royal trains and they did not have priority over express trains unless special instructions were issued.' Thomas missed the point that Meakin intended to send the local service between the two expresses but his comment adds further stress to the extreme difficulties confronting the signalman – both on 22 May and at Coroner Strong's inquest.

James Tinsley could not, of course, escape entirely from the fierce line of questioning. He was still very much in the frame and the coroner did not shirk in his frequent references to the rule book from reminding the jury of Tinsley's own transgressions. He quoted, for example, from the rule which forbade all but the locomotive crew to ride on an engine without specific permission. Tinsley had no such permission when he hitched his footplate ride to work from Gretna en route to his disastrous shift.

The probability that stationmaster Alexander Thorburn, despite his constant vagueness on this and other matters, saw Tinsley clamber onto the engine from the Gretna platform, all but confirmed by Roger Kirkpatrick's evidence (see chapter nine), does not appear to have raised an eyebrow.

Cautioned by the coroner, as Meakin had been, about incriminating himself, Tinsley's grasp of what had happened on the 22nd was again shown to be poor – at best. The *Cumberland News* reported his recollection, in reply to questioning, that the shunted local train was in full view of the signal box while it was stationary.

His next statement was that 'Hutchinson, the guard [a reporting error – he was actually, of course, the local train's fireman], had signed the [train register] book and, if [Tinsley's] entries had been made up in the book from six o'clock he would have seen the signature to remind him that the local train was there.'

This was presumably what Tinsley had told the court. But it simply wasn't the case. He had confirmed at the Board of Trade inquiry that he had given Hutchinson the register book to sign – albeit, it transpired, on the wrong page – after his late arrival in the signal box around 6.35. From that moment Hutchinson's signature *was* there to remind him of the stationary local train – the very same train Tinsley had got off minutes earlier.

A quick check of the register by the coroner – it had been brought to court – would have clarified this piece of key evidence. Strong failed to ask for it. As for his questioning of Tinsley about his forgetfulness, the coroner barely managed to scratch the surface. 'Now tell us – take plenty of time over it – how was it you did not remember the train on the up line?' he asked.

'I forgot all about it, sir,' was Tinsley's unhelpful statement of the obvious! And that was that – no further questions from Strong on this key issue.

The only reference to Tinsley's health, for what it was worth, came from his solicitor in an exchange with the signalman concerning his late start arrangement with Meakin and a possible reason for implementing it on 22 May:

Lightfoot: 'Were you in your usual health that morning?'

Tinsley: *'Yes'*

'Where were you the night before?'

'At my home.'

'Not in Carlisle?'

'No'

There had apparently been local speculation that Tinsley had spent the evening before the accident drinking in Carlisle. This would explain Lightfoot's line of questioning but the suggestion did not re-surface to any extent in the subsequent investigative process. Lightfoot certainly took it no further – and neither did he or the coroner question Tinsley on his abject failure to respond to events following the initial collision which were clearly the behaviour of a man who was very far from being in good health.

For the first time, local train fireman George Hutchinson, who lived in Carlisle, took centre stage. That he too was now seen as a candidate for a share in the blame was confirmed when he received the same caution from Strong regarding incriminating responses that Meakin and Tinsley had earlier been given. The ever watchful *Dumfries & Galloway Standard* reported his evidence in full, confirming that Tinsley had climbed down from the train's locomotive as it was crossing onto the up line. Hutchinson had then followed the late-arriving signalman into the signal box.

Lightfoot: 'Did you remind the signalman of the position of the local train?'

Hutchinson: *'No sir.'*

'Why not?'

'I did not think it was necessary.'

'Because he had gone [travelled] with you?'

'Yes.'

The coroner quoted the company rule which stipulated that Hutchinson, as fireman of a train shunted across to the 'wrong line,' should have checked that the signal collar was affixed to the lever in order to protect it.

Strong: 'You did not ask for that assurance?'

Hutchinson: *'No sir.'*

'You did not see the lever collar on the home signal?'

'No sir.'

'On previous occasions when you have been on this train and it has been crossed to the up line, have you gone to the box?'

'Yes.'

'Have you ever seen the lever collar on?'

'No sir.'

'Then why did you go to the box?'

'Just to sign the book.'

The questioning of Hutchinson now turned to the situation in the signal box.

Juryman: 'Do you know which signalman was on duty?'

Hutchinson: *'I took Tinsley to be on duty.'*

'Had you any conversation in the box with Tinsley?'

'Nothing at all until after the 5.50 [the departure time from Carlisle of the Edinburgh express] *had passed. Tinsley just said, "We will have to keep you for the 6.05* [the Glasgow express].*"'*

Lightfoot (taking over the questioning): 'Was Tinsley standing at his desk?'

'Yes, he was reading telegrams.'

The probability, though it can be no more than that, is that Tinsley was actually reading the notes on train movements which Meakin had compiled for him, by arrangement, on the reverse of telegraph forms before his late arrival for work.

Of the two brakesmen in the signal box prior to the first collision, the goods train's Thomas Ingram and the empty coal train's William Young, it was the latter who contributed the more telling evidence to the inquest, though Ingram did help Meakin by confirming that the signalman had briefed Tinsley on his arrival of the situation on the line. Otherwise, Ingram was noticeably cautious in his responses – he hadn't seen a newspaper in the box or heard any war news while he was there, and neither had he witnessed any of the signalling operations that were taking place around him.[9]

According to the *Cumberland News* , William Young was on the receiving end of the coroner's authoritarian manner almost as soon as he began telling of his visit to the signal box – as Hutchinson and Ingram were leaving – to check how long his train was going to be kept in the passing loop. In reply to Strong he said he had not signed his name in the train register.

The coroner, consulting the rules, pounced. 'It says you *should* sign in the book.'

Young stood his ground. 'It does not say so in the appendix,' he replied – correctly.

Strong was having none of that. 'It's quite clear, isn't it? In future you must sign your name.' The coroner's authority had been challenged – hardly surprising as he had greatly exceeded it here – and he now resorted to his caustic wit in an apparent attempt to bring Young down a peg or two after the brakesman insisted his only question to James Tinsley was about his train's delay – the question which the signalman either ignored or didn't hear.

Strong: 'You did not ask about the war?'

Young: *'No.'*

'You did not want the war news? What were you doing?'

'Looking at the pictures on the wall.'

'The cocks and hens in the corner.'

Just about every line of this exchange was greeted with laughter in the courtroom. In fact, as noted in chapter five, Young had a genuine interest in poultry but the coroner's patronising tone had left him sounding foolish, an unreliable witness. Shamefully, Strong ignored the possibility that the brakesman might be telling the truth – it wouldn't fit with the theory that Tinsley had been distracted from his duties by animated chatter in the signal box.

There was little of consequence from remaining witnesses as the first day of the inquest drew to a close. When it reopened the next morning a trio of railwaymen provided graphic but non-contentious accounts of the disaster before the time came for Gretna stationmaster Alexander Thorburn to give his evidence.

Much of what Thorburn told the court has been described in the context of his evidence to the Board of Trade – his early involvement in rescue coordination, his imprecise recollection of his signal box inspection regime, his professed ignorance of the illicit shift change arrangement, his denial that he ever saw Tinsley, when late for work, hitch a lift from Gretna on the local train and his highly questionable explanation as to how he had missed this. Unlike his frequent quoting of company rules when Meakin, Tinsley and Hutchinson, the three men under suspicion, were being examined, Coroner Strong apparently did not resort once to this course in response to Thorburn's answers.

Thorburn told the coroner he had never visited Quintinshill signal box at 6am. Asked why not, he said it was 'an untimely hour for me seeing the time I leave at night.' Agreeing that six in the morning, coinciding with the hour the men should have been changing shifts, might have been an important time for a visit, he told Strong it had never occurred to him to do so.

Confirming that he checked the train register periodically and that the signalmen's signatures gave the impression that they had changed shifts at the authorised hour, Thorburn should have found himself in a very tight spot when Strong asked him if he compiled reports of his visits for his superiors. He had not done so, of course, a breach of the rules of which his employers were now well aware. The stationmaster needed to be rescued. On the face of it, not an easy task for Caledonian solicitor, Forgan.

The company's lawyer had to admit they hadn't brought any written reports from the stationmaster to the court. It hardly mattered, he implied, as the evidence of his visits was recorded in the signal box's train register book.

Somehow Strong did not see fit to force the issue. He certainly should have done. This was critical evidence of system failure, a serious flouting of the rules. Strong let it go and it stands as one of the most glaring examples of how the Caledonian Railway, aided by virtually non-existent interrogation of its more senior operatives, was allowed to get away with any hint of corporate misdemeanour or fragility. Given the lamentable imbalance in the coroner's attitude towards witnesses, it comes as no surprise that he did not challenge Thorburn either on his laughable explanation for repeatedly missing Tinsley's furtive approach to Gretna station – behind the railway... behind the water tank – when late for work.

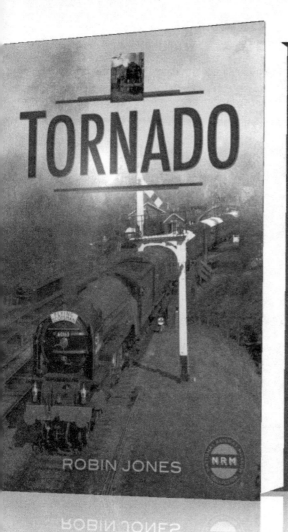

TORNADO

ROBIN JONES

HB 9781844681204 •
208 pages • Fully integrated
with colour pictures • £19.99

fficially endorsed by the A1 Steam locomotive trust, Tornado is the official account of the building of itain's first main line steam locomotive for 50 years, how it took a team of volunteers 18 years to ise more than £2-million to build it and its international headline-grabbing debut on the main line, ith a royal visit thrown in for good measure.

The book looks at the history of the A1 class and the East Coast Main Line which they were built run on, the man who designed them, Arthur H Peppercorn, the preservation movement which olved from a handful of volunteers saving a cash-strapped steam railway in central Wales in 1949 to e point where it could build a main line express passenger locomotive, and how the dream of ilding Tornado came to fruition stage by stage at Darlington. Tornado is lavishly illustrated with both chive and contemporary photographs bringing the story up to date.

HAT THE CRITICS SAID:

compelling story of the new build A1.'
ITISH RAILWAY MODELLING

HB 9781845631451 •
Epub 9781783409952 •
Kindle 9781783406319 •
176 pages • Fully integrated
with colour pictures • £19.99

Following the success of the first two rebuilt 'Claughton' class engines, the London Midland & Scotti
Railway (LMS) in 1932 embarked upon a building programme of fifty more 'Patriot' class 5
locomotives. The new 4-6-0 locomotives were at first referred to as 'Baby Scots', until officially nam
the 'Patriot' class in 1937. Two batches of the new 3 cylinder engines were built simultaneously, forty
Crewe and ten at Derby. In 1948 British Railways took all fifty-two 'Patriot' class engines into stock a
subsequently eighteen of the class were rebuilt as '7P' locomotives. Although successful in traffic a
popular with engine crews and enthusiasts alike, no example of these trains survived into preservatio

This definitive work looks at the details associated with each member of the class and archi
images of all fifty-two locomotives are featured. In addition to looking back this comprehensiv
researched and highly informative account of the LMS 'Patriot' class also details the plan to build t
53rd member of the class, to be known as locomotive No 45551 THE UNKNOWN WARRIOR.

WHAT THE CRITICS SAID:

'This book would be a welcome addition to the bookshelves of any exponent of the LMS.'
Steam Railway Magazine

'Providing a detailed account of it's history and packed with plenty of photographs, it makes
fascinating read.'
Best of British Magazine

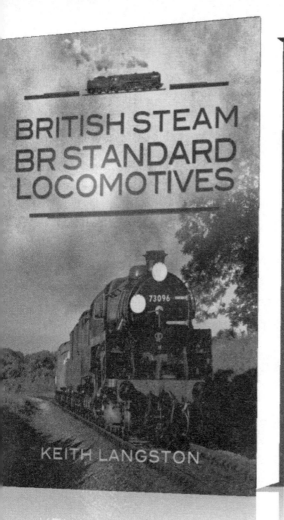

HB 9781845631468 •
Epub 9781783408016 •
Kindle 9781783404377 •
320 pages • Fully integrated
with colour pictures • £25.00

e strains of maintaining rail services during the Second World War had taken its toll on Britain's
am locomotive fleet. On 1 January 1948, the British Transport Commission was formed, which
ced all existing railway companies under the control of one government organization. This would
on to spawn British Railways.

The railway infrastructure had suffered badly during the war years and most of the steam
omotives were 'tired' and badly maintained. Although the management of British Railways was
ady planning to replace steam power with diesel and electric engines, they still took the decision
build more steam locomotives as a stop gap. Cometh the hour, cometh the man! That man was
bert Arthur Riddles; he had more than proved his worth during the war years overseeing the rapid
ation of War Department locomotives. Some 999 Standard locomotives were built in twelve classes
ging from super powerful express and freight engines to suburban tank locomotives. The
omotives were mainly in good order when the order came in 1968 to end steam, with some
omotives being only eight years old.

This comprehensive publication details all the BR Standards and three Austerity type engine
sses associated with Riddles. The locomotive specifications are illustrated and presented in a
nner that will appeal equally to enthusiasts, model makers and railway historians.

AVAILABLE FROM ALL GOOD BOOKSHOPS
OR TO ORDER DIRECT
PLEASE CALL **01226 734222**

OR ORDER ONLINE VIA OUR WEBSITE:
WWW.PEN-AND-SWORD.CO.UK

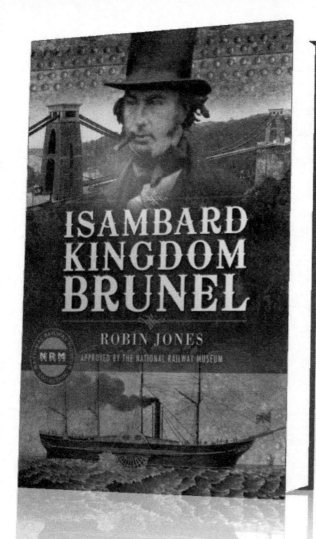

ISAMBARD KINGDOM BRUNEL

ROBIN JONES

APPROVED BY THE NATIONAL RAILWAY MUSEUM

HB 9781844681211 •
Epub 9781783461035 •
Kindle 9781783407392 •
224 pages • Fully integrated
with colour pictures • £19.99

Isambard Kingdom Brunel. Three names. Three people in one. Born in Portsmouth on 9 April 180
there was Brunel the great engineer, who would habitually throw out the rule book of tradition ar
established practice, and start again with a blank sheet of paper, taking the technology of the day
its limits – and then going another mile.

Then there was Brunel the visionary, who knew that transport technology had the power to chan
the world, and that he had the ability to deliver those changes. Finally, there was Brunel the artist
who rarely saw technology as just functional, and strove to entwine the fruits of the Industri
Revolution with the elegance and grace of the neo-classical painter. His bridges, tunnels and railwa
infrastructure have entered a third century of regular use, and the beauty of their design and structu
has rarely been equalled.

The three decades, from the 1830s to the 1850s, saw an explosion of technical excellence, and it wa
Brunel who in so many cases lit the blue touch paper. He did not always get it right first time, and
was left to others to reap the fruits of his many labours. Nevertheless, his actions fast-forwarded th
march of progress by several decades.

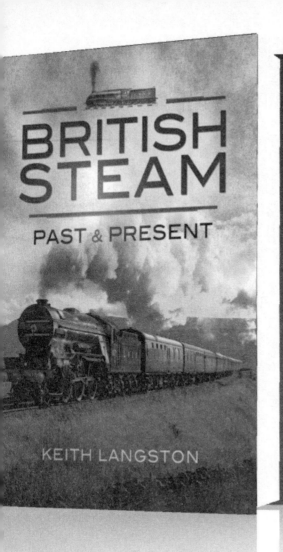

HB 9781844681228 •
Epub 9781781598160 •
Kindle 9781781598177 •
176 pages • Fully integrated
with colour pictures • £19.99

itish Steam - Past and Present contains an evocative mix of specially commissioned modern steam
ages and steam era archive pictures, the majority of which have never been published before.

The work of accomplished steam photographer David Anderson is highlighted in three special
ocation in Focus' features, studies of 1950s and 1960s steam workings at Oxford and on the mighty
attock Bank. In addition there is the photographic record of a 1959 visit to Belfast, with unique
ages of steam on the Belfast – Dublin (ex GNR route).

Original photographic studies from the preservation era included in this book are: David Gibson
ho features the Churnet Valley Railway, Paul Pettitt who features the Bluebell Railway and Southern
gion locomotives, and Fred Kerr who presents an eclectic mix of Main Line Steam images, are all
cluded. Freight locomotive preservation is not forgotten and is featured, using modern and archive
ages. Together with many archive and new images from the author's own collection these images
esent an enthralling window on steam, which is totally unrivalled.

HAT THE CRITICS SAID:

n in-depth account...with wonderful archive pictures bringing our steam heritage vividly to life.'
:ST OF BRITISH MAGAZINE

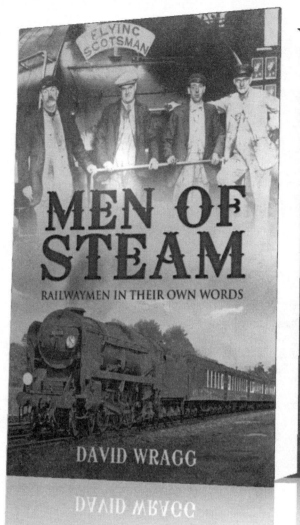

MEN OF STEAM
RAILWAYMEN IN THEIR OWN WORDS

DAVID WRAGG

HB 9781845631338 •
Epub 9781783831450 •
Kindle 9781783031443 •
8pp B&W plates •
224 pages • £19.99

Few modes of travel have the enduring appeal of steam railways. Today preserved lines, locomotiv
and rolling stock attract not just expert enthusiasts but more casual visitors who are keen to savo
the distinctive atmosphere of a lost era in transport history. Yet these relics are but one aspect of th
long story of steam, for they cannot reveal the human side of working life on the railways – th
experience of the railwaymen who operated the machinery of the steam age.

It is this, the human aspect of railway history, that David Wragg has chosen as the subject of th
landmark book. He has selected extracts from the personal reminiscences of railwaymen to create a
all round portrait of the industry in its prime. He records their memories, anecdotes and insights, an
he brings the routines of the steam railway vividly back to life.

Fortunately for us, the railwaymen of that time shared their experiences with one another throug
their employee magazines and their books, so they have left behind them a fascinating record of the
work, their attitudes and concerns. The observations, eyewitness accounts, operating procedure
complaints, anecdotes, and simple descriptions of the long-lost daily routines of the steam railway a
the raw material for David Wragg's remarkable book.

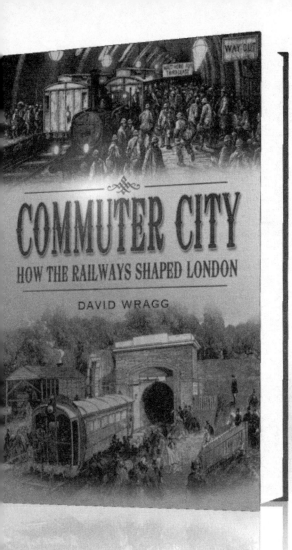

COMMUTER CITY
HOW THE RAILWAYS SHAPED LONDON

DAVID WRAGG

HB 9781845631093 •
Epub 9781844685264 •
Kindle 9781844685271 •
8pp B&W plates •
304 pages • £19.99

n the eve of the railway age, London was the world's largest and most populous city and one of the
most congested. Traffic-clogged roads and tightly packed buildings meant that travel across the city
was tortuous, time-consuming and unpleasant. Then came the railways. They transformed the city and
set it on a course of extraordinary development that created the metropolis of the present day. This is
story that David Wragg explores in his fascinating new book. He considers the impact of the railways
on London and the Home Counties and analyses the decisions taken by the railway companies,
Parliament and local government. He also describes the disruptive effect of the railways which could
not be built without massive upheaval. His study of the railway phenomenon will be thought-
provoking reading for anyone who is keen to understand the city's expansion and the layout of the
capital today.

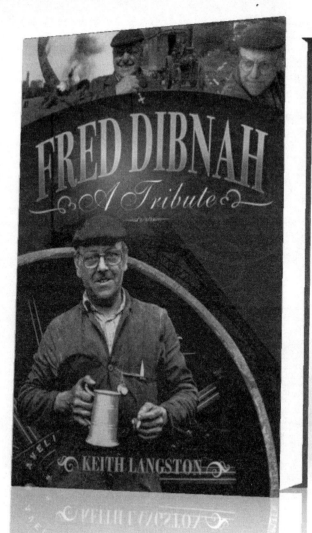

HB 9781845631154 •
Epub 9781783409877 •
Kindle 9781783406234 •
272 pages • Fully integrated
with colour pictures • £25.00

Mid-Cheshire based heritage transportation specialist, photographer and feature writer Keit
Langston travelled extensively with Fred Dibnah during the filming of his last TV series, 'Made i
Britain.' Following Fred's untimely death, Keith embarked upon the creation of a book, drawing n
only on his experiences with the Bolton born steeplejack and TV presenter, but in addition talking t
a representative cross section of those persons who numbered themselves amongst Fred's mar
friends. Fred became a high profile media personality and the fame which accompanied that statu
never affected him, or in any way changed his down to earth demeanour. He will be remembered n
only for his many practical achievements, but also for encouraging thousands of others to care abou
our industrial heritage. The steam bug infected Fred at a very early age, possibly following his illic
visits to his father's place of work, a bleach factory. Encouraged by one of his ex teachers, Fred starte
what he described as 'a steeplejack business'. When he turned to presenting his own programmes h
blunt, no nonsense style made a welcome change from the so called television professionals. H
genius lay in being able to communicate with the audience in simple, direct, colloquial English.

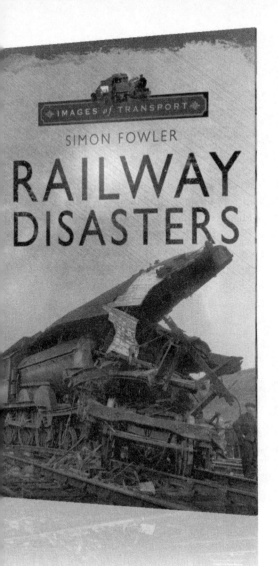

PB 9781845631581 •
128 pages • Fully integrated
with B&W pictures • £12.99

...AILWAYS KILL! British railways are one of the safest ways of travelling. That they are so is the result ...f painful lessons learnt over many decades, for there have been many hundreds of railway disasters.

This book looks at some of the most famous as well as some that have been all but forgotten, ...atching graphic illustrations with eyewitness accounts of people who were there and the ...onfidential reports of the accident investigators who worked out what had gone wrong.

The book explores the reasons why accidents happen. Some are due to the carelessness of staff, ...thers due to equipment failure or poor signalling. Yet others still baffle the experts.

Simon Fowler is a long-standing Pen & Sword author having written many books on family and ...ilitary history. He is a also a professional researcher and tutor.

EXPLORE MORE RAILWAY
AND TRANSPORT TITLES
ALSO AVAILABLE FROM
PEN AND SWORD BOOKS

Pride of the Caledonian. Cardean class 4-6-0 locomotive 907 nears the summit at Beattock at the head of a London–Edinburgh express before its ill-fated trip with the local train from Carlisle on 22 May 1915.

The troop train's locomotive, McIntosh 4-4-0 number 121, pictured on an earlier working near Floriston with a Glasgow to Liverpool / Manchester express.

Lead engine 4-4-0 number 140 of the London-Glasgow express which ploughed into the wreckage of the initial collision is pictured in its original condition before removal of the smokebox whiplash.

Pictured piloting a northbound express away from Carlisle, 4-4-0 number 48 was the fourth Caledonian locomotive involved in the Quintinshill tragedy – as train engine behind number 140 at the head of the Glasgow sleeper.

Fire and smoke belch from the Anglo–Scottish express's sleeping car, the train's fourth vehicle, at the height of the blaze which followed the second collision.

A fire hose is trained on the sleeping car as the blaze is finally brought under control.

Virtually nothing remains above the underframe of the gutted sleeping car.

The wrecked leading coach of the local train in which Rachel Nimmo and her baby died. On the right is the undamaged locomotive of the empty coal train.

Burning debris spills over the wagons of the empty coal train in the passing loop (right) from the tender of local train locomotive 907. Water, which could have been used to fight the blaze, was lost when damaged tenders were split open.

Stationary in the southbound passing loop, the train of empty coal wagons (like the northbound freight in the other loop) suffered considerable damage. Trucks that escaped were later used to remove debris.

In the fields on either side of the railway rescuers tended the many victims of the disaster. This is the scene on the down (northbound) side.

The barn in the background was used as a makeshift mortuary but, with so many fatalities, this and other buildings were soon filled and the fields bordering the railway had also to serve as a collection point for the dead.

Uninjured men of the 7th Royal Scots are prominent in this picture as their wounded comrades are loaded onto the train which will take them to hospital.

The arrival of the Caledonian's ambulance train brought medical personnel and equipment to the remote scene of the disaster.

Some of the few Royal Scots who escaped uninjured from the troop train assemble solemnly in a field alongside the scene of the disaster to have their names taken by their commanding officer, Lieutenant Colonel William Carmichael Peebles, who had gallantly led the rescue operation.

A bacon curer's cart from Carlisle takes on an unusual load as it is stacked with coffins containing the bodies of crash victims at one of the makeshift mortuaries.

Having cycled to the scene, local people gaze disbelievingly at the fire-ravaged London-Glasgow express's pilot locomotive, number 140. Also pictured is the tender of the troop train's engine which the express had violently propelled through the wreckage from the initial crash. On the far left a crane lifts the tangled piles of debris. Several hours after the crash, smoke is still clearly visible.

A breakdown crane crew pose for the photographer after securing the remains of the two locomotives involved in the original head-on smash, 121 (left) and 907, on the track ready for removal. Neither engine could be repaired.

Debris has been pushed down the shallow embankment so that the cranes of the breakdown crews can restore derailed carriages to the tracks and clear the way for a remarkably quick restoration of train services on the busy main line.

Soldiers and residents of Edinburgh and Leith line the streets for the three-mile funeral procession on 24 May for men of the 7th Royal Scots who had lost their lives two days earlier. They are being taken for burial with full military honours at Rosebank Cemetery.

The funeral procession in the Etterby district of Carlisle for the highly-respected troop train driver Francis Scott and his fireman James Hannah.

Driver Francis Scott, killed instantly when his troop train locomotive ran into the stationary local train at Quintinshill.

A gaunt-looking James Tinsley (centre) walks through the streets of Carlisle to the opening of the Board of Trade inquiry at the city's County Hotel.

At Carlisle's Cumberland Infirmary soldiers of the 7th Royal Scots pose with staff who had nursed their wounds.

Laughter is the best medicine! Wounded soldiers of the 7th Royal Scots are photographed with nurses at the Cumberland Infirmary. The majority have swopped uniforms, the soldiers dressed as nurses and vice-versa, for the picture.

Evidence of epilepsy? The seventh line on this note of a telephone message jotted down in the Depute Procurator Fiscal's office in Dumfries records how the initial attempt to arrest signalman James Tinsley was thwarted because, according to a local GP, he had been suffering from epileptic fits and could not be moved.

Lieutenant Colonel Edward Druitt RE, the officer appointed to hear the Board of Trade's public inquiry into the rail disaster. He opened his investigation in Carlisle three days after the accident – but was he prevented by higher authority from carrying out a comprehensive independent assessment of the facts?

The County Hotel in Carlisle where Colonel Druitt held his one-day public hearing on 25 May on behalf of the Board of Trade. The hotel is pictured (left) as it was at the time, alongside the city's main Citadel railway station.

Signalman James Tinsley (left), the first man arrested in connection with causing the Quintinshill disaster, photographed with his solicitor, Lionel Lightfoot, during a visit to the crash site.

Very few photographs have survived of George Meakin. He is pictured here (left) with James Tinsley at the Board of Trade inquiry a few days after the disaster.

Carlisle Coroner Thomas Slack Strong (far right) and the jury visit the scene of the disaster on 23 June 1915 prior to the opening of the inquest in the city. Quintinshill's by now infamous signal box is pictured on the left.

James Tinsley at the time of the June 1915 inquest in Carlisle. His healthy appearance contrasted so vividly with his look and demeanour a month earlier that photographs taken of him at the inquest have often been wrongly identified as depicting his fellow Quintinshill signalman, George Meakin.

Robert Killin, the Caledonian's Assistant Superintendent of the Line, proved a competent spokesman for the company throughout the investigative process – but the evidence suggests that, in his defence of the railway and its procedures, he was economical with the truth.

Quintinshill signal box. Although pictured several decades after the disaster, the cabin's appearance had changed very little.

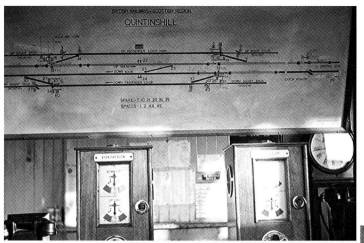

Inside Quintinshill signal box. The track diagram above the instruments is exactly as it was when George Meakin was faced with the complexities of accommodating five trains in quick succession on the fateful morning of 22 May 1915.

A signal collar of the type used at Quintinshill box in May 1915. When in position (as in this picture) it prevented a forgetful signalman from pulling the lever and allowing access to a section of track which was obstructed. George Meakin's failure to use the collar was a key issue during the investigation.

The Springfield area of Gretna as it was at the time of the disaster. The pointer identifies the Maxwell Arms, the pub run by George Meakin's wife. Trade was brisk there on the weekend of the crash and some have questioned Meakin's sensitivity in choosing to help his wife serve the flood of thirsty sightseers.

William Dickie, editor of the *Dumfries & Galloway Standard*, who singularly sought to widen discussion on the causes of the disaster via the letters page of his newspaper, in defiance of an apparent government clampdown.

Herbert Asquith, the UK's Liberal Prime Minister when the Quintinshill crash in May 1915 served as a disaster too far for his beleaguered administration. It helped to force him into coalition with the opposition parties.

Thomas McKinnon Wood, Secretary of State for Scotland at the time of the Quintinshill disaster, whose Glasgow constituency included the Caledonian Railway's St Rollox workshops. The politician most closely involved with the outcome of the decision to prosecute the railwaymen in Scotland and the subsequent campaign to free them from imprisonment. He left office in July 1916.

James Condie Sandeman, defence advocate at the Edinburgh High Court trial of railwaymen James Tinsley, George Meakin and George Hutchinson in September 1915. His oblique reference in court to an epileptic fit supports the likelihood of a deal with the prosecution to withhold key evidence from the jury.

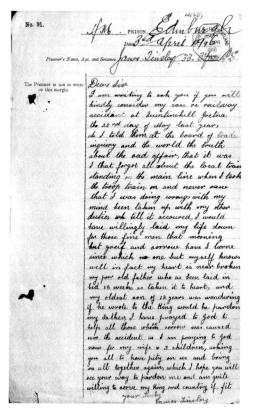

A shaven-headed but elegantly dressed James Tinsley poses for a two-profile picture for the prison records at Peterhead jail following his September 1915 trial and conviction.

A grief-stricken James Tinsley writes from Peterhead prison in April 1916 seeking from the Secretary of State for Scotland his release from jail and expressing his willingness to enlist in the armed forces – a request that fell on deaf ears.

The wily rail union activist Jimmy Thomas MP played a key part in the campaign to free jailed signalmen Tinsley and Meakin – at one stage threatening the troubled Asquith government with a virtual general strike.

An inscribed plaque records the unveiling in May 1995 by the Scottish area of the Western Front Association of a cairn memorial at Gretna Green to the memory of all those who were killed at nearby Quintinshill eighty years earlier.

1914-1918
REMEMBERING

IN MEMORY OF
214 OFFICERS AND SOLDIERS OF
THE 1/7TH ROYAL SCOTS
(THE ROYAL REGIMENT)
WHO, TOGETHER WITH A FURTHER
13 RAILWAYMEN AND OTHER
PASSENGERS, DIED IN THE
QUINTINSHILL RAIL DISASTER,
ON 22ND MAY 1915.

THE CRASH SITE, ABOUT HALF A
MILE TO THE NORTH CAN BE SEEN
FROM THIS SPOT.

ERECTED BY
THE SCOTTISH AREA OF THE
WESTERN FRONT ASSOCIATION.
MAY 1995.

Rachel Nimmo and her baby son Dickson, the youngest victim, both died in the local train at Quibntinshill. They are buried at Elswick Cemetery in Newcastle–upon–Tyne.

This magnificent memorial at Rosebank Cemetery on the Edinburgh-Leith border was dedicated in May 1916, the first anniversary of the disaster, above the mass grave for officers and men of the 7th Royal Scots who lost their lives at Quintinshill.

Mrs Rachel Buchanan, whose mother Rachel Nimmo and younger brother Dickson were both killed at Quintinshill, escaped with her father unhurt and, as the last survivor of the disaster, returned to the area as an 83-year-old in May 1995 to unveil the new memorial to the many victims at Gretna Green.

Quintinsill in recent years. The signal box has gone but passing loops remain in use beneath the wires for the now electrified West Coast Main Line as a Virgin Voyager unit passes on a southbound Anglo-Scottish express. The area retains the air of rural remoteness it possessed on that fateful Saturday in 1915.

Strong seemed to be relishing his time in the nation's spotlight, happy to throw in the odd bit of levity at intervals to lighten the gloomy mood. A good example of this came when Thorburn told him he had not had occasion to speak with either Meakin or Tinsley as to the hours they were keeping. 'Both were steady men,' said the stationmaster to explain his inaction.

Strong: 'Strictly temperate?'

Thorburn: *'Not strictly temperate, I don't suppose.'*

'I mean, not given to drink?'

'Not at all.'

'Too much to ask a Scotsman that he should not take any whisky?'

'Quite so.'

The coroner's caustic wit was again greeted with peals of laughter around the courtroom. It is not recorded how Meakin and Tinsley reacted to the joke. Neither of the signalmen was actually Scottish; both were born in England – Tinsley, as noted, at Ripon in 1883 and Meakin a year later in Carlisle!

Still, Thorburn had gone some way to establishing their good character with his response. He added that the pair had always carried out their duties satisfactorily and his visits to their box had not shown up any default.

But the fact that he had never inspected the box at 6am was awkward for Thorburn. Company solicitor Forgan stepped in at this juncture to assist with a series of questions presumably aimed at clarifying why he had not done so. In reply, Thorburn explained that it was sometimes ten o'clock at night before he finished work, sometimes an hour later than that – not exactly conducive to an early morning inspection visit to Quintinshill. There was also the need – twice in the week of the accident – for him to be at Gretna to see the slow passenger train leave the station at 6.29. Early morning checks on Meakin and Tinsley were further limited by the fact that they did not always work the shifts either side of six.[10]

Jury foreman Fred Telford may have appeared somewhat bemused by signalling technicalities the day before but he had no trouble following the stationmaster's reasons for never carrying out 6am inspections at Quintinshill – and spotted an obvious weakness in what Thorburn had said.

Telford: 'Don't you think their changing at that time to suit their convenience was because there would be no fear of them being inspected at that hour?'

Thorburn: *'I expect so.'*

That was enough for Coroner Strong. Alexander Thorburn was not going to be interrogated in his court. He intervened to ease the stationmaster's plight:

Strong: 'Mr Thorburn could not be there at every hour.'

Telford: *'I am not blaming Mr Thorburn at all.'*

The jury foreman had bowed to the pressure. His point, which had validity, would be taken no further. Once again, Strong had stopped a strand of inquiry which threatened to expose failure at a higher level than that of the three men already in the frame. Thorburn was allowed to stand down.

Company representatives in the court were no doubt relieved when he was replaced in the witness stand by Assistant Superintendent of the Line Robert Killin, a man they could rely upon to shore up a robust corporate defence by reinforcing once more the rules and regulations – or at least his selective interpretation of them – to the detriment of the three targeted men.

Killin's long statement to the court mirrored to a large extent his evidence to the Board of Trade inquiry. Again he drew attention to the lack of the lever collar, skated around the rule on blocking back so that George Meakin's defence for not using it remained, as was now becoming the routine, ignored, and made great play of the (incorrect) 'fact' that the indicator in the signal box was showing 'line clear' when the first of the two collisions occurred. Maybe in an attempt to allay any suspicion that he was out to get Meakin and James Tinsley no matter what, he acknowledged that both signalmen had 'been long in the service and had good characters.'

Then, possibly with a piece of rehearsed corporate strategy, the knife was twisted again into the pair via an intervention from Forgan, the company's lawyer. 'I take it… the result of your evidence here is that in particular there were three things in operation [in theory] as precautionary measures. There was the lever collar, the blocking back and the indicator. Yes?'

Killin confirmed this was the case but added that 'there was a fourth thing that you must not forget – that the "line clear" signal should not be given unless the line is clear, and the signalman, before giving it, should see that the line is clear.' That was surely clear to everyone! Why make such an obvious statement. Was Killin implying that Tinsley should have taken more care to check the line was not obstructed by glancing out of the window of the signal box overlooking the track? Whatever it was, his words no doubt succeeded in piling up the minus points against James Tinsley.

Aided by Strong, Killin was then able to remind the jury of George Hutchinson's apparent laxity, confirming that under the rules the fireman of a train halted by the signal box, as Hutchinson's local service had been, had a duty to come up to the box and satisfy himself that the necessary safety precautions were being taken to protect it. The clear implication here, given the subsequent events, was that Hutchinson had failed to do so.

And then the proceedings, uninterrupted by the coroner, descended from any pretence of investigative objectivity into something more akin to what modern-day observers might call a Caledonian Railway 'love in' as Robert Killin waxed lyrical about the virtues of state-of-the-art signalling systems which he said were kept under constant supervision, and how his employers in particular were constantly striving to keep ahead of the game.

The press reported him as saying that his boss, Thomas Pettigrew, superintendent of the line, 'had had great experience in the matter and was for a long time a member of a committee of experts. Having regard to everything that human forethought could do, the arrangements at the Quintinshill box were

as perfect as could be. It was thoroughly up to date and had been passed [as satisfactory] by the Board of Trade inspector in 1904.'

Company solicitor Forgan then provided a timely cue for a further plaudit, this time aimed at Robert Killin himself for having taken the jury to the signal box the morning before and explaining to them the workings.

'I am sure we are all indebted to Mr Killin for his lucid demonstrations,' the coroner was moved to comment. It seemed like a job well done for the Caledonian's arch rule-quoting – when it suited him – defender of the faith.

But there was a sting in the tail. It was now that Killin was forced to go back on his insistence at the public inquiry (see chapter seven) that it had been the responsibility of George Meakin, having at the end of his shift signalled the train of empty coal wagons into the southbound loop, to give the 'train out of section' signal. Put on the spot for once by the men's solicitor, Lionel Lightfoot, Killin conceded that there was no rule to compel Meakin to continue any signalling operation once he had handed over to his mate, 'but he must see that his mate thoroughly understands the state of matters.' Meakin had done that. Killin failed to score on that one.

It was now time for Thomas Slack Strong to begin what he would certainly have regarded as the most important address he had ever made in a courtroom. Fittingly, he began his summing-up by setting the grim historical context and underlining the appalling scope of Quintinshill's tragedy.

'There have been coroners of our city for certainly seven centuries, probably much longer,' he said, 'but I doubt whether any predecessor of mine over that long period was ever faced with an inquiry which involved such disturbing features as this. Technically we are assigning a cause to twenty-seven deaths, which in itself is a record in point of number for the city, but the [overall] deaths from the same causes are at least seven, and it might be eight, times as great. Then, over and above that, are the maimed.

'We might count heads in this fashion by way of comparison with former disasters, but all comparisons break down hopelessly when we attempt to realise the dreadful scene which immediately followed the collision. The gruesome details are too horrible for recital. It is sufficient to say the demon of destruction had piled up the wreckage and the passengers in a confused heap, and had stirred it up by hurling a second express [sic] into it. He lighted the pile and let loose all the terrors of hell to complete his work.'

While today it carries an air of melodrama, it is right to see those words as an eloquent expression by the coroner of a city's horror at a disaster just ten miles to its north which had so quickly, comprehensively and heroically engulfed its citizens in its sad aftermath. Strong got this bit right.

He continued in much the same vein as he soberly contemplated the disaster's implications: 'So much for the direct results, but in the presence of such horrors we are apt to forget the far-reaching indirect effects on family and business ties

so rudely shattered, all the grief and distress and all the other consequences. We might ponder them but we can't fathom them.'

The coroner now turned to what he and the public at large rightly saw as the crux of the matter before the jury. 'This accident happened on one of the main arteries of our railway system on which many valuable lives of all classes are passing to and fro, particularly in the west coast expresses that run between London and the north. It is vital for this traffic that, before all other considerations, it should be safe. It is essential that it should be protected by all possible safeguards.'

'At present,' he continued, 'the block system of signalling is the safeguard which stands between the travelling public and the horror such as we are investigating. It is their charter and it is your duty as representatives of the public to investigate any infringement of it with very great care. You will be impressed by the way in which it provides for all eventualities that are likely to arise, and more particularly by the duplicate, triplicate and even quadruple precautions for safety which it imposes.'

On the face of it, inarguable. He added: 'After considering the system carefully in the light of all the explanations that have been given, you could not but be of the opinion that, if the human element necessary to its working only carried out the duties assigned to it, no accident would be possible, and in this inquiry you have to consider whether it was this human element that fulfilled its trust or whether it has failed – and if so, how?'

The coroner then made the first of what would prove a catalogue of misleading statements: 'The responsibility,' he said, 'rests on three men.'

Contributory responsibility for the disaster extended well beyond Tinsley, Meakin and Hutchinson right through the Caledonian Railway's supervisory regime to the company hierarchy – and beyond – but this hadn't been recognised by Strong and he wasn't about to change his mind now.

'On the evidence you will find no trace of any default on the part of the signalman at Kirkpatrick or the signalman at Gretna. They seem to have carried out their duties with scrupulous accuracy,' he said. 'You will find nothing in the facts against the drivers of any of the trains affected. They obeyed only too well the signals given to them.' This was undeniably true.

'The responsibility seems, subject entirely to your judgment, to rest with three men only, the signalmen at Quintinshill and the fireman of the slow passenger train, and you will weigh all the evidence as it affects these three men fairly and dispassionately and give due weight to the points in their favour which have been brought out.' Sadly for the three railwaymen those favourable points had been somewhat few and far between.

Strong now sought to 'simplify your labours and avoid confusion.' He urged the jury to concentrate their attention on the up (southbound) line and the signalling of the traffic upon it and to 'dismiss from your view the trains on the down line, because the proximate cause of the disaster is to be found in the

working of the up line, and if you do that the material facts are small compass and there is no real conflict of evidence upon them'

This was a simplification too far. There were a number of issues relating to the down line, not least of which was the fact that the Caledonian's reconstruction of the tragedy had shown that the second collision could probably have been avoided had Tinsley thrown his signals to danger immediately the first crash happened – and prevented the Glasgow-bound express, approaching on the down line, from smashing into the wreckage. That key reconstruction had received not a mention throughout the inquest.

The coroner now reminded the jury of the track layout and signalling at Quintinshill – they had a plan before them to assist in the process – and summarised the train movements there prior to the first crash. In doing so he made a crucial error. Recalling how the empty coal wagon train had made its laborious way to Quintinshill from the north, he concluded by noting that it had 'proceeded from the up line into the loop' and then added that 'practically at the same time' the slow passenger train from Carlisle had arrived on the down line and been halted there by George Meakin.

Here we have one of the classic misinterpretations of the events which led to the disaster. Had the empty wagon train already been installed in the passing loop when the local service arrived it would have cleared the main line and made it possible for Meakin to apply to Kirkpatrick box for permission to block back and prevent the onrushing troop train from entering the section north of Quintinshill. The reality was that, mindful of the need to avoid delaying the first of the two express trains from London, he had shunted the local train across to the up line before the empty wagons had cleared the main line – and company rules prevented Meakin from blocking back once he had moved the slow passenger train across.

It is a point worth repeating. Conflicting Caledonian policy over troop and express train priorities had left him in a near impossible position. The company rule book stopped him from fully safeguarding the solution he chose.

Coroner Strong carried on regardless. The signal box's train register, he told the jury, showed that the two shunting manoeuvres were practically simultaneous. 'You will see on looking at the train register that both of [the trains] are entered as arriving at the same time, 6.30, and the evidence of the men in charge of these trains is that neither was brought to a standstill but proceeded immediately on its arrival to its allotted place.'

There are two points of contention with this statement. First, the train register was, as we have noted, riddled with errors made by the confused Tinsley – hardly a reliable piece of documentary evidence. Second, the coroner implies here that, following their 'practically simultaneous' arrival, the two trains were brought to a standstill at the same time. It would, of course, have taken the slow-moving rake of empty wagons far longer to reach its 'allotted place' in the loop than it would the much shorter passenger train to clatter through the crossover onto the line

opposite. So, even if their respective arrival trains outside the signal box had been identical, the local train would have been there first.[11]

Meakin was being repeatedly let down by the coroner's summation. There was to be no let-up as Strong plunged yet another thrust of the knife into him.

The signalman's decision to replace one obstruction on the up main line, the empty wagons, immediately with another, the local train, struck the coroner as 'a singular thing to have done unless he expected that he had time to let the two expresses pass and afterwards return the slow train to its proper line before the troop train arrived. Had he thought the matter over for a moment it must have occurred to him at least one of the expresses must be brought to a standstill if the troop train was to have precedence.'

This was a disgracefully unwarranted attack on Meakin. Consistently, in his formal statements and in his totally misunderstood evidence the previous day, he had tried to explain that his, perfectly reasonable, plan had been for Tinsley, when he relieved him, to pass the local train on from Quintinshill as soon as the first express had passed through and before the second arrived. This would have significantly delayed neither the troop train nor the expresses – the local train could have been held further down the line to allow the Edinburgh service to pass it. Given the circumstances, it was the best possible solution to an awkward problem which would no doubt have succeeded had James Tinsley been properly alert.

While clearly unimpressed with Meakin's simultaneous shunt, which he had completely misinterpreted, Strong dismissed it as 'a minor matter' and insisted that, no matter what course of action Meakin chose, 'safety would have been secured immediately' had he followed company rules. 'The crossing of a train on to the opposite running line is regarded as an operation which demands extreme care because it is fenced round with precautions which, if observed, absolutely preclude any accident,' he added.

The coroner then took the jury through the various precautions employed by the Caledonia company to safeguard its trains. Having quickly dealt with the signalling itself, he moved on to the 'simple' lever collar rule. 'The obvious result [of using it] is that the signalman, however forgetful, cannot withdraw the signal which protects the obstruction without being directly reminded of the consequences. The lever collar was not used [on 22 May] and it was Meakin's duty to use it.' Strong told the jury this was an issue 'of the utmost importance to your deliberations.'

He did not add the point that Meakin undoubtedly felt that Tinsley should not have needed the collar to remind him of the presence of a train he had just hopped off. So far as the coroner was concerned, Meakin's guilt in this matter was as simple as the rule itself. It had been broken. That was enough.

Meakin had begun the inquest with a far better defence for his failure to block back. Sadly for him, he had succeeded only in confusing the whole matter with his muddled evidence. By the time the coroner's review of the Caledonian's safety

precautions reached the blocking back rule, his chances of a fair hearing on this particularly vexed issue had all but evaporated. They were dead and buried by the time Strong had finished talking.

The fact that the jury had earlier had the rule explained to them, and were advised by the coroner that they could have it read to them again during their discussions, was highly unlikely to have helped the beleaguered signalman. They would very likely have had only Robert Killin's edited version, without the section that would have supported Meakin's case, to rely on.

It was easy for Strong to make the case that, if Meakin had blocked back to Kirkpatrick, no train could have approached from the north until the obstruction was removed. 'The evidence is quite clear that when the slow passenger train was crossed to the up line the signal should have been given, and it is equally clear that no such signal was given. There is no doubt... that it was Meakin's duty to give this signal and he failed again in this.'

Strong now turned to the case against George Hutchinson. 'Such care has been taken in elaborating the system [of safeguards] that there is still a fourth. Rule 55, well known to all the railwaymen concerned, places an important duty on the fireman of the slow passenger train... when his train is crossed to the opposite running line he must proceed immediately to the signal box and remind the signalman of the position of his train. A subsequent part of the rule says that he must return to his train after receiving an assurance that the signalman has protected [it] by the use of the lever collar. He must sign his name in the [register] book as a further reminder.'

Referring to the evidence, the coroner conceded that Hutchinson *had* gone to the box and signed the register book but had then omitted further observance of the rule. 'If this man had done his duty the accident would not have arisen because the lever collar would have been on,' concluded Strong.

The coroner had saved his assessment of James Tinsley's role until last. 'Tinsley's part in the matter requires a little closer investigation,' he said. Never a truer statement was uttered in the entire story of Quintinshill's tragedy, and never was one made that so utterly failed to get anywhere near the ultimate truth, based as it was on evidence devoid of the vital missing ingredient – the fact that Tinsley had been seriously unwell on 22 May.

It was, of course, true that, by clandestine arrangement with Meakin, he had flouted the morning shift change regulations by coming in for work late – 'habitually' said Strong, supporting the likelihood that it was Tinsley, rather than his mate, who most often had an extra half-hour in bed.

Also true were the coroner's references to Tinsley's illicit ride to work on the local train, the fact that it had then been parked a matter of yards away, 'right under his nose,' for the sixteen minutes he was in the signal box prior to the accident, and 'the subterfuge [the copying of the notes of missed train movements into the train register] by which Meakin and he arranged to cloak their breach of the rules.' These were inarguable facts.

'It is for you to consider how his late arrival and the subsequent hurry to get his book up to date contributed to the accident,' the jury were told by Strong. 'However that may be, the fact remains that Tinsley completely overlooked the slow passenger train standing in full view of him in spite of all that had been done to remind him of it. The absence of the blocking back signal enabled him to give the 'line clear' signal to Kirkpatrick and the absence of the collar permitted him to lower his signals from danger.' Put like that, Tinsley – and once again, Meakin – were sunk without trace.

'If the blocking back signal and the lever collar had been made use of,' continued the coroner, 'he could not have caused the accident as he did. On the other hand, his part in the matter is so glaring that it is difficult too see what excuse there can be for him. But you must be fair to him and view his conduct in every possible light.'

Except, of course, the light of any medical evidence to explain Tinsley's extraordinary lapses of memory. The coroner didn't mention that at all – the jury didn't consider it.

Coroner Strong's lengthy summing-up was finally drawing to a close. He now addressed the jury on degrees of negligence as they applied in this case.

'If you find as a result of deliberations that the rules and safeguards have been broken by one or more of the railwaymen concerned or, in other words, there has been negligence, there remains one other point which you must decide, and that is this: is this negligence of such a character, having regard to all the surroundings, as to be culpable negligence – in other words, gross negligence. If so, it was manslaughter.' Strong explained that the gross term in this context simply meant 'very great negligence'.

Winding up to a crescendo, he urged the nineteen men to consider if there could be any greater negligence on the part of railwaymen than to 'disobey explicit rules which are a vital part of this important system – a system which any ordinary man must know is framed to protect your fellow subjects from a death such as presented to your minds in this disaster.'

Strong cautioned the jury to consider each man's case in turn, advised them of the two optional verdicts open to them, either accidental death without culpable blame or manslaughter against one or more of them, and urged that they should leave any suggestions for change – his example was the question of the continuing use of gas in trains – to the Board of Trade.

Fred Telford and his colleagues – 'hard-headed business people with all the innate shrewdness of the northern man', as Strong put it in his parting words – retired at 12.40pm and returned just under an hour later at 1.35.

Their verdict, unsurprisingly, was that the twenty-seven deaths on which they had been asked to deliberate were the result of gross negligence on the part of Tinsley, Meakin and Hutchinson. Clearly some of the jury had been unconvinced about Hutchinson's guilt – seven had voted against an indictment in his case while twelve were in favour. 'Twelve is all I want,' said Coroner Strong, apparently unperturbed by such a sizeable split.

Before the corner could continue the men's solicitor, Lionel Lightfoot, made his last stand – and a good point. 'I would not be doing my duty by the men concerned if I did not formally protest against what I assume will be your next step – to commit these men for trial. You no doubt understand that my protest is based on want of jurisdiction. There are some facts in this case that are perfectly obvious, and the first is that the criminal act that any of these men might have committed was in Scotland…'

'Partly,' interjected Strong, although which part of the disaster he considered had taken place in England remains a mystery to this day. Perhaps he was thinking of Tinsley's late departure for work on 22 May from his home near the station in Gretna, just south of the Scottish border!

Ignoring this unwarranted interruption from Strong, Lightfoot picked up his thread: 'The act was committed in Scotland; furthermore, in respect of one of the men – Tinsley – the position is that the King has already proceeded against him. Tinsley has already been arrested for the crime of manslaughter. It would be absurd to arrest him twice for the same offence.'

Tinsley had actually been charged in Scotland with culpable homicide but the absurdity remained. On the defensive, Strong maintained that, as deaths had occurred in Carlisle, he was within his rights to investigate. That was hardly the point but the coroner wanted no further argument. He formally indicted the three men to stand trial for manslaughter at the Cumberland Assizes, granting their release on bail of £50. Was he right to do so?

Not according to research provided for this book by the Coroners' Society of England and Wales which has revealed a series of irregularities about Strong's handling of the inquest. This has shown that, while he did have a perfect right to investigate, the 1887 Coroners' Act made clear that he was seriously in breach of section five which stated that 'when a coroner's inquisition charges a person with the offence of murder or of manslaughter or of being accessory before the fact to a murder, the coroner shall issue his warrant for arresting or detaining such person – *if such warrant has not previously been issued* [authors' italics].' Tinsley's earlier arrest on a charge of culpable homicide means Strong was in the wrong.

There was another particularly curious irregularity about the Carlisle inquest. Surviving documents reveal that jury foreman Fred Telford had been permitted by Strong to add his comments and questions on depositions prepared for the hearing. His remarks, reproduced as part of the typescript, are not dated but it would appear that he made them before the inquest opened and was thus able to analyse and query the statements provided by key witnesses before he heard a word of their evidence in court!

Many questions could be asked about Coroner Strong's inquest with regard both to its narrowness of focus and its procedure. But Strong was not dishonest; he did not lack integrity. The Carlisle coroner had been duped and manipulated by the Caledonian Railway. Had he been made aware of this during his lifetime there is little doubt he would have been appalled.

Notes

1. Solicitor Thomas Slack Strong served as coroner for Carlisle for more than thirty years, from 1915 – his inquest into twenty-seven of Quintinshill's victims was among his first – until he stood down in 1947.
2. The jury at the Leeds inquest into some of the victims of the 1913 disaster at Ais Gill added riders to the effect that others, in addition to driver Samuel Caudle, shared culpability for the accident.
3. Under the Coroners Act 1988 a jury is only required in cases where a death occurs in prison, in police custody or in circumstances which might affect public health or safety.
4. Reference for Home Office file released in 2012 following FOI request – HO 144/22520.
5. Considerable stigma surrounded the little understood condition of epilepsy in the early twentieth century.
6. As part of the probable pact, Hannah Tinsley was found employment in Carlisle and the family was allowed by the Caledonian Railway to return to company-owned premises – see chapter fourteen.
7. Some of the press reporting the inquest spelt troop train brakesman Charles Leggat's surname as Leggett, however it is the former which is recorded thus in the Board of Trade's inquiry report.
8. Gretna Junction's signal box was exempt from blocking back as it did not have the facility to cross a train from one running line to the other, thus creating an obstacle which would need to be protected.
9. We may conjecture that brakesman Ingram's caution might have stemmed from the letter in the *Dumfries & Galloway Standard* suggesting wider culpability in the signal box – see chapter eight.
10. In his evidence Alexander Thorburn referred to Meakin and Tinsley changing shifts at 6am on just one week in every four. This was not strictly correct. They actually formed the team who worked the late (night) and early shifts every other week, but alternated between the two.
11. It seems from Strong's words that the jury was given the train register to inspect? If so, it should have been obvious from the errors made by Tinsley that something was wrong with him.

Chapter 11

Collusion and Conviction

*'It would not have been criminal negligence if he had
fallen down in an epileptic fit.'*

*James Condie Sandeman KC, defence advocate at
High Court trial, 15 September 1915*

Unsurprisingly, the outcome of the Carlisle's coroner's inquest was badly received in Scotland. There was widespread concern north of the border that Thomas Slack Strong had exceeded his authority by indicting the three railwaymen for trial in England. It wasn't long before Scottish anger and frustration over the matter had reached the corridors of power in London.

The deeply patriotic St Andrew Society, formed in 1907 to study and promote all things Scottish, blamed the Home Office for permitting the situation to develop and directed its protest all the way to Prime Minister Asquith. Unhappy that a coroner's inquest in England was allowed at all and furious at the Home Office's 'instructions... to the English coroner to commit certain of those concerned for trial at the Cumberland Assizes,' the society's vigilant committee asked Asquith to press for an apology from the Home Office for what they considered had been 'unconstitutional action.'[1]

James Tinsley's committal from the Carlisle court in particular made little sense to anyone. In the House of Commons Scottish MP Hugh Watt asked who had given the instruction for Tinsley's second arrest – as a result of the coroner's indictment – in Carlisle. He was told by Sir John Simon, the Home Secretary, that no definite instructions had been given by anyone in his department. He declined to intervene, stating that deaths had occurred in Carlisle.

'Is it fair that this man should be liable to be apprehended twice for the same offence?' asked Watt. Simon ducked the question, resorting to speculation about whose trial would prove the first – the English or the Scots.

With the Scottish Lord Advocate, Robert Munro, reportedly perturbed by the stalemate – which was probably putting it mildly – the Scottish authorities decided to take matters into their own hands. Warrants were issued for the arrest of George Meakin and George Hutchinson by the Depute Procurator Fiscal at Dumfries. Now the Scots had all three accused railwaymen in their grasp. The

two nations' legal powers consulted and commonsense finally prevailed. The trial would be held in Scotland.

It opened on 14 September 1915 at the High Court in Edinburgh. With the investigative focus now wrested back from England, the interest in Scotland was substantial as the proceedings began before Alexander Ure KC, Baron Strathclyde. the Lord Justice General. The courtroom bristled with what the *Dumfries & Galloway Standard* called 'a great array of legal gentlemen engaged in the case'. Press and public were inevitably also well represented in the crowded chamber. 'Many of the public who turned up failed to gain admission,' the *Standard* reported, but those who did get in included 'a number of ladies.' Whether those women were relatives of the disaster's many victims or just sightseers was not recorded.[2, 3]

Leading for the prosecution was the Lord Advocate himself. Handed the tricky brief of defending all three accused, as solicitor Lionel Lightfoot had done at the earlier hearings, was the distinguished Scottish barrister James. Condie Sandeman KC, a man with no illusions about the task ahead of him which would test to the full his renowned ability for coolness under fire.[4, 5]

Once more proceedings would be dominated by the omnipresence of the Caledonian Railway. It was again their officials who would provide all the evidence relating to railway technicalities. No independent expert witnesses would be called. With the sole exception of Charles Morrison, the police inspector who had arrested James Tinsley, all those who would give evidence were on the Caledonian payroll and none were there to assist the defence. Sandeman would be left to question as best he could, hampered by having little real knowledge or understanding of railway matters.

The Caledonian was thus able, once again, to make misleading statements unchallenged to the detriment of the men in the dock. An early example came with the evidence of senior company engineer W.A. Patterson who fired a broadside at Tinsley by insisting his view of the local train on the southbound track would not have been obstructed by the presence of the empty coal train in the passing loop between the signal box and the main line.

While on the surface this was true, Patterson had ignored completely the fact that the box's design dictated that Quintinshill's signalmen worked with their backs to the railway so, unless Tinsley had turned round, he would not have been looking out of the front window and would not have this visual reminder of the stationary local service on the up line. At no time was the court made aware of this, a significant factor in the accident.[6]

Thus the prosecution already had a head start when Robert Killin waded in with a lengthy re-run of what was effectively the case for the prosecution. George Meakin's failure to adopt the prescribed safety devices was an easy uncontested 'kill' and for good measure Killin added that, in his opinion, Meakin's decision to shunt the local train in the first place had been 'an error of judgment'. There

was, of course, again no mention that the signalman's plan was sound and would have avoided delays.

It was easy for Killin to skip over the hurdles as he tore through the evidence. Ignored once more were the inconvenient bits of the blocking back rule which had prevented Meakin from using it. Brushed to one side was Alexander Thorburn's rule-breaking failure to compile records of his signal box inspections – it didn't matter Killin stressed again, they had been recorded in the train register – and he supported Patterson's misleading assertion that Tinsley had a clear view of the track from the box.

And so it went on. Killin could say what he wanted. He was the expert in that courtroom. He possessed the technical expertise that demanded respect. There was no one to question his interpretation and opinion. Condie Sandeman made no attempt to challenge him. The judge sought no clarification, content no doubt that this well-educated senior official of the Caledonian Railway must be telling the truth and would not stoop to the sort of deceit resorted to by the wretched trio of railwaymen under trial.

Such an assumption was misguided. Killin was a wily character – though it seems fair to speculate that the suppression in court of one key piece of evidence of which he was fully aware must have required a degree of collusion from the Crown. In precognition Killin had noted, in a handwritten addition to his statement, the obvious mistakes James Tinsley had made in the train register – a clear indication of his confusion prior to the accident. This was never raised during Killin's time on the witness stand.

Sandeman finally intervened, rising to object when Killin began telling the court how he had asked Tinsley in the signal box what had caused the accident. The defence advocate, it appears, suspected Killin had used his position of authority to elicit from the signalman the answer he, and the company, wanted to hear. Sandeman didn't want the exchange repeated in court but, after discussion on the legalities. he was overruled by Judge Ure.

So judge and jury were told of Tinsley's stark admission that he had simply forgotten about the local train and, as a result, had brought on the troop train to its tragic fate. Prosecutor Robert Munro asked if that had been the extent of the conversation. 'Yes, [that was] all at that time,' Killin replied.

'Did he give that freely and promptly?' asked the judge.

'Yes,' said Killin, adding that later in the day, when he had quizzed Tinsley more thoroughly, the signalman had told him, enigmatically, that he had known the local train was there, 'but it escaped his memory entirely'.

Possibly anticipating questions in the court about Tinsley's mental state at the time of the accident, Killin added that 'both [men] were in an ordinary state of health but were very much upset. Otherwise they appeared all right.'[7]

Under cross-examination from Sandeman, Killin admitted, as he had at the inquest, that 'they were experienced signalmen – they were good signalmen and men of good character,' but he immediately stripped some of the gloss from this

by adding that, 'apart from the war conditions, the cabin was not one of the busy cabins. They would have a train every ten minutes.'

If this was an attempt to skirt around the demands of the additional wartime traffic that had played such a critical role in the disaster, Robert Killin for once was halted in his tracks. Sandeman grabbed his chance. 'Do the war conditions not really put more head work on the men?' he asked.

'There is a small amount of extra work, but not very much,' was Killin's misleadingly distorted response – there had actually been a forty per cent increase on train movements through Quintinshill as a direct result of the extra wartime traffic. Killin wasn't challenged and the court was never told of this.

The Assistant Line Superintendent got away with further distortion before he stood down. In his view Meakin should have sent the local train on to Kirkpatrick instead of halting it at Quintinshill. Arguably, he could have done so, but it would have meant delaying the following Edinburgh express in contravention of company policy. Killin made no mention of that.

Then, in response to a question from the Lord Advocate, he was reported in the press as claiming there really had been 'no complexity about the particular position of affairs at Quintinshill that morning. He was sorry to say that the complexity was introduced when Tinsley came on duty at half past six and had to enter up from a slip of paper the various times entered by Meakin between six and six-thirty.' To suggest there had been no complexities was shockingly misleading – par for the course with Killin.

When William McAlpine took the stand Condie Sandeman managed at last to make some sort of impression for the defence. The accused men's advocate asked the district traffic manager if it was his duty to see that lever collars were being used in the signal boxes within his area of control.

McAlpine agreed that this was his responsibility. He added that, whenever he visited boxes, the collars were 'regularly used.' In fact, he added, he had 'never gone in a box and seen that the collar was not on when it should have been.' The case in question was therefore 'quite unique'.

Of course, cynics would argue that signalmen were almost bound to do everything by the book when a manager was carrying out an inspection but at least this was apparent evidence from a senior Caledonian official supporting the view that the men in the dock – Tinsley and Meakin at least – just might have been rather more inclined to rule book adherence than the evidence was suggesting. McAlpine had added in a precognition statement that the Quintinshill men 'do not require to use them [collars] very often, of course, because of the loop lines being there.' This might have helped Meakin's mitigation but the High Court trial was never told of it.[8]

Another element of McAlpine's precognition statement denied to the court was his – erroneous – belief that it would have been possible for Meakin to have blocked back to Kirkpatrick after he had shunted the local train. Presumably, the

prosecution were keen to avoid the potential risk of cross-examination on any reference by witnesses to the blocking back rule.

As for McAlpine's part in the systems failure which had allowed Alexander Thorburn to get away with neglecting to keep records of signal box inspection visits, this too was never pursued at the Edinburgh hearing. With, as noted in chapter nine, the evidence taken in precognition from Andrew Binnie, the company's chief inspector, also considered too risky to use in view of its conflicting interpretation of who did what in the signal box, it is clear the prosecution had gone to some length to exclude from the High Court jury anything which threatened the simplicity of its case.

There was little comfort for the accused men from the evidence given by fellow signalmen Thomas Sawyers and Roger Kirkpatrick which in both cases mirrored what they had told Coroner Strong's inquest three months earlier. Sawyers was, metaphorically speaking, kicked about a bit by Sandeman, finding it hard to follow his line of questioning, which seemed to be aimed at attacking the signalman's credibility. At one point Sawyers admitted that he simply didn't understand what the advocate was getting at.

'If you don't understand that, I am surprised you are a signalman,' said Sandeman scornfully. What specifically had led to this exchange was not recorded but Sawyers was an odd choice for Sandeman to put the boot into.

Kirkpatrick might have been a better candidate – though far from the most obvious – but Sandeman seems not to have raised a challenge when the Gretna signalman implied poor practice on the part of his Quintinshill colleagues over their failure to follow the blocking back or lever collar rules.

Alexander Thorburn escaped unscathed, too. Had he known about the change of duty arrangement between Meakin and Tinsley, said the stationmaster, he 'would have stopped it at once'. Neither Sandeman nor the judge asked the obvious question – how could he possibly not have known of it, living only the shortest of distances from Tinsley's Gretna cottage?

As with Killin before him, Thorburn took the opportunity once more of stressing that he had found Tinsley 'sober and in good health' when he had visited the signal box soon after the accident on 22 May. Again the stationmaster praised Tinsley – this time as 'a satisfactory and capable man' – and said the box he and Meakin had manned was 'the most modern and commanded a good view'. In other words, there had been no indicators before it actually happened that an accident might be on the cards.

With brakesman William Young adding nothing to his statement at the Carlisle inquest and a raft of other witnesses contributing very little of relevance to a criminal trial, the first day's proceedings were brought to a close at 4.30pm when fifteen of the thirty-two prosecution witnesses had been heard.

There wasn't much in the way of courtroom drama, either, when the other brakesman in the story, Thomas Ingram, was called to get the following day's

evidence under way – again it was a virtual repeat of what he had told the inquest, equally vague about who had said what to whom in the box.

The train drivers' evidence was dramatic enough – it could hardly have been anything else – but it contributed nothing of consequence to the business of determining guilt. Neither did Charles Morrison's evidence, which covered his experiences at the scene of the crash but nothing at all about his role as the police officer involved in James Tinsley's subsequent arrest. The omission of Morrison's evidence about Tinsley's fragile health when the arrest was first attempted, abortively, on 28 May – a statement given in precognition but never referred to at the trial itself – is a particularly disturbing aspect of the High Court proceedings. (See chapter six).

It was at this juncture that things took a truly dramatic turn for the first time. Local train fireman George Hutchinson's indictment on the same charge as the signalmen had been particularly harsh. He certainly had transgressed company rules but making a case of culpable homicide against him stick was asking a lot of the prosecution despite the apparent willingness of the Caledonian Railway to facilitate the process. Hutchinson, after all, had every reason to suppose Tinsley would have remembered his local train – with or without the aid of a signal lever collar.

On Hutchinson's behalf, Condie Sandeman formally invited the judge to instruct the jury to dismiss the case against the fireman. Naturally, Lord Strathclyde asked the Lord Advocate for his take on the matter. Munro said that he had 'made up his mind to make such a proposal' but added that the proper time to do so would be after the case for both sides was heard.

This made perfect sense but Sandeman, probably to the surprise of most in the courtroom, advised Judge Ure that he did not propose to lead any evidence. Not only were there to be no witnesses in support of the accused men, it was now clear that they would not themselves be giving evidence.

There was therefore little point in delaying the matter. The Lord Advocate announced that, based on the evidence already before the court – and in Hutchinson's case nothing material had been added to what had been revealed at the earlier inquiry and inquest – he considered it his duty not to press the case against the fireman. Hutchinson would be able to walk free.

It wasn't enough for Sandeman. He submitted that the fireman was entitled to a formal verdict of not guilty. The Lord Justice General raised no objection. He told Sandeman that he proposed later on to ask the jury to return a verdict of not guilty. And with that the trial moved towards its finale with the advocates rising to address the jury with their respective cases.

Those closing speeches were high on emotion. There was nothing especially unusual about that in 1915. Counsel either side of the border developed a distinctive style of trademark eloquence and used this to full effect in their closing submissions. Judges followed suit, saving the best to last as some of them very probably saw it. If the Lord Advocate was going to outshine the Lord Justice

General in this case – let alone Sandeman – he was going to have to produce something memorable. In this he certainly succeeded. Even by the standards of the day, the opening thrust of Munro's speech to the jury for the prosecution was perhaps over the top.

'It is manifest,' he began reasonably, 'that this case is one of extreme importance because of the awful loss of life which resulted from the collision....' Preamble out of the way, Munro was fully into his stride as he grabbed the undivided attention of judge and jury with an extraordinary outpouring of high-octane courtroom melodrama which the newspaper reporters saw fit to record virtually word for word. This was, in its contextual setting, a veritable *tour de force* by the Lord Advocate.

'You have only to reflect on the fields of Gretna which on that bright summer morning were like the fields of Flanders. You have only to reflect for a moment on the high hopes in these brave hearts [the soldiers of the Royal Scots] which were quenched suddenly that morning, and the desolation that was brought to countless homes, in order to appreciate at once the awfulness of the catastrophe, the cause of which it is your duty to ascertain...'

The lives of the travelling public, he said, were entrusted to railway servants. The accused men were not from the criminal classes; they were 'men of ripe experience' with an unblemished record of railway service. As with all signalmen, a great responsibility had been placed upon them, a responsibility governed by the rules and regulations of their employers. 'Your duty is to ascertain on this occasion whether the rules of the company – nay more, the rules of commonsense and common prudence – were flagrantly violated, and if so, by whom,' the Lord Advocate told the jury.

It was the Crown's case, Munro added gravely, that 'these vital rules were flagrantly disregarded on this occasion'. Simple – as clear cut as that.

Munro then outlined the specifics of the charges against each man in turn. He began with the allegation of George Meakin's flouting of the Caledonian's rules governing both the lever collar and the blocking back procedure, commenting that 'if ever a breach of duty was clearly proved, it is this one.' Meakin had failed to do 'two supremely important things'.

The allegation against Meakin was therefore one of omission. That against James Tinsley, on the other hand, was one of commission – of having done 'two highly dangerous and improper things to the dictate of prudence and commonsense'. It was a nice turn of phrase by Robert Munro, but hadn't Tinsley's forgetfulness about the train been a glaring omission too?

Probably in recognition of his adversary's acute predicament in trying to represent the interests of two clients whose evidence did not always coincide – especially over the question of which of them had cleared the indicator lock – the Lord Advocate added that 'it would not do on the part of the defence to juggle with the respective duties of Tinsley and Meakin. Most of this trouble arose because of the clandestine arrangement between the two men and it would be an

extraordinary thing if they should profit rather than lose by such an arrangement'. Was this fair comment?

In fact the dispute over the indicator lock had no direct connection with the late change-over of shift. It could be argued that, even if Tinsley had arrived on time, there would still have been a dispute as to who did what.

Munro was being mischievous with this point. He was on safer ground when he spelt out his view of Tinsley's two key errors. 'He accepted the troop train in the circumstances then existing, then lowered the signals to enable the troop train to pass. He said, "I forgot" and that is all he had to say about it. Wasn't that just an amazing lapse of memory? Forgot about the existence of a train by which a few moments before he himself had travelled!'[9]

There was no disputing this. Without any medical explanation it would certainly, and understandably, have been regarded as amazing by the jury.

'[Tinsley] forgot about the existence of a train which, if he had looked out of the window, he could have seen within a few feet of him. He gave the "line clear" signal and, whether he admitted to it or not, his own figures in the train register book show that the troop train was accepted at 6.46. It was a grave breach of duty to do so. The local train was under his very eye – on the line for which he gave the "line clear" signal for the troop train.'

Munro must surely have seen the train register. He would have noted Tinsley had given Hutchinson the wrong page to sign – the action of a befuddled man. Anything Tinsley had scribbled down in the register that morning should not have been regarded as reliable evidence. But Munro did not pause to consider that. He repeated that what had been done was 'a gross breach of duty, and Tinsley was the man who was responsible for it'.

Moving on to the lowering of the signals to clear the troop train's advance, the Lord Advocate made what should have been a highly telling remark: the evidence, he said, was straightforward – that it was Tinsley's duty to be sure that the southbound line was clear before the signals were pulled.

'It should not have been necessary for him to look out of the window [to check that the way was clear]. If he had looked into the resources of his own memory he would have seen that the local train was on the up line.'

Exactly! Had he been functioning properly on 22 May, Tinsley should have needed no visual or, indeed, mechanical aid to remind him of the exposed local train on which he had ridden to work. Forgetting its presence just outside the box would have been inconceivable. In a few words Robert Munro had arrived at the causal crux of Quintinshill's tragedy.

Tinsley's memory should have been enough to avert disaster. The fact that it hadn't should have been the clearest indication that something was wrong with him – something that adversely affected his responses to what was happening around him and his capacity to recall virtually anything that had just happened. Munro took it no further and it slipped past the jury.

So far as the Lord Advocate was concerned the origin of the disaster lay not in Tinsley's confused mental state but in his 'clandestine arrangement' with Meakin for arriving at work half-an-hour later than he was supposed to.

The prosecution had no time for any hint of underlying causes. It was black and white for Munro as he declared that 'every eye and ear should have been alert in that signal cabin' and launched another broadside against the signalmen for allowing their attention to be so seriously diverted.

At a time of 'unexpected complexity' caused by the demands of so many trains, 'Tinsley was, to use a phrase from another walk of life "posting his ledger" and the other signalman was reading a newspaper. I think you will agree that this was quite intolerable if valuable human lives, lives dear to their friends and valuable to their country, should be imperilled and sacrificed.

'Why?

'In order that a signalman might spend half-an-hour more between the sheets on a particular morning. That, I think, is not overstating the case in regard to Tinsley. I suggest that, but for that clandestine arrangement, none of us would be here today and much valuable life would have been preserved.'

Munro urged the jury to bear in mind that 'a verdict in favour of the accused would rightly be regarded as a charter of indemnity to railway officials to disregard the rules provided by the company if they so pleased' Resorting to the grandiloquent, the Lord Advocate added as his finale:

'If you look simply and solely at the evidence which has been led, and if you survey that evidence, as no doubt you will, without prejudice and without passion, and without quixotic sentiment, you will feel constrained by virtue of the oath you have taken to return a verdict of guilty as libelled.'

How would Condie Sandeman respond to the prosecutor's finely worded submission? The signalmen's defence lay entirely in his hands. What case could he make? The way the evidence had been presented, and Munro had summed it up, on the face of it at least, appeared to demand guilty verdicts. But Sandeman was very far from chastened when he rose to speak.

'I have not the Lord Advocate's gift of eloquence to talk of the fields of Flanders, the desolate homes, the sacrificing of human life to spend more time beneath the sheets, and charters of indemnity, and I am really rather glad because it seems to me that if one had a gift like that one might exercise it to produce prejudice – and to produce prejudice is to try to induce people to decide cases not on the evidence before them but on things in their minds. Emotional feelings should be absent from courts of justice.'

It was a brilliant opening riposte, inviting the jury immediately to reconsider the legitimacy of the Lord Advocate's argument and to ask themselves whether his emotive language really had obscured some of the facts. His theme clearly established, Sandeman continued in similar vein:

'The help I can offer you, the jurymen, is the help of a humble lawyer trying to bring before you clearly what it really is you have to decide, apart altogether

from the outside question of what you might feel next time you go to London. I want to show you what really is the evidence and direct your intention to the real importance of the case, which of course for you and me is naturally Meakin and Tinsley and nothing else at all.

'Yesterday the men were described as workmen of the higher class who had spent their lives from boyhood doing their duty as signalmen [not true in Tinsley's case – see chapter eight]. For periods of ten and eight years they had done their duty faithfully. Today the Lord Advocate asked you to find that these men were criminals and to have them sent to prison where they would be of no use to any person and their careers would be ruined.

'All criminals are judged by their intention to commit the crime; that is a rule of universal application, but there is an odd exception. In dealing with criminal negligence or culpable homicide a man might do a thing a dozen times and be called a careless fellow, and if the thing he did happened to result in the death of a fellow human being, he would become guilty of a crime. But a little negligence would not do – it would have to be some very gross negligence which directly contributed to the result.'

Having started strongly, Sandeman then lost momentum with an obviously weak statement in defence of Meakin's admission [to Killin] that he had not put the collar on the signal lever as he should have done. 'But,' argued the defence lawyer, 'there was no admission by Meakin himself that he should have put the collar on. There appears to be a difference of opinion as to whether the collar ought to have been put on and you have to make up your minds to be sure that Meakin should have put it on.'

Quite why Sandeman should have tried that one is a mystery. There was no doubt whatsoever. The rule was clear. Meakin should have used the collar.

The defence advocate was now punching way below his weight as his defence of Meakin continued to deliver no meaningful blows in the signalman's favour. He raised inconclusive points over the question of whether it was Meakin or Tinsley who gave the 'train out of section' signal and then failed to question the misleading evidence on the blocking back rule. It hadn't amounted to any real defence at all. Would James Tinsley fare better?

Sandeman opened his case for Tinsley by reaffirming that his second client had accepted the troop train when the local service was standing on the same line. He could hardly argue otherwise. Then Sandeman asked the jury if this had amounted to negligence or something else, reminding them that, when asked about it, Tinsley had replied that he had simply forgotten the 'local'.

That, Sandeman insisted, did not amount to negligence. 'It was one of those curious failures of memory which were so completely recognised by the railway companies that they added two or three precautions to try to secure what they saw was necessary when the human element was introduced. It is ridiculous to say that the man was in neglect for not looking out to see a train he had just come off. It was just some temporary defect.'

Could Sandeman really brush it off that easily? Could it really be dismissed as just one of those things? Could any normally functioning human being – and so far as the jury knew Tinsley was in good health at the time – really be capable of so extraordinary a lapse of memory as this? Was Sandeman about to enlighten the jury as to Tinsley's true state of health?

Arguably his next statement was the most significant in the trial – indeed, in the entire investigation into the causes of Britain's worst-ever railway disaster. But it is probable that it was not regarded as such by the jury at the time and certainly not at all in the subsequent attempts to interpret the tragedy throughout the century that has all but elapsed since. Oblique in the extreme, Condie Sandeman barely allowed it to penetrate into the consciousness of most of those who crowded out the Edinburgh chamber.

Had it really been criminal negligence on Tinsley's part? Sandeman asked. 'It would not be criminal negligence if he fell down in an epileptic fit.'

Which of course it wouldn't. Was Sandeman suggesting this is what had happened? Whether or not this was the case, he took it no further. Neither did the judge mention it in his summing-up. It would remain the only public reference to epilepsy during the investigative process. So why did Sandeman make this comment at all? Was he just using epilepsy as an illustrative example for his argument against the prosecution's case of gross negligence? Or did he have an ulterior motive? Was this a reminder to Munro, Alexander Ure and possibly others in higher authority that he knew the truth but would not pursue it at the trial? In other words, had a deal been done?

'Tinsley,' added Sandeman, 'had the further misfortune that there was no collar against the lever and that he found the [block] indicator showing that the line was clear, which helped to mislead him. In other words, the very perfection of the system was against him. He did not get the jogs he should have got.' Whether or not this would assist Tinsley's defence, a statement like that was going to do nothing for Meakin's chance of an acquittal – a good example of the lawyer's difficulty in representing both men.

'It is very easy for the Lord Advocate to say that the fact spoke for itself,' added Sandeman. 'An unhappy combination of events had contributed some part to the ultimate catastrophe, but that will not do for me and you. You have to say if the particular faults charged by the Lord Advocate are proved.'

Sandeman then rounded off his speech with another highly enigmatic choice of phrase. 'Of course there was fault,' he remarked, 'but if the means are not before you for seeing who was responsible for that fault then, as far as I can see, no course is open for you but to return a verdict of not guilty.'

What were the jury to make of that? Was this curious comment meant for them at all? Were the real targets, once again, the prosecutor, judge and officialdom beyond – a second oblique reference to evidence being deliberately withheld from the jury by a pre-trial contract? We believe there must have been such

an agreement in place. It is a matter, crucial to understanding the truth about Quintinshill, best left for the book's final analysis.

Alexander Ure, the Lord Justice General, predictably began his summing-up with his own take on the unparalleled gravity of the disaster – and what he was keen to portray as the straightforward nature of determining its causes.

'I suppose that rarely, if ever, in the annals of this court has there been a sadder case brought before it, and rarely, if ever, has there been a clearer and simpler case. Happily, as Mr Sandeman has observed, it is not part of your duty to dwell upon the horror of the awful tragedy enacted on that May morning in the neighbourhood of that signal box, by which many valuable lives were lost. I suppose a more heartrending episode has never before occurred since railway trains began to run.

'Your duty is confined exclusively to say who was to blame, on whose shoulders lies the responsibility and on whose shoulders, the guilt. If you are satisfied that. through the gross negligence of these men, those valuable lives were lost, you must, I'm afraid, find the prisoners guilty as charged.'

George Meakin had been badly served throughout the trial, the validity of his mitigation brushed aside as the knife was mercilessly twisted into him. Now he was about to get the cruelest cut of all as Lord Strathclyde added: 'They gave the signal to the north that the line was clear, that there was no obstruction on the line, and that the troop train might safely come on.'

This was grossly unfair on Meakin. He had not been accused of any such thing. The Lord Advocate himself had stressed that the Crown regarded Meakin's guilt as that of omission – the things he *hadn't* done. Possibly the judge was generalising, implying that the troop train had been invited on because of the collective failings of the two men, but his choice of words was at the very least misleading. His next remarks were more specific.

'One of the men in the box had actually left that local train a few minutes before, just at the time when it was being shunted onto the up main line. The other... had, a few minutes before, actually directed the local train from the down line and shunted it onto the up line. That is the staggering fact that confronts you. If you can explain that fact consistently with these two men having faithfully and honestly discharged their duty, you must acquit them. If you cannot explain that fact... then you must convict them.'

The judge added that 'instantly the [local] train was put on the up line it was in a position of danger.' This was a statement of the obvious. Any train stopped in a block section would be in potential danger regardless of its position, irrespective of whether it was on the up or down line. Meakin had no choice if he was to comply with company policy – crossing the 'local' to the up line was, in theory, dangerous but it was not an irresponsible act. He had no reason to think Tinsley would forget it was there.

In reviewing the Caledonian's precautions for ensuring the local train's 'absolute safety and the safety of any other train which might come from the

north at that time,' the Lord Justice General correctly rebutted Sandeman's ambiguity over the signal collar. There had, he said, been 'no choice about it'. Meakin should have 'at once placed the collar on the lever, and so prevent any man from drawing the lever and lowering the home and distant signals,' thus allowing a southbound train to reach the 'local'.

This was always a weakness in George Meakin's defence. Sandeman's meagre hope of muddying the waters over the rule's application had been flushed out by the judge. Altogether a different matter, however, was the blocking back issue.

Ure repeated the point he had made on the signal collar – blocking back was not a matter of choice; it *had* to be done – but he, like Munro, allowed no concession to Meakin over the impossibility of implementing the rule once the local train had been moved. Instead, he told the jury that the blocking back signal should have been sent as soon as the collar was affixed, so Meakin had compounded his error. It was as black and white as that. This was highly debatable and the hapless Meakin was then dealt yet another body blow by the judge.

'It was the plain duty of the man who directed the local train from the down line to the up line to take these precautions. You will easily see for yourself it would never do to leave such a duty so imperative and insistent as that to any subsequent incomer. It is the man who deliberately creates the danger whose duty it is to instantly take precautions against risk...'

This was wrong on two points. First, Meakin did not deliberately cause danger. He was merely trying to resolve a complex problem imposed on him by company policy on train priorities. Second, it had already been established at the Carlisle coroner's inquest that he was perfectly within his rights to hand over to Tinsley at the time he did, providing he had made his incoming mate fully aware of the situation – and there had been third party evidence during the earlier investigative hearings that he had done so. At no point during the trial was any mention made of this latter point.

With Meakin's hopes of leaving the court a free man sinking fast, the judge broke off to carry out his earlier promise of formally instructing the jury to acquit George Hutchinson. This done, he turned his attention to Tinsley.

It is clear that Alexander Ure saw the case against Tinsley as being as open and shut as it had been against Meakin. Having reviewed the evidence, he told the jury that Tinsley had been 'asked to accept the troop train from the north. He accepts it and signalled back that the line was perfectly clear, that there was no obstruction on the line, and the troop train was to come on. It is for you to say if that was not gross negligence of duty.

'In answer to Mr Killin, he said that he had forgotten about the local train. It is for you to say if you accept such an excuse from a highly intelligent man, a man who knew his duty thoroughly, a man who had been many years at this work – and remember this obstruction was under his eye, and... was the train he himself had just left a few minutes earlier. It is for you to judge.'

Added Ure, 'You will perhaps come to the conclusion that there was a much simpler explanation of this unaccountable lapse of memory. Meakin and Tinsley made the arrangement that morning together – perhaps not for the first time – that Tinsley should come on duty some time later than the appointed hour. That arrangement was a gross breach of the regulations.'

It was, the jury was told by the Lord Justice General, 'an arrangement to which I hope you will give no sanction – an arrangement very dangerous to the travelling public. The rules state that signalmen must exchange their duty only at the appointed hour and the accused asked no permission from their superior officer for this change. It was done surreptitiously and clandestinely... I suppose nothing would have happened if these two men had not laid their heads to deceive their superior officer – to conceal the arrangement.'

Like those who had sat in judgment at the previous investigative hearings, Ure saw it simply – the arrangement had relied on Tinsley copying into the register the train movements he had missed which had been left for him by Meakin. While he did so, Meakin was reading the paper.

The judge was not going to delve into the realms of mitigation. He was not interested in trying to understand the dilemma, which was not of his making, facing Meakin when the 6.17 local train from Carlisle arrived at Quintinshill. He was certainly not going to say anything about Tinsley's health. Instead, he said the court had been told 'the simple facts of the case.'

In conclusion, Ure told the jury it was 'now for you to judge whether or not these men failed to do their duty. It has been said, and quite properly said, that the men have been many years in the service of the company, and in the past have discharged their duties satisfactorily. They are capable, sober men, and up to the day of the accident gave satisfactory service. Indeed, had that not been the case, they would not have been there, for railway companies cannot afford to put in responsible positions men who are not skilled, who are not sober, and who are not efficient servants.

'It is not your duty to inquire into their past character and career. You simply have to say whether on that day, at that time, they were guilty of the gross neglect of duty which brought about these deplorable results.'

At 12.40pm the jury retired to consider their verdict – and were back in the courtroom after an absence of just nine minutes. The foreman announced that, unanimously, they had found Meakin and Tinsley guilty as charged. The formality of a not guilty verdict against Hutchinson was noted.

For the fireman the ordeal was over. He stood down, leaving just the two signalmen in the dock to await their fate. There was, unsurprisingly, an immediate plea for leniency from Sandeman's junior counsel, Smith Clark.

'Each of these men, since the dreadful occurrence, has suffered in the most shocking fashion,' he said. 'Each of them has had complete nervous breakdown and suffered regularly from sleeplessness. Apart altogether from considerations on health, I would ask your lordship to keep in view that the future of these men

is completely cut off now, and to mete out to both the accused as moderate a punishment as you think reasonably proper.'

Later events would make clear that Lord Strathclyde did not consider the sentences he then passed to be moderate. 'I will... say nothing to add to the bitter feeling of remorse you must feel at the thought of the awful consequences which have followed those breaches of duty of which you have been convicted unanimously,' he told the two men. 'I see room for drawing a distinction on your cases and I accordingly pass sentence on Meakin of eighteen months and on Tinsley of three years' penal servitude.'

As he spoke, press reporters noticed that Meakin and Tinsley stood with bowed heads. 'Tinsley appeared to be on the verge of collapse, but by an effort each controlled himself, and they left by way of the trapdoor amid an impressive silence,' the *Dumfries & Galloway Standard* recorded soberly.

Notes

1. The St Andrew Society is still in existence, describing itself as a 'patriotic and neo-political' society which incorporates the World Federation of Scottish Societies and many individuals.
2. Edinburgh High Court was founded in 1672 though its origins date back to the College of Justice set up in the city in 1532 and to the medieval royal courts and barony courts. The courtroom in which the Quintinshill railwaymen were tried remains in use, now as the court of appeal.
3. Liberal politician and judge Alexander Ure (1852–1928), became a Queen's Counsel at the end of the Victorian era in 1897. A controversial legal career saw him installed as Solicitor General for Scotland in 1905 and then as the country's Lord Advocate in 1909. Found in the same year to have misled the court at the Oscar Slater murder trial (see chapter thirteen), Ure suffered political defeat four years later when he lost the Livingstone parliamentary seat he had held since 1895. His fortunes were restored a year later when he was elevated to the peerage as 1st Baron Strathclyde and assumed the role of Lord Justice General, remaining in office until 1920. The title became extinct on his death but was recreated in 1955 and remains in use.
4. Robert Munro (1868-1955) was admitted to the Scottish Bar as an advocate in 1893. He became a King's Counsel in 1910, the year he was elected Liberal MP for Wick Burghs in the far north of Scotland. In October 1913 he was appointed Lord Advocate, remaining in post until December 1916, the month his political status rose in stature when he was appointed Secretary of State for Scotland in the new Lloyd George Cabinet, a position he held until the end of coalition government in 1922. He then served as Lord Justice Clerk (1922-1933), having been raised to the bench as 1st Baron Alness. Munro too was embroiled in the fall-out from the Slater murder trial when in 1914, as Lord Advocate, he indicted on a trumped-up charge the detective who had expressed misgivings over Slater's conviction – eventually quashed.
5. James Condie Sandeman (1866-1933) was born in Perthshire, studied law at Edinburgh University and was admitted to the Scottish Faculty of Advocates in 1899, becoming a KC in 1909. Regarded as a powerful advocate capable of remaining remarkably cool under fire,

he was said by his contemporaries to wield to an unusual degree 'the rapier of satire' in the courtroom.

6. Although other signal boxes of similar design shared the feature with Quintinshill, it was contrary to usual Caledonian Railway practice for the lever frame to be located at the rear of the box rather than the front, forcing the signalmen to work with their backs to the line. In 1978, some years after his book on the disaster was published, John Thomas acknowledged this was so. 'This simple fact might well have been the cause of the disaster,' he wrote in a letter, having been shown the evidence in a newly discovered Caledonian document – see chapter twelve.

7. It is possible that Killin interviewed Tinsley and Meakin not in the signal box but later on and may have formed part of Depute Procurator Fiscal James Kissock's initial investigation.

8. In his precognition statement McAlpine expressed his surprise on learning that the lever collars were not always used. We can probably conclude from this that he was not in regular contact with some of his counterparts on the rival Glasgow & South Western Railway – see chapter eight.

9. This particular quote from Robert Munro is taken from *The Scotsman*. It was not carried in the *Dumfries & Galloway Standard*, the source of most of the quotes reproduced in this chapter.

Chapter 12

Inquisition and Soul-searching

*'My opinion is that, if this irregularity can go on in this
signal cabin for twelve months. it might go on in other
signal boxes. I think some action should be taken to see
that it is not continued.'*

John Barker, Burgh Surveyor, Dumfries,
at the fatal accident inquiry, 4 November 1915

The investigations into the accident held in Carlisle and Edinburgh may
have grabbed the headlines but there were a further three examinations of
the tragedy's causes which, in varying degrees, did succeed in broadening
the issues and uncovering some of the key underlying truths. However, for
different reasons, none had any material effect on the demonisation of James
Tinsley and George Meakin as the only men held culpable for the disaster.

A second inquest had taken place at Penrith on the edge of the English Lake
District in the historic county of Cumberland. It was held to look into the death
of Royal Scots Lance Corporal Robert Dawson who had succumbed in the town's
hospital to the wounds he received in the accident. As the inquest was held before
the High Court convictions of Tinsley and Meakin and the acquittal of George
Hutchinson all three attended to give evidence. Robert Killin was also among
those called to Penrith.

The inquest produced just two notable strands of evidence. In the first Tinsley
said he would only have seen the local train outside the signal box had he looked
to the south, thus confirming that Quintinshill's signalmen relied only on the
box's side windows rather than the one at the front.

More illuminating was the questioning of Hutchinson by the three men's
solicitor, Lionel Lightfoot, about his signing of the box's train register book.
'What did you do in addition to writing your name?' Lightfoot asked him.

'I signed my name and wrote "Rule 55" and the number of my engine,' he
replied.

'Was the object of putting "Rule 55" to draw the attention of the signalman
to your train?' Hutchinson was asked. He replied that it was – the clearest of

reminders to Tinsley of the presence of the train on which he had just ridden to work.[1]

Hutchinson's evidence made no difference to the inevitable conclusion of the inquest; once again it was gross negligence by the railwaymen in Quintinshill signal box.

The last public investigation into the disaster, the long-awaited Scottish fatal accident inquiry, finally opened in Dumfries on 4 November 1915 before Sheriff George Campion. The now jailed Tinsley and Meakin were notable absentees, declining an approach, made through the prison authorities, for their attendance. What could this Scottish version of an inquest possibly contribute to the protracted process of examining the causes?[2]

As it turned out, the inquiry proved rather more significant than might have been expected. It provided a platform for the first and only effective cross-examination of Robert Killin, who had been allowed, along with his employers, to get away with so much up until then. Another factor which elevated the inquiry above the status of an academic exercise was that it was heard, unlike the Carlisle inquest and Edinburgh trial, in full knowledge of the findings of the now published report from the Board of Trade.

Although allowing the Caledonian Railway to wriggle free of any corporate blame, that report had raised doubts over certain aspects of the tragedy. The unconvincing evidence of stationmaster Alexander Thorburn was high on that list but, in Dumfries at least, there was evident concern that the testimony of others further up the chain of command had not been tested.

From most of the sixteen witnesses called by Depute Procurator Fiscal James Kissock there was practically nothing that hadn't already been heard before, by now several times over. The outstanding exception was Killin.

This was almost certainly not his intention when he began giving evidence with his well-rehearsed line on the signalmen's failures to observe company rules. There was certainly nothing new in that but, unlike the situation today, fatal accident inquiries sat with juries in 1915 and, when the Caledonian's assistant superintendent of the line submitted to cross-examination from two members of the Dumfries jury, the comfort zone within which he had operated ever since the disaster all but evaporated. First to test him was the town's burgh surveyor, John Barker.

'You appear to attach considerable importance to the fact that the signalmen did not change their shift at the proper time. How long had this irregularity been going on?' he asked in the first of a series of awkward questions for Killin.

'Of course,' the Caledonian official replied in his typically confident style, 'we knew nothing about it, but they admitted themselves that it had been going on for about a year, on and off [although] it was not going on every morning. They are on that shift once every four weeks and the men stated to me that probably two or three mornings out of the four weeks they might change their shift at six-thirty instead of six. Apparently, it was just as they happened to rise in the morning.'

The door had been opened for Barker. He wasn't going to let the opportunity pass. 'Are these signalmen not under the charge of some local official?' he asked.

Killin was now on the defensive: 'They are under the charge of the stationmaster, but it would be impossible for him to see that every signalman changed his duty at the proper time. They are in a place a fairly good distance from the station [at Gretna] and the stationmaster has the supervision also of all other signalmen round and about. There is a district inspector and a check is made on the signalmen by [virtue of] the time they sign off in the train register book.'

If Killin thought this would be enough to satisfy the Dumfries surveyor he was quickly disabused of the notion. John Barker had the bit firmly between his teeth.

Barker: 'It seems extraordinary, surely, that this irregularity should have been going on for twelve months without detection.'

Killin: *'An irregularity can go on for a long time if there is a deliberate attempt to hide it, as was done in this case. If an irregularity is going on openly it is comparatively easy to find it out by supervision, but if the men set themselves deliberately to hide it from their superiors and falsify their books, it is very difficult to find out.'*

'But I understand one of these signalmen travelled by train to his work during the whole time the irregularity went on. Was that so?'

'Oh no. He says himself he only travelled two or three times by the train. If the stationmaster had been on duty the signalman would have been out of his sight as he got on the local train on the side, away from the platform.'

'My opinion is that, if this irregularity can go on in this signal cabin for twelve months, it might go in other signal boxes. I think some action should be taken so that it is not continued.'

'You may rely on it that it will be looked after. This was most unusual and I can assure you that it has not been going on in other signal boxes.'

Robert Killin had hopped, skipped and jumped away from this sort of interrogation at all the previous hearings to which he had been called to give evidence. Suddenly, the game seemed to be slipping away from him. At last he had been put under pressure, and not by a clever lawyer, a High Court judge or a Board of Trade railway inspector. Killin was finally under fire from a local government officer who was making more of an impact on him than all of his previous questioners at all the earlier proceedings put together. If Killin was relieved when John Barker finally ceased firing, he was given no time to savour it.

One tormentor was immediately replaced by another as juryman Robert Laidlaw opened up a new broadside with a question that began with a misunderstanding but quickly had Killin back on the defensive: 'There was a message sent from the station to the box, "the boy will get a ride this morning." Does that not indicate that the officials at the station knew about it?' Laidlaw asked.

Correctly, Killin pointed out that the message had actually been sent by Meakin at Quintinshill to Gretna signalman Roger Kirkpatrick 'at the junction near to the station.' (The Gretna cabin was located at the divergence of the Glasgow

& South Western's route from the Caledonian main line north of the station platform.) The message exchange, therefore, had not involved the station officials at all, Killin told the inquiring juryman. Though this was technically true, Killin was drawing something of a fine distinction here – Roger Kirkpatrick's signal box was only a matter of yards from the station and Kirkpatrick himself was managed at Gretna by stationmaster Alexander Thorburn.

'You can understand that one signalman is not going to give away another when he finds him doing anything which is slightly at fault,' Killin told the jury.

Slightly at fault! Much of the case against the signalmen had been built on the illicit shift change arrangement. The prosecution at the High Court trial had gone to some lengths to stress that it was the reason, in Robert Munro's words, 'most of the trouble arose... but for that clandestine arrangement, none of us would be here today.' The judge had called it 'an arrangement very dangerous to the travelling public.' Was Killin, the man who had so consistently drawn attention to the flaunting of company rules, now implying that Tinsley's train ride from Gretna, already some minutes after he should have relieved Meakin at Quintinshill, was actually nothing more than a minor breach?

Killin had slipped up. He was wriggling, having for once to give responses to questions he had not rehearsed beforehand. Laidlaw was proving a tenacious inquisitor as he widened his probing to seek clarification on issues of responsibility – and Killin's former sure-footedness very quickly deserted him again.

'On whom does the responsibility rest for deciding whether a local train is sent on from Gretna to be shunted at Quintinshill?' asked Laidlaw – an easy one for Killin.

'There are fixed margins laid down as to what time a local train is allowed to run ahead of an express at different points on the line,' he replied, confidence restored. 'If the signalman finds that the local train has not the requisite margins it is his duty to shunt it. These margins are laid down in the timetables and there are telephones and telegraphs to guide [signalmen] in such matters. The responsibility in this case lay on the signalman at Quintinshill to shunt the local train.'

This was true – but it failed to quell the ever questioning mind of juryman Laidlaw. 'Do you think that is a satisfactory arrangement, to put that responsibility on a signalman? Here he was dealing with five trains at almost the same time. Would it not be better to have a higher official, say at Carlisle or Gretna, to decide where the train should be shunted? After all, if this train had been shunted at Gretna, this accident would never have happened,' he asked Killin.

Bruised and battered, Killin fell back on what he probably saw as the chief weapon in his defensive armoury – superior knowledge. Condescendingly, he told his persecutor, 'You must bear in mind that a railway system is a very complicated affair, but all these things have been thought out. Although the signalman had five trains in his section... he was only dealing with one train at a time.'

This was arrant nonsense. In shunting the local service across, George Meakin was dealing not only with that train but simultaneously with the empty coal train entering the loop, the two northbound expresses and the southbound troop train, juggling his options, trying to make room for them all on Quintinshill's tracks.

According to Killin this did not represent 'any real difficulty, although to a man not acquainted with railway work there would appear to be difficulty'. For good measure, he assured Laidlaw that 'it had nothing to do with the accident,' a remark which must surely have caused a massed raising of the eyebrows in the court.

Robert Laidlaw had made a perfectly valid point in suggesting a more centralised system for controlling train movement. Train controllers were an established feature on the UK rail system, having been pioneered by the Midland Railway in 1907. Despite the boasts from Caledonian managers at previous hearings of state-of-the-art signalling at Quintinshill, the company had yet to follow suit, something Killin was probably not especially keen to mention.

The pressure on him was unrelenting. Laidlaw was not going to let him off the hook. 'In view especially of the fact that the passenger train had to be shunted from one main line across to the other and that at a time when the lines were busy, does it not occur to you that it was a mistake to allow that passenger train to start from Gretna... should it not have been allowed to remain there?' he asked.

'I don't admit that it was a busy time,' Killin retorted, 'but, apart from that altogether, the machinery for working all these things out and regulating the running of trains in the way you have described is connected with signal boxes and it is part of a signalman's duties. There is a system of telephonic communication... to the signal boxes to acquaint them as to how trains are running... if a train is running so many minutes late and requires to be shunted a signalman has no difficulty in making up his mind as to what should be done.'

All things are relative but Killin was surely unwise to argue that it had not been especially busy at Quintinshill on the morning of 22 May. It may not have been extraordinarily so, but of course it was busy. His point about signalmen normally being able to deal with such situations was valid though. Meakin had had no difficulty deciding what to do that morning, and it would have worked, irrespective of mechanical safety precautions, had Tinsley not forgotten the 'local'.

Effective though his volley of questions had been, Robert Laidlaw was, at the end of the day, a layman without any real degree of railway operational knowledge. As he continued to harass Killin about the shunting of the 6.17 it would have been clear to the latter that the juryman had not done his homework about the track layout at Gretna. It allowed him to recover and wriggle off the hook.

Laidlaw: 'Does it not occur to you that it was very inadvisable to shunt a train through to the [up] main line when it could have been avoided by keeping the train at Gretna, particularly in view of the fact that the train had only to proceed a mile and a half [to Quintinshill] after leaving Gretna?'

Killin: *'I don't agree with you that it could have been avoided by keeping the train at Gretna.'*

'Is there not more accommodation for shunting at Gretna than there is at the Quintinshill siding [sic].'

'I am sorry to say there is not. If a train had been held at Gretna it would have been necessary to put it through the road [the crossover] *or run it forward to the Glasgow & South Western junction and let it stand on the main line there. In either case they would have been in exactly the same position.'*

James Kissock (intervening): 'I suppose if there had not been gross carelessness there would have been no accident at all.'

'No.'

Thus, with the help of the Depute Procurator Fiscal, Killin stood down, no doubt relieved that, despite his long overdue and difficult examination, the last words in the bruising exchange once again had settled on carelessness by the two signalmen in Quintinshill's now infamous cabin. Just the way he would have wanted it. But the Dumfries jurymen were far from finished. Next in their target sights was the Gretna stationmaster, Alexander Thorburn. How would he fare?

Thorburn began by contradicting his evidence to the Board of Trade inquiry. Responding to questioning from Barker he said that on the morning of the accident he had gone on duty at 6.55, his 'usual time'. If this was the time he normally started work, how could he have seen the local train leave Gretna at 6.29 on at least two mornings in the week prior to the accident, as he had told the board's inquiry? He had made no mention in his evidence of these being earlier than usual starts for him; he'd merely said he had been 'on duty' at that time.

Thorburn had now given three different accounts in his outrageous attempt to show he had not seen Tinsley leave for work on 22 May – lying to save his skin.

He further complicated the issue by adding that he was 'not necessarily on duty' when the local train left Gretna, but was 'occasionally so' – not that he ever saw Tinsley travel on the train. 'Of course I am only on that shift one week in a month.' Somehow Thorburn got away with this. The otherwise diligent jurors failed to spot these inconsistencies. Strangely, Laidlaw persisted instead with his questioning about the wisdom of sending the train on from Gretna.

Thorburn, for once on safe ground, was able to parry the questions by repeating Killin's answer that it would have served no purpose holding the train at Gretna. It would have ended up on the southbound line just as it was at Quintinshill as there was no siding at Gretna into which it could have been shunted.

'Does that not seem inadequate?' asked Laidlaw. Whether or not Thorburn gave a reply is not recorded. It hardly matters, that line of questioning was going nowhere.

There was little else of any consequence from the remainder of the evidence. Barker and Laidlaw had done their best to unsettle and undermine the Caledonian's defence but the corporate bastion had, just about, withstood the

siege. It was left to Sheriff Campion to address the jury. The company could relax.

Dealing first with the questionable need for a fatal accident inquiry – 'the Crown authorities were of the opinion that it should be held in accordance with the law' – Campion told the jury that 'the railway companies have devised a very complete system of rules and regulations which have been made after many years of valuable experience and which, if observed, will safeguard the public.'

He added that, 'if there is any point which you can bring to the attention of the companies, I have no doubt... their officials will give it their serious attention.' This was commendably sensible and in total contrast to Coroner Strong's instruction to his Carlisle jury to refrain from commenting on wider considerations. The sheriff had an immediate suggestion for the jurymen to ponder: 'Apparently, one signalman went on duty at ten o' clock at night 'til six o'clock in the morning... probably a question for consideration in the discharge of such important duties is to ask, had this not been too long a duty at one stretch?'

Campion accepted what the court had been told by Killin and Thorburn about the pointlessness of shunting the local train at Gretna – and that was that. The Dumfries inquiry fizzled out like the proverbial damp squib when the jury returned a unanimous finding that, had it not been for the flouting of company rules and regulations by Tinsley and Meakin, the accident would never have happened. The public investigations into Quintinshill's disaster were finally over.

But there had been yet another examination, this time held entirely in private, which had yielded a far more revealing interpretation of the causes than any of the other inquiries. The investigating authority was the Caledonian Railway itself.

Remarkable documentation relating to this had lain in virtual obscurity for decades until in 1978 it resurfaced and was referred to Quintinshill historian John Thomas, for whom it sadly came too late for inclusion in his 1969 book. Comprising the record of a meeting of senior Caledonian officials in 1916, together with related letters and other written material, it was in essence, a 'scrapbook' of internal soul-searching collated by W.H. Blackstock, the company's district superintendent at Carlisle. It appears to have been passed by Blackstock's widow on his death to a Mr Hay of Glasgow who showed it to Thomas before donating it to the archival service of Dumfries and Galloway Council. It has since been stored among the records at the Ewart Library in Dumfries.

Largely forgotten, these fascinating documents were once more brought to light by the council's archivists early in 2012 in connection with research for this book.

The meeting which formed the focus for the archive was held in the Caledonian's station hotel at Glasgow Central on 20 March 1916. The memorandum produced from it shows that it was attended not only by senior management but also by the various members of the company's inspection team, its target. Much of the content is highly technical in nature – see appendix two – but many of the general points noted can usefully be summarised here.

Chairing the meeting, Robert Killin explained that it had been called to discuss various points raised in the Board of Trade inquiry report about the non-observance of the company's rules and regulations, and to consider whether anything could be done, through supervision or otherwise, to prevent a repeat of the disaster.

'While the proximate cause of the accident is quite clear,' the report records Killin as saying, 'there has come to light in the course of several inquiries made into the case several irregularities in the carrying out of minor, although important, instructions which demand the serious attention of all concerned.'

Leaving aside Killin's questionable use of the adjective 'minor', his statement turns out to be code for systems failures on the Caledonian Railway network which extended way beyond the confines of Quintinshill signal box – the very things he and senior company colleagues had striven to keep out of the public domain.

The examination opened at 'ground level' with a reference to the failure of Gretna signalman Roger Kirkpatrick to report Tinsley's persistently bad timekeeping on the early morning shift, and to Kirkpatrick's clearly pre-arranged indication to the Quintinshill man that the local train was to be shunted at his signal box on the morning of the accident. There was, the meeting noted, a clear need for company officials to remind men under their supervision of their obligation to assist in the carrying out of rules and regulations, and to report 'any infringement thereof, or any occurrence... affecting the safe and proper working of the line.' On the surface, an inarguable point.

The logical extension would have been to question stationmaster Thorburn's probable complicity in the rule infringement, which had been highlighted by Colonel Druitt, convinced Thorburn must have been aware of it, in his Board of Trade report. However, if this was specifically mentioned at the meeting, it was not minuted.

An admission that inspection visits were in need of tightening up in order to stamp out irregular shift changes came with recommendations that supervisory visits should be made at the official changeover times or, failing that, telephone calls should be made to signal boxes to check by voice recognition who was on duty. The meeting also discussed a rule change which would force a signalman to leave his box as soon as his shift was completed. Killin agreed to consider this.

There was agreement that the riding on locomotives by unauthorised staff was in need of enforcement, but of rather more significance was lengthy discussion around the monthly reports stationmasters were supposed to compile on their supervision of signal boxes – the company's rule 96. It would appear from the memorandum that the procedure required the reports to be sent by stationmasters for administration by the clerk in charge of the company's staff department, whose duty it was to report any irregularities to the district superintendent. His role, in turn, was periodically to examine the reports and act accordingly.

From the evidence given to the various investigative hearings, it is clear that the procedure had not been adhered to, in the case of Quintinshill at least.

Thorburn had failed to compile the reports so the clerk was given nothing from him to administer and the district superintendent, nothing to periodically examine. And, it would seem, nothing had been done to rectify the situation. Clearly this shoddy state of affairs lay behind a recommendation that in future stationmasters should be issued with a printed form on which to record their visits to the boxes. Why this had not been thought of before is something of a mystery.

Reference to the error-strewn recording in the train register by James Tinsley on the day of the accident – surely evidence of his dysfunctional behaviour – had been studiously avoided by Caledonian officials during the 1915 inquiries, but this was evidently a matter for some earnest discussion at the March 1916 meeting. Examination of the box's registers 'showed that the recording of block signals etc had been performed in a careless manner generally'. Inspectors would be urged to tighten up on this and specifically to make sure that entries made on scrap paper for copying into the book 'should be deleted and put a stop to'.

Bizarrely, the meeting identified as another example of bad practice in Quintinshill signal box the display of the infamous pictures of poultry which had so fascinated coal train brakesman William Young on the morning of the accident. Quite what those images had to do with the events that followed remains a mystery, but the poultry had to go – along with all other pictures hung in signal boxes. Supervisory inspectors would be ordered to remove the lot!

Brakesmen, firemen and all other external staff were also to be banished from the Caledonian's boxes as soon as they had been given the information they needed by the signalman and, without exception, had signed their names in the register.

The meeting decided the company should look afresh at the apparent anomaly of allowing a 'train out of section' signal to be given, as was done with the empty coal train at Quintinshill, at a time when the section of line in question was actually blocked by another obstacle, as the up line at Quintinshill had been. Amendments would also be made for the same reason to the 'line clear' signal.

George Meakin's admitted failure to use the signal lever collar on 22 May 1915, and the Quintinshill signalmen's previous neglect in conforming to the rule, had been presented as something unique to this particular signal box. That this was not the case is evident from the record of the March 1916 meeting. There had clearly been wider disregard for the rule's correct application – not only was the collar not being used in some cases, in others it was being affixed 'in circumstances other than those specified in the regulation'. Inspectors would be urged to impress upon signalmen the importance of acting strictly in accordance with the rule – but evidently this was not thought at the meeting to be enough.

The rule was in a mess. District superintendents would now be instructed to consider the whole matter with the inspectors under their control, reporting to

the company's superintendent of the line with their recommendations for the future.

Remaining points covered by the meeting were really matters of comment. Robert Killin's was that Meakin would have been wiser to have sent the local train on to Kirkpatrick station 'where it could have been shunted in a siding clear of the running line, in which event the possibility of delaying the troop train could have been avoided'. On the face of it, this sounded a reasonable argument, but Meakin would have been well aware of the undesirability, to say the least, of reversing the local train into a goods siding controlled by unlocked points. Parking it in Kirkpatrick's siding would have been the option of last resort when no others were available. Odd that Killin should have suggested this, having repeatedly denied at the fatal accident inquiry that it was 'a busy time.'

What was seen, or rather, not seen, from the signal box that morning was an obvious issue for discussion. The fact that Quintinshill's signalmen worked with their backs to the line – the point that most interested author John Thomas when he was sent the documentation in 1978, concluding that this might have actually caused the disaster (see also chapter eleven) – was certainly a relevant topic.

Had Tinsley, despite his confused state, seen the local train as he pulled the levers to clear the up line, it could be argued that the accident would not have happened. The design of the box was the problem in this case, not James Tinsley.

Because of this, the Caledonian's repeated insistence that the train was standing in full view of the signalman was either disingenuous or a sign of remarkable ignorance by senior management of the layout of this particular design of cabin. The record of the Glasgow meeting did not indicate which of the two it was, but it was suggested that visibility could be improved at Quintinshill, and at other boxes with the same layout, if the company adopted a North British Railway design which incorporated the extension of side windows to floor level.

One final point, never mentioned at any of the 1915 inquiries, was noted. No other railwayman at the scene had noticed that the up line signals had been cleared for the troop train's approach before it was too late. It was now, of course, too late for Meakin and Tinsley for this, and so many other contributory factors, to be brought to wider attention. But then this apparently had never been the intention. Reviewing such matters in March 1916 was, on the surface, the action of a responsible railway company trying to learn from its mistakes and those of its employees, but this obscures the fact that the failures in the company's supervisory structure were profound and should certainly have been acknowledged before the two Quintinshill signalmen were made to take all the blame.

Notes

1. Rule 55 was universally applied by all British railway companies at the time and for many decades afterwards. It had been introduced in the nineteenth century following a series of accidents caused by signalmen forgetting – as James Tinsley did at Quintinshill – that

a train was standing on a running line in the vicinity of a signal box. The rule required a member of the train crew to go to the signal box and ensure that the signalman was aware of the halted train's presence. He had also to check that all available precautions had been taken to protect the train.

2. Fatal accident inquiries (FAIs) became part of the Scottish legal process under the terms of the Fatal Accident Inquiry (Scotland) Act 1895. Under current legislation – the Fatal Accidents and Sudden Deaths Inquiry (Scotland) Act 1976 – certain deaths demand a compulsory FAI while others are held on a discretionary basis. Initiating an FAI is the responsibility of the procurator fiscal following an investigation into the circumstances of the death.

Chapter 13

The Fight for Justice

'The whole history of this case shows a deplorable miscarriage of justice has been perpetrated.'

J.H 'Jimmy' Thomas, National Union of Railwaymen,
16 April 1916

For nearly a century speculation and mystery shrouded in an impenetrable veil the events leading to the release of the two imprisoned Quintinshill signalmen in December 1916.

The extraordinary truth lay unseen among Scotland's archival records, locked away, beyond public reach, for seventy-five years following the deposit in 1916 and 1918 of the documents which held its startling evidence. Now, for the first time since these historical records were finally opened for public inspection at the end of the twentieth century, the veil can be lifted so that the illuminating truth is at last clear.

It is a complex drama-filled truth – an interwoven story of political intrigue, the threat of what would have been a devastating nationwide strike in the critical mid-war year of 1916, probable corruption and, above all, the legacy of injustice.

It is also a story that cannot be divorced from the prevailing social attitudes of the period and the rigid class system inherited from the Victorian and Edwardian eras. With deference to one's supposed 'betters' set firmly at its core, this was a structure characterised often by a complete and, to the twenty-first century mind, incomprehensible trust in the integrity of those in authority and government – a trust strengthened by patriotism and a jingoistic attitude buoyed up by the war.

As noted in chapter one, it was not until the numbing truth about the military disasters of Gallipoli and the Somme in 1915-16 filtered through to an incredulous British nation that the possibility of fallibility on the part of those in control of the country's titanic conflict on the European mainland began to dawn.

The imprisonment of George Meakin and James Tinsley, the working class railwaymen held entirely responsible by the British establishment for the slaughter at Quintinshill, was a *fait accompli* long before such doubts began to surface.

When Alexander Ure, the Lord Justice General, handed down the prison sentences on 15 September 1915 satisfaction was expressed in prominent quarters that the men's incarceration represented, at least in part, repayment of the debt for the terrible deaths of – to paraphrase Lord Advocate Munro's indignantly emotive words – those 'brave hearts so suddenly quenched' for no other reason than to allow a signalman another thirty minutes between the sheets.

In its leading article the morning after the trial's conclusion *The Scotsman* newspaper in Edinburgh was quick to adorn itself with the cloak of moral justification on behalf of the tragic Scottish soldiers who had accounted for the vast majority of the death toll at Quintinshill. 'The fields of Gretna on that bright summer morning were like the fields of Flanders,' its editorial noted. While this borrowed heavily from the most quotable line of Munro's closing speech, it was fair and fitting comment, encapsulating in a few words the awful irony behind the fate on 'home soil' of the battle-bound men of the 7th Royal Scots.

Having graphically set the scene, the influential Scottish daily delivered its own unequivocal pronouncement on the signalmen now convicted of causing the slaughter.

'As long as the war is recalled,' it declared gravely, 'it will be remembered that half a battalion of the 7th Royal Scots were almost wiped out by the fatal errors of two signalmen. The two men who were responsible for this great and moving calamity… have received the penalty for their offence, and it is no greater than the magnitude of their crime deserved. It is not agreeable to apply harsh terms to men who up to this time enjoyed a reputation for efficiency and good work and who may have been guilty of no more than a temporary – though fatal – aberration, but it is impossible, on the evidence, to avoid the conclusion that they were justly convicted of a most serious dereliction of duty.'

The consequences for Meakin and Tinsley, added *The Scotsman* with seemingly inarguable insight, would 'haunt them for the remainder of their lifetime'.

While noting that 'the failure of the human mind at critical moments' had been responsible for nearly all accidents in British railway history prior to 1915, the Scottish newspaper pointed out that, in the case of the Quintinshill disaster, there had been 'aggravating circumstances which increased the guilt of the two signalmen'. First in line was the men's undeniable rule-breaking 'private arrangement' for delaying the day shift hand-over. *The Scotsman* was in little doubt that this was a key factor in the tragedy. 'Had the second signalman come on duty at six o'clock, as he should have done, he would not have had his attention distracted by the necessity of writing up back entries in his record book to conceal his late arrival. While he was doing this, the man whom he relieved was sitting by, reading a newspaper, and at that moment the accident occurred.'

This, in general terms, was pretty much the prevailing view, fostered by the long investigative process, a notion not at all disabused by the Caledonian Railway. But, when it came to specifics, *The Scotsman's* interpretation was awry.

Despite the misleading implication, Tinsley was not writing anything at the moment of initial impact. He had finished copying Meakin's notes into the train register. This was ignored by *The Scotsman's* leader writer, as was the fact that the very act of copying the notes should have served as a reminder to Tinsley of the stationary local train's presence on the southbound main line. But then, this had not occurred to any of the 'neutral' commentators in the aftermath of the accident.

None of them had been concerned with peeling away the 'outer wrappings' of the catalogue of events which preceded the initial collision. *The Scotsman* was making a point that, more or less, was universally accepted. 'It is at least probable that the accident would have been avoided but for this breach in rules,' the paper asserted. On the face of it, that was how it undoubtedly seemed.

The prompt, decisive, yet ultimately unsuccessful, steps taken by George Meakin to prevent the catastrophe of the second collision merited no mention in the article. Instead, he was condemned afresh for 'grave omissions of duty' in the lead-up to the initial crash. 'When he put the local passenger train from Carlisle on the up main line, along which the troop train was running, he ought to have placed a collar on the signal lever to show that the line was occupied, and he ought to have given the blocking back signal to the neighbouring signal box.'

Simple, straightforward, no room for doubt – the conventional prevailing wisdom. In letters to the paper, *The Scotsman's* readers expressed much the same view.

However, in parallel with the outrage-fuelled approval of those adamant that Meakin and Tinsley had received their just desserts, disquiet quickly spread among railway workers equally convinced that the punishment handed down by the trial judge was both unduly harsh and unjust – particularly in the case of Tinsley.

On a Sunday evening in Carlisle Theatre, four days after the trial's conclusion on 15 September, members of various National Union of Railwaymen branches in the area met as the Carlisle Vigilance Committee, passing a motion which called for their union's executive to press for a reduction in the signalmen's sentences.

Corresponding meetings were held over a wide area and similar motions passed urging the NUR leadership (and, in some cases, the Labour Party) to intervene with the Government on behalf of Meakin and Tinsley. The NUR executive responded. During October a total of thirty-nine motions calling for reduced sentences were submitted to the Scottish Office. A national railwaymen's petition was organised in support. It maintained that insufficient allowance had been made at the trial for the additional strain on railway staffs owing to the war.

All of this apparently came as no surprise to the Scottish civil service. 'I expect we will hear more on this case,' noted an official in a handwritten letter, now archived.

Interestingly, while the railwaymen's appeals sought clemency for both signalmen and generally made no attempt to apportion blame between them,

the basis for the initial NUR motion passed in Carlisle seems to have been that Meakin was the more culpable of the two in that he had effectively 'set Tinsley up to fail' by not making him fully aware of the position of the traffic in the vicinity of Quintinshill signal box and leaving the block on the southbound line open. This flew in the face of evidence which had established the very opposite.

'The foundation of this opinion,' reported the *Dumfries & Galloway Standard*, which had interviewed one of the union men at the NUR meeting, 'is that it was Meakin who ought to have seen that the train he put 'through the road' [the crossover between the lines] was properly protected before handing over the box to Tinsley as the man on duty. Tinsley certainly took over the duties but ought to have been made aware by Meakin of what had taken place before he began to tamper with either the block or the levers'.

If the newspaper's interviewee really was voicing the collective opinion of his colleagues it was a view that was surely a product of the rumour mill which, inevitably, would have been churning out gossip and speculation in the border region for weeks. Meakin had briefed his mate fully on the situation before handing over. Even by those people acting in his interests he was still being badly served.

The *Standard's* informant clearly went further in pressing Tinsley's case. The newspaper's account of the interview continued, 'Neither did the train register show any blocking back signal'. How could the union man, or any of his colleagues, have known whether this were true or not unless, of course, he or they had been shown the book? Not inconceivable, but gossip seems the more likely explanation. Whatever the truth of that, Meakin was getting a bad press.

Still quoting from its union source, the *Standard* added that, 'in these circumstances Tinsley was entitled to assume that the line was clear for the troop train. Of course, it may be said that Hutchinson should have reminded Tinsley that there was a complication, but it is probable that the fireman hesitated to cross-question him as to the placing of a collar on a certain lever, recognising his own small knowledge of signalling'. A good point to end with but why the interviewee imagined that Tinsley had every right to assume the line was clear when he knew the local train was blocking the way is a mystery. It seems the NUR at local level had decided solidly to press his case.

In the thirty or more appeals for clemency eventually sent from union branches around the country there were references to lax enforcement of regulations by railway companies generally. The branches also challenged the Caledonian's claim that Quintinshill signal box was completely up-to-date by referring to the lack of track circuiting, an electrical device used to detect the presence, or absence, of a train on the line, but it was the apparent assertion that Meakin should have shouldered more of the blame than Tinsley that is of special interest.

It was an argument that eventually gathered credibility and, it appears, was later encouraged by the Caledonian Railway itself as the campaign for the men's release gathered momentum. This poses an interesting series of questions.

Strip away the natural public desire for retribution and the emotions which surrounded it, the prison sentences in both cases had been harsh. Whatever their failings in the signal box, neither Tinsley nor Meakin had set out to harm anyone on 22 May 1915. There had been no criminal intent. The crash at Quintinshill had been tragic, terrible, catastrophic – but an accident all the same.

Had those harsh penalties handed down to the signalmen surprised the railway company, well aware, even if the public were not, of its own contributory role in the disaster? Apart from his complicity in the illicit shift change and his failure to make use of the signal collar – the Caledonian of course knew it had 'stitched him up' over blocking back – George Meakin had acted properly in the box and had done everything in his power to prevent the unfolding catastrophe as soon as he realised the seriousness of James Tinsley's fatal error in allowing the troop train to proceed southwards into the path of the local service.

At the same time the Caledonian's high command knew fully of Tinsley's catalogue of errors and were only too aware from the protracted legal proceedings since the accident how unreliable his evidence had been. They would also have had serious grounds to suspect his medical condition was a key – *the* key – factor at the time of the accident. So why were they, and others, pursuing the line that, of the two signalmen, Meakin had been the more culpable?

Was the company worried that the longer Tinsley remained in jail, the greater the risk that the truth would be teased out? Would he crack? Would the public then learn of a deal to keep Tinsley's health difficulties, embarrassing for the company, under wraps in exchange for a promise that he and his family would be looked after in the future? Would Condie Sandeman and others join the mounting campaign for the men's release? How far would the NUR take things?

If this was how the railway company saw things, the stakes were high.

Scottish Secretary Thomas McKinnon Wood, the Caledonian's St Rollox works at the heart of his Glasgow constituency, was effectively 'their man'. If he, as must be strongly suspected, had been party to the deal with Tinsley and the clampdown on any press coverage that threatened to expose the signalman's apparent illness, the embarrassment factor was potentially huge. McKinnon Wood surely would not have acted alone – he would have been backed by the Government and would not have been out of step with the public mood exemplified by *The Scotsman* in helping to ensure the rule-breaking Quintinshill duo were locked up – but it clearly would have reflected badly on him, his party, the Government and the Caledonian had a conspiracy to limit the truth come to light.

The Scotsman was unrelenting in its outspoken support for the prison sentences. On 29 September, two weeks after the penalties were handed down at the High Court trial, the newspaper attacked the growing campaign for clemency.

'It does not seem to occur to the originators and supporters of this agitation that the public requires to be protected against the repetition of such gross breaches of duty as led to the Gretna Green [the nearest place of note to Quintinshill] calamity.' This, of course, was entirely in keeping with the Lord Advocate's

encouragement to the jury to avoid handing to the signalmen 'a charter of indemnity'.

Somewhat grudgingly, *The Scotsman* conceded that there was a distinction to be drawn between the men's misdemeanours and offences committed with intent, but added that, 'while some errors are excusable... others, which begin with breaking the rules of the company, are culpable in the highest degree: and no one considering the evidence with an impartial mind can honestly believe the men were hard done by.'

Point made, the paper vented its annoyance on the NUR.

'Agitations such as the movement for the release of the... signalmen are, in fact, a grave public danger, and the danger is all the greater when it comes from the organised body of trades unionism. In such cases there is a suspicion that the appeal is not one of justice, but of intimidation... the railwayman's union are not disinterested parties in this question. They are not raising the agitation in the interests of the convicted men only, but in the interests of their whole class.

'They are, in short, on a question of this kind, naturally opposed to the public and for themselves. An agitation emanating from them is, therefore, suspected from the beginning, and it would have been much better if they had left the question alone, recognising that the public also have an interest in the matter and that the public interests are predominant.

'The exercise of pressure by trade unions to defeat the ends of justice is, unfortunately, only too familiar... such cases create an impression that a trade union has only to threaten loudly enough to have its demands granted; while they cannot but have an injurious effect upon the administration of justice.'

Thus, the Quintinshill disaster, or at least its aftermath, had become a game of political football – the railwaymen's trade union versus the Scottish establishment. The slant of *The Scotsman's* editorial probably tells us much about the rush to arrest the signalmen and their convictions as the only men held culpable for the tragedy. Politics and the class struggle characterise this story.

It is right to say that, at this stage, the campaign for release had not found much support outside the railway community. For a second time the story was dropped by the press. The NUR's appeals, despite the weight of collective pressure, fell on deaf ears at the Scottish Office where it seems likely they were treated once more with suspicions of being motivated by political gain, pity or both. Without the need to concern themselves with wider agitation for the men's release, the Scottish authorities clearly saw no need to act on the matter at all.

So the Quintinshill signalmen remained in their respective prisons. George Meakin had been sent to Barlinnie in the north-east of Glasgow. James Tinsley went initially to Edinburgh, spending much of his time splicing cord, but was then transferred to the much harsher environs of Peterhead Convict Prison in Aberdeenshire. Unlike Meakin, he had been sentenced to a term of penal servitude, but why the decision was taken to move him to this notorious jail, accommodating many of Scotland's most dangerous offenders, remains utterly

inexplicable. He was clearly no threat to society, no career criminal. While his prison records survive, they offer no clue as to why Peterhead was chosen for him.

What is known is that Tinsley, on arrival, was assigned to the prison labour force working the granite quarry at Stirling Hill. Why it was thought that this type of hard labour was appropriate is another mystery. Looked at from this perspective, it is little wonder the NUR was anxious to have him set free. The fact that the quarry was connected to the prison by its own railway is unlikely to have made life any easier to bear – a constant reminder of what had brought him to this sorry plight. Fortunately, an injury sustained while breaking the quarry rock allowed him to escape the appalling rigours of Stirling Hill. He was instead given lighter work, probably sewing mailbags for the rest of his term.[1]

We know of his injury from the prison's surviving medical records. But these are incomplete. The quarry accident apart, the only statement relating to Tinsley's medical condition, apparently made at the time of his admission to the prison service, records that his health, both past and present, was 'good.' For a man reported to have been suffering from epileptic fits prior to his incarceration, this is palpably and ridiculously false. The conclusion must be that the Scottish authorities' denial of his true medical condition was both deliberate and total. Tinsley may have gone to prison in a far better medical state than he had endured in the immediate wake of the disaster, thanks presumably to treatment he received in the interim period, but to claim his health was, and always had been, 'good' is indicative only of a thorough cover-up.

The surviving prison records, held at the National Archives of Scotland, reveal one other interesting piece of information which adds further to the bewilderment over the nature of his incarceration. It comes in what amounts to a good character reference from Inspector Charles Morrison, the Annan police officer who supervised Tinsley's arrest at Gretna.

Morrison describes him as 'honest, with no criminal perspectives, a respectable workman, steady and industrious'. We are left to wonder whether the time the inspector spent observing Tinsley as he waited for the go-ahead to arrest him had left a lasting impression on the officer characterised perhaps by a deep sense of injustice at work.

It is clear from the records that Tinsley continued to act responsibly while at Peterhead. A man of deep religious conviction, he worked hard and was a member of the prison choir. In a letter sent from the jail to his wife he expressed deep remorse and prayers for forgiveness for his role in the tragedy.

Meanwhile, the NUR's campaign for release was being stepped up. Thirty-nine petitions from branches far and wide were submitted in support, many on the grounds that the two signalmen had already 'suffered grievously' and further punishment was not justified. It seems probable that the nationwide campaign was orchestrated by the union's principal activist, the redoubtable Jimmy Thomas.

His part in the Quintinshill story has never before been revealed, but it was of huge significance. Overcoming a difficult start to life – he was born, illegitimate, into poverty at Newport, South Wales in 1874 and was raised by his grandmother – Thomas began a railway career in his early teens and was soon an active member of the Amalgamated Society of Railway Servants, helping to forge its merger with two other unions to form the NUR in 1913. Although effectively the union's leader for some time beforehand, it would not be until 1917 that he was elected general secretary, a post he held until 1931.

Thomas was also involved in the wider political sphere. Starting as a local councillor in the Wiltshire railway town of Swindon, he was elected Labour MP for another stronghold of the rail industry, Derby, in 1910. Thus he was in a position to exert influence both as a trade union leader and as an MP at the time of the campaign for the release of the Quintinshill signalmen, but it was in the former capacity that this passionate, strong-willed, clever and charismatic champion of the working class would carry the most clout and have the most effect.

Thomas had played a pivotal role during the national rail strike of August 1911. His negotiating skills had gained him the admiration of David Lloyd George, then Chancellor of the Exchequer, who acted as a mediator to bring an end to the dispute, and, perhaps more interesting, the respect of Sir Guy Granet, the Midland Railway's general manager, who represented the employers. Garnet regarded Thomas as a tough but fair-minded negotiator with whom he could do business. The general view, however, was that the NUR's leader was a man most would welcome as an ally in any sort of argument – and opponents would fear.

His first discernible comment on the Quintinshill trial's aftermath had come late in November 1915 when, in a letter to the Scottish Secretary, he wrote that practically every NUR branch in Scotland was 'praying for a mitigation of the sentences', but there is evidence of a much deeper involvement on Thomas's part.

In the fragment which survives of his letter to McKinnon Wood, Thomas pointed out that no railwayman had ever faced a criminal charge with regard to an accident prior to the prosecution in 1907 of driver George Gourlay in the wake of the December 1906 Elliot Junction disaster near Arbroath (see chapter six). Thomas might have been expected to press the rarity of prosecution issue, but his letter then referred to something surely just as rare, an extraordinary enclosure that would almost certainly have come as a surprise in the Scottish Office.

'I enclose a petition signed by the foreman and eight members of the jury… who themselves clearly point out, which we have abundant evidence to prove, that both the unfortunate prisoners are men of unblemished character and sobriety.'

Calling for the signalmen's early release, the petition had been sent to the NUR's solicitors but was ultimately marked for the attention of George V himself. It can be safely assumed that the wily NUR leader was not merely acting as a

messenger here. He would have played a part in organising this show of support for Tinsley and Meakin from many of the men who only months earlier had delivered the guilty verdicts which had led to their imprisonment. But for such a large number of the jurymen to have signed the petition was surely indicative of a genuine sentiment among them of unease at the harshness of the sentences handed down by Lord Strathclyde, the trial judge.

The jurors' petition quoted the outcome of the Elliot Junction trial as precedent. Although driver Gourlay was held to be primarily responsible for the twenty-two deaths, the judge in his trial acquiesced to a plea for clemency from the jury and restricted the sentence to five months' imprisonment. As with Quintinshill, the Elliot Junction inquiries had revealed contributory fault by others and a generally lax state of affairs on the North British Railway. It was a good parallel.

Endorsing the point in Thomas's covering letter about the Quintinshill pair's good character and sobriety, the former Edinburgh jurors added that, at a time when the country was in need of every available man, 'these two young men, who are not really criminals and whose release would not be a danger to society, would be more useful to the nation... if they were given freedom at an early date'.

Condie Sandeman had made much the same point in his closing submission at the trial. Did he also play a part in orchestrating the jurymen's petition for release? This can only be speculation – though it seems well-grounded – but whoever was involved in this extraordinary appeal, it did not have the desired effect.

A handwritten draft of a letter survives in the archives, presumably the work of a civil servant at the Scottish Office, who confirms to Thomas that his letter and the accompanying jurors' petition had been shown to the Secretary of State and adds that, 'Mr McKinnon Wood has given careful consideration to the cases... but in view of the grievous negligence shown by the prisoners, leading to terrible consequences, which was clearly proved at the trial, he does not feel justified in advising His Majesty to accede to the prayer of the petitions.'

The writer tells Thomas that 'the petition of certain members of the jury in the case [it was actually two-thirds of them!] forwarded with your letter has been laid before the King and... H.M. was not pleased to issue any command thereon'.

It is highly improbable that the King was ever given a proper opportunity to consider this petition. He would have been bombarded with war papers and a civil servant, or indeed the minister himself, could easily have slipped it past him.

Politics were at play. This was not merely an issue about the imprisonment of Tinsley and Meakin; it far exceeded that. Herbert Asquith had clung on to the premiership thanks to the coalition deal struck in May but he and the Liberal Party were hardly in a secure position. The re-emergence of the Quintinshill case, in a manner which cast doubt over the severity of the signalmen's sentences and once again brought into question the whole issue of wider responsibility, was clearly not going to help the weakened Prime Minister's cause.

McKinnon Wood would certainly have had this in mind when news of the jurors' petition reached him. He would also have harboured suspicions about Jimmy Thomas's motives. The NUR leader had a high regard for Asquith but was also on good terms with fellow Welshman Lloyd George, who had been Minister of Munitions since the coalition's formation and would eventually replace Asquith as Prime Minister in December 1916. McKinnon Wood was no friend of Lloyd George, who would kill off Wood's governmental career in 1916.

A year earlier, did the Scottish Secretary regard Jimmy Thomas as subversive – a threat? Very likely. Did he consider the union leader's campaign for the signalmen's release to be part of the perceived wider socialist agenda? Almost certainly.

Whatever the political nuances, the campaign for release appears to have lost momentum for a while as Thomas found his attention diverted by the debate over armed forces conscription, which saw him criss-crossing the country to speak at meetings and in Parliament in his dual capacity as NUR leader and MP.

Then, in March 1916, politics took a back seat as the campaign acquired a poignantly personal note in a letter from James Tinsley's married sister, Jane Ann Johnson, to the Home Secretary, the recently appointed Liberal, Herbert Samuel. In an impassioned plea for her brother's release, she wrote that he 'wasn't really to blame for his loss of memory'. Tantalisingly, she offered no explanation as to why this might have been the case, but it is not difficult to draw the conclusion that she was referring to Tinsley's medical condition, something that, as a close relative, she almost certainly would have been aware of.

The letter explained that Tinsley's father had become seriously ill as a result of the sorrow he had experienced since the conviction and imprisonment of his son.

'He has been struck down by a stroke and will never get up again. But he longs for a sight of his son. It is more than sad to see and hear him calling for him to come before he dies… I dare not write to the King or Queen, but I feel sure if they knew our sorrow they would do something for my brother, such a good son he has been till this sorrow… I know it was a dreadful accident, but for ten years he made no mistake. If you cannot get him off or his sentence reduced, does it lay in your power to let him come down and see his father who is on his deathbed?'

She hoped the Home Secretary would 'excuse the liberty I have taken of writing to you and may God grant my request for the prayer of a heartbroken sister'.

The letter did not succeed in winning back Tinsley's freedom but it was, of course, in the power of the Home Office to accede to the heartfelt plea for temporary release. Despite some misgivings, for the first time in the sorry story of Tinsley's incarceration, compassion was at last shown. On 31 March he was escorted south by a prison warder to Edinburgh and thence by rail across the English border to his birthplace at Ripon. Tinsley was at his father's home in the town for more than three hours. The Scottish prison service noted that, during his day release, 'he caused no trouble to the escort and behaved well throughout'.

On 2 April his sister wrote again to the Home Secretary on behalf of the family. With gratitude and despair in equal measure intermixed with an element of hope, she thanked Samuel 'for the great kindness shown to James Tinsley, the signalman of the Gretna disaster... my father got the last wish he has craved for and we... thank you for what you have done, and if it ever lays in your power to reprieve him or shorten his sentence, I hope you will do so for the sake of his wife and three children. We all know the disaster was a terrible thing, but he has suffered much and no mistake. He takes it very hard because he is one of thirteen children and not one of them has been in prison nor brought trouble to our home. This is our first great grief, which makes it harder to bear for us all...'

Jane Johnson would get nothing further from the Home Secretary; her brother was staying where he was. The renewed appeal for clemency was summarily dismissed in a single handwritten sentence which survives in the archives and presumably represents Herbert Samuel's view at the time. 'I don't think we need take up with this woman the question of remission to which she alludes.' it reads.

It would not be so easy for the Government to similarly shake off the tenacious Jimmy Thomas. He was a different proposition altogether and in April he was dramatically back on the Quintinshill case. The gloves were about to come off.

Tinsley, meanwhile, had written to the Scottish Office. Dated 3 April, his letter expressed, in heartrending terms, overwhelming remorse for his role in the tragedy.

'I would have willingly laid my life down for those fine men that morning, but grief and sorrow have I borne since which no one but myself knows well – in fact my heart is near broken,' he said in his neatly written one-page letter before telling of the deep distress caused to his father and adding poignantly that 'my oldest son of twelve years was wondering, if he wrote to the King, "would he pardon my father?" I have prayed to God to help all those whose sorrow was caused over the accident as I am praying to God now for my wife and three children, asking you all to have pity on us and bring us all together again.'

In closing, Tinsley reiterated his hope that 'you will see your way to pardon me,' and then added that he was 'quite willing to serve my King and country, if fit.'

This request to enlist for the armed forces in an understandable bid to ease the burden of guilt that was obviously tearing him apart had very little chance of succeeding. Tinsley must have known that, his closing reference to questionable fitness something of a giveaway, but it is probable that his offer was genuine. There is nothing known about his character that would suggest it was an empty gesture. He was a man desperate to do something to redeem himself.

The Scottish Office brushed it aside. 'It is ridiculous of this man to think that he might be of use in the army,' was the derisory note of the official who dealt with it.

But was there some hope for Tinsley – Meakin as well – when the Scottish Secretary issued an instruction that their cases were to be 'brought up for

consideration' in three months' time? McKinnon Wood had written to Jimmy Thomas in connection with this. Dated 14 April, the letter, which survives in the archives, makes clear that the two men had already been discussing the matter.

McKinnon Wood referred in the letter to an earlier conversation with the NUR leader and wrote that 'I have refreshed my memory regarding the facts'. Commenting on the sentences handed down, he said the signalmen 'have only served about six months and, before deciding on the question of remission of sentence, it is in accordance with the usual practice that I should consult the judge who presided at the trial, and I think that it would be premature to do so at this stage. I have, however, given instructions that the case is to be brought to my notice again later on, so you may rest assured that it will not be overlooked.'

If the Secretary of State supposed he could fob off Jimmy Thomas MP in such a patronisingly dismissive manner, he was very much mistaken. At the least it was politically naïve; at the most, contemptuous. The NUR leader responded immediately – and it couldn't have made pleasant reading at the Scottish Office:

'The whole history of this case shows a deplorable miscarriage of justice has been perpetrated,' thundered Thomas piercingly, 'and having regard to the sentence these men have already served, I do feel that the circumstances warrant their immediate release. As I explained to you, tremendous feeling exists in the railway service, but we quite appreciate that no good purpose would be served by simply putting questions in the House. I do hope you will give the matter your immediate consideration with a view to their early release.'

Thomas had chosen his words carefully. He clearly wanted to maximise their impact. There was an implied threat in what he had written. It would be unwise of McKinnon Wood to kick the ball in this game into touch. Thomas had upped the ante.

He knew his adversary had a weak spot – and had gone straight for it in the opening line of his letter. In 1914 McKinnon Wood had ordered a private inquiry into the case of Oscar Slater, a disreputable German immigrant who was convicted in 1909 for the brutal murder of an 83-year-old spinster in Glasgow. The prosecution was deeply flawed. Although initially sentenced to death, Slater escaped execution when the sentence was commuted to life imprisonment. He eventually served nineteen years at Peterhead prison before, in 1928, his conviction was formally quashed on the grounds that the judge in the case had not properly directed the jury as to the irrelevance of Slater's previous character. The Slater affair was truly a can of worms for McKinnon Wood.

The Scottish Secretary's 1914 inquiry had revolved around a detective in the case, John Trench, who had provided information which threw doubt on the conviction but was allegedly concealed by the police from the High Court trial. The inquiry, however, found that the conviction was sound. The unfortunate Trench, in turn, found himself dismissed from the police force and prosecuted on totally trumped-up charges. He was later acquitted but the sorry Slater-

Trench affair had done nothing for the reputation of the Scottish legal system and had proved a major embarrassment for Secretary of State McKinnon Wood.

He had only reluctantly set up the inquiry and had done nothing to prevent it descending into a farcical charade which was always going to end with the one, wrong, outcome. 'The Honourable Gentleman acted dishonourably,' wrote author Richard Whittington-Egan in his 2001 book, *The Oscar Slater Murder Story.*[2]

Now, in 1916, he was confronted with Jimmy Thomas's allegation of another major miscarriage of justice in the Quintinshill case. Potential embarrassment again loomed large for McKinnon Wood, especially as the Quintinshill trial had several links, in terms of personnel, with the Slater case and its disgraceful sequel.

Alexander Ure, judge at the Tinsley-Meakin trial, had prosecuted Slater in 1909 when serving as Scotland's Lord Advocate. He had played fast and loose with the evidence, had indulged in a savage character assassination of the accused man and had clearly prejudiced the jury in his apparent desire to see Slater hang, behaviour for which he had been widely censured – not that any of this had prevented his appointment as Scotland's Lord Justice General following his elevation to the peerage as Baron Strathclyde in 1914.

Also linked dishonourably to the Slater affair was Ure's successor as Lord Advocate, Robert Munro, who prosecuted the Quintinshill signalmen. He had been criticised for his poor – many called it criminal – conduct in the appalling treatment of John Trench. It was Munro who had indicted the innocent detective on the manufactured charges which, rightly, were later thrown out of court.[3]

Jimmy Thomas was no political 'rookie'. He was a shrewd operator who had battled against corruption and misdemeanour in high places for years. It is probable that he was aware, or at least suspicious, that the prosecution of Tinsley and Meakin had concealed evidence potentially damaging to those in high authority. He would certainly have known how to turn this to suit his own ends.

McKinnon Wood's reaction to Thomas's letter was predictable. If the union leader wanted to talk tough, then he would do so too. Angrily, he told Thomas he was 'surprised to note that your representations in favour of these men are now based upon the new and serious allegation that "the whole history of this case shows a deplorable miscarriage of justice has been perpetrated." I can find no warrant for this allegation in the report of the proceedings at the trial. On the contrary, it seems that the jury were amply justified in arriving, as they did, at a unanimous verdict of guilty, and the justice of that verdict has not been hitherto impugned.'

This was as ridiculous a statement as it was outrageous. McKinnon Wood knew full well that, just four months previously, he had received a petition from nine members of the jury which, by implication at least, clearly impugned the justice of what had transpired at the High Court. Whether or not they felt they had been misled by the judge's summing-up is open to question, but they clearly

thought the sentences handed down by Lord Strathclyde were unjustifiably severe. McKinnon Wood, of course, was also aware that Thomas knew about this.

He closed his reply of 26 April to the NUR leader with the defiant ultimatum that, 'if there is going to be any reconsideration of the cases at a later date it must be on a different ground from which you urge'. War had been declared!

Within a week Thomas had responded. His tone more conciliatory, he wrote on 1 May of his regret that the Secretary of State had appeared to have 'misunderstood the purport of my letter of 15 April. What I meant was: those – the railway company and we – who know all the circumstances connected with the technical working of the railways are unanimous in the opinion that the heavier sentence [has been handed] to the man who is least responsible for the accident' – a surprising return to the NUR's case that Meakin was the more guilty.

'I hope' he added, 'this explanation will enable you to realise this aspect of the case, but I quite appreciate that in soliciting your kind intervention it must necessarily be on the grounds that we feel the penalty these men have already suffered would warrant a re-consideration of their cases, and it is upon that ground I urge your compassionate intervention.' It was a complete change of strategy.

So what was his game plan now? Ever the opportunist, he had cleverly implied that he now had the support of the Caledonian Railway. It was a risky strategy, of course, particularly as it threatened the chances of an early release for Meakin, but letting McKinnon Wood know that he was working in concert with the company was bound to leave the Scottish Secretary in a very tight spot.

Frustratingly, his reply to Thomas's May Day letter – assuming he made one – does not survive in the Scottish archives. There was a lengthy gap, anyway, in the 'debate' as Thomas's attention was again diverted by other union-related issues. Conscription, which had come into force in March, was extended to include married men with the passing of a second Military Service Act on 3 May, the NUR leader reluctantly agreeing to cooperate over this – in contrast to continuing opposition from other union activists. Then, in July, national attention became focussed on the start of the British and French Somme offensive.[4]

A week later, on 9 July, McKinnon Wood, now 60, was moved by Asquith from his Scottish post to assume the twin roles of Chancellor of the Duchy of Lancaster and Financial Secretary to the Treasury. Taking over as Scottish Secretary was Herbert Asquith's brother-in-law, the 50-year-old Scottish Liberal, Harold Tennant. Elected an MP for Berwickshire in 1894, Tennant had been given various governmental roles by Asquith since he came to power in 1908 but the Scottish job was his first – and would turn out also to be his last – Cabinet post.

Back on the Quintinshill case, Jimmy Thomas seized on Tennant's comparative lack of experience and questionable political mettle. It would not take him long to pounce.

The newcomer was briefed on the situation by civil servants on 17 July and advised that his predecessor had left instructions for the case to be reviewed. In

a surviving memo, Tennant's Parliamentary Under Secretary, Sir James Dodds, advised the Scottish Secretary, 'the one thing that would justify remission of a portion of the sentence is that there was no criminal intent and I think that the Lord Justice General might now be consulted on the subject of remission'.

Here, at last, the critical matter of criminal intent had been raised by the Scottish Office and with it the question of whether or not the prosecutions were legal.

In a further memo dated 19 August, Dodds recorded that, three days earlier, he had seen Thomas and NUR colleague, Jimmy Williams, the union's general secretary since 1910, 'in regard to this case… and agree that the Justice General should be consulted'. It looked as if a breakthrough was now on the cards.[5]

On the same day Dodds dispatched a formal letter to Lord Strathclyde, the trial judge, formally seeking his opinion. The reply was not long in coming, dated 21 August, but strangely it arrived in the form of a personal, and presumably private, letter. The judge explained that the reason for Tinsley's heavier sentence was that he was 'the man actually on duty. He gave the fatal signal that the line was clear when he knew it was not' – an apparent suggestion that Tinsley deliberately pulled the signals to clear while knowing that the line was blocked.

This flew in the face of the evidence. There had been absolutely no proof that Tinsley had done anything of the sort. He did not know the line wasn't clear for the troop train. He had repeatedly said that he had forgotten all about the local train.

Was Alexander Ure thinking straight when he wrote to Dodds? It is tempting to ask, was his lordship entirely sober? If that seems shockingly uncharitable, what other interpretation can there possibly be? His words were crass, utter nonsense. The learned judge continued his explanation in similar vein, adding that 'the other man had gone off duty, although he still remained in the signal box, and when he went off duty the danger signal was up, so no mishap could have occurred had not Tinsley given the signal, "line clear". The sentences were… severe but, in my opinion (shared by the jury, I believe), the case was much stronger than hitherto known. It was really very gross. The train which blocked the way was lying just beneath the man's eyes; they both knew it was there.'

This was appalling gibberish. Once again the judge was suggesting wrongly that Tinsley knew the 'local' was there but had deliberately ignored its presence. As for the jury sharing his view on the severity of the sentencing, most had since made clear this was not the case, though it is possible that Alexander Ure had not been told of the jurors' petition and it had simply been 'buried' by McKinnon Wood. Whether or not this was the case, seldom can a High Court judge in Britain have so hopelessly misinterpreted the evidence in a trial at which, less than a year earlier, he had presided over. Increasingly it seems that he was desperately trying to justify a process which he knew was flawed.

Just two days after sending this private missive to Dodds, Lord Strathclyde wrote again to the Parliamentary Under Secretary. This time his letter was formal.

It consisted almost entirely of an expanded justification of his decision to impose the sentences he had. 'The case of Tinsley and Meakin which I tried in the High Court last September was the most serious of its kind which has occurred either in Scotland or, as far as I am aware, in England,' he asserted. This was, of course, true. 'The precautions taken by the railway company to avoid accidents of this kind appear to me to be perfect. No suggestions to the contrary were made at the trial. Both men were thoroughly acquainted with them.'

This was markedly less accurate. Had the trial addressed the failures in supervision or properly tested the evidence of the Caledonian's Robert Killin and Alexander Thorburn the very suggestion of perfect safety precautions would have been laughable. The judge, however, was technically correct when he added that 'no excuse of any kind was offered for their failure to observe them.' The excuse – or at least, reason – for Tinsley's many lapses was never raised.

'Neither of the men went into the witness box,' added Ure. 'Their negligence was very gross and was wholly destitute of excuses. The jury apparently found no difficulty in the case.' Hardly surprising given the tone and content of his summing-up! 'After an absence of only eight minutes they returned a unanimous verdict of guilty.' Well, he had made sure of that – but this statement is further indication that the judge was unaware of the jurors' subsequent change of mind and the extraordinary action they had taken in a bid to redress things.

Yet another inaccuracy was to follow: 'There were no recommendations to leniency.' Condie Sandeman and his defence team had pleaded for precisely that at the trial. Blithely sidestepping this obstacle to his argument, the judge asserted that, 'having in view the exceedingly gross character of the men's negligence, a very severe sentence must be pronounced. Penal servitude, it is true, has never, so far as I am aware, been given in similar cases. But, of its kind, this was the gravest case of neglect of duty which has ever come before the courts.'

He then reiterated his reasoning for handing down the stiffer sentence to Tinsley, yet again repeating that the signalman had known the up line was not clear. This brought Lord Strathclyde to his final paragraph. Given the content and thrust of the main body of his text, it is astonishing to read that paragraph today.

'Having in full view of the circumstances of the cases, I think we and the Secretary of State for Scotland might now recommend the liberation of both men.'

Having effectively just accused James Tinsley of murder, the judge was now recommending that both he and George Meakin should be given early release from prison! It was truly a staggering change of stance. What could lie behind it?

The probability must be that Alexander Ure, Lord Strathclyde, had received from what must have been, given his status as Scotland's Lord Justice General, very high authority an instruction to go against his own judgment and recommend the remissions in sentence. In a muddle, he had imposed penalties on Tinsley and Meakin that had, in terms of severity, surprised a great many people. Again,

it is hard not to conclude that the powers-that-be now wanted the signalmen, Tinsley in particular, out of prison to minimise the chance of the truth behind the Quintinshill disaster emerging. For this to happen, the acquiescence of the trial judge was essential. Ure surely had been 'got at'. Had he now been told the truth about Tinsley's underlying illness?

By whom it is hard to say, but this seems a plausible explanation for his statement that, 'in full view of the circumstances,' he was recommending early release.

Yet, it seems, he had wanted to go down with a fight – hence his despairing, if shamefully ill-judged, defence of his action at the High Court in September 1915.

Sir James Dodds quickly alerted Secretary of State Harold Tennant to the new situation, attaching to his memo Ure's second letter with its amazing twist in the tail.

'He intimated to me in his note of 21 August that the Lord Justice Clerk [second in rank to the Lord Justice General] was at hand and he would confer with him about the propriety of remission,' wrote Dodds. 'I take it, therefore, that the Lord Justice Clerk may be taken as concurring in the opinion of the Head of the Court.' But Dodds advised Tennant that 'it does not follow that you are bound to act on this opinion. All it conveys is that the judges would not consider that the ends of justice had not been served if the men were now released.'

In other words, double negative aside, Scotland's top two judges were now happy, or at least prepared, to set the signalmen free. But Dodds saw things differently.

'I confess I have grave doubt as to the propriety of immediate release. I fully believe that the prisoners must have suffered grievously from the knowledge that such a terrible catastrophe was caused by their gross and criminal carelessness and I have no doubt that the pressure which has been used to get them out of prison is due to a natural sentiment of pity,' he told the Secretary of State.

How Dodds reached that conclusion is hard to understand. No doubt pity played a part in the campaign for release but the Under Secretary would have been aware of Jimmy Thomas's letters to McKinnon Wood about the unfairness of the sentences and the alleged miscarriage of justice; he would have known from the same source of the Caledonian Railway's support for getting Tinsley, at least, quickly out of jail; and he must have seen the jurors' petition in favour of freeing men who were 'not really criminals.' Could all this be motivated by pity alone? Dodds seemed to harbour no doubts as he developed the theme by adding:

'The question is, how far should such sentiments be allowed to interfere with the course of justice? I see no special object in taking the great trouble and expense of an elaborate prosecution in the criminal courts if a sentence which, when put beside the terrible effects of their crime, seems very moderate indeed, is to be materially reduced because it is to be demanded by an extremely powerful trades

union. I am somewhat alarmed by the way in which the railway organisations take up these cases. The ordinary criminal has no such support.

'It will be answered, of course, that these men are not ordinary criminals. I admit they are not, and that they had, presumably, no criminal intent; but if this argument is rigorously pushed to its logical conclusion, it would be not to prosecute in such cases at all, but to leave the man to his conscience and public opinion.'

What a curious line of argument by Sir James. If Tinsley and Meakin had harboured no criminal intent, which of course they hadn't, they could not, by definition, be said to be criminals at all, whether 'ordinary' ones or otherwise!

'Normally,' continued Dodds' memo, 'a penal servitude convict [as in the case of Tinsley] earns… one-fourth remission, and an ordinary prisoner, one-sixth. Tinsley should therefore get out in the ordinary course, about 15 December 1917 and Meakin, 15 December 1916, earning nine months' and three months' revision, respectively. I do not personally see why they should get any extra remission. It is obvious [that] if they were both now discharged they would benefit very unequally. I also believe that public opinion would resent their discharge.'

Dodds possibly had a point there. Starved as it was by full and proper knowledge of the facts, sections of public opinion might well rail against the men's early release. His memo, though, is more illuminating for the insight it provides into the widening political confrontation between the British establishment and the expanding trades unions and Socialist movement in general, a recurring theme of the Quintinshill story. Whether by design or default, Edinburgh High Court had seen something of a political show trial in 1915.

But public opposition to the men's release was far from total – a factor that might have been an optional, or possibly additional, explanation, had he got wind of it, for the content of Judge Ure's second letter to Sir James Dodds on 23 August.

Around the same time Jimmy Thomas had weighed in again, presenting a new 110-page petition to the Scottish Office with at least 2,000 signatures calling for the signalmen's release. This was apparently forwarded to Judge Ure, though he would already have sent his second letter to Dodds before it reached him.

More petitions quickly followed. 'I herewith enclose the latest bundle of petitions regarding the case of Tinsley and Meakin… which will give you some indication of the tremendous feeling and sympathy existing for these poor men,' Thomas wrote to Harold Tennant on the 23rd. This time the signatures were not those of NUR members. The significance of their origin was profound.

'When I point out that these petitions were signed primarily by the citizens of Edinburgh, where the trial took place and where the majority of the unfortunate victims were resident, you will realise the importance of them,' Thomas told the Scottish Secretary. 'I would beg you to urge His Majesty the King to extend his gracious act of clemency, as I am satisfied these two men have already undergone sufficient punishment to have more than met the demands of justice.'

It is not known who organised the Edinburgh signatures and whether there was some link to the jurors' earlier petition from the city. Was this latest petition orchestrated, or at least supported, by Thomas himself? It cannot be ruled out. Whoever was responsible, this intervention carried a considerable measure of weight.

Around this time Thomas and Jimmy Williams were evidently granted an interview with Tennant. Thomas referred to it in a letter he sent to the Secretary of State dated 11 September. The meeting had clearly not provoked any particularly swift action on Tennant's part. 'I shall be extremely obliged if you can now let me know whether anything can be done as the anxiety in these cases is tremendous,' Thomas told the Scottish Secretary. 'I feel sure that you will recognise the severe punishment these unfortunate men have already suffered.'

Six days later came the reply. It was not the answer Jimmy Thomas wanted to hear. Tennant told him that he had held a conference in Glasgow with the Lord President of the Court of Session and the Lord Advocate, 'and went very carefully into the cases of Tinsley and Meakin. I have decided, on this careful review, that I should not be justified in recommending the release of these men just now.

'I have given instructions for these cases to be bought up for reconsideration towards the close of the year. I am sorry I cannot say more at present.'

Harold Tennant was indulging in a high risk political game. Closely aligned with Asquith on the right of the Liberal Party, he was vulnerable to the growing threat posed to the leadership by David Lloyd George. The latter had adopted a conciliatory stance in his response to industrial disputes, yet here was Tennant apparently prepared to take on one of the most powerful, resourceful trades union officials in the country. Incurring Jimmy Thomas's wrath was political naivety.

The re-emergence of Lord Advocate Robert Munro in the story is interesting. He had clearly played a pivotal role in persuading Tennant to oppose the case for remission, effectively overruling the Lord Justice General. It would seem from this that he did not share the Caledonian Railway's apparent desire to get Tinsley away from Peterhead as soon as possible. Was professional pride his motive?

Jimmy Thomas turned up the heat on 23 September. 'I hardly need to say that I am keenly disappointed at your inability to do anything at this stage,' he told Tennant. 'I will refrain from doing anything further until I have the opportunity of seeing you.' The implied threat of stepping up NUR action should have been heeded.

No record survives of a further meeting between the two men. If there was one, it had evidently not succeeded in resolving the matter by the time Thomas wrote again to the Secretary of State on 18 November, reminding Tennant of his undertaking on 17 September to reconsider the case towards the end of the year.

'I am sorry to have to trouble you again [but] as you will be aware these men are still serving their terms of imprisonment and from the information I am getting from all parts of the country there is a growing indignation at the treatment [they]

are receiving,' he wrote. 'Surely, having regard to the offence and the punishment they have received, justice will now have been met by arranging their immediate release.' Point made, the NUR leader turned the screw.

'My difficulty is aggravated by the fact that, against all opposition, I have prevented drastic action being taken by our men. In view of all the circumstances of these cases I would beg you to step in and exercise your authority.'

This was a typical Thomas ploy. He was giving the impression that he alone was desperately trying to prevent serious industrial action by his members of which he was probably the instigator – if the threat really existed at all at that stage. Morally dubious perhaps but, at the same time, this was also shrewd political manoeuvring. With Jimmy Thomas MP, the ends always justified the means.

The threat was ignored, a civil servant at the Scottish Office merely reminding Thomas that a review had been promised and, anyway, 'Meakin's time is nearly up.'

Faced with this intransigence, on 25 November Jimmy Thomas delivered the killer blow in a further letter to the Secretary of State.

'I have been making every effort to see you this week without success,' he wrote, 'and therefore I am writing this private letter because I am beginning to be alarmed at the state of feeling existing in Scotland with regard to the treatment of Tinsley and Meakin, not only among railwaymen but also among transport workers and miners.

'As you know I have prevented so far our members taking any action, notwithstanding their impatience and eagerness to stop work. Of course I saw the danger of allowing an agitation on a question of this kind, and felt quite satisfied that these were cases which would appeal to you.

'Unfortunately, I am now left with no alternative than to submit the whole question to my executive committee who are meeting on Monday next week, when I am perfectly satisfied that they will take the matter into their own hands.

'You will remember the petitions I sent to you in August last which contained the signatures of even the jurymen themselves. Whilst treating this as a private letter I do hope that you will realise the state of the country [as regards the war] and the burning indignation of the railwayman on this matter, more especially (as they keep reminding me) when they compare the Tinsley and Meakin case with the railway blunder in India and the difference in the punishment in that case.'[6, 7]

Harold Tennant was now facing the threat of a paralysing national strike by the three unions which in 1914 had formed a powerful Triple Alliance – the NUR, the Miners' Federation and the Transport Workers' Federation of dockers, seamen, road haulage workers and tramwaymen. It was just about the last thing his beleaguered brother-in-law at the helm of the war-weary government needed.

Desperate to head this off, Tennant turned for help to Arthur Henderson, leader of the Labour Party and, since formation of Asquith's coalition administration in May 1915, a member of the Cabinet in his capacity as President of the Board of Education. Evidently the two men had discussed the worsening situation, presumably by telephone, on 1 December. Later the same day the Scottish Secretary wrote to Henderson, revealing that he had 'again thought over the matter in relation to J.H. Thomas's intervention on behalf of Tinsley and Meakin'.

He told the Labour leader he had as a result 'altered my mind to some extent and have put a small protest in writing. It is very mild in comparison to what I feel.

'I send you a copy of what I have written. I do not wish my letter to be in any way a substitute for what I hope you will say to him. Rather, I wish your letter and my letter to be confirmatory of each other and complementary to one another.'

Despite his 'small protest,' Tennant had in fact caved in to the pressure. In the letter he had sent to Thomas, and copied to Henderson, he told the NUR leader he had now reconsidered the case for the signalmen's release 'and in view of a favourable report from the learned judge who tried the case [which he had actually had since September], I have now decided that I shall be justified in releasing Tinsley at a date which anticipates the normal date of discharge by a year.'

Taking into account the one-fourth earned remission, which would have seen Tinsley set free in December 1917, Tennant informed Thomas that he had issued instructions for the signalman's release 'on or about 15th instant'. Within a fortnight, James Tinsley would be bidding farewell to his grim prison environs.

For George Meakin the Scottish Secretary's change of heart had come too late for a release date earlier than the one-sixth earned remission on his nineteen month sentence. He was due for release on 15 December anyway and would be out by that date. It only remained for Harold Tennant to record his small note of protest:

'I feel that I should add that the remission in Tinsley's case must not be taken as implying that I regard the sentence as excessive; and also that the difficulties of a Minister whose duty it is to give unbiased consideration to the revision of criminal cases are much increased when he has to face suggestions of organised agitation by sectional interest in the event of his not following a particular course.'

Thomas is unlikely to have been at all agitated by the Secretary of State's rebuke.

Arthur Henderson replied to Tennant on 4 December from the London office he occupied as Labour adviser to the Government. 'I will speak to Thomas on the matter, supplementing what you have said in your letter,' he told the Scottish Secretary. What he said to Thomas was not recorded but it is unlikely to have amounted to much of a reprimand. He might not have entirely approved of the

NUR man's methods – there is some evidence to support his reservations in this regard – but the outcome would certainly not have displeased the Labour leader.

Tennant had handled the situation poorly from the start. News of this would have been passed immediately to Asquith. The premier's fury can be imagined. His brother-in-law's inexperience, incompetence and prejudice had brought the country close to a potentially devastating industrial dispute at a time of national crisis.

When Asquith was ousted from the premiership on 5 December, Harold Tennant was simultaneously sacked by the incoming Lloyd George, never to return to front line politics. He would lose his Parliamentary seat at the 1918 general election and, despite an attempt to win it back at Glasgow Central in 1923, his career as a politician was finished. How much of a contributory factor his inept handling of the Quintinshill affair was to the fall of Asquith is arguable.

Jimmy Thomas would never refer publicly to his key role in the release of the signalmen. The probability is that some aspects of this, and the case in general, were known to only a very few people and it was decided to keep it that way. On 15 December 1916 James Tinsley and George Meakin were freed from prison.[8]

Notes

1. Quarrying at Stirling Hill for the distinctive red Peterhead granite – regarded as excellent for decorative and monumental purposes – began in 1815. In 1884 the Admiralty commenced construction of breakwaters for Peterhead Harbour. The private railway was built to link the Admiralty quarry at Spring Hill with Peterhead prison to transport both convict labour and the quarried granite. The stone was crushed in the prison yard and made into large concrete blocks. This massive project was not completed until 1956. Today just one quarry remains on the hill.
2. *The Oscar Slater Murder Story* by Richard Whittington-Egan, published by Neil Wilson Publishing, 2001 – ISBN 10-1897784880.
3. J. Condie Sandeman provided yet another link between the Slater affair and the Quintinshill trial. He was Detective Trench's defence advocate before representing Tinsley and Meakin.
4. The liability for conscription was further extended by a third Act in 1918 which increased the upper age limit to 51.
5. Jimmy Williams was officially the NUR's general secretary from 1910 until his retirement from ill health in 1916 when Jimmy Thomas took over the post. It is clear, however, that Thomas was effectively fulfilling the duties of general secretary for a lengthy period prior to this.
6. It may have been a slip of the pen by Thomas but was he suggesting that the Edinburgh jurors – possibly the entire jury – had signed the August petitions in addition to the earlier petition which had first raised their unease at the severity of the Lord Justice General's sentences?
7. The Indian railway accident occurred on 30 August 1916 between Ambala and Saharanpur on the main line to Lucknow when a mail train ran into a goods train, killing two non-commissioned officers of the British 2nd Wessex Brigade on their way to a month's holiday

in Mussoorie. Unlike the Quintinshill disaster, none of the railwaymen involved were sent to prison.

8. James Henry 'Jimmy' Thomas (1874-1949) remained a controversial character in later life. He briefly served twice as Secretary of State for the Colonies (later Dominions) under Labour's Ramsay MacDonald in 1924–1931, and again as part of Conservative Stanley Baldwin's National Government in 1935–36, though his decision to join the National Government had led to his expulsion from both the Labour Party and the National Union of Railwaymen. His political career ended abruptly in May 1936 when he became involved in stock exchange speculation and was found to have dropped hints about tax changes planned in the Budget. Despite this, Jimmy Thomas had earned considerable cross-party respect.

Chapter 14

The Final Analysis

'Human truth is always soiled with falsehood.'

Austin O'Malley, Keystones of Thought, 1914

The preface to this book set out its prime purpose – to tell the story of Britain's worst-ever railway disaster in a manner which exploded the myth behind it that has stood for nearly a century. The cause of Quintinshill's tragedy was far more complex than the straightforward tale of two careless signalmen, one of them extraordinarily forgetful, who disobeyed rules. Though generally accepted in 1915, that simplistic interpretation of what happened has never made any sense. It makes no sense today. Yet, until now, no one has seriously challenged it.

For that myth to develop and become enshrined, immediately and enduringly, as fact required at its heart a sophisticated deceit which relied only on those parts of the Quintinshill story which suited its ends. Meanwhile, the remaining aspects were buried in a highly successful bid to blame the whole thing on those two working class men in the signal box.

In other words, it was a cover-up, and for this to succeed it would had to have been blessed with the approval of high authority in the crisis-torn government of wartime Britain. It is in the construct of that major crisis in the spring of 1915 that the digging for evidence to justify this thesis begins.

As detailed in chapter one, May 1915 was a disastrous month for Herbert Asquith's Liberal administration and the nation it was tying to lead ten months after the start of the Great War. Bad news engulfed Britain. A flawed, failed invasion in the Dardenelles, precipitating the fall from grace of Winston Churchill, was quickly followed by the sinking of the *Lusitania* and then, on the 14th, *The Times*'s war correspondent, Colonel Charles Repington, reported profound criticism of the Government's handling of the war from the man commanding the British Expeditionary Force.

The British Army was losing battles because it was short of ammunition. That was the essence of Sir John French's verbal attack on the War Office – War Secretary Lord Kitchener in particular – and it is worth reiterating what a shattering effect his words had on the country. That 'our boys' may have been

sacrificed for want of such a fundamental requirement was profoundly shocking. The dramatic political upheaval which then erupted in the wake of what is now recalled as the 'shell crisis' is fundamental to understanding a key underlying aspect of the Quintinshill story.[1]

Asquith was under severe fire even if the enemy in France was not. The very last thing he needed in the final week of May was another disaster. Then news filtered through on the 22nd that more than 200 Gallipoli-bound Scottish soldiers had been killed in a train crash on the English border before they could even reach their port of disembarkation. The Government exercised executive control over the nation's railways in wartime.

It was the final calamity in a month which had seen one piling on top of another. Within days Asquith had been forced to surrender the Liberal Party's total control of the Government in favour of an unwanted coalition with the other parties in the Commons, principally the official Conservative opposition. It saved his status at the helm of the country for the time being but Herbert Asquith was now a desperately weakened premier.

One shock after another. It wasn't just the political elite who were feeling the effects of that crisis-ridden month. Across the nation, the stunned British public were looking for reasons, looking for people to blame. The political situation was perplexing to many, but at least with the disaster at Quintinshill it appeared there were a pair of ready-made culprits for the taking.

Fired by fiercely patriotic emotions, it was easy for the public, initially at least, to blame James Tinsley and George Meakin for the loss of the soldiers, among others, especially after the opening of the Board of Trade inquiry in Carlisle seemed to leave no room for any doubt as to their guilt.

The signalmen were easy targets; men of the people themselves, and the people understood that organisations like railways were governed by rules. The signalmen had clearly broken these. At least with this disaster the public did not need to concern themselves with the uncertainties of criticising the respected great men of influence and breeding who ran the country.

And the great men themselves were able to sit a little more comfortably on their benches, at least with this issue, safe in the knowledge that the heat was off. It appeared a cut and dried case of negligence in the signal box.

Then the apparently straightforward nature of the case was complicated by reports in the press of James Tinsley's arrest in an ambulance. Could this just be put down to extreme stress – shock at what had happened? *The Scotsman* newspaper in Edinburgh hinted at something else. Tinsley, it reported, was 'subject to fits.' It was a reminder that Tinsley's health at the time of the accident had been raised at the inquiry. He was adamant that he had been 'all right' but it seemed there was now some doubt about this. The public weren't to know that the police in Dumfrieshire, having received medical advice, were attributing the fits to epilepsy but the press in Scotland had come very close to suggesting this

as a possibility. What did it mean? Was this case really as straightforward as it had seemed?

Sensitive to any possibility of hostile public reaction, did Asquith's newly-formed coalition take immediate action to halt in its tracks this unwelcome twist in the tale? The potential reaction to the employment of a man who might have been suffering from epilepsy in a signal box on one of the country's most important rail routes – a man whose illness might have been the main reason for the deaths of the Scottish soldiers – would have been of major concern.

At a time when public morale was at a very low ebb, was the decision taken to bury the story as far as was practically possible and prevent further press comment?

As we have shown this would appear to have been the case. Presumably using its powers under the Defence of the Realm Act of 1914, the Government seems to have imposed an immediate ban on all newspaper reporting of the case which was apparently effective until the first of two inquests got under way in Carlisle on 23 June. But not entirely so. In tracing what really happened in this tragic case, the seemingly brave defiance of the ban, if ban there was, by the *Dumfries & Galloway Standard*, which voiced its concerns via its letters page, was of immense value.

It raised the question – should the Caledonian Railway, on whose tracks the disaster had occurred, be sharing the blame? Had shortcomings in its supervisory regime been a major factor? Did this amount to a systems failure?

The Government may have exercised executive influence over the railway network but the powerful rail companies still ran the trains. Mighty institutions with considerable political clout, they sought at all times to protect their own interests. The Caledonian's were now under threat, not least because it was they who had recruited James Tinsley.

There are, of course, many indisputable facts in the Quintinshill story. At the head of these, beyond any doubt, is that on that fateful morning in May 1915, a time-served, experienced and respected signalman, who had graduated through the Caledonian ranks to work on the prestige cross-border West Coast Main Line, had inexplicably pulled signals to 'clear' on a blocked line. In so doing, James Tinsley had ushered in unspeakable horror. Was it credible that he had simply forgotten the local train standing outside his box in the way of the troop train?

It is, and always has been, the crucial question in the Quintinshill story. Others have answered it in the affirmative. We have argued that this was simply not the case. Signalmen from time to time do make mistakes. They *do* forget trains. But seldom, if ever, do they forget a train standing just a few yards away in which they have minutes earlier travelled to work.

The two most widely suggested reasons for Tinsley's extraordinary lapses of memory are highly questionable. The one accepted at the time was that he was distracted by copying up George Meakin's notes on train movements since the

official 6am shift change time. This has stood the test of time and is still regarded as the established 'truth'. It was, as we have said, a gift to those in 1915 intent on pinning the lion's share of the blame on his shoulders.

But it was based purely on a speculative remark attributed to Tinsley in the Board of Trade's report. It enabled the illicit shift change arrangement to be brought into the equation as the probable underlying cause of the accident. Because of the need to mark up the train register and cover up his late arrival, it is argued, Tinsley's mind was not focussed on what was happening on the line.

The unofficial arrangement allowed him, and his equally experienced mate, men with hitherto unblemished records, to be painted as dishonest and unreliable workers. The fact that the Caledonian had apparently done nothing to expose the irregularity and had allowed disreputable employees – as Tinsley and Meakin now seemed to be – in such responsible positions to work on its main line somehow was lost on those charged with investigating the causes, just one of the many missed opportunities to get to the truth. But was getting to the truth ever the real objective?

On its own the note copying theory does not stand up to scrutiny. While it was Tinsley himself who allegedly floated it in the first place, he never actually used this at the public inquiry as an excuse, or reason, for his chaotic failures and he appeared to duck the question at the coroner's court. It is found only in narrative form – no direct quotation – in the board's official report, and how much credibility can be placed on a document that failed so completely to look into any of the many wider issues?[2]

As discussed in chapter five, a key question is – how long would it have taken Tinsley to copy the notes? It was said that he had to make thirty entries in the register. On the face of it, this sounds a long task. But these were far from complex – just eight brief train descriptions with twenty-two times alongside. A simple experiment using pen and ink from an inkwell indicated that, providing Tinsley was functioning normally, it would have taken him no more than four minutes to carry it out.

Having to juggle this task with running the box no doubt would have been tricky but Tinsley had done this many times before and insisted that he had completed the copying exercise on 22 May before the initial crash occurred. If this were true, the theory of distraction at the critical time fails. Nobody investigating the disaster's causes saw fit to put this to the test.

If the note copying was a relevant factor it had to be linked to something else. Almost certainly, it was. It is clear from the evidence that he was struggling with the task, simple though it should have been, and not making a very good job of it. We have only copies made by the company of the relevant pages from the register to go on – the originals have never resurfaced – but it appears that he had left one set of figures out altogether. A comparison with the concurrent train registers from neighbouring signal boxes suggests there were also a large number of timing discrepancies, probably due (though it's hard to be certain of this) to

further errors in Tinsley's copying exercise, an aspect explored in Keith Walter's technical appraisal (see appendix two).

On the face of it, then, not the best attempt at a forgery on the part of Tinsley, but hardly surprising given the inept book-keeping that followed. We have drawn attention to the fact that he offered local train fireman George Hutchinson the wrong page of the register to sign. Hutchinson might be forgiven for not spotting this, but it was a major error by Tinsley. Even if it had been the correct page, he indicated to the fireman entirely the wrong place.

While it is now clear that the inspection regime in the Caledonian's southern district was lamentable, and that the book-keeping in Quintinshill signal box, according to Robert Killin, may have left a lot to be desired, if this slapdash marking-up of the train register was typical of Tinsley's train recording on the days he started work thirty minutes late, it surely should have been discovered well before the accident.

But we very much doubt that it was typical. There has to be another explanation, and the only plausible one is that Tinsley was *not* functioning normally that morning. Far from it. Had he been, the copying exercise would not only have been simple, it would have served not as a distraction but as a reminder of the traffic on the line. He saw in Meakin's notes the reference to the slow train from Carlisle, the train he had just left, being left on the 'through road' – the main line – and duly entered this into the register. Hutchinson's signature, albeit on the wrong page, was, or certainly should have been, a further reminder to him. Clearly, something was seriously wrong with Tinsley that day.

It is impossible to say whether the note copying theory was subjected at the time to wider scrutiny or any kind of proper investigation – Killin's observations do not clarify the matter – but it was accepted by just about everyone as the reason Tinsley was allegedly distracted from his duties at the critical time. Evidence to support this was, and is, lacking but the theory is taken as fact. We believe it is itself a distraction from the underlying truth.

The second theory, that he was distracted by animated discussion with various train crew in the signal box, is interesting in that it has a story of its own. It is a relatively modern creation that seems to have its origins in John Thomas' 1969 book on the disaster. The theory is based on a throwaway response to questioning made by George Meakin at the Carlisle Coroner's Court – 'yes, we were all talking together'. At no point in the drawn-out investigative process was this seriously pursued as a key causal factor. With very good reason – there is no real evidence for it.

According to the records, the only protracted conversation following Tinsley's arrival would appear to have lasted for between four and five minutes when firemen Hutchinson joined the signalmen and brakesman Ingram in the signal box. As we have pointed out, this was the only time that the box was occupied by four men. Tinsley took no real part in the chatter. Brakesman Young arrived as Hutchinson and Ingram were leaving. Tinsley ignored him, even when the

brakesman asked how long his train of empty coal wagons would be kept in the loop. Young went to the back of the box to study the poultry pictures while Meakin read his newspaper. There were never five men in the signal box as has been suggested and at no time was Tinsley distracted by indulging in chat about the war news. The theory fails.

We need spend no time considering the possibility that Tinsley was an incompetent signalman. This was never suggested; indeed, the comments made about his past record were all to the contrary. That brings us back to the only remaining explanation for his erratic behaviour in the box. James Tinsley was unwell. He hardly knew what he was doing. He may well have had a serious illness.

There is no absolute proof that this was epilepsy – the medical records that would have proved it one way or the other have either been lost, deliberately destroyed or, as in the case of his prison record, almost certainly falsified to eliminate any hint of a chronic condition. So is epilepsy really a credible explanation for Tinsley's shambolic performance and fatally flawed memory in the signal box? Is this the one theory that does stack up? There is, we believe, a credible case in support of this.

The evidence is compelling. *The Scotsman's* generalised reference to 'fits' was quickly followed at the time of Tinsley's arrest by the local doctor's warning to the police that, if care was not taken, 'his brain might be affected,' and then by the disclosure from the police to the prosecuting authorities that the doctor had advised them his patient 'had had epileptic fits since [the] collision'. Clear and specific. We need to be cautious here. The condition was still relatively little known in 1915 and it is right to allow the possibility that the GP's diagnosis might have been wrong. But if it was correct – and it was never apparently challenged – Tinsley was suffering from epilepsy.

At least, according to Dr Carlyle, he was in the period *after* the accident. Obviously, the lack of any formal medical records to substantiate the notion that this was a pre-existing condition is a stumbling block, but expert medical opinion on the nature of epilepsy and the history of treating the disorder has confirmed this to be a plausible hypothesis. If epilepsy was at the root of Tinsley's difficulties, it is likely that he had been diagnosed with the condition in childhood – a far from easy thing to handle.

Management of epilepsy in 1915 was restricted. At the time the condition was commonly treated with the anti-convulsant and sedative properties of potassium bromide (KB), the first effective medication for the disorder. The assumption is that Tinsley was being treated with bromides at the time. Possibly his treatment was erratic. The photographs taken of him just after the accident – even allowing for the appalling stress he must surely have been experiencing – suggest a very sick man, someone markedly older than his 32 years. Just a month later, as described in chapter ten, he looked the picture of health at the coroner's court.

As we have argued, a transformation as dramatic as this in such a short space of time strongly indicates he had been very well looked after in the interim. Had

the Caledonian, in whose care he seems to have been placed, ensured that he was given the best possible treatment for his condition in a bid to hide any suggestion of a pre-existing illness? We think this highly likely.

One obvious objection to the epilepsy theory is – how did Tinsley cope with it, apparently without mishap, before the catastrophe of 22 May 1915?

For an answer to this, it is necessary to look at the operation of Quintinshill signal box in the pre-war period. It was not a particularly difficult box to manage in peacetime. Located neither at a busy junction nor a station which would regularly present difficult operating decisions, it was merely a passing place providing accommodation for slower moving trains. Most of the traffic simply ran through. But the war changed everything – traffic was increased by forty per cent on that section of the line.

Railway historians acknowledge that the 'business as usual' policy of the companies operating the trains in the early part of the war was completely unsustainable, given the need simultaneously to incorporate the huge amount of additional wartime traffic. Indeed, the policy was dropped completely later in the conflict. It had imposed considerable strain on staff.

Were those extra demands a factor in the crash? Did they impose intolerable stress on Tinsley? He was known to be obsessive about his work. According to a young railwayman to whom he was passing on the skills of his job, Tinsley was constantly checking and re-checking everything he did, apparently fearful of accidents. This can only have increased the pressure on him. Did this exacerbate his condition? It would seem so. As is the case with many other conditions, epilepsy symptoms can worsen under prolonged stress. Tinsley may well have been able to cope with his illness before but had it now become too much to handle? We suspect that very probably it had.

Another aspect of the condition is relevant. People with epilepsy were, and are today, advised to avoid shift work as disturbed sleep patterns can result in seizures, especially first thing in the morning. Was this the main reason behind the signalmen's late shift change arrangement? The evidence suggests that it was James Tinsley who made the most use of it.

It takes time to recover from a seizure; the brain does not instantly re-adjust. Tinsley said he had overslept that morning; he only just caught the local train from Gretna at 6.27 and was at work just a few minutes later. Assuming that he had suffered a seizure that morning, which seems a realistic hypothesis, it is perhaps something of an irony that, had he not caught the train, he might have had sufficient time to recover during the walk to work.

Having arrived there by the local train, his behaviour was erratic in the extreme. He said he forgot all about the 'local' as soon as he left it, but the evidence paints a picture of a man whose confusion was more profound. His awareness of the train was very sporadic. He remembered it, forgot it, remembered it again and then, fatally, forgot its close proximity once more.

Meakin clearly, and properly, did outline the traffic situation to Tinsley as soon as he arrived in the box. This, of course, included the presence and position of the local train. Tinsley failed to retain the information. He also appears to have completely forgotten Meakin's instructions to send the 'local' on to Kirkpatrick between the two northbound expresses from London.

Add to this his difficulty in marking up the register, his failure, twice, to notice Hutchinson's signature clearly set out in the book in front of him, and his critical errors in acknowledging and accepting the troop train into the obstructed section to the north, and Tinsley's chaos is patently obvious.

Experienced railwayman with whom we have discussed this were unanimous in expressing astonishment that Tinsley did not react automatically to the collision. Each of them said it would be an instantaneous response – all signals to danger. Immediately! Had Tinsley done this, he would probably have averted the second crash. Sadly, he was in a world of his own. When the troop train he had invited on ploughed headlong into the 'local' his instincts deserted him.

He ran to the window, completely unable to comprehend what had happened, incapable of responding. It was left entirely to Meakin to stop a catastrophic second collision. Incredibly – at least it would have been incredible in anything other than these extraordinary circumstances – Meakin had to tell Tinsley what now needed to be done in order to protect incoming traffic on the main line in both directions, specifically the fast approaching London-Glasgow express. But Tinsley failed to respond.

Instead, utterly confused, he managed to send a routine message to Kirkpatrick, the signal box north, as if nothing untoward had occurred, after Meakin had desperately thrown all of Quintinshill's signals to 'danger'.

These were the actions of a man adrift from reality. Frankly, given the facts, it is ridiculous to attribute his astonishing failures that morning to a need to copy a few notes from a piece of paper or to an imagined chat about the war – or to anything other than an illness which left him incapable of behaving in a manner that came anywhere close to normality.

Before looking further at how that illness and its deeply tragic consequences almost certainly triggered the high-level cover-up and conspiracy we firmly believe has thrown a smokescreen over the Quintinshill disaster, we should first examine more closely the roles of Meakin and Hutchinson, the other two key railwaymen in the story.

It could be argued that Meakin should not really have had a case to answer at all. He handed over responsibility for the box, presumably unwittingly, to a man who was in no fit state to take it over. It was then the accident happened – on Tinsley's watch. Meakin was off duty but did everything in his power to restrict the outcome. Sadly, he had no real time.

He was, as we have shown, badly served by just about everyone involved in the investigative process. His complicity in the illicit shift change apart, virtually all the criticism and blame levelled at him was deeply unjust.

It was alleged in the Board of Trade report that he passed control of the box to Tinsley on the morning of the disaster 'in a casual manner'. This was nonsense. It is quite clear from the evidence that he gave his mate a comprehensive briefing on the status and position of all trains in the vicinity and there is no reason to believe he did not tell Tinsley about his plan to dispatch the local train northwards after the first express had passed the signal box.

There is also absolutely no proof that, as has been repeatedly suggested, it was Meakin who sent the 'train out of section' signal after the empty wagon train was installed in the passing loop – indicating that he was in charge of the box at that time. The only evidence that he had done so came from Tinsley, whose recall of events was shown to be unreliable, to put it mildly.

Meakin's alleged failure to use prescribed safety measures were the main reasons for his conviction – rightly according to just about everyone who has studied the disaster. We have argued that it was never as black and white as it seemed.

Indeed, the criticism he faced over his non-application of the blocking back rule was nothing short of malicious falsehood on the part of the Caledonian Railway. We have shown that, by shamefully selective reference to its regulations, the company was able to make the case on this issue against a man who had actually followed the rules to the letter. This will forever remain a stain on the integrity and reputation of this highly regarded Scottish railway.

This leaves the vexed question of the signal lever collar. Meakin never denied that he had failed to affix it and there is no doubt whatsoever that, under the rules, he should have done so. Our argument in this instance is based on the mitigation that was never extended to him in 1915. He had no reason for thinking that Tinsley would forget the presence of a train he had only just got off, thus rendering a lock on the lever somewhat irrelevant. Possibly he thought that the act of applying the collar might have been taken by Tinsley as an affront to his competence and integrity.

Meakin's case was compromised, of course, by his inability to use blocking back to protect the line. In such a situation, the importance of the lever collar's availability increases. This might explain why no clear defence was offered by his legal representatives on this aspect. In a sense, then, he was taking a risk, but it was taken in the context of what he must have imagined was a secure safety net – there was surely no way that Tinsley would unrestrictedly allow another train to approach the box on the southbound track whether or not there was a collar in place on the lever.

Had Meakin been able to rely on legal representation dedicated solely to his defence, had he have been able to count on the support of independent railway expertise, these mitigating factors surely would have been explored.

As important, if not more so, is that the use of lever collars was clearly inconsistent across the Caledonian network. The company had done little to enforce the rule – a very definite systems failure. It was of course the railway's

responsibility to ensure its rules were followed and all staff were properly trained in accordance with them. The Caledonian was exposed to press criticism on this issue but never to any kind of formal censure.

In this sense the company was fortunate to be operating a railway system in 1915. In today's environment, its failure to enforce the collar rule – and the serious shortcomings in its inspection regime which lay behind this – would be seen as major factors and would leave the company in line for allegations of corporate incompetence leading almost certainly to criminal charges. But even in 1915 the Caledonian had reasons to be fearful.

It was facing public opprobrium and commercial embarrassment if it became widely known its supervisory inspections had failed and its rules had not been properly enforced. On top of this, the Caledonian had failed to detect James Tinsley's apparently serious medical condition. Technically, of course, he should not have suppressed it. Realistically, if epilepsy was the problem, he would have stood little chance of meaningful employment anywhere had he 'come clean' on his illness.

Whether the Caledonian management – indeed, almost anyone in 1915 – would have fully understood the effects of an epileptic seizure is debatable. The condition was generally misinterpreted. But the risk of a signalman developing fits, irrespective of their cause, while on duty would surely have been obvious. Yet the company had recruited James Tinsley apparently without any real examination of his medical condition and history.

This had to be concealed – but the Caledonian had a problem. It knew what Tinsley had done, or not done, in the signal box on 22 May but, if he had to bear the responsibility alone the likelihood that his illness would emerge as a factor was high. Unwittingly, George Meakin came to the rescue.

Both signalmen had broken the rule on shift changes and Meakin had additionally broken another over the non-use of the lever collar. It would not be difficult to present these as factors that contributed to the accident. Meakin could share the blame with Tinsley. The risk to Caledonian credibility would decrease with careful management. It is our belief that this was the prime consideration for bringing a charge of criminal negligence against Meakin.

Why the trumped-up allegation of failing to block back was added is open to speculation – probably it was to strengthen the case against him. In any event, based on the strength of the available evidence, it seems that bringing Meakin into the equation was nothing but a cynical defensive ploy.

It could be argued, and indeed it was, that Meakin 'set Tinsley up to fail… Tinsley did not get the jogs he needed' – the words of defence advocate Condie Sandeman at the trial. If this were the case, Tinsley's behavior could, in part at least, be explained, thus reducing suspicions of an underlying reason for his extraordinary errors. There appears sufficient justification to ask – was Meakin framed?

Never properly considered before in the Quintinshill story is the indictment of George Hutchinson. In essence, the charge of criminal negligence against the fireman rested on just the one point – that, having gone to the signal box to check the signal collar was on the lever, in breach of his duty he left the box without doing so.

At the trial it was said that there was insufficient evidence to proceed against Hutchinson, and this was clearly agreed with the defence before proceedings began. Many have since said that, as the Quintinshill signalmen rarely used the collar, he would not have expected to see it in use that morning. But would he have expected to see it in use elsewhere? Had Quintinshill been the one glaring example of a failure to observe the collar rule – a suggestion that was actually made in at least one precognition statement – then surely train crew working the main line would have had cause for concern at this signal box for their own safety and that of their train.

As noted, the evidence now to hand shows that the use of collars on the Caledonian was sporadic at best. It does not seem unreasonable to assume that, had the case against Hutchinson been pressed, this would have been raised. Was this yet another example of the Caledonian Railway, and we may suppose, those in higher authority, protecting their own interests?

If so, this was far from the only relevant evidence that was never properly examined in 1915. Had the disaster occurred today, a major factor would be the condition, speed and gas lighting of the troop train.

The use of gas-lit trains and its obvious potential for causing fire in the event of an accident was of increasing public concern in 1915. There had been three previous instances of this happening in the preceding five years. Now it had proved a very material factor in the deaths of so many of Quintinshill's victims. The *Cumberland News's* leader column had specifically echoed public outrage about this, but within a week the apparent ban on any newspaper comment on the disaster had come into force.

These were further factors likely to detract from the 'simple' case of signalling negligence that, it seems, were deemed unsuitable for public consumption. This was a disgrace. The train carrying the Royal Scots was unfit for purpose. That the point was not pursued was an insult to the soldiers who died. Why were they confined in that antiquated rolling stock? Just a day later modern first class coaches were quickly commandeered to take the survivors to Liverpool. The contrast was immense – no chance of a repeat disaster – but for the Royal Scots the damage had been done.

If it really was the case that those wretchedly pathetic carriages were all that could be found for the battalion on 22 May, why on earth were they permitted to be hauled along at express train speeds for which they were obviously not suited? It was highly dangerous. It was asking for trouble.

Whose fault was this? The blame here falls on the overseeing Railway Executive – the Government's strategic wartime authority. It was the executive

who provided, or at least organised, the train. It was they who ordered the Caledonian to run it to a prescribed time beyond its capabilities. A timetabling clerk, presumably unaware of the train's pitiful condition (it wouldn't have been his responsibility to know of this), worked out the schedules as if this were a state-of-the-art main line train and nobody, absolutely nobody, thought or bothered to check the reality.

Driver Scott, acting on the instructions he had been given, blamelessly attempted against all the odds to carry out his orders, running his train into a deathtrap, for himself and so many others, at a speed which touched 70mph.

Sins of omission. Yet, apart from a generalised repeat in the Board of Trade report of recommendations from an earlier accident, the question of how much of a factor all this had been was never the issue it should have been. It was treated virtually as an irrelevance, hushed up, shamefully ignored.

We have examined at length the Board of Trade's involvement in the process of determining the disaster's causes. Its eventual report, forwarded to the Caledonian Railway on 17 September, was a whitewash, embodying all the things that pointed the accusatory finger at Tinsley and Meakin and 'airbrushing' everything that did not fit in with this official version.

We have acknowledged that to suggest, even to those with no more than a passing interest in British railway history, that the board's fabled railway inspectorate in 1915 was either incompetent or susceptible to corruption and political control – perhaps all of these things – is likely to come as a profound shock.

Weaned as they have been on the works of eminent railway historians such as L.T.C. Rolt and O.S. Nock, most would regard the reputation of the railway inspectors as beyond impeachment. However, in more recent times, specialist historians David Howell and Robert Strange have demonstrated clearly that this is something of a rose-tinted perspective. Both have revealed the extent of considerable political influence at the Board of Trade.[3, 4]

In *Respectable Radicals* Professor Howell has thrown much new light on the involvement of the railway inspectorate's involvement in the 1913 Ais Gill disaster inquiry, identifying inadequacies in the process.

'At Ais Gill there were serious issues about cheaper and inadequate coal and the effectiveness or not of lubrication systems, yet the report effectively ignored the claims of railwaymen and union officials.

'The discussions at Board of Trade investigations can be contrasted with those at coroners' inquests and criminal trials where the debate seems broader. This reflects that [railway] inspectors and company officials shared much in terms of culture, values and an understanding of what counted as expertise.

'Moreover, the authority structure of the industry and the wider society helped to shape the hearings and outcomes. Perhaps most decisively, inspectors regarded disasters as attributable to individuals who could and should be held responsible. They had little sympathy with, or perhaps understanding of, the

view that managerial policies could have significant unintended consequences and that such relationships could not be captured in the language of individual responsibility.

'By 1914 the trade unions were beginning to develop an alternative view but as yet their influence was limited. The attempts by companies to marginalise their input into Board of Trade hearings should be seen in this context, although unions had achieved a firm foothold…'

Was Colonel Druitt competent to investigate the Quintinshill disaster on behalf of the board? Like all of his fellow inspectors, he was recruited from the Royal Engineers. Unlike most of them, men with railway experience gained usually from working on networks in one of Britain's many overseas colonies, the evidence indicates that Edward Druitt's military background was essentially that of an engineer involved with fortifications. This was far from being irrelevant to his role with the Board of Trade – his expertise would be essential to the board as it had the dual responsibility of inspecting civil engineering work on the British rail network.

But was Quintinshill asking too much of him? From the records we have been able to examine, while he had been involved with many accident investigations, this would appear to have been his first major incident inquiry.

His line of questioning at the public inquiry suggests a degree of naivety about railway signalling but the most serious charge against him is his failure to properly interrogate Caledonian officials on the blocking back rule.

We have made the point that the company's presentation of the rule was conveniently selective. The proof of this can be found in archival records. Copies of the relevant rule 13 have been cut from a rule book and pasted to a report the company sent to the board. As explained in chapter nine, only two of the four parts of the rule have in this way been prepared for forwarding. The critical section which would have shown George Meakin was correct in not adopting the rule on 22 May clearly was not sent.

Druitt sought no clarification on this, referring in his conclusions at the end of the board's report only to the parts of rule 13 the company had sent.

Neither did he ever follow up his suspicions about the veracity of stationmaster Alexander Thorburn's claims to have been completely unaware of the shift change irregularity at Quintinshill. Druitt wrote in the Board of Trade report that such claims were 'hard to believe.' They were indeed but the inspector, like so many other investigators, let Thorburn off the hook.

Similarly, the report contained no reference whatsoever to the Caledonian's rules governing the inspection of signal boxes; no reference to the condition of the troop train or to its being timetabled at express speeds; and no adequate reference to the use of gas lighting. Indeed, the devastating effect of the gas in turning a wreck into a blazing inferno was underplayed in the report. Very noticeably, as

we have said, unlike almost all other reports of a major accident, there were, no recommendations for change arising specifically from the Quintinshill tragedy.

It was all about pinning the entire blame on the rule-breaking signalmen. Many since have regarded the Board of Trade report as the definitive guide to what happened that morning. It was nothing of the sort. It was a whitewash. A sham.

Perhaps the most critical – and astonishing – omission is Druitt's apparent ignoring of Tinsley's failure to respond to the emergency at the time of the initial collision. The Caledonian's own investigation into the crash made clear that, had he responded correctly and immediately, he would have prevented the subsequent collision. There is no mention of this in Colonel Druitt's Board of Trade report. Instead, Tinsley's own analysis was allowed to stand unchallenged: 'After the first collision there was nothing I could have effectively done to prevent the second one, there being no time.'

Druitt knew this was untrue. Seconds counted, but it had little to do with a lack of time. It was really about Tinsley being utterly incapable of reacting. For Druitt to have acknowledged this, of course, would have opened the door to wider questions about Tinsley's health. So, was the report effectively hijacked as part of a conspiracy to prevent any of the wider issues from being raised?

There are good reasons for thinking so. Beyond any doubt, following Druitt's public hearing in Carlisle on 25 May, the inquiry was continued – or possibly a different inquiry altogether was held – in secret, almost certainly at Caledonian premises in Glasgow, and the railway company exercised considerable influence over its findings and the way in which these were presented, even though the colonel formally signed off the report.

Druitt almost certainly intended his inquiry to continue in public at a later date. He did not close it at Carlisle – that would have made Quintinshill the only major disaster in British railway history to have been examined at a public hearing lasting only a single day – and to this day it has never been formally declared as being closed. Instead, he adjourned it. Whether the Board of Trade regarded the completion of the secret hearing and the subsequent report as an official closure can only be guessed at.

The board was justified under procedural rules in 'going private' because James Tinsley had been charged with a criminal offence but we are left to conjecture whether Druitt actually had a role in the secret session. If he did, then he must have been part of the whitewash. But if this were so, did he willingly acquiesce to it or was he ordered by higher authority to comply? Unsurprisingly, no records have survived to provide an answer to this.

As to who orchestrated the whitewash, we can only conclude that it must have had the approval of government, anxious to keep the whole affair simple and avoid being dragged into damaging political fall-out. Protecting the Caledonian Railway's interests was unlikely to have been the main aim, though we can surmise that the company was more than happy to co-operate. Avoiding an extended

public hearing and apparently given free rein to manipulate the evidence and findings to its advantage was a gift for the Caledonian but the Government had its own strategic interests rooted in the political uncertainties and unrest of the period.

If the inquiry was a sham, what can we say about the Carlisle inquest and the High Court trial in Edinburgh? We might question the practice of indicting people at a coroner's court for criminal trial – and it was clearly ridiculous in the case of the already charged James Tinsley – but, while highly problematical, this was not irregular procedure at the time. There are, however, a raft of serious issues to address, none more so than the fact that evidence was undoubtedly withheld from the Carlisle hearing (and from the inquest in Penrith, for that matter) as well as from the later trial.

To take the Carlisle inquest first, the irresistible question is – did higher authority judge Coroner Strong well and effectively use him to pursue its goal?

Here was a man guaranteed to demonstrate the general distrust and lack of respect for the working class that was such a feature of the divisive politics of the era. It would be unfair to suggest that Strong was dishonest but, as a man of his time, he was highly likely to be pre-disposed to accept without question the evidence provided by a powerful railway company and have little regard for signalmen who appeared to be careless, rule-breaking workers. The outcome was inevitable in Strong's court.

The Scottish trial is a more complex issue. It would appear that James Tinsley is the only railwayman in British history to have been charged in connection with an accident on the line before an exhaustive investigative process (inquiry, inquest etc) has taken place. His arrest after only the briefest of legal investigations was extraordinarily rushed – no doubt as a knee-jerk reaction to public outrage at the deaths of so many people.

It was premature but the die had been cast and the prosecuting authorities in Scotland were determined to see it through. It remains a matter for conjecture how this rush to judgment was received in London. Probably the Government, concerned at what might be revealed, would have preferred not to have been confronted with a high-profile criminal case – a 'can of worms'.

A biased trial was the outcome with the aim of keeping the lid on the proverbial bottle. As with the public inquiry, there are many questions to be asked. One mystery surrounds the legal advice given to the NUR's Jimmy Thomas. It seems he was cautioned that, in the best interests of the two signalmen, each of them should be represented in court by their own counsel.

Meakin, at least, would stand a good chance of acquittal. So why did Thomas reject the advice? Could it be attributed solely to financial considerations? This seems unlikely. We believe other factors were at play. His character is important in this context. To quote David Howell, 'Thomas's negotiating skills were founded on flexibility and pragmatism. He was adroit, economical with the truth and… blended a flair for publicity with a readiness to cut private deals.

During the war he saw himself as protecting the national interest through his role in the NUR.'

While the union's minutes book reveals that Thomas referred to Tinsley's arrest in some detail, there was no mention of the medical complication. Did Thomas know of this? Was his decision to employ only the one advocate part of an elaborate deal to serve the best interests of Tinsley, at least?

It left Condie Sandeman, the man appointed to lead the defence at the trial, with few options in the courtroom. Tinsley's evidence might threaten Meakin's defence and vice-versa. But if Thomas had indeed cut a deal – and it would have to have been at a very high level – Sandeman would of course have been aware of it. We have drawn attention to a major clue that he very probably had acquiesced to an agreement brokered with the prosecution. Surely his comment that 'it would not have been criminal negligence if [Tinsley] had fallen down in an epileptic fit' was no throwaway remark.

We are persuaded that it was a reminder to the prosecution of the key truth behind the cause of the accident – and that a deal was in place to keep it quiet, just as one was clearly agreed to acquit George Hutchinson on his charge.

The probable nature of the deal would ensure that the signalmen, as the only culpable parties, took whatever penalty was handed down and no complication factors – especially the nature of Tinsley's illness – would be pursued by the defence. In exchange, Tinsley's family would be looked after by the company and he would be spared the appalling prospect of being rendered virtually unemployable through disclosure of his condition which, assuming it was epilepsy, carried considerable stigma. The workhouse would be avoided.

Meakin's situation was different and complex. Was he to be 'thrown to the wolves', sacrificed in the wider interests? He was certainly not properly defended by the NUR or in court. The existence of a deal would explain why so many points which could have been raised by the defence were not pursued but this was particularly harsh on Meakin. We have shown how the case against him was based largely on allegations that were grossly unfair.

Tinsley, of course, was equally falsely accused. The allegation that he hadn't 'run to the window' every time a train was dealt with was a betrayal of the fact that, because of the signal box's design, checking for what was happening in this manner was not practical and neither was it the custom. But at least he stood to gain from being the apparent beneficiary of a deal. What Meakin stood to gain from it is another matter. We will return to this later.

The Caledonian's culpability on these falsehoods was profound; they were without foundation. Yet the company was allowed to mislead the court.

It might not have been difficult for a clever advocate backed by independent railway expertise to have demolished the case against both men, but in Tinsley's case particularly, this was risky. Had this defence failed, what would be left? Tinsley's medical condition might have been exposed.

This, as we have argued, would have suited nobody – George Meakin probably excepted – as the whole charade would have fallen apart with both the Government and the Caledonian seriously embarrassed and Tinsley facing ruin. As a hypothesis, cutting a deal with him appears credible.

However, the plan, if plan there was, hit a problem – the judge went too far. No records appear to have survived of the Government's reaction to the severity of Alexander Ure's sentences, particularly the three-year term of penal servitude handed down to Tinsley. The suspicion is that it came as much of a surprise to the coalition administration as it did to those members of the Edinburgh jury who responded quickly with their brave petition.

This, in turn, very probably prompted Jimmy Thomas, who more than likely had expected similar sentences for both signalmen, to join and very soon lead the increasingly popular campaign for the two men's release. Assuming he did know the truth about Tinsley, he would have regarded the judge's decision as highly unjust. Further motivation would have come from Thomas's need to respond to the members' demands for action.

And Thomas being Thomas, he would also have seen some mileage in using the campaign for release as a means for pressing his political aspirations at the expense of Asquith's leadership of the unstable coalition.

It is clear that Thomas played his hand well, waiting as he did for the right moment – with a weak Scottish Secretary in post and a Prime Minister about to be evicted. No one would have bothered to check the veracity of his claims that a widespread strike was imminent; the threat of a catastrophic dispute, causing absolute panic to everyone walking the corridors of Whitehall and Westminster, would have been more than enough.

It was a gamble on Thomas's part but one that was cushioned by the fact that the petitions coming in from Edinburgh clearly showed growing public sympathy for the signalmen. It would leave Harold Tennant a politically damaged Secretary of State, but this was of little concern to Thomas – and within days Tennant would be out of office anyway, ousted with Asquith.

It was a final chance to get the signalmen out of prison. It worked and it could be argued that, with the exception of Meakin, whose sentence had reached its natural conclusion thanks to the remission he had earned, it suited all interested parties. Tinsley could rejoin his family. The risk of his cracking under the sustained pressure of imprisonment and the truth being revealed had been eliminated. The Caledonian Railway and the Government had been spared potentially serious consequences. But to conclude the interests of justice had been served would be wide of the mark.

They certainly hadn't been for the many victims of the tragedy, whose loved ones were denied – as their descendants have been ever since – from knowing the full circumstances behind their deaths. It is deplorable that so long a time has elapsed without anything in the way of official acknowledgment that the long accepted version of events is wrong.

In conclusion, it is interesting to compare the contrasting fortunes of those most closely involved in the story. The Caledonian Railway was left to quietly and secretly address its own failings (see chapter twelve). Thereafter, reputation intact, it continued in being during the difficult years that followed the war's conclusion in 1918, but for only another five years. In 1923 it was swept away in the nationwide grouping of Britain's railways, becoming part of the vast network of the London, Midland & Scottish Railway.

Alexander Thorburn, the Caledonian's hapless stationmaster at Gretna, who had through his shaky evidence threatened to blow the whole conspiracy asunder, received what might be called just deserts from the company. His supervisory record had been woeful and it was nonsense to suggest that he knew nothing about the illicit shift change. He must have done, living as close as he did to both Tinsley and Gretna signalman Roger Kirkpatrick in the station community. Even with the station long closed, a visit today to the cottages at the site would confirm just how ridiculous a notion this was.

Thorburn was demoted by his unimpressed employers, finally realising he was not up to the Gretna job. He was banished from the Caledonian's main line, effectively sent out to graze at the South Lanarkshire station of Biggar.

As for his superiors, little is known. Carlisle District Superintendent, W.H. Blackstock, who diligently preserved the outcome of the Caledonian's private investigation; apparently ended his career at Oban, terminus of the scenic West Highland Line's surviving branch. Whether or nor this was by choice remains a matter for speculation. It is interesting to ponder why he kept the records of the meeting. Possibly it was to make sure the truth came out one day or maybe it was a result of his annoyance at suffering the indignity of what appears to have been a demotion.

What of the key players? Re-employed by the Caledonian on his release, Tinsley never returned to signalling. Instead, he became a lampman – looking after lamps. A mundane job, way below the work of a main line signalman, it very probably was regarded by the company as safe employment for a man whose health was seen as a threat. Tinsley later became a porter, a job equally devoid of risk, at Carlisle Citadel. It is worth noting that, while he was in prison, his wife, Hannah, following a plea from Jimmy Thomas, was employed in the station cloakroom at Citadel.

Was this expedient? Almost certainly it was. She and the three children had remained in Caledonian property, presumably benefitting from company support as a result of the deal struck earlier. This being the case, it surely would have aroused suspicion had she not been on the payroll. The job would have given her a legitimate right to stay in the family home.

It would appear from what records are available that she died at Carlisle in 1935. Tinsley, it seems, had two further marriages, first to Ada Leil, who died in 1949, also at Carlisle, and very soon afterwards to Jane Graham.

Anecdotal evidence suggests that, while quite reserved, Tinsley was well liked, a man who made regular donations to charity. There is a suggestion that he made occasional visits to the Quintinshill memorial at Leith, although this is hard to corroborate. Understandably, it also appears that he never spoke of the accident after leaving prison. Judged by the overwhelming remorse he evidently felt while at Peterhead – his letter to the Scottish Office is testimony enough of this – we can speculate that, sadly, he probably carried his guilt and its associated secrets to the grave.

That grave, at Carlisle's Stanwix Cemetery, is unmarked. It has remained so since his death in the city from natural causes, aged 77, in 1961. It is hard not to feel enormous sympathy for him, his reputation tarnished by a probable illness that few knew about but which will forever link him with an appalling disaster.

It is difficult to be precise about some aspects of George Meakin's later life story. He had already suffered tragedy through the loss of both of his daughters in infancy and, extraordinarily, on the day after the disaster at Quintinshill he was involved in a motorcycle accident which resulted in the death of a local child. But Meakin, it seems, managed to lead a very full life after his release from Glasgow's Barlinnie prison at the end of 1916.[5]

He never worked as a signalman again but he too was re-employed by the Caledonian, in a more responsible position than was found for Tinsley – as a second man in the guard's vans of freight trains. Eventually made redundant, he started up a coal business in Springfield which eventually failed and later found employment as a clerk in part of Gretna's massive munitions depot south of the Scottish border at Longtown, earning promotion as head of office.

Mystery surrounds him though. Always impeccably dressed, Meakin was well-liked by some. However, local anecdotal evidence suggests that he was prone to arrogance, 'with a certain swagger'. Was this his way of coping?

Or did it hide another truth? Was he compensated by the Caledonian for being made the main scapegoat for the accident? There are grounds for believing this was so. A key indicator is the fact that Meakin acquired and was able to run a car at a time when car ownership was almost entirely the preserve of the very well-off. Where did the money come from?

Quintinshill historian J.A.B. Hamilton suggests in his book that the purchase was financed by the State Management Scheme of 1916 which allowed the state to take over the brewing, distribution and sale of liquor in three areas of the UK. One of these was the Carlisle and Gretna scheme which had acquired and then closed the pub business owned by Meakin's wife. This cannot be ruled out, but neither can the possibility that Meakin was, to put it crudely, paid off as part of the Quintinshill deal.

We will probably never know, but if he was paid to keep quiet about Tinsley's illness and accept his sentence, even if he did not consider himself culpable (which to a large extent he wasn't), it might explain why he apparently remained – at least in public – silent on the matter of his subsequent comparative wealth.

George Meakin died in 1953 at Springfield and is buried locally at Rigg Cemetery with his two infant daughters and his wife, Isabella, who died in 1960.

Without knowledge of Tinsley's illness and the suspicion of a deal to cover it up, previous Quintinshill historians have found it difficult to square the long accepted version of events with the men's re-employment, in any capacity, by the Caledonian. Why on earth would the company take back onto its payroll men who, according to the perceived wisdom, had been instrumental in causing on its network what was, and remains, the worst-ever railway accident the United Kingdom has ever known.

J.A.B. Hamilton was mystified. 'Their subsequent stories are strange indeed. I had always pictured them being called up into the armed forces after their release and afterwards cherishing a lifetime's remorse,' he wrote in 1969.

'It did not happen that way at all. Both returned from gaol to jobs on the railway. Why they were not called up is a mystery. It is difficult to believe that two youngish signalmen should both be unfit for military service. One can only suppose that the railway company managed to obtain exemption for them. Tinsley did not even lose his railway cottage, in which his family continued to live during his imprisonment.'

Other commentators have sought to explain the apparent mystery of why the pair were not enlisted by claiming that no ex-convicts were called up for service. This is untrue. Convicts could apply to be released for military service, just as Tinsley did. Some served their country with distinction.[6]

The real reason Tinsley's appeal to join up failed was almost certainly his medical condition. As noted in chapter fourteen, he hinted at this himself in his letter to the Scottish Office. He had no previous criminal record, was no danger to society and was obviously an intelligent man. In all other respects, he *was* fit for conscription. His illness, whatever its precise nature, was clearly the real barrier.

His condition, however, did pose a serious problem for high authority. Tinsley was not fit to serve his country. Meakin was. Awkward questions would have been asked if Meakin was conscripted and Tinsley was not, returning instead to the railway. The men had to be treated the same when they left their prison cells. They both had to rejoin the Caledonian's payroll.

These we believe to be the true facts behind the Quintinshill disaster. Admittedly, there are still some uncertainties – precisely who was involved at government level in the probable cover-up for one, although Scottish Secretary of State Thomas McKinnon Wood is very obviously a prime candidate – but we can now say with confidence that this was very far from being a simple, albeit tragic, story of negligence in the signal box. It was a convoluted tale of secrets and conspiracy designed to conceal the full facts, one which has stood unchallenged for virtually a century.

In a sentence, this was the shocking story of how truth joined the death toll on the Anglo-Scottish border at Quintinshill signal box on 22 May 1915.

Notes

1. Repington's article came about as a result of Chancellor David Lloyd George's fervent belief that a radical shake-up of the country's munitions industry was both achievable and essential to the war effort. Lloyd George persuaded Lord Northcliffe, powerful publisher of *The Times* and *Daily Mail*, to use one of his newspapers to press home the Chancellor's case. It proved a master stroke when Repington was able to quote in *The Times* Sir John French's frank criticism of ammunition shortage for the BEF in France, triggering political upheaval and change.

2. Tinsley offered no excuses at any of the public hearings for his erratic behaviour on 22 May other than his repeated confession that he had simply forgotten about the stationary local train.

3. *Respectable Radicals: Studies in the politics of railway trade unionism* by David Howell, published by Ashgate Publishing, 1999 – ISBN 10-1840146903.

4. See also *Who sank the Titanic? The final verdict* by Robert Strange, published by Pen and Sword Maritime, 2012 – ISBN 10-1848844700.

5. With regard to George Meakin's motorcycle accident, the evidence suggests that he was assisting his wife at the Maxwell Arms, her pub in Springfield, which was doing good business with the many sightseers who visited the crash site on Sunday, 23 May, the day after the accident. The pub had run out of beer and Meakin was sent on the motorbike to fetch some more. On the journey the motorbike collided with a child, who subsequently died. The anecdotal evidence indicates that Meakin was a pillion passenger and was not therefore in charge of the vehicle. Be that as it may, his presence in the pub that day continues to surprise many.

6. A memorial to prisoners who fell in the Great War can be found at the chapel at HMP Parkhurst, Isle of Wight. Among those named is William Mariner, who was awarded the Victoria Cross for outstanding bravery in France against a German machine gun post on the same day as the Quintinshill disaster – 22 May 1915.

Chapter 15

Truths, Myths, Legends and Memorials

'I saw a train packed with soldiers. Some wore tartan but most of them had on a dullish uniform with diced bonnets. They seemed to be local boys, and they were travelling south to go abroad.'

The premonition of Stirling housewife Kathleen Kennedy – 1896

Around all disasters, both man-made and natural, legends and myths inevitably emerge, some assuming a false – or at least speculative – mantle of truth over the years. The 1915 tragedy at Quintinshill is no exception. The railway's *Titanic* has an extraordinarily diverse catalogue of them.

Kathleen's Vision

According to legend, Kathleen Kennedy had a particular gift for premonition. The former children's educational magazine *Look and Learn* (1962-82) featured a spectacular vision of Kathleen's dating back to the nineteenth century:

'One evening in the spring of 1896, a Scottish housewife was sewing in the living room of her home in Stirling. Suddenly, she groaned and fell to the ground, shouting, "The screams! I can't stand the screams! It's horrible! It's on fire!"

'She continued to babble about death, destruction, pain and fire. When she eventually calmed down she told her husband that she had experienced another terrifying vision. "I saw a train packed with soldiers," she stated emotionally.

"Some wore tartan, but most of them had on a dullish uniform with diced bonnets. They seemed to be local boys and they were travelling south to go abroad. But they never reached their destination. Their train crashed. I think it was somewhere near Gretna Green and the coaches caught fire. Scores of young soldiers were crushed to death and many more burned alive. I could hear them screaming for mercy." At this, Mrs Kennedy broke down again.

'Her husband helped her upstairs to bed. Kathleen was convinced that, sooner or later, hundreds of innocent people were to suffer agonising deaths.

Often the memory came back to her and she murmured, "Those soldiers, I feel sorry for those poor soldiers"...'

There is, of course, no proof that Kathleen really did have this vision, but if she did and it truly happened in 1896, it is worth bearing in mind one particular aspect – her reference to 'dullish uniforms'. In 1896 khaki uniforms, as worn by the 7th Royal Scots when disaster struck their train nineteen years later, were not in regular British Army use. Red was still used by most military units.[1]

Rumours of Desertion

A rumour in the border region persists that a few soldiers deserted at the scene of the crash. Local researcher Denis Muir investigated the claims and revealed that there were unconfirmed reports of three or four men running across the fields away from the railway.

It is impossible to verify these claims but it seems unlikely that those soldiers did desert. These were not conscripts; they were volunteers – a close-knit battalion of territorials. The evidence suggests high morale among the Scots and an enthusiasm to get to the front.

If the reports have any substance, the likely scenario is that the men – most probably boys – were understandably traumatised by the accident. There is clear evidence in the contemporary press reports that some of the Royal Scots were affected in this way. Probably these young soldiers were found, though it may have been some time later, and were then quietly returned for the roll call.

We have seen no record of disciplinary action against any of the soldiers at the time or later. If there was any such action, it can only be hoped that the men were dealt with sympathetically. They had clearly suffered enough.

It is highly improbable that any deserter could have remained incognito for the rest of the war, especially in a case like this. They would have needed some external assistance, a lot of protection from their family, and probably a false identity – leaving them liable for call up as conscripts later on.

Unless other evidence emerges. this story must be viewed as the result of misinterpreting an observation. The explanation almost certainly was trauma.

The Unidentified Victims

One story that sadly is true still has an element of myth attached. It relates to five unidentified victims of the disaster, four of them thought to be children, who were buried together at Glasgow's Western Necropolis (see chapters three and four). It is a story that has gained much prominence over the years as various attempts have been made to uncover the truth behind it.

Among the theories put forward is that the tragic victims came from the Maryhill district of Glasgow and had somehow stowed away on the troop train. Partly prompted by this, a local council in 2011 generously paid for a memorial at the Necropolis – but does this story really stand up to scrutiny?

It is acknowledged in Glasgow that corroboration is lacking. The only references to the children, if children they were, in the contemporary press accounts come in the reports of the arrival of two coffins at Glasgow Central station on the evening of 24 May. The reports differ in detail but follow the same general line that one of the coffins was labelled, 'unrecognisable' and the other, 'three trunks, possibly children.' They had been forwarded from Leith in the, ultimately forlorn, hope that the pitiful remains could be identified.

As we have noted, there were also references to the body of a woman removed from the London-Glasgow express, who was buried as unidentified with the others.

The origin of the stowaway story is a mystery. Neither of the two accounts of the disaster published in the 1960s refer to it so it's probable that it has emerged more recently – and it is hard to see that it has any real credibility. Even the possibility that the unofficial passengers were bound for a ship in Liverpool is flawed.

The destination of the troop train was known only to the railway and military authorities. It was a security-tight wartime operation and where it was headed was never made public. To suggest that any civilians, let alone children, in Maryhill or, indeed, at Larbert, location of the train's originating station, were aware that it was bound for the Mersey is almost certainly little more than a fantasy.

It can be assumed that a train carrying military equipment, including ammunition, would have been provided with a round-the-clock guard and would definitely have been locked while in the storage sidings. How would any stowaways have got on it? As for the suggestion that a young family, possibly four children unescorted, would not have been noticeable among a battalion of soldiers as they boarded the early morning train, it is utterly inconceivable.

They couldn't have been travelling on the troop train. So who were they, where had they come from, where were they bound and which train were they really on?

There is no doubt that the remains of a woman and at least one child were discovered among the wreckage of the express. This initially suggested the possibility of a young family from Belgium bound for a wartime refugee settlement at Falkirk. But another, more likely, option has since come to light.

A story handed down within an Irish household insists that four members of the McClure family had perished in a train crash in 1915. Birth certificates survived for them but no death certificates could be traced. The four were named as Margaret Jane (60), her daughter, Matilda (29) and Matilda's two children, John, aged seven, and his three-year-old sister, who shared her mother's first name. It appears they were planning to emigrate to Canada and were possibly en route to Glasgow to pay a farewell visit to relatives in Maryhill.

This seems a highly plausible explanation to the mystery, the most convincing put forward. It would mean, of course, that the idea of there being five unidentified civilian victims should probably now be reduced to four, and that the theory of four children dying together in the crash is only partially correct.

The reference to 'three trunks, possibly children' on the second of the coffins can probably be explained by the pitiful state of so many of the bodies retrieved from the wreckage. Wrong conclusions were virtually inevitable. One of those in the coffin could have been that of a young adult – the children's mother? – and another might well have been that of a young soldier. This will remain a mystery.

The Tragic Nimmo Family

The tragic story of the local train's only fatalities, Rachel Nimmo (28), from Newcastle, and her son Dickson, less than two years old and the only identified child victim of the disaster, has been described in chapter three.

Having travelled overnight from Newcastle, boarding the local train at Carlisle, they died near the front of the sparsely-filled three-coach train because Mrs Nimmo had left her husband and the couple's two young daughters further down the train in an effort to calm her restless son. Her draper husband, also called Dickson, and the girls, three-year-old Rachel and her slightly younger half-sister, Annie, survived with little physical harm but their experience in the crash's immediate aftermath was shockingly sad.

The stories told of their anguish are sadly almost certainly not myths. In their rear coach compartment, the impact was relatively minimal. Mr Nimmo was thrown forward and under the seat opposite, injuring his hip. Mercifully, the little girls suffered only minor knocks. With the coach virtually undamaged, all three were able to leave it quickly and head for the field alongside the line. Naturally though, they were deeply concerned for Mrs Nimmo and baby Dickson. Initially, the news appeared to be good.

With his daughters taken to the home of a family friend in South View, Gretna, Mr Nimmo was assured by a railway guard that his wife and son were safe and had been sent back to Carlisle. Collecting the girls, he and they set off to catch a train at 3.06pm, presumably from the Glasgow & South Western station at Gretna, to travel the short distance south to Carlisle.

On their way to the station they saw a motor wagon beside the village church. The wagon was loaded with a number of dead bodies covered by a sheet.

'My daughter called my attention to a portion of hair that was not covered,' recalled Mr Nimmo, 'and she exclaimed, "that is mother!" I went to the wagon and lifted the sheet – and I saw the dead body of my wife. I identified her by her face, her clothing and jewellery.

'After the dead bodies had been removed from the wagon into the church, I saw the charred remains of a child, which I presumed was the body of my son, as I did not see any other child on the train.'

Having identified the bodies and provided local police with particulars, the distraught man made arrangements for them to be conveyed to Newcastle. They were buried at the city's Elswick Cemetery on 25 May.

Local anecdotal evidence suggests that, having done that, Mr Nimmo stayed with his friend in Gretna for a short time. While there, it is said, he wandered alongside the Quintinshill crash site, unable to take in the enormity of what had happened there and the loss of both his wife and son.[2]

A Shot at the Signalmen?

We have referred in chapter three to the probable mercy killings by Royal Scots officers of hopelessly trapped soldiers before the flames engulfed them.

A local story suggests that one of those officers, incensed with rage at what had happened, stormed into the signal box and attempted to shoot the signalmen he felt sure had caused the slaughter of so many of his men.

It is impossible to verify any of this. However, it is possible that the story emanates from a newspaper report that one of the signalman – thought to be Tinsley – had been arrested at the scene. This was later discounted but, with feelings running high among the soldiers, it cannot be ruled out that one, or both, signalmen were escorted from the site by police for their own safety, perhaps giving the impression of an arrest to anyone who witnessed it.

Questions of Sabotage

It is clear from documents only recently declassified at The National Archives in Kew that rumours of sabotage by German agents or sympathisers were seriously considered as a possible cause of the disaster.

Astoundingly, George Meakin was a suspect. A Home Office memo from 1915 refers to a suggestion that an investigation into Meakin had been undertaken to ascertain if he had German connections. The correspondence is incomplete but it would appear that no evidence was found.

Another investigation into possible sabotage was taken very seriously and is an interesting story in its own right. Dated 15 September 1915, a letter from a Miss Theodora Dury of Earl's Court, Tunbridge Wells, survives in the archives. It is not clear to whom it was addressed but it would appear that the recipients were the Metropolitan Police. It is an extraordinary document.

Miss Dury recounted a story told to her by a woman residing at 35 St James's Road, Derby. One of her sons, who worked for an aviation company, had been ordered to go to Scotland by the express that was involved in the disaster. While at King's Cross, she had told the letter writer, her son had been handed a telegram telling him not to join the train.

It should have been spotted at the time that, if her son was at King's Cross, he was obviously intending to catch an East Coast express rather than use the West Coast route from Euston, from where the doomed express had left.

The writer suggested that the origin of the telegram was a mystery. It had not come from the son's company; the sender was unknown. It led her to add that, 'by this it certainly seems as if the wrecking of the trains was no accident – but someone who knew wished to save this man's life.' She went on to assure the recipient that her informant was a 'respectable woman'.

The police considered this worth investigating. They contacted the woman's son, George Henry Robertson, who told them he worked for the Sopwith Aviation Company at Kingston upon Thames in southwest London.

In his surviving statement dated 19 October he confirmed that he had been instructed by the company to visit Fort George, north of Inverness, to erect aircraft for the Admiralty. Originally told to travel overnight on 21 May he had then been instructed at the last minute to delay his journey until the 24th. Returning to King's Cross that evening, he was told, apparently by a friend, that a telegram had been received asking him to telephone for further instructions before leaving London. He left that night.

And that was that. The mystery telegram had not been mysterious at all and it had been sent two days after the disaster. 'The only explanation I can give respecting the confusion over the date on which the telegram was received is that a misunderstanding must have occurred between my sister and my mother,' the statement from an embarrassed Mr Robertson added.

Wrong date. Wrong railway line – clearly a tale that 'improved' with the telling!

An American Fantasy

In his 1969 book on the Quintinshill tragedy J.A.B. Hamilton quoted from Len Guttridge, a contributor to *The Stag*, an American adventure magazine.

Born in Bournemouth in 1918, Guttridge served in the RAF in World War Two, later emigrating to the USA where he became a writer. In the Sixties *The Stag* published an article he had written based on the Quintinshill disaster.

It is difficult to understand why Hamilton bothered to include excerpts from what was nothing more than fanciful nonsense. It included a fabricated conversation in which Meakin is supposed to have phoned Tinsley from the box at 4.30 on the morning of the accident, advising him that he could have a lie-in as the expresses from London were running late!

Another extract featured an imaginary conversation between Tinsley and his wife at breakfast that morning during which she expressed concern at the shift change arrangement with Meakin. Tinsley was portrayed as being casual about the whole thing, merrily whistling the tune to the song *Tipperary* as he leisurely strolled to catch the local train at Gretna station.

One part of Guttridge's story, however, does seem to have become part of local folklore. Stricken with remorse, he wrote, James Tinsley insisted on helping in the rescue. Guttridge described how Tinsley witnessed mercy killings. While there is no record of him leaving the signal box to help – almost certainly another piece of nonsense from *The Stag* – there is a link to a story quoted by local historian Gordon Routledge in his 2002 book.

According to Routledge, a large woodman's axe had hung on the wall of Quintinshill signal box for many years after the accident. It was known as 'Tinsley's axe' and it was said that it had been used in the rescue. A legend may have grown from this that Tinsley had used it himself as, in line with Guttridge's story, he desperately tried to help with the rescue after the crash.

Alex Jackson, a local signalman who many years later worked for a time in the signal box, recounted a strange twist to the story of the axe. Early one morning, as an express passed the box, the axe fell from its mounting with a thud. According to Routledge, signalman Jackson shouted out, 'Tinsley's back!'

Appreciating the funny side of the incident, he was in no way perturbed by it until, glancing at the newspaper he had brought with him to the box, he saw immediately a story headlined, 'Memories of George Meakin.' Routledge described how 'a shiver went through him as he read the date – 22 May.'[3, 4]

In Memoriam

Although the 1915 disaster has now passed from living memory it is recalled today through memorials to the fallen in Leith and on the Anglo–Scottish border.

The unveiling in May 1916 of the disaster's principal memorial at Leith's Rosebank Cemetery, dedicated to the officers and men of the 7th Royal Scots who lost their lives, is described fully in chapter four. The impressive granite monument is beautifully maintained and a remembrance service is held there every year.

However it is far from being the only permanent tribute. Over the past two decades other memorials have been erected in Scotland and in the border region.

In May 1990, the Scottish area of the Western Front Association organised a service on the line-side at Quintinshill to commemorate the 75th anniversary of the crash. It was suggested then that a permanent memorial should be provided as close to the site as possible. A successful appeal for funds was launched via publicity in local and national newspapers and the railway press.[5]

The location chosen for the memorial was the north side of the car park at the famous Old Blacksmith's Shop at Gretna Green. From there the crash site can be seen half-a-mile to the north. The memorial's design incorporates a bronze Royal Scots badge on the north side of a plinth, with one in stone on the reverse. On top, a plaque bears an inscription explaining that the memorial commemorates not only the soldiers killed but also those railwaymen and passengers who perished, something that all too often is ignored.

The 80th anniversary (actually held on Sunday, 21 May 1995) was chosen as a suitable date for the dedication and unveiling of the memorial. An article about this had caught the eye of 83-year-old Rachel Buchanan, the former Rachel Nimmo, in Newcastle. Alerted, the association invited her to perform the unveiling ceremony. Happily, she accepted. As the last survivor of the disaster, there was nobody more suitable to undertake the task.

Conducted by Gretna's minister, the Reverend Bryan Haston, the dedication service was attended by around 200 people, including a detachment of Royal Scots and Sir Hector Monro, MP for Dumfries, whose maternal grandfather, General Sir Spencer Ewart, was GOC Scotland at the time of the disaster, hurrying from Edinburgh to help co-ordinate the rescue work.

Rachel Buchanan's recall of the disaster was clearly not going to be substantial owing to her age – just three – when it occurred. 'My only memory... was of soldiers lying injured on mattresses in the field, and of one of them giving me chocolates... I never knew my mother. There was no great trauma for me since I was so young and my half-sister brought me up,' she told local writer Gordon Routledge (though the reference to being brought up by her half-sister throws doubt over Annie's age – reportedly slightly younger than Rachel).

'But,' she added, 'whenever it gets to that time of year, 22 May, I wake up about the time of the accident. It must be at the back of my mind.'

Also in 1995 a memorial plaque was installed at the former Caledonian Railway station at Larbert, from where the 7th Royal Scots had set off on their doomed journey eighty years earlier. The station, near Falkirk, is still in use.

Worthy of note is the work of the Devil's Porridge Exhibition at Eastriggs near Annan. The museum's main feature is its display of exhibits recalling the former Gretna munitions factory but it includes another dedicated to the rail disaster.

Back at the site of the crash, Springfield and Gretna Community Council raised funds to install a plaque at Blacksyke Bridge which overlooks the site – it was this bridge that obscured driver Scott's view of the stationary local train.

On Sunday, 26 September 2010 around 100 people gathered at the bridge for the plaque's unveiling. It is inscribed with words written by local poet and historian, the late Denis Muir, who did much in recent years to keep the memory of the disaster alive. Two years later, the community council established a Quintinshill trail as a further reminder of the tragedy.

Quintinshill was an accident of its time – trains lit by gas are long gone, live coals from steam engines will never again light the fuse for such appalling carnage. Modern technology has made the West Coast railway a safer place for all who travel and those who work on it. Never again will a lone signalman in a state of utter confusion be able to usher in such an awful tragedy.

In notes that accompany his poem on Quintinshill, Denis Muir states that 'no ghosts of soldiers – but there are of questions. Therein lies the attraction of Quintinshill. So many unanswered, so many have never been solved and never will be.'

Regrettably, the answers provided by this book have come too late for Denis. But as the Quintinshill disaster approaches its centenary, the commemorations will for the first time be held in the light of the true story of what happened on 22 May 1915.

QUINTINSHILL
by Denis R. Muir

Blacksyke Wood awakens still to the sound of a blackbird's merry trill.
His lonely tribute to the dawn is to remind us of that fateful morn
for eighty years have slowly passed since Madam Fate her five die cast
to fall at random where they may on a perfect, cloudless, sunny day
– at Quintinshill.

She chose the place. she set the scene, near quiet, peaceful Gretna Green.
A train of Royal Scots, 'Leith's Own,' were battle-trained and leaving home.
Innocents but in their prime and eager for a distant clime.
From Larbert then, excitement high, they'd watched the lowlands passing by
– as day began.

In long descent the 'Special' roars,
the rhythmic rails drum wooden floors
as a farm of fluorescent white
ghosts by in early morning's light.
An over-bridge's shadow casts
its hint of gloom but flashes past.
The rattling sound of sleepered joints;
a sway of unexpected points
– then CRASH.

With a roaring, deafening, shattering thud,
the trains compressed to splintered wood.
Men crushed to death without a noise
or flung away like ragged toys.
Some scramble blindly, half in dreams.
bewildered by the wretched screams
to stare at what was once their train,
while trying to focus in the brain
– the question 'WHY?'

CRASH

A second fearful rending sound
comes ploughing through the cindered ground.
Men thankful once to be alive
are mown like corn before the scythe.
A blade of death – of flying steel,
distorted rails and fractured wheels
then, adding further to the strife,
a lazy flame explodes to life
– escaping gas!

The kindled coaches blaze alight;
adrenalin flows through fear and fright
as anxious helpers hear the cries
and fight to where their comrades lie.
Explosions – shots —the scorching heat
and cinders hot beneath their feet.
The panic of the searchers, crying
which petrifies the trapped still lying
– within the flame.

Survivors laid upon a field
succumb to death and quietly yield.
Midst dandelion; daisy; clover; vetch;
a pall of death as soldiers retch.
Men of War struck down by chance
far from the poppied fields of France
or a muddy, bloodied Belgian trench
instead, a sickening, searing stench
– on Scottish soil.

Lost with the men – the Battalion Roll,
proof of the Scots' horrific toll.
Nameless men for ever more
but known by God at Heaven's door.
One sombre photo says it all;
their remnants mustered by a wall.
With staring eyes they line and wait,
distraught in grief yet ramrod straight
– the 7th Royal Scots.

There live yet men who remember well
the piercing screams and mangled hell;
the line-side poles all burnt away; gun-metal tarnished bluish-grey.

The horrendous aftermath of fire with carriages for a funeral pyre.
Two hundred soldiers in the sun found death before their war begun
– in friendly fields.

Hardly anything now remains. Just empty loops and ghosts of trains.
Nothing but the 'Guinness' book to remind us of the lives it took.
No memorial – no marble stone to mark the loss of boys half-grown;
no signal box – no bells that ring, but in Blacksyke Wood a blackbird sings.
– at Quintinshill.

Notes

1. Khaki was adopted by the British Army as campaign dress in 1897 and was first used in the Second Boer War (1899-1902).
2. This account was recalled by the Davies family, to whom – along with Springfield Community Council – we extend thanks for drawing it to our attention.
3. The infamous signal box at Quintinshill survived largely unchanged for just over seventy years before its demolition in 1975 when the main line was electrified. Although alterations have been made to the trackwork, the passing loops have long outlived the box and remain in regular use today.
4. The Western Front Association was established in 1980 by noted military historian John Giles. Its aims are not to justify or glorify war. Its object is to educate the public in the history of the Great War with particular reference to the Western Front.
5. Poem reproduced by kind permission of Denis Muir's widow.

Quintinshill's Death Toll

TROOP TRAIN
7th Royal Scots

Officers:
Major James D.L. Hamilton
Captain John Mitchell
Lieutenant Christian R. Salvesen

Sergeants:
William Allan
James Anderson
James Gear
Alexander S. Gibson
William Hutchinson

Lance Sergeants:
William Flett
David Peters

Corporals:
Samuel Allison
Jack David
Michael Kerr
William Milton
George McKay
James Sime
Alexander Somerville
George Storic

Lance Corporals:
Robert Angus
George Bellman
Charles Bonnar
John Brass
George Brown

Archibald Cairns
Peter Campbell
Robert Dawson
William Mennamann
David McLean
Robert Nicholson
Robert Ramsey
George Shaw
Walter A. Simpson
John Suttle
Alexander White

Drummers:
William Blackwood
Alexander Grant
John Inglis

Bugler:
John Malone

Privates:
James Adams
Thomas Allan
James Anderson
David R. Angus
Thomas Arnold
David Archibald
John A. Auld
Andrew F. Baillie
William Ballie
John W. Ballantyne
Thomas Barnet
Thomas W. Barnet
William N. Barret
Robert Batey

Francis Batten
Archibald Baxter
Andrew Bell
Peter Bird
Alfred J. Bird
William Bissett
James A. Blair
John Blair
Robert Borthwick
George Bremner
Frederick Brookshaw
Andrew Brown
James Brown
Robert Bruce
Robert Brunton
Douglas Burke
James Burnet
John Burnet
Henry S. Cairns
Andrew Campbell
Richard Carlin
John Carter
Alexander Clark
William Clark
Arthur B. Colville
Lister S. Combe
James Cranston
John Cumming
John Cummingham
George Dalgeish
Albert Dallas
James Dick
Thomas C. Dougherty
George Duff
Robert Duff
Robert C. Dugdale
Thomas Edmond
John Falconer
John Finlays
Joseph Forrester
Robert R. Fraser
Daniel Frew
John Fyfe
Michael Gaffiney

Robert Gibb
Alexander Glennie
John Goodwin
James Grady
Sydney Hadden
Archibald Hamilton
Thomas Hamilton
Percy Hampson
James F. Hannah
William H. Hannah
Hugh Hart
Robert Hay
John Henry
Lawrence Henry
James Herd
George Hogg
James W. Hollgrin
George Houliston
Robert Hunter
George Johnston
Andrew Keir
Napoloeon B. Kerr
Thomas King
Daniel Laing
William H. Laing
John Lang
Robert Little
William Love
George M. Lunny
Charles Main
William Main
George Marr
Archibald Mason
James Mather
James Maxwell
John May
William Melville
Walter Mighton
John Moran
Edward Morgan
George Muir
Andrew Murray
Thomas Murray
William Murray

George Macaulay
Henry Macaulay
David McDiarmid
George A. McDiarmid
Henry McDonald
John Macdonald
William McEwan
Alexander McIntyre
Alexander McKay
William McLaughlan
Daniel Macnamara
Charles Macpherson
James McSherry
John McSorley
George Nairn
John Neilands
Alexander Nicol
William Niven
Thomas Ormiston
Charles Orr
William E. Park
William Patterson
David Pearce
William Pettigrew
Alexander Ponton
Donald Porteuos
James Purves
Robert Renwick
David Ritchie
Peter Ritchie
David Robertson
James Robertson
Duncan Ross
George Schumacher
Duncan Scott
James Scott
William Scott
Robert H. Sime
George Simpsom
Thomas Singer
William Skidmore
Robert Smart
George Smeaton

John Smith
Peter Smith
Thomas Smith
Archibald Spencer
Robert Stevenson
James Stewart
John Stewart
William Stewart
Arthur G. Summers
John Suttie
Robert Swan
James Symons
Adam S. Thomson
William Tinlin
James Tindale
Adam S. Turnbull
John Vass
Robert Walker
William West
George White
Robert White
Daniel Whiteman
Robert Wilkie
Andrew Williamson
Thomas Williamson
William Williamson
George Wilson
Thomas I. Wilson
Andrew Young

8th Highland Light Infantry (Attached)
James Cook
Robert Leckie

Railwaymen
Francis Scott (Driver)
James Hannah (Fireman)

EXPRESS TRAIN
9th Argyll & Southern Highlanders
Captain Robert Findley
Lieutenant James Bonner

Lieutenant John Jackson
Naval personnel
Lieutenant Commander Charles Head
Assistant Paymaster William Paton

Railwayman
Samuel Dyer (Sleeping Car Attendant)

Civilians
Herbert Ford
James MacDonald
Four unidentified

LOCAL TRAIN
Civilians
Rachel Nimmo
Dickson Nimmo

TOTAL FATALITIES
230

Signalling Operations, 22 May 1915

A technical appraisal by Keith Walter, C.Eng, MIET, MIRSE

T his appendix looks at the signalling that was in use at Quintinshill in 1915, the rules and regulations that should have helped prevent the accident, and how these were applied – or not – on the morning of 22 May that year.

Signalling at Quintinshill in 1915

Quintinshill signal box opened on 25 September 1903, replacing an earlier signal box on the main line of the Caledonian Railway between Carlisle and Glasgow. It had up and down passing loops and a trailing crossover connecting the main lines in front of the box. Each loop had a dead-end siding, referred to as a shunt spur, at each end and there was a second dead-end siding at the north end of the up loop.

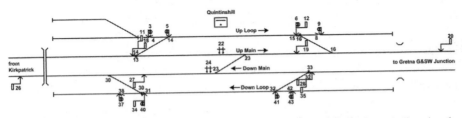

Fig 1: Signalling plan of Quintinshill, 1915 Longitudinal scale is accurate for main line signals and crossover, the signal box, and the bridges; Distant signals are omitted.

Quintinshill worked absolute block to Gretna G&SW Junction in the up direction (1 mile 34 chains) and Kirkpatrick in the down direction (2 miles 65 chains). Both these sections were worked with standard Caledonian Railway block instruments.

There were, in fact, two styles of 'Caley Block', one mounted on a vertical board (which is believed to be the style at Quintinshill in 1915) and one designed to sit on the block shelf (see fig.2). The only significant difference was the mounting of the bell and the separate bell key; functionally, the two styles were identical.

Fig 2: Caledonian Railway block instrument. (a) Normal (b) Line Clear (both directions) (c) Train on Line.

These instruments were combined 'peg' and 'non-peg' instruments with a window on the front, behind which was a representation of a signal post with the front view of a signal arm near the top and the rear view of another lower down. The upper arm was the 'non-peg' part, i.e. it was controlled by the signalman at the adjacent signal box and was for trains going away from this signal box. The lower arm was for trains coming towards this signal box and was controlled by two plungers below the window. The upper, red, plunger set the signal to danger, the normal position. The lower, white, plunger set the signal to clear, the Line Clear position. These indications were repeated by the upper arm on the instrument in the adjacent signal box.

When the red plunger was operated, this also set a round indicator on the left-hand side of the instrument to ON, with a red background, indicating Train on Line. Pressing a small plunger on the side of the instrument returned the indicator to OFF on a white background. Both the red and the white plungers rang the block bell in the adjacent signal box. When it was necessary to ring the bell without operating the indications the signalman could use a separate bell key.

These were therefore basically two-position block instruments, but with a Train on Line indicator for approaching trains only. For this reason, they were sometimes referred to as a three-position block, but this name is really only appropriate for instruments which indicate Train on Line on the instruments in both signal boxes.

Quintinshill had two of these instruments: one linked to Gretna G&SW Junction and the other to Kirkpatrick. The process for a down train would normally be as follows:

Gretna G&SW Junction calls Quintinshill's attention by ringing a single beat on the block bell using the bell key. Quintinshill acknowledges this by repeating it back, also using the bell key.

Gretna G&SW Junction offers the train to Quintinshill by ringing a series of beats on the block bell, using the bell key: e.g. three beats, pause, one beat (written 3-1) for a local passenger train, four consecutively for an express passenger train, 3-2, 1-4, or 4-1 for the types of goods trains that were in the area on the morning of 22 May 1915. This code is known as Is Line Clear.

Quintinshill accepts the train by ringing 1-2, using the white plunger, which sets the white signal to clear. The signalman at Gretna G&SW Junction watches to see the red signal in the instrument change to clear. Each man records the time in his train register. More recently, this response has been changed to a repetition of the Is Line Clear code, giving the signalman at Gretna the opportunity to detect any error in Quintinshill's interpretation of the bell code.

As the section from Gretna G&SW Junction to Quintinshill is quite short, Quintinshill immediately calls attention and offers the train to Kirkpatrick in the same way. If the section was longer, the signalman would wait until the train passes Gretna G&SW Junction.

Once Kirkpatrick has accepted the train and each signalman has recorded the time train register, Quintinshill clears all signals for that train: the Down Advanced Starter, no. 26, the Down Starter, no. 27, the Down Home, no. 28, and the Down Distant, no. 29.

As the train passes Gretna G&SW Junction, the signalman there gives two beats consecutively on the bell key, meaning Train Entering Section. Quintinshill responds with one beat on the red plunger, returning his own white signal and Gretna G&SW Junction's red signal to danger and changing his own Train on Line indicator to ON. The time is again recorded at each signal box.

As the train passes each signal the signalman returns it to danger.

As it passes the signal box, he sends two beats to Kirkpatrick to signify Train Entering Section. He also watches the train to see that there is nothing wrong with it and, once he has seen the tail lamp to prove that the train is complete, he calls attention to Gretna G&SW Junction. On getting a response, he rings 2-1 to signify Train out of Section, at the same time pressing the small plunger on the side of his instrument to return the Train on Line indicator to OFF. He records the time for Train Entering Section to Kirkpatrick (in a column headed dep/pass) and Train out of Section to Gretna G&SW Junction. If the train stops at Quintinshill, its arrival time is also recorded, as there is often a delay after the train arrives before the conditions are met for giving Train out of Section.

Finally, when Kirkpatrick sends the Train out of Section code, Quintinshill acknowledges this with a single beat on the bell key and records the time in the train register.

In the event of a train being offered to the next signal box but, for one reason or another, not being accepted immediately, it seems that the practice was to record the time it was offered rather than the time it was accepted. Some railways designed their train registers with separate columns for each of these two times.

Signalling regulations

In 1915 the concept of Blocking Back was still relatively new and the implications of the situation at Quintinshill had clearly not been fully considered. When the Welsh coal empties arrived in the up loop, Regulation 10, as it was at that time, stated that Train out of Section could be given as soon as the signalman was sure that the complete train was clear of the up main line (Fig. 3).

However, Regulation 13 required Blocking Back to be done before the local train was put onto the up main line (see fig. 4). This was impossible as it was already there. The only way it could have been possible would

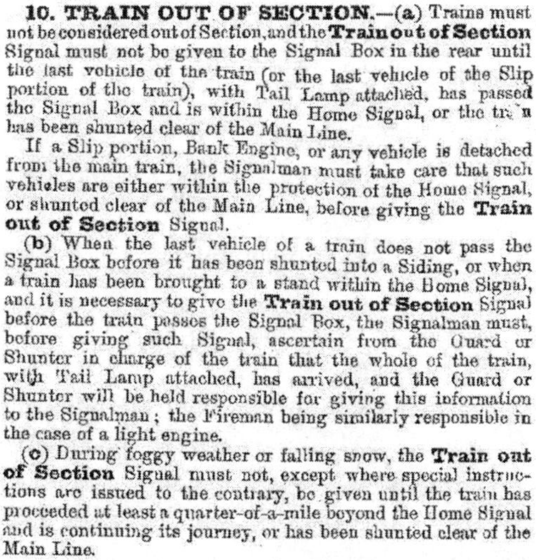

Fig 3: Caledonian Railway regulation 10, 1915.

10. TRAIN OUT OF SECTION.—(a) Trains must not be considered out of Section, and the **Train out of Section** Signal must not be given to the Signal Box in the rear until the last vehicle of the train (or the last vehicle of the Slip portion of the train), with Tail Lamp attached, has passed the Signal Box and is within the Home Signal, or the train has been shunted clear of the Main Line.

If a Slip portion, Bank Engine, or any vehicle is detached from the main train, the Signalman must take care that such vehicles are either within the protection of the Home Signal, or shunted clear of the Main Line, before giving the **Train out of Section** Signal.

(b) When the last vehicle of a train does not pass the Signal Box before it has been shunted into a Siding, or when a train has been brought to a stand within the Home Signal, and it is necessary to give the **Train out of Section** Signal before the train passes the Signal Box, the Signalman must, before giving such Signal, ascertain from the Guard or Shunter in charge of the train that the whole of the train, with Tail Lamp attached, has arrived, and the Guard or Shunter will be responsible for giving this information to the Signalman; the Fireman being similarly responsible in the case of a light engine.

(c) During foggy weather or falling snow, the **Train out of Section** Signal must not, except where special instructions are issued to the contrary, be given until the train has proceeded at least a quarter-of-a-mile beyond the Home Signal and is continuing its journey, or has been shunted clear of the Main Line.

have been to keep the local on the down main line until Train out of Section had been given for the Welsh coal empties – this would almost certainly have delayed the first down express.

13. BLOCKING BACK.—(a) When it is necessary, after the passing of one train, and before permission is given for another to leave the Signal Box in the rear, to obstruct the Line **inside** the Home Signal by allowing vehicles or a train to be crossed from one Line to another, or to leave a Loop Line or Siding for the Main Line for shunting purposes, or before the **Line Clear** Signal is received from the Signal Box in advance, the **Blocking Back** Signal (2—4) must, unless instructions are issued to the contrary, be given to the Signal Box or Boxes in the rear on the Key which raises the Block Semaphore Arm to danger, and the same must be acknowledged by repetition on the Ringing Key.

(b) When a Signalman requires permission to occupy the Line **outside** his Home Signal, he must give the **Blocking Back** Signal (3—3) to the Signalman at the Box in the rear, and the latter must, before acknowledging by repetition the **Blocking Back** Signal (3—3), satisfy himself that he can with safety give such permission, and that he has not allowed a train to approach his Signal Box from the Signal Box in the rear under Rule 3, unless there is a distance of at least half-a-mile between his Home Signal applicable to such train and the Signal Box from which he has received the **Blocking Back** Signal, or, if at a junction, he has set his Facing Points for another Line, and that Line is clear according to these regulations.

(c) The Block Indicator must be maintained at the **On** position until the Line or Lines are again clear.

(d) If, when a Signalman gives the **Blocking Back** Signal for the purpose of asking permission to occupy the Line, the Signalman at the Box in the rear is not in a position to give such permission, he must not repeat the **Blocking Back** Signal, or acknowledge it in any way.; and until the Signal has been acknowledged, the Line must not be occupied.

(e) Unless special permission is given by the District Superintendent, no train or vehicle must be placed outside a Home Signal where the Line is on a falling gradient towards the Signal Box in the rear.

(f) When the obstruction has been removed and the Main Line or Lines are again clear, the **Obstruction Removed** Signal must be given to the Signal Box in the rear.
   When the **Blocking Back** Signal is given and acknowledged, the **Is Line Clear?** Signal must not be forwarded by the Signalman in rear until he has received the **Obstruction Removed** Signal from the Signal Box in advance, unless the latter is a Station at which the **Section Clear but Station or Junction Blocked** Signal is in operation, and when the **Blocking Back** Signal has been authorised for Shunting operations **inside** the Home Signal at such places, the Signalman in rear is not prohibited from sending the **Is Line Clear?** Signal for Trains which are authorised to be accepted under Block Rule 5.

(g) The Signalmen forwarding and receiving the **Blocking Back** Signal must make a note of the circumstance in their Train Register Books.

Fig. 4: Caledonian Railway regulation 13, 1915.

This problem was realised in the aftermath of the Quintinshill accident, and was discussed at a meeting of the Caledonian Railway on 20 March, 1916 (see fig. 5). Although the notes of the meeting show that fourteen items were discussed, most were related to improving supervision to enforce the existing rules and regulations, and only two suggested the need for any change to the signalling regulations.

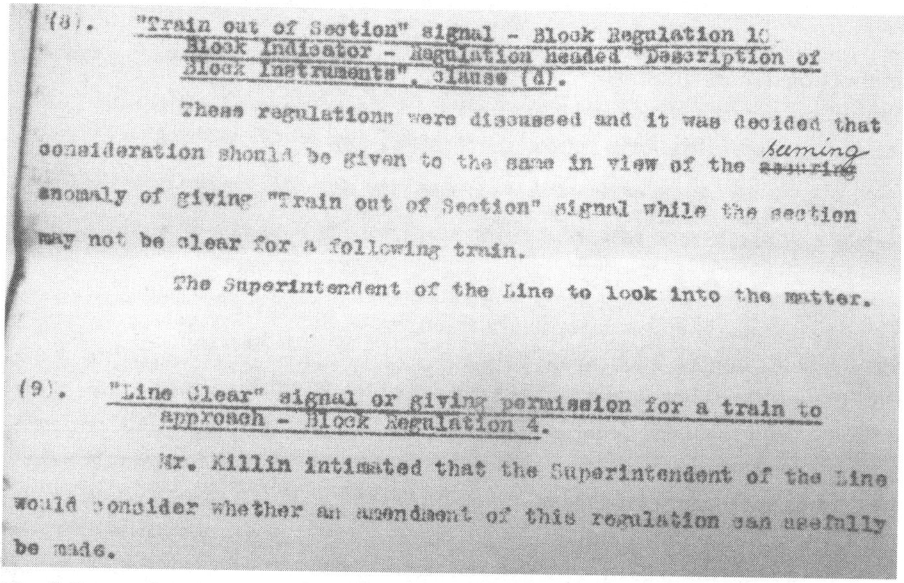

(8).   "Train out of Section" signal – Block Regulation 16
       Block Indicator – Regulation headed "Description of
       Block Instruments", Clause (d).

       These regulations were discussed and it was decided that consideration should be given to the same in view of the *seeming* anomaly of giving "Train out of Section" signal while the section may not be clear for a following train.

       The Superintendent of the Line to look into the matter.

(9).   "Line Clear" signal or giving permission for a train to
       approach – Block Regulation 4.

       Mr. Killin intimated that the Superintendent of the Line would consider whether an amendment of this regulation can usefully be made.

Fig. 5: Extract from notes of Caledonian Railway meeting on 20 March 1916.

Later versions of the signalling regulations required the line to be clear for 440yds beyond the home signal before Train out of Section was given when junction points were changed but, incredibly, even today this is not a requirement when the train has been put into a siding. The current book of Absolute Block Regulations, available on the Railway Group Standards website, instructs signalmen to give Train out of Section 'when the train has passed beyond the clearing point, or passed beyond a facing junction and you have set the points for another line which is clear to the clearing point of that line or has been shunted clear of the running line'.

If a regulation had existed instructing signalmen to give Train out of Section 'when the train has been shunted clear of the running line *and* you have set the points for another line which is clear to the clearing point of that line', Train out of Section should not have been given for the Welsh coal empties until the 'local' had returned to the down main line after the passage of the two down expresses and the signalman at Kirkpatrick would not have been able to ask for a Line Clear for the troop train until then. When some recent/current signalmen were asked

how they would act in such a situation, they said that this was how they would implement the regulation anyway.

Another problem with the signalling regulations was that, in theory at least, the signalman at Kirkpatrick could have refused to allow Blocking Back on the grounds that it would delay the troop train. This would have led to a 'Mexican stand-off', though, obviously, the signalmen would have sorted it out by telephone.

A second regulation that was relatively new in 1915 was one that required a lever collar to be placed on the lever of the signal controlling access to a section of line occupied by a stationary train. This collar acted as a reminder of the stationary train by preventing the signal from being cleared without the signalman taking the extra action of removing the collar. However, the evidence is that it was not regularly used on at least this part of the Caledonian Railway.

22 May 1915

The passing of trains was recorded in the train register at each signal box. After the accident, copies were made of the registers at Gretna G&SW Junction, Quintinshill and Kirkpatrick. These were certified by Robert Killin, but there are some discrepancies. What is not possible without the original train registers is to say whether these discrepancies existed in those registers or whether they were the result of errors made when they were copied. In the case of Quintinshill entries relating to the period from 6am until Tinsley took over, it is also not possible to say whether any errors were made by him in copying from Meakin's piece of paper.

Figures 6 and 7 show combined versions of the information taken from those copies; the down direction is in figure 6 and the up direction in figure 7. The information from Quintinshill is shown in bold and is laid out as in the original document. The information from Gretna and Kirkpatrick is shown in light and italic type, respectively and has been moved to the column where it can be

DOWN		code	ILC G-Q	TES G-Q	ILC Q-K	arr Q	dep/pass Q	TooS G-Q	TooS Q-K	remarks
	Gretna	3.2	5.58	6.1	-	-	-	6.6	-	C.R.
[previous Down train]	**Quintinshill**	**1.4**	**5.57**	**6.0**	**6.4**		**6.5**	**6.5**		Slowed
	Kirkpatrick	3.2	-	-	6.6	-	6.6	-	6.17	
	Gretna	4.1	6.6	6.10	-	-	-	6.16	-	C.R.
Down goods	**Quintinshill**	**4.1**	**6.5**	**6.10**		**6.14**		**6.14**		Looped
	Kirkpatrick	-	-	-				-		
	Gretna	3.1	6.23	6.28	-	-	-	6.33	-	C.R.
local	**Quintinshill**	**3.1**	**6.20**	**6.26**		**6.30**		**6.31**		Through Road.
	Kirkpatrick	-	-	-				-		
	Gretna	4	6.33	6.36	-	-	-	6.38	-	C.R.
first express	**Quintinshill**	**4**	**6.33**	**6.36**	**6.33**		**6.38**	**6.38**	**6.42**	
	Kirkpatrick	4	-	-	6.33	-	6.38	-	6.42	
	Gretna	4	6.47	6.49	-	-	-	-	-	C.R.
second express	**Quintinshill**	**4**	**6.46**	**6.48**	**6.46**		Cancelled			
	Kirkpatrick	4	-	-	6.47	-	6.53	-		
	Gretna			Danger signal from Quintinshill 6.53						
	Quintinshill						Obstruction danger signal given.			
	Kirkpatrick		-	-	-		-	-		

Fig. 6: Combined train register extracts – down.

UP		code	ILC K-Q	TES K-Q	ILC Q-G	arr Q	dep/pass Q	TooS K-Q	TooS Q-G	remarks
[previous Up train]	Kirkpatrick	1.4	5.50	5.59	-	-	-	6.4	-	Empties
	Quintinshill	1.4	5.50	6.0	6.0		6.4	6.4	6.6	W. Empties
	Gretna	1.4			5.59	-	6.3		6.6	Empties
	Kirkpatrick									
	Quintinshill			(Signed)	"G. Hutchinson, Rule 55, Engine 907"					
	Gretna									
Welsh empties	Kirkpatrick	1.4	6.17	6.25	-	-	-	6.34	-	Empties
	Quintinshill	4.1	6.15	6.22	6.14	6.30		6.34		See Kingmoor, looped.
	Gretna	-	-	-	-			-		
troop train	Kirkpatrick	4.4.4	6.43	6.47	-	-	-		-	X18
	Quintinshill	4.4.4	6.42	6.46	6.46					Collision, 6.50 a.m. passed Lockerbie, 6.32 a.m.
	Gretna	4.4.4	-	-	6.47	-	Cancelled 7.2 to border			X18
[next Up train, at 7.3]	Kirkpatrick	3.2			-	-	-		-	Put into siding
	Quintinshill				-	-			-	
	Gretna		-	-	-	-		-		
	Kirkpatrick									
	Quintinshill						Obstrruction danger signal given.			
	Gretna			Rule 12 from Quintinshill 6.53						

Key:

ILC	Is Line Clear
TES	Train Entering Section
TooS	Train out of Section
G	Gretna G&SW Junction
Q	Quintinshill
K	Kirkpatrick

Fig. 7: Combined Train Register Extracts – Up.

compared directly with the equivalent information from Quintinshill. Column headings have been amended to be more useful to the modern-day reader and an extra column has been added on the left to show to which train each set of information refers.

Discrepancies of one minute have been ignored as being insignificant. Those of two minutes or more or in bell codes are highlighted in light shading. The inexplicable Train Entering Section sent from Quintinshill to Kirkpatrick after the collisions is highlighted in dark shading.

The first trains shown in each direction were the last to pass Quintinshill before those involved in the accident. Everything happened smoothly apart from a slowing of the down train. However, the bell code recorded for this train at Quintinshill differs from that recorded at the other two signal boxes. Given the extremely low probability that mirror-image errors would be made by the two signalmen, it is unlikely that Meakin would genuinely have thought he was dealing with a 1-4 train rather than a 3-2. This makes it clear that at least one error occurred either when Tinsley copied details from Meakin's scrap of paper or when the copy certified by Killin was produced.

A further discrepancy exists for the bell code of the Welsh empties on their way to the up loop. Thus we cannot be certain that the remaining information is accurate and so, with discrepancies of up to three minutes, the relative timing of some events will never be accurately known.

Between 6:05 and 6:16, the down goods was offered by Gretna, accepted by Quintinshill, ran through the section, and entered the down loop. The records from Gretna and Quintinshill differ as to the time of Train out of Section being given by two minutes, but this does not materially affect subsequent events.

According to the certified copy of the train register, the next entry on the up direction page at Quintinshill was George Hutchinson's signature with the words, 'Rule 55, Engine 907'. Assuming the copy was made correctly, this entry was on the wrong page – an understandable error by someone other than a signalman, particularly as the details of his train were not yet in the train register – and also preceded the entry for the Welsh empties, which should have been made before it, but which, in reality, would have been copied into the book shortly after.

The entries for the Welsh empties and the 'local' show the most inconsistencies between the times recorded in the different signal boxes and even within the Quintinshill train register on its own. The first time noted for the Welsh empties relates to Quintinshill asking Gretna if the line is clear for it. This can hardly be accurate, as Quintinshill had not yet been offered the train from Kirkpatrick! In any case, Gretna was unable to accept the train and it had to be put into the up loop.

In both cases, the Is Line Clear and Train Entering Section times differ by two to three minutes between Quintinshill and the preceding signal box. This creates some doubt about the arrival times recorded as being written in the Quintinshill book – 6:30 for each train. However, if we take it that the arrival time for the 'local' relates to it stopping in front of the signal box, a four minute journey from Gretna seems reasonable and, with all the staff aware that they had to move quickly to avoid delaying the first express, another minute to move the train onto the up line and give Train out of Section to Gretna also makes sense.

Meanwhile, the Welsh empties train would have approached Quintinshill slowly, hoping to avoid actually stopping; 6:30 would therefore be a reasonable time for it to have arrived at Quintinshill up home signal (no. 18). It could then easily have taken four minutes to enter the up loop, for the points to be returned to normal and Train out of Section to have been given to Kirkpatrick. This also accords with witness statements that say the local train was on the up main line before the Welsh empties entered the up loop.

There is no record of any Blocking Back bell code being given to Kirkpatrick. It is also clear from the evidence given by those present that no lever collar was used.

According to the details copied from Gretna's train register, the first express was offered to Quintinshill immediately after Train out of Section was received for the 'local'. Compared with the details for other trains, this seems more likely to be correct than the two minute delay suggested in the details copied from the Quintinshill train register. Either way, the records agree that it was offered to Quintinshill at 6:33, passed Gretna at 6:36, Quintinshill at 6:38 and Kirkpatrick at 6:42, all without incident.

If the decision had been made to run the local train to Kirkpatrick between the two expresses, it would have been brought back to the down main and allowed forward to the advanced starting signal, no. 26, as soon as the first express had passed that signal and it had been returned to danger. The signalmen would then have exchanged the necessary bell codes as quickly as they could and the 'local' would have been sent on its way well before Gretna asked Is Line Clear for the second express.

The 'local' would then have reached Kirkpatrick at about 6:48, a minute after the troop train had passed, and could have been shunted again to the up main line or to a siding by 6:50, probably causing the second express to have to slow down at Quintinshill, but not to stop. Sadly, this was not done. Almost as soon as Kirkpatrick had belled Train out of Section for the first express, he asked Quintinshill Is Line Clear for the troop train?

We then find four events that happened so near to simultaneously that each signalman showed them as happening at the same time: 6:46 according to Quintinshill and 6:47 according to the other boxes. These were: (1) the troop train passing Kirkpatrick, as shown by the Train Entering Section code; (2) Quintinshill asking for and being given Line Clear for the troop train to proceed to Gretna; (3) Gretna asking for and being given Line Clear for the second express to proceed to Quintinshill; and (4) Quintinshill asking for and being given Line Clear for the second express to proceed to Kirkpatrick. Quintinshill would then have cleared all signals on the up and down main lines, allowing both trains to proceed at full speed.

Two minutes later, Gretna belled Train Entering Section to Quintinshill for the second express and, in the absence of anyone realising that anything was wrong, disaster was now inevitable.

Following the first collision, it would have been almost a reflex action by an experienced signalman to immediately have thrown all signals to danger, starting with the down distant and then the down home. There would then have been some chance of preventing the second collision or at least reducing the impact speed, as the crew of the second express would have done everything to stop their train as soon as they saw the signals going to danger.

The signalman's next actions should have been to give the Obstruction Danger bell code, six beats consecutively, on both block instruments simultaneously and then to use his telephone to summon all necessary assistance. Instead, the signals were not replaced to danger until far too late, it was about three minutes before Obstruction Danger was sent to Gretna and the only recorded message to Kirkpatrick was the inexplicable Train Entering Section, also three minutes after the collision.

Acknowledgments & Bibliography

It would have been impossible to collate and compile the multi-faceted true story behind Britain's worst railway disaster without the help of a great many people – experts in their respective fields – and the ability to consult a large number of newspapers, libraries, internet sites, journals and archival collections. The authors are indebted to them all and wish to thank them for the time, enthusiasm and expertise they have generously given.

To understand the complexities which underpin the story we sought help and advice from a number of eminent specialists and owe them a particular debt of gratitude. They include Dr Edward Reynolds (Charles Sykes Epilepsy Trust), a specialist in the history and treatment of the condition; Lord Chief Justice Colin Tyre, Scottish Supreme Court; David Howell, former Professor of Politics at York University; and Keith Walter, signalling engineer with Atkins, who has contributed the technical appendix. All have provided us with the benefit of their extensive experience and breadth of knowledge in their respective fields.

Others who have made considerable contributions include Carlisle historians Ashley Kendal, Denis Perriman and John Huggon. Without their input we would not have been able to access valuable background information relating to the crash and the rescue operation that followed, in which the city played an immense part – and we would certainly not have had the opportunity to include the selection of pictures depicting the crash and subsequent events in 1915.

We are also grateful to Lorna and Peter Strong, who were able to provide a fascinating insight into the character of their ancestor, Thomas Slack Strong, former Carlisle coroner, who conducted the main inquest into the fatalities.

In the Gretna area itself, enthusiastic support for, and assistance with, the project came willingly from local author Gordon Routledge, Isabella Tranter and Graham Thompson (Springfield and Gretna Community Council) and historian and lecturer John Cameron, who also provided the images of memorials, Rachel and Dickson Nimmo and modern day Quintinshill.

Others who have helped enormously with specialist areas of our research include Colin Divall. Professor of Railway Studies and Head of the Institute of Railway Studies and Transport History, run jointly by York University and the National Railway Museum which is located in the city.

We should also mention the help given by Jim Tweedie (Leith Historical Society); Morag Williams (Dumfries Historical Society), Joe McClure, for his information on the unidentified victims of the tragedy; Caledonian Railway Association members Jim MacIntosh, Alec Inglis and John Lindsay; Philip Crome (Great Central Forum); Keith Long, for permitting use of a rare

photograph; Rob Hoon; Kay Shaw, Matt Searle and his wife, Sarah, for their help with ancestry research; Matt, too, for his invaluable help in preparing the illustrations, and Sarah for her superb location map and crash sequence diagram.

Last but certainly not least, our thanks go to Jon Wright and colleagues at Pen and Sword for entrusting us with this project, and to Irene Moore, our editor.

Archival Sources

Extensive use has been made of the archival records held by a large number of authorities and organisations. Special thanks are extended to Cathy Mills and Graham Roberts at Dumfries and Galloway Council's records office for their help in uncovering documents essential to an understanding of the story.

Acknowledgment must also be made of the help provided by the Charles Sykes Epilepsy Trust and staff at the National Archives, Kew; the National Archives of Scotland, Edinburgh; the Cumbrian Archives, Carlisle, and Carlisle Library Service, with special thanks to Stephen White; Richard Brodie and staff at the Devil's Porridge Exhibition, Annan; the Ewart Library, Dumfries; the National Railway Museum; the Royal Scots Museum, Edinburgh; the University of Warwick; the Western Front Association; Springfield & Gretna Community Council; and the British Library's Newspaper Library at Colindale, London (see below).

Archival picture credits: The National Archives of Scotland (police note re. epilepsy and images from Peterhead prison records); V&A Lafayette Negative Archive) Thomas McKinnon Wood); *The Railway Magazine* (Robert Killin); *Dumfries & Galloway Standard* (William Dickie); *The Scots Law Trial* (James Condie Sandeman).

Newspapers

Key to unravelling the crucial events in 1915 and beyond has been the extensive collection of local and national newspapers held at Colindale. Newspapers consulted have included the indispensable – in this context – *Dumfries and Galloway Standard and Advertiser* and the following titles:

National:
Daily Express
Daily Mirror
Illustrated London News
The Scotsman
The Times

Provincial:
Annandale Observer
Carlisle Journal

Cumberland News
Edinburgh Evening News
Edinburgh Weekly Journal
Glasgow Herald
Leeds Mercury

Journals

Look and Learn (Issue 965)
Railway Gazette (1915)
Railway Magazine (1916)
Scots Law Times (1933)

Books

Adamson, Duncan & Sheila – *Kirkpatrick Fleming, On the Borders of History* (Dumfries & Galloway Natural History Society, 2011)

Adelman, Paul – *The Decline of the Liberal Party* (Pearson Education)

Hall, Stanley – *Railway Detectives* (Ian Allan Publishing, 1990)

Hamilton, J.A.B. – *Britain's Greatest Railway Disaster: The Quintinshill Blaze of 1915* (George Allan & Unwin, 1969)

Hamilton-Ellis, C. – *1915: The Trains We Loved* (Macmillan, 1971)

Howell, David – *Respectable Radicals: Studies in the Politics of Railway Trade Unionism* (Ashgate Publications, 1999)

Leventhal, F.M. – *Arthur Henderson Lives on the Left* (Manchester University Press, 1989)

Macdonald, Lyn –*1915. The Death of Innocence* (The John Hopkins University Press, 2000)

Marr, Andrew – *The Making of Modern Britain* ((Macmillan, 2010)

McKibben, Ross – *Parties and People: England 1914-1915* (Oxford University Press, 2011)

Nock, O.S. – *Historic Railway Disasters* (New ed. Arrow Books, 1986,)

Rolt, L.T.C. – *Red For Danger: The Official History of British Railway Disasters* (New ed. The History Press, 2009)

Routledge, Gordon – *The Sorrows of Quintinshill: The Harrowing Account of Britain's Worst Rail Disaster* (Gordon Routledge / Arthuret Publishers, 2002)

Strange, Robert – *Who Sank the Titanic?* (Pen and Sword Maritime, 2012)

Thomas, J.H. – *A Life for Unity* (Frederick Muller, 1964)

Thomas, J.H. – *My Story* (Hutchinson & Co., 1937)

Thomas, John – *Gretna: Britain's Worst Railway Disaster* (David and Charles, 1969)

Toughill, Thomas – *Oscar Slater: The Mystery Solved* (Cannongate Books, 1993)

Whittington-Egan, Richard – *The Oscar Slater Murder Story* (Neil Wilson Publishing, 2001)

Wolmar, Christian – *Engines of War* (Atlantic Books, 2012)

Online Sources

The Great War Forum (with a special thanks to the many who answered our questions)
The Railway Forum
The Signal Box
Wikipedia

Index